T5-AEZ-911

EARLY ENGLISH MANUSCRIPTS IN FACSIMILE

VOL. XVI

THE DURHAM RITUAL

(Durham Cathedral Library A. IV. 19)

Edited by

T. J. BROWN

University of London

with contributions by

F. WORMALD

University of London

A. S. C. ROSS

University of Birmingham

and

E. G. STANLEY

University of London

*

Printed in Denmark by
Det Berlingske Bogtrykkeri
Copenhagen

*

Collotype by
Nordisk Kunst- og Lystryk
Copenhagen

EARLY ENGLISH MANUSCRIPTS IN FACSIMILE

CHIEF EDITOR

PETER CLEMOES
University of Cambridge, England

ASSOCIATE EDITORS

KEMP MALONE
Johns Hopkins University, Baltimore, U. S. A.

KNUD SCHIBSBYE
University of Copenhagen, Denmark

Sixteenth Volume

ROSENKILDE AND BAGGER
INTERNATIONAL BOOKSELLERS AND PUBLISHERS
COPENHAGEN

For The British Commonwealth except Canada
GEORGE ALLEN & UNWIN LTD
LONDON

For The United States and Canada
THE JOHNS HOPKINS PRESS
BALTIMORE

EARLY ENGLISH MANUSCRIPTS IN FACSIMILE

Volume I The Thorkelin Transcripts of BEOWULF
Edited by Kemp Malone, Johns Hopkins University, U.S.A.
233 pp. in collotype plus an introduction of 43 pp.

Volume II THE LENINGRAD BEDE
Edited by O. Arngart, University of Lund, Sweden.
323 pp. in collotype plus an introduction of 36 pp.

Volume III THE TOLLEMACHE OROSIUS
Edited by Alistair Campbell, Balliol College, Oxford.
174 pp. in collotype plus an introduction of 27 pp.

Volume IV THE PETERBOROUGH CHRONICLE
Edited by Dorothy Whitelock, St Hilda's College, Oxford.
184 pp. in collotype plus an introduction of 43 pp.

Volume V BALD'S LEECHBOOK
Edited by Cyril E. Wright, British Museum, London.
255 pp. in collotype plus an introduction of 32 pp.

Volume VI THE PASTORAL CARE
Edited by N. R. Ker, Magdalen College, Oxford.
204 pp. in collotype plus an introduction of 34 pp.

Volume VII TEXTUS ROFFENSIS. Part I.
Edited by Peter Sawyer, University of Edinburgh.
242 pp. in collotype plus an introduction of 23 pp.

Volume VIII THE PARIS PSALTER
Edited by John Bromwich, University of Cambridge
N. R. Ker, Magdalen College, Oxford
Francis Wormald, University of London
Kenneth Sisam
Celia Sisam, St Hilda's College, Oxford, and
Bertram Colgrave, University of Durham.
187 pp. in collotype (reproducing 374 MS pp.) plus an introduction of 20 pp.

Volume IX THE MOORE BEDE
Edited by Peter Hunter Blair, Emmanuel College, Cambridge.
258 pp. in collotype plus an introduction of 39 pp.

Volume X THE BLICKLING HOMILIES
Edited by Rudolph Willard, University of Texas, U.S.A.
153 pp. in collotype (reproducing 300 MS pp.) plus an introduction of 72 pp.

Volume XI TEXTUS ROFFENSIS. Part II.
Edited by Peter Sawyer, University of Birmingham.
234 pp. in collotype plus an introduction of 42 pp.

Volume XII THE NOWELL CODEX
Edited by Kemp Malone, Johns Hopkins University, U.S.A.
116 pp. in collotype (reproducing 232 MS pp.) plus an introduction of 120 pp.

Volume XIII ÆLFRIC'S FIRST SERIES OF CATHOLIC HOMILIES
Edited by Norman Eliason, University of N. Carolina, U.S.A., and
Peter Clemoes, Emmanuel College, Cambridge.
430 pp. in collotype plus an introduction of 38 pp.

Volume XIV THE VESPASIAN PSALTER
Edited by David H. Wright, University of California, U.S.A.
3 colour plates and 325 pp. in collotype plus an introduction of 101 pp.

Volume XV THE RULE OF ST BENEDICT
Edited by D. H. Farmer, University of Reading.
1 colour plate and 157 pp. in collotype plus an introduction of 29 pp.

Volume XVI THE DURHAM RITUAL
Edited by T. J. Brown, University of London.
178 pp. in collotype plus an introduction of 92 pp.

THE DURHAM RITUAL

A SOUTHERN ENGLISH COLLECTAR
OF THE TENTH CENTURY
WITH NORTHUMBRIAN ADDITIONS

DURHAM CATHEDRAL LIBRARY A. IV. 19

EDITED BY

T. J. BROWN
University of London

WITH CONTRIBUTIONS BY

F. WORMALD
University of London

A. S. C. ROSS
University of Birmingham

E. G. STANLEY
University of London

ROSENKILDE AND BAGGER
INTERNATIONAL BOOKSELLERS AND PUBLISHERS
COPENHAGEN 1969

PREFACE

The main contents of the original portion of the manuscript here reproduced constitute the earliest surviving collectar written in England, an expert and ingeniously decorated copy of a probably continental exemplar. Also original is a long series of benedictions. This first work—collectar and benedictions—was produced at an important centre in southern England during the first quarter of the tenth century. Its script shows the pointed Anglo-Saxon minuscule of Alfredian manuscripts at a uniquely late stage of development; its decoration skilfully utilizes the full range of motifs characteristic of contemporary English art.

Within fifty years this collectar was in the possession of the community of St Cuthbert, at that time at Chester-le-Street, and today, a thousand years later, it is still owned by that community's successors. Early in this ownership it was much augmented, mainly in a single campaign by six scribes c. *970. These additions comprise further liturgical texts, some educational ones and a vernacular gloss to almost all the original contents and to some of the additions. Essentially the manuscript remained a priest's book. Some of the additions are among the earliest material showing what portions of the daily office in England were like, and others—as has been shown by Professor H. Gneuss in his book,* Hymnar und Hymnen im englischen Mittelalter *(Tübingen, 1968, published since the introduction to the facsimile was written)—are the earliest extant evidence for the introduction of the 'New Hymnal' into England during the tenth century: it may well have been the newness of the hymns that caused them to be included here. Linguistically the gloss, written by the Aldred who had earlier glossed the Lindisfarne Gospels, forms one of the three main sources for our knowledge of tenth-century Northumbrian. The handwriting of these additions of* c. *970 shows that the scriptorium of the community of St Cuthbert was at that time influenced less by Caroline minuscule, the Latin script of the southern-based monastic reform, than by older traditions.*

The exceptionally thorough introduction to the facsimile (including, at pp. 44–51, a useful list of the manuscript's multifarious contents) does full justice to the manuscript both as a representative product of southern England at a time for which evidence is scarce and as a key book for an understanding of Chester-le-Street as a northern centre. Professor Brown has provided this introduction, apart from those sections specifically attributed to others, and has been responsible for supervising the preparation of the facsimile. I am greatly indebted to him for all the care and scholarship which have gone into his work. The manuscript has been a particularly difficult one to reproduce. It has suffered a great deal from damp, which has caused much offsetting between facing pages, and there has been severe rubbing at the structural junctions of the additions: only about half the pages in the manuscript are satisfactorily legible; about a quarter of them are very bad. The irregularly spaced words of Aldred's gloss, written in a small, somewhat informal script, in red ink and with a fine pen, have been especially vulnerable to loss. If to these limitations are added those of an excessively tight binding, the severity of the task facing the photographer and the printer can be appreciated. I am grateful to Messrs John R. Freeman and Co. Ltd, the photographers, and to Mr Simonsen, the printer, for making every possible effort to achieve the maximum success. The introduction greatly aids the legibility of the facsimile by including numerous citations and especially by providing a classified list of all the linguistic forms of Aldred's gloss that Professor Ross and Professor Stanley have been able to discern in the manuscript itself.

My sincere thanks are extended to the Dean and Chapter of Durham Cathedral for their permission to reproduce this manuscript and to transfer it for a period to the University of London Library so that it might there be photographed and studied by the editors; to Canon Couratin, Durham Chapter Librarian, for his kindness in twice making the journey to London, once to bring the manuscript and once to fetch it; to Mr J. H. P. Pafford, who was at that time Goldsmiths' Librarian of the University of London, for offering safe-keeping for the manuscript and for providing excellent conditions for its proper photography and convenient use; to Miss Joan Gibbs, of the Palaeography Room of the University of London Library, for her helpfulness; to Mr E. M. Dring, of Messrs Bernard Quaritch Ltd, for valuing the manuscript for insurance purposes. The publishers, as always, have been of the utmost helpfulness throughout.

The current prospectus contains information about the volumes proposed for the future. The subject of the next one is expected to be B. M. Cotton Nero A. i.

PETER CLEMOES

CHIEF EDITOR

CONTENTS
OF THE INTRODUCTION

INTRODUCTION

GENERAL

The nucleus of Durham, Cathedral Library, A.IV.19—the 'Durham Ritual'—is a collectar (1r–61r10), in Latin (except for a few lines of Anglo-Saxon, 55r–57v *passim*), written in Anglo-Saxon minuscule of the early tenth century, apparently in the south of England. In the late tenth and early eleventh centuries the original collectar received extensive additions in Latin and Anglo-Saxon (61r11–88v),[1] mostly liturgical in content and all apparently made in the community of St Cuthbert, which, formerly of Lindisfarne, was at Chester-le-Street from 883 until it moved to Durham in 995. The main body of these additions was written *c.* 970 by a group of scribes, one of whom, 'Aldred the provost', signed and dated (10 August 970), in an Anglo-Saxon colophon, the four Latin collects for St Cuthbert which he copied on 84r 'for Ælfsige the bishop'—evidently the one who governed Chester-le-Street from 968 to 990.

1. The manuscript is misbound, with gatherings IX and X transposed; but the pages are reproduced here in their right order, and the gatherings and folios concerned are given a double numeration, in which the right (facsimile) reference precedes the actual (manuscript) one, the latter being placed within square brackets: IX[X] (66[70]–72[76]) and X[IX] (73[66]–76[69]). The leaves have been both foliated (1–89) and paginated (1–178) in modern times. Wanley (see below, next note) used the foliation; others the pagination. The manuscript pagination does not correspond to that of the text in Lindelöf and Thompson's edition (see below, p. 12, n. 4), to which philologists have usually referred since 1927. This table converts the manuscript pagination to our foliation, in the two misbound gatherings:

MS pages		our folio	MS pages		our folio
131–2	=	73[66]	141–2	=	67[71]
133–4	=	74[67]	143–4	=	68[72]
135–6	=	75[68]	145–6	=	69[73]
137–8	=	76[69]	147–8	=	70[74]
139–40	=	66[70]	149–50	=	71[75]
			151–2	=	72[76]

Aldred's contribution includes liturgical (66[70]r–67[71]v5 and 77r–84r) and educational (85r–88v) texts in Latin, all but a few lines of which he glossed in Anglo-Saxon, and an Anglo-Saxon gloss to most of the original collectar and to the first few lines of the later additions (1r–53r and 54v–61v10). To judge by his handwriting, Aldred also wrote and signed, as a priest, the Anglo-Saxon gloss in the Lindisfarne Gospels (B.M. Cotton Nero D. iv; colophons at 89v and 259r) and wrote the unsigned Latin glosses in an eighth-century manuscript of Bede on Proverbs (Oxford, Bodleian Library, Bodley 819). There is no evidence to suggest that the 'Ritual' has left the custody of the community of St Cuthbert and its successors at any time since the late tenth century.

The first mention of the 'Ritual' in print is in Edward Bernard's *Catalogi manuscriptorum Angliae et Hiberniae* (Oxford, 1697).[2] It is described in the catalogue of manuscripts in Anglo-Saxon by Humfrey Wanley[3] and in that by N. R. Ker;[4] in the Durham Cathedral catalogue of Thomas Rud,[5] compiled early in the eighteenth century, and in that of R. A. B. Mynors;[6] and in *The Palaeographical Society: Facsimiles of Miniatures*

2. Vol. II, p. 10, no. 362: *Liber Collectarum Ecclesiasticarum, cum interpretatione Saxonica. Liber mutilatus. 4to.*

3. *Librorum veterum septentrionalium catalogus* (Oxford, 1705), vol. II of George Hickes, *Linguarum vett. septentrionalium thesaurus*, pp. 295–8.

4. *Catalogue of Manuscripts containing Anglo-Saxon* (Oxford, 1957), no. 106, pp. 144–6.

5. *Codicum manuscriptorum ecclesiæ cathedralis Dunelmensis catalogus classicus* (Durham, 1825), p. 71.

6. *Durham Cathedral Manuscripts* (Oxford, 1939), no. 14, p. 25, and pls. 12 (50v and 51r) and 13 (76[69]r and 84r).

and Inscriptions, ed. E. A. Bond and E. Maunde Thompson, series I (1873–83), pls. 240–1 (82r and 84r). E. A. Lowe, *Codices latini antiquiores,* II (Oxford, 1935), no. 151, describes fol. 89 and illustrates part of 89r. N. R. Ker has discussed the relationship between Aldred the Provost and the Aldred of the Lindisfarne Gospels;[1] and T. J. Brown, A. S. C. Ross and E. G. Stanley have discussed the date of the 'Ritual' gloss and its relationship with the Lindisfarne Gospels and Bodley 819.[2] The first edition of the text, published in 1841 by Joseph Stevenson,[3] was superseded in 1927 by that of U. Lindelöf, which includes an introductory chapter by A. H. Thompson on the contents and on the Anglo-Saxon colophon.[4] Between these two editions John Lingard discussed the manuscript;[5] W. W. Skeat published a collation of the glosses with Stevenson's text, a collation of the gatherings (by Henry Bradshaw) and notes on the colophon etc.;[6] and W. H. Frere printed a summary description of the manuscript and of its contents.[7]

THE PALAEOGRAPHY OF THE MANUSCRIPT

PHYSICAL STRUCTURE

Of the 'Ritual's' eleven gatherings I–VIII (fols. 1–65) belong to the original collectar, the text of which stops at 61r10 and is followed immediately by the first of the later additions. The original first gathering of the collectar, which presumably contained ten or more leaves, is lost:[8] its scribe wrote the numbers *ii, iii, v, vii* and *viii* in the bottom left hand corners of the last pages of the present gatherings I, II, IV, VI and VII (9v, 17v, 24v, 44v and 53v).[9] Gatherings IX[X], X[IX] and XI (fols. 66 [70]–88) and the single end-leaf (fol. 89) were added later.

The gatherings of the original collectar are mostly made up of five sheets, each folded to make two leaves, plus one or more half-sheets, making one leaf each. I (fols. 1–9), originally of five sheets, has lost one leaf before fol. 1. II (fols. 10–17), originally of 4½ sheets, has lost the half-sheet after fol. 15. Of III (fol. 18), once presumably a normal gathering of about ten leaves, only one leaf survives. IV (fols. 19–24), originally of five sheets, has lost four leaves before fol. 19. V (fols. 25–33), originally of 5½ sheets, has lost the half-sheet after fol. 30 and one leaf after fol. 33. VI (fols. 34–44) is of 5½ sheets (the half-sheet is fol. 38). VII (fols. 45–53), originally of 5½ sheets (the half-sheet is fol. 47), has lost two leaves before fol. 45. VIII (fols. 54–65) is of six sheets. The sheets, prepared in the Insular fashion, are not all arranged uniformly; but flesh sides seem to face outwards as a rule, so that hair faces flesh in most openings. The gatherings were pricked after folding, in the Insular fashion, for a pair of vertical lines, about 6 mm. apart, at each side of the single column of text and for hori-

1. 'Aldred the Scribe', *Essays and Studies by Members of the English Association,* XXVIII (1943 for 1942), 7–12.

2. In *Codex Lindisfarnensis,* 2 vols (Olten and Lausanne, 1956–60), ed. T. D. Kendrick, T. J. B., R. L. S. Bruce-Mitford, H. Roosen-Runge, A. S. C. R., E. G. S. and A. E. A. Werner; vol. II (1960), bk II, pp. 25–33; pls. 57 (details of 67[71]r and 82r), 58 (details of 17v, 81r and 84r), 59 (84r) and 60 (Bodley 819, details of 11r and 25v). This work is cited henceforth as *Cod. Lind.,* all references being to vol. II.

3. *Rituale ecclesiae Dunelmensis,* Surtees Society, X (1840 [1841]).

4. *Rituale ecclesiae Dunelmensis. The Durham Collectar,* Surtees Society, CXL (1927), henceforth cited as *Rit.;* pls. I (36r), II (66[70]v) and III (85v).

5. *The History and Antiquities of the Anglo-Saxon Church* (London, 1845), II, 359–66.

6. *Transactions of the Philological Society,* 1877–9, app. II, pp. 49*–72*.

7. *The Leofric Collectar compared with the Collectar of St Wulfstan,* Henry Bradshaw Society, LVI (1921), xx–xxi.

8. Wanley, *op. cit.,* p. 295, stated that the manuscript was mutilated at the beginning, in the middle and at the end. When he saw it, it was bound in the present, incorrect order.

9. The ink of the numeration is generally paler than that of the main text; but the shape of *v* is the same as in the main text.

zontal lines about 9 mm. apart. The prickings lie on the inner vertical lines. Gatherings were ruled in dry point on the first recto and then on one or more later rectos as required. The number of lines to the page varies, sometimes within the same gathering: twenty-two or twenty-three lines are usual, but twenty-one and twenty-four also occur. The width of the written space, between the inner verticals, varies between 120 and 125 mm. approximately, and its depth varies between 180 mm. (twenty-one or twenty-two lines) and 190 mm. (twenty-three or twenty-four lines) approximately. In the top left hand corner of 11v the original scribe (apparently) wrote *xb (Christe benedic* or *Christus benedictus)*.

The last three gatherings are additions to the original collectar; no numeration survives, but the contents show that the first and second of them have been transposed by a binder. IX[X] (fols. 66[70]–72[76]) is of 3½ sheets (the half-sheet is fol. 69[73]). X[IX] (fols. 73[66]–76 [69]) is of two sheets. XI (fols. 77–88) is of six sheets. All the membrane is of much the same quality; some hair (of a calf?) survives round a small hole on 84r. The flesh side of the sheets faces outwards, so that flesh mostly faces hair within the gatherings. The various scribes who wrote 61r10–88v ruled the leaves as required for the various sections of text, always with a dry point and after folding: in VIII fresh ruling can be seen on 61r, 61v, 63v and 64r (two sets); in IX[X] on 66[70]r, 67[71]v and 68[72]v; in X[IX] on 73[66]r and 76[69]v; and in XI on 77r, 80r, 82r, 85r and 85v. Ruling is for a single column except at 64v17–28 (for three) and 65v, 78r–84r and 85r–88v (for two). The number of lines to the page varies considerably throughout the additions: VIII (fols. 61–65) has between twenty-two and thirty-two; in IX[X], 66[70]r–67[71]r have twenty-one, 68 [72]v–70[74]v have thirty-two and the rest between twenty-six and thirty; in X[IX], 73[66]r–75[68]r have twenty-five and the rest between twenty-three and twenty-nine; in XI most pages have twenty-three and the rest between twenty-four and twenty-six, except 84v with thirty-five. The written space in the additions constantly varies in size, often from one page to the next; but it always roughly corresponds to that of the original collectar (120–140 mm. approx. × 180–200 mm. approx.). In the top left hand corners of the first pages of IX[X] (66[70]r) and XI (77r) Aldred wrote *xb (Christe benedic* or *Christus benedictus)*; and at 73[66]r (first page of X [IX]) scribe C[1] made a cross.

A pencilled collation of the gatherings on a sheet of paper guarded in at the beginning is in the hand of Henry Bradshaw (1831–86); and the paper slips with collations in ink pasted to the first pages of the gatherings are in the hand of Sir James A. H. Murray (1837–1915). None of these is reproduced here.

From fol. 22 onwards the top right hand corners of the leaves are stained with water; the effects are worst in fols. 76[69] and 77, and this shows that the manuscript was already misbound when the harm was done. Towards the end of the manuscript general dampness has caused a good deal of light offsetting between facing pages. A reagent has been applied at 21v10–14.

In 1927 Lindelöf[2] ascribed the then existing binding to the nineteenth century. Since then the manuscript has been quarter bound in brown, and sewn much too tightly.

THE CONTENTS IN RELATION TO THE STRUCTURE

This summary description of the main contents of the 'Ritual' is designed to show their relationship to the construction of the manuscript. The first column includes references to the full textual description, below, pp. 44–51. The four textual divisions of the original collectar (α) run straight on through gatherings I–VIII

1. See below, pp. 15 and 29–32.
2. *Rit.*, p. xliii.

in the normal way, regardless of the construction of the manuscript. The additions (β), excepting those within the text of the original collectar (β4), fall into three sections (β1–3) which correspond to the construction of the manuscript: changes of hand occur between β1 and β2 (at VIII–IX[X], 65v–66[70]r) and between β2 and β3 (at X[IX]–XI, 76[69]v–77r), but not at the junction between gatherings in the middle of β2 (at IX[X]–X[IX], 72[76]v–73[66]r). Excepting the educational texts copied by Aldred the Provost on 85r–88v, the contents of the additions are homogeneous: a single, if miscellaneous, series of liturgical supplements to the original collectar.

Contents	*Folios*	*Gatherings*	*Notes*
α. The original collectar	1r–61r10	I–VIII	
1. The Temporale (p. 44)	1r–21r		Some eleven leaves lost before fol. 1, one after fol. 15, nine(?) around fol. 18 and four before fol. 19.
2. The Sanctorale (pp. 44–7)	21r–38v		One leaf lost after fol. 30 and one after fol. 33.
3. The Commune Sanctorum (p. 47)	38v–45r21		Two leaves lost between fols. 44 and 45.
4. Benedictions etc. (pp. 47–8)	45r21–61r10		The *halsuncge* at 55r is in Anglo-Saxon, as are the rubrics at 55r6 and 20, 55v15, 56r4, 56v4 and 15, 57r10 and 57v1 and 19.
β. The additions			
1. A group of liturgical texts written by several hands (p. 48)	61r11–65v	VIII	These occupy the part of the last gathering of the original collectar that was left unwritten.
2. Another similar group (pp. 48–9)	66[70]r–76[69]v	IX[X] and X[IX]	66[70]r–67[71]v5 were written and provided with a gloss in Anglo-Saxon by Aldred the Provost. The rubric at 72[76]r3 is in Anglo-Saxon. The lines in the bottom margin of 75[68]v refer to Ealdhun, bishop of Chester-le-Street 990–1018.
3. Liturgical (77r–84v) and educational (85r–88v) texts, mostly written, and glossed in Anglo-Saxon, by Aldred the Provost (pp. 49–51)	77r–88v	XI	Aldred's four Latin collects for St Cuthbert, with his signed and dated colophon in Anglo-Saxon and a memorandum in Latin and Anglo-Saxon, are on 84r. The passages not written by him are 77v19–25 and 84v.
4. Additions within the text of the original collectar			
(a) Aldred the Provost's Anglo-Saxon gloss to the	1r–53r and 54v–	I–VIII	Aldred also added two Latin rubrics (3v and 17v) and numerous initials

original collectar and to the first few lines of the additions	61v10		omitted by the original scribe. He left 53v and 54r unglossed.
(b) *Auctor salutis unicus* (p. 50)	53v	VII	Written over erasure of a page of the original collectar, a few words of which survive in the middle of lines 11–13.
γ. The end-leaf (p. 37)	89		Part of a leaf of an eighth-century Northumbrian lectionary.

THE WRITERS OF THE MAIN ADDITIONS

Palaeographical notes on the more important of the scribes who contributed to the 'Ritual' follow at pp. 18–34, and these include my reasons for ascribing various passages of the additions to particular scribes. The minor marginal and other entries are listed below, pp. 34–6.

Scribe O,[1] who wrote and partly decorated the original collectar (1r–61r10), seems to have done his work in the early years of the tenth century in the south of England. He belonged to a far more up-to-date milieu than the six scribes who wrote the bulk of the additions, each of whom was a backward, but not necessarily an incompetent, provincial.[2]

The six main writers of the additions are:

Aldred the Provost,[3] who wrote most of the Anglo-Saxon in the 'Ritual' and gives an exact date, 10 August 970, for the four collects on 84r in β3. At the beginning of β2 he wrote the Latin text and Anglo-Saxon gloss of 66[70]r–67[71]v5. He wrote, and glossed in Anglo-Saxon, most of β3 (77r–88v). He also glossed the whole of the original collectar, except one pair of facing pages, and the first few lines of β1 (β4(a); 1r–53r and 54v–61v10); and added to the collectar two Latin rubrics (3v and 17v) and numerous initials omitted by the original scribe.

Scribe B,[4] who wrote, very clumsily, the addition next after the end of the original collectar (β1; 61r11–22).

Scribe C,[5] who wrote, in a skilled and greatly varied hand, most of β1 (61v–63v4, 64v1–16 and 65rb18–65v) and of β2 (67[71]v6–76[69]r).

Scribe D,[6] who wrote 63v5–64r8 in β1.

Scribe E,[7] who wrote, in Caroline minuscule with more or less frequent lapses into Insular, 64r9–17 in β2, 84v (apparently) in β3 and 53v in β4(b).

Scribe F,[8] who wrote, in a frank mixture of Caroline and Insular forms, 64v17–65rb17 in β1 and 76[69]v in β2.

Because of their importance for the localization of the additions as a whole,[9] I mention here three rather later scribes who made only minor contributions:

Scribe M1,[10] who wrote the sentence about Bishop Ealdhun in the lower margin of 75[68]v, in β2, in a fine Caroline minuscule.

Scribe M2,[11] who wrote 77v19–25 in β3 in a space left blank by Aldred.

Scribe M3,[12] who wrote a liturgical direction in Latin and Anglo-Saxon in the margin of the original collectar at 47v and (apparently) corrected 68[72]r–70[74]v in β2.

That Aldred and scribes B–F wrote in the same scriptorium, and at much the same time, follows from the complex order in which their work occurs in the first three sections of the additions. In β1 scribe C (61v–63v4) follows B (61r11–22), gives way to D (63v5–64r8) and

1. See below, pp. 18–23.
2. See below, pp. 23–34.
3. See below, pp. 23–9.
4. See below, p. 29.
5. See below, pp. 29–32.
6. See below, pp. 32–3.
7. See below, p. 33.
8. See below, pp. 33–4.
9. See below, p. 17.
10. See below, p. 34.
11. See below, pp. 34–5.
12. See below, pp. 35–6.

then E (64r9–17), reappears (64v1–16), gives way to F (64v17–65rb17), and then finishes the section (65rb18–65v). In β2 scribe C (67[71]v6–76[69]r) follows Aldred (66[70]r–67[71]v5) and is followed by F (76[69]v). In β3 scribe E apparently writes one page (84v) in a gap in the middle of Aldred's work (77r–84r and 85r–88v). In β4 scribe E writes one page (53v) over an erasure in the gap in Aldred's gloss to the original collectar, and Aldred glosses B's work (61r11–22) and the first few lines (61v1–10) of C's.

Aldred and C-F must have been exact contemporaries. Poor, inexpert B, as writer of the first addition only, may have worked rather earlier than they did; but it is just as likely that he was allowed to fill a gap left by C at the end of the original collectar, before Aldred began to gloss it.

The exact order in which the additions were written is not always certain. β1 was presumably written first by B-F, using up the remainder of the original collectar (VIII; 61r11–65v) and apparently following each other without leaving gaps (unless C left a gap in which B wrote slightly later[1]). In β2 (66[70]r–76[69]v) the text is continuous between IX[X] and X[IX]; and Aldred and C and F followed each other without leaving gaps. Since C wrote the lion's share of both β1 and β2, they were probably made in a single campaign; and since he chose a short gathering (X[IX]) in which to finish his contribution to β2, it looks as if the campaign ended with the completion of β2. The last page of this block of texts (76[69]v), written by F, who had already written a passage—firmly embedded in work by C—at 64v17–65rb17, is badly rubbed and has a partly erased inscription[2] running upwards in the left margin. It has evidently been, at some period, more exposed than it is now; and it is natural to suppose that the harm was done before β3 (XI) was added to the manuscript. But we know that β2 is at least roughly contemporary with β3, because Aldred contributed to both; and since the text is discontinuous at the beginning (65v–66[70]r) and at the end (76[69]v–77r) of β2, β2 may in fact have been placed after β3, when the three additional gatherings were first attached to the original collectar. Three points can be made against this possibility. First, 61r11–76[69]v look as if they were produced more or less at one time, since they are dominated by scribe C.[3] Secondly, the educational texts that Aldred copied in β3 (85r–88v), after a gap of one leaf, come most naturally at the end of an otherwise strictly liturgical volume. Thirdly, there are more or less severe signs of rubbing at all the structural junctions in the additions (65v–66[70]r, 72[76]v–73[66]r, 76[79]v–77r, 88v and both sides of the end-leaf, fol. 89): which means that everything after gathering VIII was for a long time less securely bound in than I–VIII themselves, where there are no such signs at the junctions.[4] Perhaps we may conclude that the order in which the additions are reproduced in this facsimile was the original one; but that for a long period in and perhaps after the Middle Ages, when the 'Ritual' had probably lost at least its back cover,[5] gathering X[IX] stood right at the end, to be replaced later on, but in front of instead of after IX[X]. Since the text is discontinuous between β2 and β3, they may have been written simultaneously, whatever was the order in which they were first bound up.

In β2 Aldred preceded C, opening in grandiose fashion the first of the gatherings added to the original collectar (IX[X]; 66[70]r–67[71]v 5). In β4, where all his glossing seems to have been done in a single campaign, starting at 1r, he followed C, since he glossed C's work at

1. See above.
2. See below, p. 36.

3. See above.
4. It therefore looks as if the original collectar reached Chester-le-Street as a bound volume, the sewing of which remained intact when the three additional gatherings and the end-leaf were inserted.
5. The *back* covers of medieval bindings, which often had projecting pins to take the ends of the clasps, became particularly offensive to librarians when books began to be stored upright on tightly packed shelves.

61v1–10 in β1. In β3 Aldred again seems to have done all his work in a single campaign, leaving a short gap at the bottom of 77v (filled later by M2) when he changed over from one column to two, and leaving a gap of one nearly complete leaf (84ra3–84v) when he changed over from liturgical to educational texts. Whatever the palaeographical differences between Aldred's work in the Lindisfarne Gospels, in Bodley 819 and in the 'Ritual',[1] all his contributions to the 'Ritual' itself were apparently written at much the same time,[2] with the obvious exception of 84r, where the pale brown ink is most unlike the superb black that he used elsewhere in β3 and in β2 when glossing 66[70]r–67[71]v5. The four Latin collects and the Anglo-Saxon colophon on 84r are the only exactly dated texts in the 'Ritual'. The barely legible memorandum at the bottom of 84ra may well have been written very soon afterwards, but it is not dated by the colophon.[3] Provided that the main additions after 61r10 were mostly written in the order in which they appear in this facsimile, and provided that Aldred had with him in Bishop Ælfsige's tent in Wessex on 10 August 970 the complete manuscript (and not just gathering XI: which is a reasonable possibility[4]), then most of the main additions will have been written before that date. The one certain exception is scribe E's passage on 84v. Possible exceptions are E's passage on 53v, B's passage on 61r, and Aldred's own gloss for 1r–53r and 54v–61v10: all three could have been done after the manuscript as a whole was completed and after the collects and colophon were added. If the two provisos set out above are rejected, then we can only say that 84v was written after 10 August 970 and that all the rest of the additions were written *c.* 970. Since the six scribes concerned, Aldred and B-F, were obviously exact contemporaries, working in the same scriptorium, there is next to nothing to lose by playing for safety and dating all the main additions *c.* 970.

There can be no doubt that all the scribes so far mentioned, except the writer of the original collectar, were members of the community of St Cuthbert. Aldred the Provost and B-F were evidently contemporaries. Aldred's collects are for St Cuthbert, and he wrote them in 970 for a Bishop Ælfsige, who can only be the bishop of that name who ruled the community, at Chester-le-Street, from 968 to 990; and he mentions St Cuthbert again in his memorandum on the same page.[5] C's Anglo-Saxon rubric at 72[76]r3 contains a characteristically Northumbrian form.[6] The end-leaf (fol. 89), which seems to have been in the manuscript since the tenth century, is of Northumbrian origin.[7] M1's inscription at 75[68]v refers to Ælfsige's successor, Ealdhun, who presided at Chester-le-Street from 990 to 995 and at Durham from 995 to 1018, and so it must have been written between 990 and 1018.[8] M2 apparently wrote, in the *Liber vitae* of the community,[9] an entry which probably dates from Ealdhun's episcopacy or not long afterwards.[10] M3, whose handwriting places him in the middle of the eleventh century, added St Cuthbert's name to a prayer for a confessor and bishop at 69[73]v 28.[11] Nothing about the rest of the minor additions[12] suggests that they were written elsewhere.

1. See below, pp. 25–7.
2. See below, pp. 25–7.
3. See below, pp. 24–5.
4. From at least the eighth century isolated gatherings were sometimes folded and so carried about, often for a long time (B. Bischoff, 'Über gefaltete HSS. vornehmlich hagiographischen Inhalts', *Bullettino dell' archivio paleografico italiano,* N.S. II–III [1956–7], 93–100; reprinted, with additions, in B. Bischoff, *Mittelalterliche Studien,* I [Stuttgart, 1966], 93–100). An English example of the second half of the eleventh century is Oxford, Bodleian Library, Auct. F. 4. 32 (S.C. 2176), fols. 10–18, containing a homily in Anglo-Saxon, reproduced in R. W. Hunt, *Saint Dunstan's Classbook from Glastonbury, Umbrae codicum occidentalium,* IV (1961). Our gathering XI was never folded; but the bishop's baggage could certainly have held it without folding.

5. See below, p. 24.
6. See below, p. 54.
7. See below, p. 37.
8. See below, p. 34.
9. B.M. Cotton Domitian vii, 47v11–15.
10. See below, pp. 34–5.
11. See below, pp. 35–6.
12. See below, p. 36.

THE HANDWRITING AND DECORATION OF THE ORIGINAL COLLECTAR

O, the scribe who wrote, rubricated and, it seems, partly decorated the original collectar (1r–61r10), was an expert writer and draughtsman. His Anglo-Saxon minuscule is basically of the set kind, written with frequent pen-lifts; but a few letters (notably *m*, 57v2, 5 and 9; *p*, 15r7 and 14; and *s*, 16r23) may be written cursively (once even a whole word; *per* at 43v 22). The quality of his writing varies greatly, with the state of his pen: neat and compressed when it was fresh-cut, open and even rough when it was worn (3v15–16, 7v9–10, 43r18–19 and 57r19–20). The character of his writing shows most clearly at 54r (Latin) and 55r7–21 (Anglo-Saxon), which are not glossed. A few of the features which occur throughout the main text will suffice to show that it was all written by the same hand: short *i* after *f* or *s* (1r20 and 60v12); cursive *m* (9v4 and 61r9); *v* for *u* (2v8 and 58r21); *x* (6r8 and 22 and 57v10 and 13); capital *Q* (15r22 and 51r17); three varieties of the abbreviation stroke (2v2 and 58r8–12); trailing *r* in the abbreviation of *-orum* (10r20 and 60v11); 'reversed' *e* in ligatures (2v19 and 57v2); scroll-like signs for runovers (1r3 and 10 and 49v21); and *oðoris* for *odoris* (2r2 and 57r7). All the rubrics in the original collectar (except Aldred's at 3v10 and 17v11) were written by O in red ink or (at 2v13, last two words; 3r7; 16r5; and 38v16–39r1) in a thick pigment now much oxidized. Between 31r and 58r they are poorly written, except at 38v–39r and 45v20; but good and bad alike are linked to the main text by such things as the occurrence of rough writing (30v3 and 6–8) contrasting with neat (30v12, 17–18 and 22); the use of a mixed capital display script (30v12 and 38v–39r; cf. 4r15 and 21r16); the isolated occurrence of capital forms (*G*, 25r18 and 55r20; and *Q*, 59v13); other characteristic forms like high *c* (14v4), short *i* after *s* (5r1 and 30r8), trailing *r* in *-orum* (21r14 and 25v8 and 12) and *v* for *u* (26v9 and 27v8). The *halsuncge* in Anglo-Saxon at 55r7–21 and the nine Anglo-Saxon rubrics at 55r6–56v15 and 57r10–57v19 were certainly written by O; and so was the unglossed Latin of 54r (note *-orum*, lines 3 and 16; and *x*, lines 21–2). O also numbered the gatherings;[1] and apparently wrote the guide-letters for initials (5v; compare *f* with main text, line 7). Many of the initials were supplied afterwards by Aldred, in the red ink that he used for the gloss (5v, excepting the *M* in line 1, written in the now oxidized pigment that O used for some of the rubrics), but O apparently executed all the initials and other drawings in brown ink. It is the same ink as that of the main text, and the initials at 1r17, 2v15, 13v14 and 18, 37v10 and 19 and 38v9 (at least) seem to have been drawn before the main text was written round them. At some points the regular placing of the brown initials (35v) or the presence of guide-letters for them (5v1, 15v21 and 30v4) shows that they were drawn after the main text of the page had been completed. The quality of the brown initials, like the quality of the script, is variable; but the ornamental repertoire and the details of the drawing are constant throughout.

Letter Forms

a: either pointed (the stem may rise a little) or square (when it may be horned at the start of the first stroke); the stem of the square form often rises very high at the beginning of a word.
æ: there are two common forms matching the pointed and angular forms of *a*; *e* with a mere tick below also occurs (3r4).
c and *e*: they may be either smoothly curved or 'horned', and both may be high (*e*, 39r8).
d: either uncial or half-uncial, and both forms may be 'horned' (21v5 and 23v6).
f: it may be high (38v10).
i: a straight subscript occurs after *e* or *t* (at 45r10 and 20v1), and a curved subscript after *h*, *m* or *n* (25v8, 38v7 and 40r10); *i-longa* is used at

1. See above, p. 12.

the beginnings of words (1r23 and 2v16), within words for the semi-vowel (1r9 and 22v23) and after a vowel (16r1).

k: see 6r7.

l: it may descend round the next letter (7r4 and 21r17).

m and *n*: they often have an upward turn at the bottom of the final minim, and at the end of a line the last minim of both often sweeps down to the left, and may be finished with a separate stroke.

q (minuscule): it may be 'horned'.

r: it is often near-uncial in form, especially at the end of a line (17v9); and the trailing form found in *-orum* may occur after *o* in words not abbreviated (43r3).

s: either round *s* or low Insular *s* is usual; long *s* is not uncommon at the start of, or within, words (1r22); elongated round *s* also occurs (13r9–10 and 37v6).

t: the crossbar may be either straight or sinuous, the latter especially at the end of a line (2r11).

u: it sometimes starts with a long, oblique stroke (7r23); *v* for *u* is very common.[1]

x: it is always oddly stiff, and the first stroke often starts high; the second stroke may be looped (4r14), hooked (6r11) or ticked (4r3) at the bottom.

y: it may be either straight or rounded (2v8), and both forms may be dotted above; *f*-like *y* occurs (38v6).

z: see 12v17–18.

The runic letter *s* occurs at 43v13.

In the Anglo-Saxon text (55r6–21) and rubrics, the bows of *þ* and wynn are angular; the bar of *ð* is continuous with the bow; *æ* is sometimes written as two separate letters (55r8); and *y* has the rounded form.

Some General Characteristics

(1) For O's tendency to write cursively, see above, p. 18.

1. See below.

(2) Any minim, *i-longa* or the first stroke of *h* may end in an upward turn to the right on the base-line; normal *i* and the second stroke of *u* are generally so treated, and often the last stroke of *m* or *n*. Minims and descenders most often end bluntly, and obliquely, as dictated by the slanting angle of the pen. Descenders, however, are quite often pointed, and may be turned to the left (especially noticeable in *q*); and the minims of cursively written *m* or *n* may be pointed (32r20).

(3) Any form of *m* or *n*, and round *s*, when they occur at the end of a line or paragraph, may be widened to fill space, and often elaborated (58r19).

(4) Wedges at the top of ascenders are sometimes split.

(5) 'Horned' forms of square *a*, of *c* and *e* (both may be high), of both sorts of *d*, of minuscule and capital *q* are fairly common.

(6) At the beginnings and ends of lines *a* or *t* may be flourished (33v4 and 32v15; 7r10 and 40v7).

(7) After *f* or low *s*, *i* or *u* is often written small (2v3, 15v1, 33r19 and 51r22–3); note small *a* after *f* at 1r3, and small *o* after *s* (26r11).

(8) A roughly made Caroline minuscule *g* occurs at 6r5.

Display Script

In the first lines of collects etc. (4r16, 21r14 and 37v19), at the ends of paragraphs (2v1, 48r14 and 58r19) and in rubrics (30v12 and 38v–39r) O used a display script in which rustic capital and uncial forms are mixed with his usual minuscule forms, making the effect of a capital script. We find capital *A, Æ, B, D, E, M, Q, T* and *V;* and uncial *E, G, L, M, N, P, R* and *S*. Any of these display forms may occur in isolation in the body of the text, especially at the beginning of a word; the commonest are uncial *M* and capital *Q* (plain or 'horned') and *V*. Uncial *N* and *V* are frequent throughout as alternatives to the minuscule forms. Uncial *A* occurs in isolation at 33r3.

Ligatures

An *e,* plain or 'horned' and frequently high, may run into *f* (18r21), *g* (10r10), *i* (14r1), *m, n, p* (5v12), *r, s, t, u* (39v8) or *x* (14v5); *e* may have the 'reversed' form before *m* (44v22), *r* or *s* (37v12; 7r9 and 19v16), or *t* (at 58v17); for *et* we find both a plain form and the ancient specifically Insular form (14r8), and *æt* occurs (13v10). Pairs of *f*s (3r2) or of low *ss* (6r4) are often ligatured; long *s* with *t* (4r14) is not uncommon; *u* with low *s* (21v16), *NT* (29v17), *eN* (57r21) and *tt* (57v2) occur.

Abbreviations

Nomina sacra are usually treated in the accepted fashion: but note *hierusł.* at 45v9; *hierosolimā* at 45v1–2; *isrhł* at 27r9; *israhel* at 31v6 (where Aldred has added an acute accent over the *e,* perhaps to restore the word's sacred quality); *sp̄s inmundus* (57v17); *sp̄itus* etc. for *spiritus* etc. at 47v3–54r20, with *sp̄itales* at 56r20–1.

A bar over *a, e* or *u* means *m*; over *i* at 5r7 it means *n*. In *-bus* and *-que* the sign is either a 'semicolon' or a '3'; note the big 'comma' at 41v21. *Con-* is generally written out; but Insular 'reversed' *c* occurs in a rubric at 50r10, and continental *c̄* at 40r14. A bar over *m* means *-en* in *lumen, nomen* or *sacramentis* at 28r10, 29v16 and 36r17. A bar above, or through, *b, t* or *u* means *-er* (3v13). A bar over the last letter of the stem of a verb means *-it.* (*dixit,* 27v19; and *dicit,* 27r1). Suprascript *a* over *t* means *-ra* in *tradentibus* at 45v20. In *-orum (passim)* the '2'-shaped *r* trails downwards. For *-unt*: either a bar over *r* (continental) (21v7) or a bar over *rt* (Insular) (29v12). A '2' over *m* (30v16) or *t* (40v11) means *-ur*. A large 'comma' placed high after *i, m, n* or *t* means *-us* (41r2).

Aput: *ap̄t* (25r18). *Autem*: either the Insular *h*-symbol (10v9) or continental *aūt* (9r23). *Enim*: the Insular symbol (6r5). *Esse*: *ēē.* (27v13). *Est*: either the Insular symbol (6r5) or continental *ē,* usually followed by a point (27r4). *Et*: usually one or other of the two ligatures of *et* (14r8), but the Insular symbol occurs at 55r7 and 56v15 in Anglo-Saxon and at 45v20 in a Latin rubric. *Fratres*: *fr̄s (passim). Illius*: *.illi.,* with or without a bar, occurs between 39r18 and 39v7; thereafter *.ll.* with a bar (41r8) is used for all cases. *Meus*: *ms̄* at 1r4. *Misericordiam*: *misecđam* at 59v11–12. *Nobis*: *nob̄* at 22v23. *Non*: *n̄* (3r5). *Noster* and *uester*: usually *nr̄, nr̄m* etc.; but *nr̄t (noster)* occurs at 38r20 and 44r22. *Omnis* etc.: the contractions based on *om-* are used throughout, including *om̄is, om̄s (omnes)* and *om̄ium*; of the contractions based on *o-, ōibus* occurs at 43r19; *om̄ (omnium),* found between 34r6 and 42r16, may be a suspension rather than an *o*-contraction. *Pater* etc.: *paī, pīr* and *prēm* occur. *Per*: either the Insular symbol (21v18) or the continental (38r22). *Pre*: *p̄. Pro*: *ꝓ* (in three varieties: 16v13, 17r4 and 17r5, the usual one). *Propter*: *ꝓpī* at 9r18. *Quae*: *q* followed by a 'semicolon', by a 'colon', or (at 44r6) by a 'semicolon' and a median point, all equally Insular. *Quam*: in *qm̄* (with suprascript *a*) at 41r3 the suprascript *a* looks like a correction, possibly by O himself; the result is Insular. *Qui*: *q* with suprascript *i* (3r11). *Quia*: *qa* with suprascript *i* (29v3). *Quod*: either Insular *q* (with sinuous bar) or continental *qđ* (23r3 and 9); note *q̄d* at 57v10 and a variety of the Insular symbol at 39v5. *Quoniam*: either *qm̄* (5r24) or *qūo* (26v15). *Seculum* etc.: *scłi* (8v16). *Secundum*: *sc̄dm* (44v7). *Sicut*: *sīc* (30v7), followed by a point at 45v12. *Sunt*: the Insular *s̄t* (29v16), followed by a point at 29v11. *Tibi*: *t* with suprascript *i* at 1v7. *Uel*: *ł* (46r3). *Uere dignum*: the monogram usually found in sacramentaries occurs as an initial at 52r2. *Ut*: *v* surmounted by a 'comma' occurs from 28v5 onwards. In the Anglo-Saxon passages, besides the Insular symbol for *et* mentioned above, we find *þe* and *þ* (55r15 and 17). The remaining abbreviations are of the capricious sort common in liturgical manuscripts: e.g. *apostolus, carissimi* (*km̄i* at 6r7), *eundem, natale, nonae, omnipotens, per Dominum...,* *quesumus* (generally *.q̄s.*) and *salutem.*

Punctuation etc.

(1) Words are generally well spaced; but monosyllables, especially prepositions, are mostly written in one with the next word. Words are mostly divided at the ends of lines in the customary fashion of Latin manuscripts (*huma/na*, *tem/pora* and *fi/as*).

(2) Down to about 21v punctuation is by a single point only, on or above the base line; thereafter ends of paragraphs often have a combination of one or two points with a comma (22r, 23v and 57v14), or with a horizontal or upright dash (52r8 and 58r21; 32v16 and 61r10). At 51r8–52r7 the more elaborate punctuation includes the 'semicolon', the *punctus elevatus* and the question mark (at 51r10–11). The hyphens at 55v17 and 56r18 may be later additions.

(3) Points are used with figures (50r3 and 54r21–2).

(4) Acute accents are used over an occasional monosyllable (27v21, Latin *do*; and 55r17, Anglo-Saxon *to*), and frequently over a pair of vowels (57r4, *isaac*; 38r, *andree*; 27r4, *meae*; and 27r20, *gaudii*).

(5) Three forms of abbreviation stroke are common throughout (2v2); a decorative form also occurs, generally at the beginning or end of a paragraph (13v14).

(6) Runovers are marked, between 1r and 49v, by a scroll-like sign, angular at 32r9; bracket-and-point signs occur at 37v15 and 51r19. The sign in red at 44r19 was added by Aldred. Runovers in the lower margin are marked by excellent drawings at 1r, 4r, 9v, 15v, 45r, 47v and 57r.[1]

Orthography

An *i-longa* may be used for the semi-vowel (1r9, 2v16 and 22v23). The Insular confusion between *s* and *ss* occurs (27v9 and 31v12); note *contullit* at 26v1 and *efectum* at 32v19. For *e* we find *æ* (19v21), *ę* (19v5) and *ae* (54v19); note *fyrto* at 49r10, *ylimento* at 59r7. Confusions over consonants include *ostem* at 50v2 and *husui* at 56v22; *obtimum* at 13v18 and *pleps* at 29r1; *cifes* (corrected by Aldred) at 39v14; *canguine* (corrected by O) at 23v4, *defentio* at 50r20, *sicientem* (after correction) at 1r12 and *benefitio* at 56v18; and a set involving *ð*, *th* and *ph*: *oðoris* at 2r2 and 57r7, *theoðori* at 25v12, *thabitę* at 28r4, *thimothei* at 32v8 and *piliphi* at 25v8.[2]

Corrections

O made a few changes in his own work: he inserted letters etc., with a comma-like caret (26r10) and at 21r18 with a sign like the Insular abbreviation for *est*, or with no mark (5r4); he expuncted with a point (30v11 and 31r6); and he reworked letters (*c* > *s*, 23v4; and *u* > *a*, 32v5). For Aldred's corrections of O's work, see below, p. 29.

O sometimes left a gap of one line for rubrics, or of two, and then failed to fill it up (1r–12r *passim*). The longer gaps at 21r, 21v and 22v appear to be the result of erasures. 53v was probably erased at Chester-le-Street.[3]

Decoration

I have suggested[4] that scribe O executed numerous initials throughout the manuscript, in the same brown ink as that of the text, drawing some at least before he wrote the text, and others afterwards. Note his sketch for an initial at 26r16. Aldred[5] added many more simple initials in the red ink of his gloss, and touched up a few of O's (4r10, 16r21 and 26r16). In gatherings I and II (1r–17v) O did few drawings; but I includes some of his best. He wrote guide-letters on most pages in I and II; thereafter they are few and far between (25v2). In I he painted many simple initials in the heavy pigment, now oxidized, in which he wrote a few rubrics in the vicinity;[6] and in II

1. See below.

2. For many further examples of the Latin orthography of the manuscript as a whole, see Lindelöf, *Rit.*, pp. liv–lvi.

3. See below, p. 33.

4. Above, p. 18.

5. See above, p. 18, and below, p. 29.

6. See above, p. 18.

he used it to fill several more elaborate initials (12r–17r *passim*). At 1r17 he put touches of red behind the necks of the upper and lower bird heads; at 2v15 he filled the dog's ball and the bands behind his neck and the bird's with yellow(?); the same yellow fills the *D* in red pigment at 7r4. What remains of III (fol. 18) is much decorated; and so are V, VI and VIII (25r–44v and 54r–61r). In VI he used the red pigment of the rubrics at 38v–39r to fill several nearby initials. In IV and VII (19r–24v and 45r–53v) he did comparatively little decoration.

Some of O's simpler initials are capital and others Insular; their stems are often hollow; and they may be decorated with a leaf (21r1), trumpet pattern (27r17 and 19), incipient spirals (25v20), or extra contours, inside or outside, incorporating scrolls (33v15 and 58v20). Initial *O* is often a lozenge filled with wide interlace (33r2; cf. 1v5 and 44v8), or a disk filled with bosses and some sort of cross (2v, 4r, 17r, 37r and 60v).

The components of the more elaborate initials are very various, and occur in many different combinations. O was a most ingenious artist, and this description of his initials accounts only for his main themes, not for all his variations on them. (1) *Complete creatures.* A fish forms the tongue of *e* at 40r, 57r and 60v. A seated bird forms *d* at 35v (animal head) and 56r (human head). At 36r a dog stands up and sticks out his scrolling tongue and his front paws to make *F*. Winged dragons form the bows of letters either alone (at 28v, with foliate tail); or with heads (at 1r, 2v, 3v, 42r and 57v); or with a mask (at 12r). (2) *Human heads* sometimes fill an *O* and are generally tonsured (at 27v1, 35v, 42r, 43r and 61r); *O* consists of a tonsured head in profile at 27v4 and of full faces at 32v (long haired) and 60v (bearded). Human heads, generally in profile, form terminals, sometimes in company with animals or within the bowl of a letter, at 14v, 18r, 25r (a woman?), 30r, 36r, 37r, 37v (twice: one wears a cap, like the head on the bird at 56r), 40v, 55r (full face; another woman?), 55v and 58v (with cap and beard). (3) *Human hands* occur at 38v (as a lappet) and 44r (as a terminal). (4) *Masks* often serve as terminals (12r) or as links between the parts of a letter (13v18); they are either lion-like (13v18), or semi-human but eared (12r); their tongues are often double and may be scrolling (15v), or foliate (28v), or (at 38v) made of fruit. At 57v the tongue and ears of a lion mask make *T;* and at 27v a fully human mask, but with double foliate tongue, makes *Q*. They make a pleasing gallery, at 12r, 13v, 15v, 16r, 16v, 18r, 26r, 28r, 28v, 29r, 37r, 38v, 41v and 57v. (5) *Heads of animals and birds* account for most of the terminals; the birds have open, hawk-like beaks (1r); the animals mostly look like dogs (2v), but like goats at 34v10 and 59v19, and like deer at 39r2 and 55v16. Extra-large heads occur at 24v, 26v, 28v, 36v, 42v, 46v and 55v. Dogs' tongues may be scrolling (at 2r and 46v), foliate (at 32v) or interlaced (at 29v); and dogs with balls in their mouths occur at 2v, 14r, 14v and 34v. A dog emerges from foliage at 13v; a bird eats fruit at 39v, and another has a fruit for a tongue (at 44r8). Angular lappets fall forward from dogs' heads at 14v, 18v, 21v, 24v, 30v and 48v; at 36r the lappet is interlaced, at 38v it is a human hand, and at 42v it is foliate. A dog will often bite the stem of an initial (1r and 3v) and sometimes coil his tongue round it (14v). Pairs of initials are linked by biting birds at 27r and by biting dogs at 28r, 28v and 32v. Bird and animal terminals are used in combination with fish (40r), with dragons (1r), with human heads (14v), with masks (13v), with foliage (6v) and with interlace (39v). (6) *Foliage and fruit.* Terminals are sometimes made of foliage, small (13v and 14r) or large (20v and 46v), or of fruit (39v, 42v and 44r). (7) *Interlace* is used to fill letters (45r); to make terminals (45v), which sometimes link them in pairs (28r4); to diversify their structure (28r20 and 28v3). It is generally wide, with two contours (39v), but may be solid (46v and 48v). (8) '*Sleeves*', some of them foliate (28v21), often occur just behind terminals (1r and 2v), on the stems of letters (28v3 and 21 and 46v17), or where the stems join (2v). (9) *Rectangular constructions* suggest wood- or metal-work (at 2r) and architecture (35v).

O's best drawings are in the margins. Run-overs in the bottom margin are marked by birds (at 1r, with foliate tail; 45r; and 47v), by a dragon with interlaced and foliate tail (at 4r), by a mask (at 9v), and by lions with foliate tails (at 15v and 57r). Note the heads finishing descenders at 32v and 33v, and the mask at 43v. The large patch towards the outer edge of fol. 59 moved O to decorate it, and so mitigate its ugliness, with drawings of figures which seem to illustrate the text. At 59r a beardless man raises his right hand to bless and with his left points to a fish, which presumably stands for the *ylimentum* (59r7) of water. (The text at this point is a *benedictio aquae.*[1]) At 59v a bearded man raises his left hand and holds a dish(?) in his right: which may refer to the rubric at 59v13, *oratio quando aqua in domo aspargitur.* Compare the fish with 60v11 and the bearded head with 60v19. A later artist copied the bird at 45r and the raised hand at 59r.[2]

THE HANDWRITING OF THE ADDITIONS

Aldred

Of the scribes who wrote the additions to the original collectar,[3] only Aldred the Provost has received much attention. N.R.Ker[4] was the first to establish by detailed palaeographical argument that he wrote both the Anglo-Saxon gloss in the Lindisfarne Gospels and the following additions to the 'Ritual': (1) the main text and Anglo-Saxon gloss of 66[70]r–67[71]v5 and of 77r–84ra2 and 85r–88v; (2) the Anglo-Saxon gloss to the original collectar and to the first few lines of the additions (1r–53r and 54v–61v10); and (3) the four Latin collects for St Cuthbert and their Anglo-Saxon colophon on 84r. T.J.Brown, A.S.C.Ross and E.G. Stanley suggested that he also wrote the memorandum at the bottom of 84ra and the Latin glosses in Oxford, Bodleian Library, Bodley 819.[5] Humfrey Wanley, who described both the Lindisfarne Gospels and the 'Ritual' in his *Catalogus,* 1705, saw that the Lindisfarne gloss and most of the relevant parts of the 'Ritual' were by the same hand, but he regarded Aldred the Provost, who wrote the collects and colophon on 84r, as distinct from, but contemporary with, Aldred the Priest, who signed the Lindisfarne gloss; and he dated both of them to the reign of King Alfred.[6] Wanley was allowed to borrow the 'Ritual' and to compare it with the Lindisfarne Gospels, then kept with the rest of Sir Robert Cotton's collection at Cotton House in the Palace of Westminster.[7] In the nineteenth century Wanley's opinion was followed more or less closely by Thomas Wright,[8] by George Waring,[9] and by Sir Frederic Madden.[10] Against him, Sir Edward Maunde Thompson maintained that the Lindisfarne gloss, the 'Ritual' gloss with parts of the main text, and the collects and colophon were written by three different hands;[11] and this opinion was followed by W.W.Skeat,[12] by Sir James A.H. Murray,[13]

1. See below, p. 48.
2. See below, p. 36.
3. See above, pp. 15–17.
4. 'Aldred the Scribe', *loc. cit.*

5. *Cod. Lind.,* bk II, pp. 26–8 and 32–3.
6. *Op. cit.,* pp. 295–8.
7. '...cujus quidem manum in hoc Codice statim atque conspexi agnoscebam, codicemque hunc Dunelmensem cum Cottoniano conferens, unum Aldredum utriusque, quoad maximam partem, scriptorem esse repperi (*ibid.,* p. 298).'
8. *Biographia britannica literaria, Anglo-Saxon Period* (London, 1842), p. 426.
9. *The Lindisfarne and Rushworth Gospels,* IV (Surtees Society, XLVIII [1865]), xlvi.
10. In a letter to Sir Henry Ellis printed in the latter's *Original Letters of Eminent Literary Men* (Camden Society, 1843), p. 267.
11. *Pal. Soc.,* ser. I, pls. 240–1; *Catalogue of Ancient Manuscripts in the British Museum,* pt II, Latin (1884), p. 16; and 'Aldred the Glossator', *Dictionary of National Biography,* I, 248–9.
12. *Transactions of the Philological Society,* 1877–9, app. II, p. 55*; and *The Gospel according to St John in Anglo-Saxon and Northumbrian Versions* (Cambridge, 1878), p. ix.
13. *Athenaeum* (1875), pp. 452–3; and *Academy* (July-December 1874), pp. 561–2.

by E. G. Millar,[1] and by U. Lindelöf and A. H. Thompson.[2]

The colophon on 84r reads as follows:-

> Besuðan wudigan gæte æt áclee
> on westsæxum on laurentius
> mæssan daegi. on wodnes dægi
> ælfsige ðæm biscope in his
> getélde aldred se p'fast
> ðas feower collectæ on fif
> næht áldne mona ær
> underne. awrat

And it may be translated as follows:–

> Aldred the provost wrote these four collects at Oakley, to the south of Woodyates, among the West Saxons, on Wednesday, Lawrence's feast day (the moon being five nights old), before tierce, for Ælfsige the bishop, in his tent.

The authors of the commentary on the colophon in *Cod. Lind.*[3] see no reason to alter the views they then expressed, which are these:

(1) The place at which Aldred wrote was Oakley Down, in Dorset, about a mile south of Woodyates, which lies on the main road from Salisbury to Blandford.

(2) The day of the year was 10 August, the Feast of St Lawrence the Martyr, and it was a Wednesday.

(3) The moon had been new on 5 or 6 August and it was the calendrical moon, not the true moon.

(4) Between 700 and 1099, 6 August was never calendrical new moon; but in the same period calendrical new moon was 5 August, and 10 August was a Wednesday, in the years 875, 970 and 1065.

(5) Since the first and last of these years are palaeographically unlikely, and there was in any case no Bishop Ælfsige in 875, the correct solution is 970, which falls within the episcopacy of Bishop Ælfsige of Chester-le-Street (968–90). The collects are for the Feast of St Cuthbert, who was patron of the community at Chester-le-Street; other additions in the 'Ritual' relate to him and to the community.[4]

The only important difference between these conclusions and A. H. Thompson's,[5] is that Thompson assumed that Aldred was referring to the true moon, which makes both 970 and 981 possible dates.

The memorandum at the bottom of 84ra is discussed in *Cod. Lind.* and reproduced from a special photograph.[6] It was apparently written after the collect immediately above it, but in ink of the same colour, whereas the ink of the colophon is somewhat darker than that of the collects.[7] The memorandum is written in a combination of capital and minuscule letters drawn from the Greek and Roman alphabets and reads as follows (a point on the line indicates a letter-space and a point under a letter indicates that the reading is more or less uncertain):

> ḍc̣ ΩM̄NIΠNC
> 7̣ MΛRIΛ 7 HEΛENA 7 CC̄C
> CVDBERTVC.........ṭe
> g̣ẹḷạṇịḍ.....ḍ

This may be transcribed as: 'D*eus* omnip*ote*ns *et*(?) Maria *et* Helena *et* s*anct*u*s* Cudbertus...te gelanid' [Aldre]d.' If the last word was in fact *Aldred*, and if the next to last was in fact *gelanid'* (= *gelanidon*) from an Old English **ge-lanian*, 'to grant' (second class weak verb), then the translation would be: 'God Almighty and Mary and Helen and St Cuthbert granted... to Aldred.' The memorandum appears to have been

1. *The Lindisfarne Gospels* (London, 1923), p. 5.
2. *Rit.*, p. lii.
3. Bk II, pp. 25–6.
4. See above, pp. 15–17. Bishop Ælfsige was apparently in the south of England between 971 and 975, when he accompanied Kenneth II of Scotland on his journey to do homage to King Edgar. See A. H. Thompson, *Rit.*, pp. xviii–xix, quoting the fragment 'De Northhymbrorum Comitibus' (*Symeonis monachi opera omnia*, ed. T. Arnold [Rolls Series, 75, 1882–5], II, 382).
5. *Rit.*, pp. xiv–xix.
6. Bk II, pp. 26–8, and pl. 58.
7. The reading of the memorandum is impeded by offsetting, due to damp, of some of the text on 83v, which gives 84r the misleading appearance of a palimpsest (cf. *Rit.*, p. 220).

written by Aldred. It is *not* dated by the colophon; but the Feast of the Assumption of the B.V. Mary falls on 15 August and the Feast of St Helen, Empress and Inventrix of the Cross, on 18 August, and it may well be that Aldred wrote the memorandum soon after the collects. Another possible explanation of St Helen's appearance in the memorandum is that it records a prayer or charm connected with the recovery of lost property. She is invoked, because she found the Cross after it had been lost, in an Anglo-Saxon charm for the recovery of lost cattle.[1]

It will be convenient at this point to quote in translation part of 'Aldred the Priest's' long Anglo-Saxon colophon to his gloss in the Lindisfarne Gospels (259r), the most recent commentary on which is in *Cod. Lind.*:[2]

> And Aldred, unworthy and most miserable priest *(presbiter indignus et miserrimus)*, glossed it in English between the lines with the help of God and St Cuthbert. And, by means of the three sections, he made a home for himself—the section of Matthew was for God and St Cuthbert, the section of Mark for the bishop, the section of Luke for the members of the community (in addition, eight ores of silver for his induction) and the section of St John was for himself (in addition, four ores of silver for God and St Cuthbert) so that, through the grace of God, he may gain acceptance into heaven; happiness and peace, and through the merits of St Cuthbert, advancement and honour, wisdom and sagacity on earth.

Against the first quoted line Aldred wrote in the margin, *ælfredi natus aldredus uocor: bonæ mulieris filius eximius loquor*. He then glossed *bonæ mulieris* with the words '*id est* tilw'', meaning *til wif*, 'good woman'.

That the whole of the Lindisfarne gloss was written by Aldred, as his colophon on 259r states, was accepted by Wanley,[3] argued effectively by Maunde Thompson,[4] and argued afresh in *Cod. Lind.*[5] Lindelöf[6] has shown that the 'Ritual' gloss is also the work of one hand. Ker[7] showed that the two glosses were written by the same man, pointing out the basic similarities between them and explaining the differences in terms of the writer's attitude towards his task in each case: in the Lindisfarne gloss he was writing formally, to match the formality of the Latin text, while in the 'Ritual' gloss he was writing informally. The authors of *Cod. Lind.* added a few points in support of Ker,[8] and gave a full description of the handwriting of the Lindisfarne gloss,[9] which—with the following modifications—will also serve to describe the 'Ritual' gloss:

(1) The 'Ritual' gloss is less formal and more cursive (and more expert): minims are seldom provided with feet; *f*, *p*, *r* and *s* are often deeply split; the descender of *r* is more often curtailed, so that it resembles *n*; and the lower bow of *g* is generally open, corresponding to the first of the five forms found in Lindisfarne.[10]

(2) Tall *f* and *s* are common, especially in the *st* ligature; and tall *e* is common in ligatures.

(3) The crossbar of *g* commonly projects further to the right than to the left, which is rare in the Lindisfarne gloss.

(4) The two simpler forms of *a*—the open and the pointed—predominate in the 'Ritual' gloss, but the other two forms found in the Lindisfarne gloss occur.[11]

(5) Where *i* follows *g* in the 'Ritual' it is usually made in one with the crossbar of *g*, or at least

1. G. Storms, *Anglo-Saxon Magic* (The Hague, 1948), no. 15 and pp. 213 and 215.

2. Bk II, pp. 5–11.

3. See above, p. 23, n. 6.

4. *Catalogue of Ancient Manuscripts in the British Museum, loc. cit.*

5. Bk II, pp. 12–24.

6. *Rit.*, p. li.

7. 'Aldred the Scribe', *loc. cit.*

8. Bk II, pp. 29–30.

9. *Ibid.*, pp. 12–21.

10. For the second form see 26r12 *usig*; for the third, 44r8 *god*, 50v12 *geafum* and 51r3 *nængum*; for the fourth, 23r19 *gisungan*; and for the fifth, 25r12 *giboensandum*.

11. For the open letter closed by a hairline across the top, see 44r6 and 7; for the 'Caroline' form, 10v8, 28r4 and 7 and 28v4.

touches it (3v5 and 80va10); the ligature *eo*, which occurs only once in the Lindisfarne gloss (125ra22), is common in the 'Ritual' from 31v22 onwards; and 'reversed' *e* in ligatures, which is not found in Lindisfarne, occurs throughout the 'Ritual' (*es*, 14v6; *er*, 67[71]r 19; and *ea*, 81rb16).[1]

(6) In the 'Ritual' gloss, as one would expect in a liturgical text in which formulas are often repeated, Aldred makes more use of capricious abbreviation.[2]

(7) The *f*-like form of *y* occurs in the 'Ritual' as an exceptional form (9r20 and 14r18), but never in Lindisfarne.

(8) Subscript letters are less common in the 'Ritual' than in Lindisfarne; and so are suprascripts (but note the rough breathing used for *h* at 26v11 and the shallow cursive *u* at 31v20).

(9) In the 'Ritual' groups of letters are sometimes linked by very long-drawn-out strokes (*oestro*, 15r4; *gifraignað*, 17v17; and *arfæstnise*, 18v9).

(10) In the 'Ritual' the crossbar of *ð* is almost always made in a separate stroke, whereas in Lindisfarne this form virtually disappears after 53r. The form in which the crossbar is made in one with the rest of the letter does, however, occur in the 'Ritual' (3r8, 9 and 11).

(11) In Lindisfarne the form of the abbreviation stroke differs in *-m* (straight with a tick at either end) and in *-er* or *-or* (sinuous); but in the 'Ritual' the sinuous form is generally used for both, although the straight form is occasionally used for *-m* over *o* (2r7 and 23) or *v* (37r15).

In the Lindisfarne gloss Aldred was obviously experimenting with script, abbreviations and spelling alike;[3] and some similar variation occurs in the 'Ritual' gloss. Lindelöf[4] has indicated striking variations in the use of *ge-* and *gi-* as prefix.[5] The quality of the gloss is rather better when Aldred is glossing his own main text (66[70]r–67[71]v5, 77r–84r and 85r–88v) than when he is glossing the work of others (1r–53r and 54v–61v10). As far as 4v open *a* is rather more frequent than pointed *a*, but in the rest of the glosses pointed *a* is the dominant form and open *a* is quite rare. Down to 23r he was rather more inclined to write wynn for *w* (especially at the beginning of a word) than afterwards, when he normally wrote *v* for *w* as well as for *u*. Note *u* for *-w-* at 3r10 and *vv* for *w-* at 25v13.

That the 'Ritual' gloss is later in date than the Lindisfarne gloss seems to follow from: (1) Aldred's use—from the first— of red ink to gloss texts in brown ink, a practice which he introduced in Lindisfarne only at 220va2, in the middle of a line (note that he used black ink to gloss his own main text, in red, at 66[70]r–67[71]v5 and for his rubrics at 83v); (2) his use of *v* for *u* and *w*, which in Lindisfarne he introduced only at 303v; and (3) his use of *wut'* etc. (3v1 and 2) as an abbreviation for *wutetlice*, which in Lindisfarne begins to replace longer forms only at 63va10. Again, he signed the collects as provost in 970; but when he wrote the Lindisfarne gloss he was only *presbiter indignus et miserrimus*, and his Lindisfarne colophon reveals that he glossed Matthew to Luke (and also paid eight ores of silver) as the price of his membership of the community.[6] Aldred's Latin

1. Aldred may have picked up this practice from the text of the original collectar (see above, p. 20). At 50r9 and 51r18 he uses 'reversed' *e* in isolation.

2. Examples are: *allm' (omnipotens)*, 1v9; *ve bid' (quesumus)*, 1v13 and 17; *middang'* and *midg' (mundi)*, 1v17 and 46r2; *broð' (fratres)*, 3v1 and 3; *ð'* (7r9 and 17) and *ð' h' c'* (13v13) for shortened versions of *per Iesum Christum Dominum Nostrum; miltheart' (misericordiam)*, 12v10; and proper names, 28v *passim* and 38v6. For Aldred's abbreviations of *-m* and *-er* or *-or* in the 'Ritual', see below § 11. He also uses ⁊ for *and* (2r5); crossed *l* for *uel*, without any points (2r13 and 23); *ꝥte* (1v2) and *ꝥ* (1v13); the rune for *dæg* (29r15; combined with an inflexion at 23r6); the rune for *monn* (29r9); *wut'* etc. for *wutetlice* (3v1 and 2). *God* and *crist* are written in full, but *drihten* and *hælend* are usually abbreviated (*drih'*, 3v11; and *hæl'*, 13v11); *irl' (Israhel)* occurs at 27r9.

3. See *Cod. Lind.*, bk. II, pp. 22–4.

4. *Rit.*, p. li.

5. *Gi-* predominates over *ge-* at 1r–61v10 and 77r–80r; and *ge-* over *gi-* at 66[70]r–67[71]v5 and 80v–88v.

6. See above, p. 25.

glosses in Bodley 819[1] apparently come between the Lindisfarne gloss and the 'Ritual' gloss.[2]

The four collects on 84r, as pointed out by Ker[3] and in *Cod. Lind.*,[4] have more in common with Aldred's main text at 77r–84ra2 and 85r–88v than with his glosses in the 'Ritual'; and his colophon on 84r is closer to the more formal Lindisfarne gloss than to the 'Ritual' glosses. The colophon may also be compared with the glosses in the margin of Bodley 819, 10r. Taking 84r as a whole, the most striking likenesses with Aldred's work elsewhere are: (1) the angular shapes of pointed *a* and of *q*, which are usual in the main text of 77r–84ra2 and 85r–88v; (2) the angular bases of *b* and *l*; (3) the occurrences of tall *f* in 84rb23 (*fif*), which link the colophon to the 'Ritual' gloss; (4) the shortness of the descender of *r*, which links collects and colophon alike with both the 'Ritual' and the Lindisfarne glosses; (5) the frequent occurrence of split *f, p, r* and *s*; (6) the shape of the abbreviation for *pro* at 84rb16 and 23 (cf. especially 81ra); (7) the initials to the collects (cf. 79r, 80r and 80v); and (8) the resemblance of the collects to the rubric at 83rb22, which lacks the long descenders that are usual in the main text of 77r–84ra2 and 85r–88v.

The best proof[5] that the main text of 66[70]r-67[71]v5 and of 77r–84ra2 and 85r–88v was written by Aldred lies in the manner in which the formal writing of these passages descends into informality, and closely resembles the 'Ritual' gloss, whenever the writer was pressed for space, as at 66[70]r–67[71]v5 *passim*; 77v5, 8 and 18, 78ra11, 78rb24, 78va1 and 2, 78vb3, 80rb26, 81rb17 (especially), 81rb26, 82va6, 85rb8 and 88rb23–4. Again, the rubric at 82ra6 is a direct link with the majuscule of 66[70]r–67[71]v5, while the rubric at 82rb12 is a direct link with the two rubrics which Aldred inserted in the original collectar at 3v and 17v, in the course of writing his gloss.[6]

Formal Minuscule. The handsome, decorative Anglo-Saxon minuscule of 77r–84ra2 and 85r–88v is Aldred's best work as a scribe. It is thoroughly expert. Minims usually have feet; descenders are sharply pointed; and *f, p, r* and *s* are often deeply split, showing that it was written cursively and with speed. The letters *a*, half-uncial *d* and *q* generally have angular bows; and the last two are often open and flourished. The stem of uncial *d* is generally low; *e* is sometimes 'horned', and may resemble *i* with head and tongue added (82rb3); after *c* or *t, i* often descends, and *i-longa* is common at the beginning of a word; for *k*, see 85va8–9; *m* is often uncial at the beginning of a word; minuscule *r* may resemble *n*, uncial *r* is very common, and a compromise minuscule form which ends in a sharp angle also occurs (85ra8); *v* occurs (77r21); and for *z*, see 86rb8–9. Subscript *a* (81ra25 and 85va23), *i* (67[71]r21, ligatured with *f*) and *t* (81rb12) occur;[7] so does shallow suprascript *u* (86rb16). Ligatures are frequent; they include: *æc, æsp* (87rb11) and *æt*; *ec, ed* (with half-uncial *d*, apparently, at 86va16), *ef* (83va15), *eg, ei, em, en, eo, ep* (78ra10), *er, es, esp, ess, est* and *ett* ('reversed' *e* occurs in *es*, 80ra12, and *est*, 86rb15 and 23; the head of *e* may be drawn out to the right, as at 80ra12 and 86vb9); *ff* and *ss* (the first of each pair generally high, as at 88ra17); *os* (86ra16); *sp* and *sti* (with the *i* curved or straight, as at 79va8 and 19); and *xp* (86vb17). Numerals have a point before and after (87r and v). Minor punctuation is by a point on the line; major punctuation by one or two such points, or by two points followed by a dash. An acute accent is often placed over a monosyllable. Insertions are sometimes made

1. See *Cod. Lind.*, bk. II, pp. 32–3, and pl. 60.
2. Bodley 819 (S. C. 2699) is probably the oldest surviving manuscript of Bede's Commentary on Proverbs. E. A. Lowe now ascribes it with confidence to the Wearmouth-Jarrow scriptorium; see *CLA*, II, no. 235; 'A Key to Bede's Scriptorium', *Scriptorium*, XII (1958), 185 and 187 and pl. 22a; and *English Uncial* (Oxford, 1960), pl. XXXVIIIe.
3. 'Aldred the Scribe', pp. 10–11.
4. Bk II, pp. 30–1.
5. See *ibid.*, p. 30.
6. See above, p. 15.
7. Subscript *e* follows *m* at 78ra13.

with no mark, sometimes with a *signe de renvoi* consisting of two (77v5) or three (79ra11) points; at 81va16 words are transposed with marks resembling abbreviation strokes. Orthography: *æ* for *e* occurs (79rb15), and so does the Insular confusion of *s* and *ss* (*assia* and *remisae*).

Majuscule. Aldred's Insular majuscule (66[70]r–67[71]v5) starts bravely, as a spectacular opening to gathering IX[X], the first to be added to the original collectar at Chester-le-Street; but he abandoned it sooner than he need have done (67[71]r14), probably with relief. Unlike scribe C, who understood the majuscule tradition very well,[1] Aldred was apparently new to it, and so failed to see that if he was to succeed with such large letters, he needed to use a much wider pen. His half-uncial *g* is a poor thing; but he had learnt, doubtless from his work on the Lindisfarne Gospels, that *a* had a special shape; that the wedges of *f* and *p* ought to be a shade lower than those of *i* etc.; that *d, n, r* and *s* could be uncial in form (he made them all uncial, which is not the canonical practice); and that the head of uncial *d* and the crossbar of *t* might have a triangular serif at the left.

Abbreviations. Aldred's Latin abbreviations are of particular interest.[2] This account of them includes both the abbreviations found in the 'Ritual' itself, and those found in Bodley 819. Where an abbreviation occurs in one of the two manuscripts only, it is marked out with [R] or [B]. In the Lindisfarne Gospels Aldred used only fourteen Latin abbreviations; four are 'capricious' and most of the rest are very common in the other two manuscripts, so that only a minority of them needs to be mentioned here.

Nomina sacra are usually treated in the accepted fashion: note *isrl* at 82va11, *hierus̄* at 88rb8 and *hierusal* at B34r.

A bar over *a, e* or *u* means *m*; note *ī* (*in*) at B32r. For *-bus* the usual sign is *b* followed by a 'comma' over a point (order reversed at B20v); but at R81v *passim* a '3' is used. For *-que* the usual sign is *q* followed by a 'colon'. *Con-*: reversed *c* (Insular). A bar over *m* means *-en* (*nom̄*, 87rb14). For *-em* [R] a bar either above (87va10) or to the right of (83ra20) the preceding consonant. A bar over *t* or *u* means *-er.* A bar over *f* means *-or* (78va21; B24r). For *-orum,* either *oꝝ* or *or̄*. Over *t* or *g* a double 'comma', arranged to look like a cursive *n* (83va17), stands for *ra*; over *g* a bar stands for *re*; and over *p* an *i* stands for *ri*. A bar over *c* or *n* means *-um*. For *-unt, r̄t* [B and L] and *b̄t* [B]. For *-ur* after *t,* either the continental '2'-symbol [R] or the Insular 'comma' [B]. For *-us,* generally a 'comma' over a point, but '3' occurs.

Apud: *ap̄*. *Autem*: the Insular *h*-symbol. *Caelum* etc. [R]: *cl̄s*. *Dicit* and *dixit* [B]: *dt̄* and *dx̄*. *Dicitur*: *dr̄*. *Eius*: the Insular 'reversed' *e*. *Enim*: the Insular symbol. *Ergo* [B]: *g̊*. *Esse* [B]: *ēe*. *Est*: the Insular symbol, with a 'comma' above the line and a point below. *Et*: either the Insular ligature of *et* or the Insular symbol (the former much commoner in R). *Frater* etc. [R]: *fr̄, fr̄s* and *fr̄ib;*. *Gloria* etc. [R]: *glō*. *Hoc* [R]: *h* with a point over the bow (Insular). *Homo* etc.: contractions based on *ho-* (but note *hōmē* at B8v). *Huius* [B]: *hs̄*. *Id est*: either normal *i* with a point at either side (in R, B and L), or *i-longa* with points (in B and L), or *i-longa* with points followed by the Insular *est*-symbol (in R and L). *Meus* etc.: *m̄s* and *m̄m*. *Mihi* [R]: *m̊*. *Nisi* [B]: *n̊*. *Nobis* [R]: *n̄* and *nob̄*. *Nomen* etc. [R]: contractions based on *no-* (but note *nomī*). *Non*: *n̄*. *Noster* [R] and *uester* [B]: normal, but note *nost̄* as well as *n̄r* for *noster* in R. *Omnis* etc.: *om̄s (omnes)* and contractions based on *o-*. *Pater* etc. [R]: *pr̄* and *pr̄is*. *Per*: either the Insular symbol or the continental. *Pre*: *p̄*. *Pro*: *ꝓ*. *Post* [R]: *p̊ (ea)*. *Proprius* etc. [B]: *ꝓpæ*. *Propter*: either *p̄p, p̄p(ea)* or *ꝓpter, ꝓpt̄*. *Qua-* and *quo-*: *q̊* [B] and *q̊*. *Que-* [B]: *q̄* (*loq̄ndo*, B40r; and *laq̄um*, B24r). *Quae*: *q* followed by a triangle of points (Insular) [R]; in B (15r and 24r) *q* with a

1. See below, p. 41.
2. See below, pp. 39–40.

slanting bar across the tail, ticked upwards on the left and downwards on the right, apparently stands for *quae*. *Quando* [B]: either *qn̄o* or *qͣndo*. *Quasi* [B]: *qͣsi*. *Quem* [B]: *q̄(cūq:)*. *Qui*: *qͥ*. *Quibus* [R]: *qͥb;*. *Quid* [B]: *qͥd*. *Quis* [B]: *qͥs(q:)*. *Quod*: *q* with either a straight or a sinuous bar across the tail. *Quoniam* [R]: *qm̄*. *Seculum* etc. [R]: *sclm̄*, *sclā* and *scƚorum*. *Secundum* etc.: *s̅c̅dm* and *s̅c̅dam* [R]; and *sdu* (with a bar through the descender of *s*) [B]. *Sicut* [R]: *sͥ*. *Sunt*: *s̄t*. *Super* [R]: *s̅r̅*. *Supra* [B]: *sr̄a*. *Tibi*: *tͥ*. *Uel*: *ƚ* without points in R; in B and L, the same letter either without points or with a point before and after. *Ut* [R]: *uͭ*.

Decoration. Aldred's initials in 66[70]r–67 [71]v5, 77r–84ra2 and 85r–88v are generally enlarged text-letters (he was fond of Caroline *a*), some of which are modestly decorated with a scroll (half-uncial *d*, 79rb9; uncial *d*, 79va15; and *q*, 78vb10); with spirals (79va7); or with rudimentary trumpet pattern (79vb4). Besides glossing the original collectar, he supplied—in the red ink of the gloss—the many initials omitted by scribe O.[1] Here the letter forms are often capital, to match O's (3r; note two-barred *H* at 23v3 and 50v16); and he decorated them with the same scrolls (1r4 and 26v19), spirals (9v19, 15v4 and 11 and 33v1) and trumpet pattern (1v; especially elaborate at 19v16). At 4r10 he added a frame to O's letter; at 16r21 he apparently filled in the contours with red; and at 26r16 he added a little to the *f* sketched by scribe O.

Corrections. His other contribution to the original collectar was corrections (not always felicitous) to the Latin text:[2] insertions with no sign (3v2, 4r1, 6r11 and 8v5 and 20), or with *signes de renvoi* of two (25r3) or three (16v5) points; deletions with a box (4r6, 27v5 and 29r 19), with a line above and below (22r14) or simply below (11v3), with a point below (37v19), or with a line through the offending letter (61r12). At 3r10 he erased and refashioned to change *ch* into *d*. At 44r19 he added a runover sign.

In the additions by scribe C,[3] Aldred made corrections in black ink at 63r2, 9, 10, 11, 13, 14 and 18, and may be responsible for a correction at 62v24.

Scribe B

The pitifully inexpert hand that wrote 61r 11–22 in Anglo-Saxon minuscule is notable for the shapes of *a* (pointed or square), *r*, *x* and *&*. Round *s* occurs (lines 15 and 20). Abbreviations are the erroneous *spīs (spiritus)* in line 11; and *oīa* and *oñis*. The writer corrected himself in lines 13 and 19; and Aldred made corrections in lines 12, 14 and 20 in red ink, while writing the gloss.[4]

Scribe C

C's additions can be divided into eight sections, some of which are continuous with the preceding section but are distinguished from it by a change in the colour of the ink, in the arrangement of the text, in the rubrication, or in the type of handwriting. C was a thoroughly competent, if not particularly elegant, scribe who understood how to write Anglo-Saxon majuscule as well as minuscule and who, like all Anglo-Saxons who had been taught to write both scripts, was prepared to mix them in various proportions, or to change over from one to the other *in media re*, as circumstances required. He wrote both scripts as set hands, with many pen-lifts, and held the pen at the same moderately slanted angle for both (an eighth-century scribe would have held it straighter for majuscule). He was a contemporary of Aldred's, working in the same scriptorium, like scribes D, E and F.[5] That he was, like Aldred, a Northumbrian follows from the presence of a characteristically Northumbrian form (*nioða* without final *n*) among the few

1. See above, p. 21.
2. See above, p. 21.
3. See below.
4. See above, p. 15.
5. See above, pp. 15–17.

words in Anglo-Saxon which he wrote as a rubric at 72[76]r3: † *nim ðæt godspel her on nioða writen is.*[1]

C's eight sections are:

§ 1. 61v–62v18, in minuscule, in dark brown ink.

§ 2. 62v19–63v4, also in minuscule, in light brown ink.

§ 3. 64v1–16, in large majuscule, his most imposing passage.

§ 4. 65rb18–65v, in near-majuscule as far as 65v1 and in minuscule thereafter.

§ 5. 67[71]v6–68[72]r16, in mixed majuscule and minuscule throughout, with rubrics and some initials in red.

§ 6. 68[72]r17–71[75]r7, in minuscule, with rubrics, fillings of initials and some initials in red.

§ 7. 71[75]r8–75[68]v, partly in majuscule and partly in minuscule, with rubrics and most initials in red down to 74[67]v6.

§ 8. 76[69]r, in majuscule.

A detailed account of the changes of script in § 7, which was evidently written in one campaign, will serve to demonstrate C's range as a scribe. He begins (71[75]r8–72[76]v) with majuscule for rubrics and main texts, and small minuscule for minor texts. Note that the first three words of 71[75]r10 are minuscule: he must have decided on majuscule for the main texts only after he had embarked on the first of them. In 73[66]r1–17, the opening lines of gathering X[IX], he wrote minuscule, excepting the rubric at line 8. From 73[66]r18 to 74[67]v3 he wrote majuscule again, except in the minor texts at 73[66]v9 and 74[67]r7. The next few lines (74[67]v4–11) exhibit a mixture of majuscule with minuscule forms (*a* remains majuscule; but *r* and *s* may be either uncial or minuscule); and at 74[67]v12, still without the slightest sign of any break in continuity, C went over to minuscule, and so continued down to 75[68]v11. Finally, starting with the last two words of line 11, again with no sign of a break, he went back to majuscule for the rest of the page, having realized, no doubt, that he had enough space left for a more or less imposing end to § 7. Note *dns' eius* in minuscule at line 21.

We may now compare 73[66]v, as typical of the majuscule in § 7, with §§ 3 (64v1–16), 4 (65rb18–32) and 8 (76[69]r); and compare 75[68]r, as typical of the minuscule in § 7, with §§ 1 and 2 (both on 62v), 4 (65v), 5 (67[71]v) and 6 (70[74]v).

Let us examine five characteristic details of C's handwriting which occur in some or all of the eight sections: (1) The abbreviation stroke usually has an upward pointing serif on the left and a downward pointing serif on the right (in § 3, 64v, note lines 2, 5, 6, 8, 15 and 16). (2) The usual punctuation mark at the end of a paragraph consists of a 'colon' followed by a dash like the abbreviation stroke (62v in §§ 1 and 2; 64v16 in § 3; 65rb32 and 65v16 in § 4; 67[71]v23 in § 5; 71[75]r18, 72[76]v5, 74[67]v4 and 22 and 75[68]r21 in § 7; and 76[69]r13 in § 8). An alternative form, consisting of a triangular arrangement of two points and a large 'comma', occurs at 61v5 and 12 and 62v18 in § 1; at 68[72]v2 in § 6; and at 71[75]r8, 74[67]v17 and 75[68]v23 in § 7. (3) Note how *amen* is written at 61v–62v in § 1; at 64v16 in § 3; and at 65v16 and 29 in § 4. (4) Note the crosses at 61v12, 15, 20 and 22 and 62r3 in § 1; 64v1 in § 3; 74[67]v22 and 72[76]r3 in § 7. (5) Note how *r* is written in *-orum* or *-or* at 63r4 in § 2; 65rb27 and 32 in § 4; 69[73]v12 and 20, 70[74]r7 and 15 and 70[74]v 7, 12 and 13 in § 6; and 72[76]v22 in § 7. In the description of C's handwriting that follows, a similar range of examples is provided for certain other features which are equally characteristic.

Letter Forms. C distinguishes his majuscule from his minuscule by writing majuscule *a* instead of square *a*, or (less common) pointed *a*; uncial *r* instead of pointed minuscule *r*; and

1. *Rit.*, pp. l–li. See below, p. 54.

round (uncial) *s* instead of pointed minuscule *s*. He might have gone further and used uncial *g* and uncial *n*; but he apparently did not. His minuscule *g* is, however, generally rather better made in majuscule passages (64v1–16, 71[75]v and 76[69]r) than in minuscule (61v, 65v and 68[72]v), where the crossbar is apt to project more to the left and the centre of the stem is apt to be angular. The following notes on particular letters relate to both forms of script.

a: generally square in minuscule, but pointed *a* occurs (65v3 and 29); high 'Caroline' *a* is often used at the beginning of a word (74[76]v4; see note on *amen* above), and sometimes within a word (68[72]v16) or at the end (70[74]r14); rustic *A* is used as an abbreviation for *Antiphona* (71[75]r8).

æ: *æ* is usual in the minuscule, *ę* in the majuscule.

c: note high 'horned' *c* at 62r5.

d: the uncial form is used in majuscule and minuscule alike, and the ascender often has a triangular serif at the left end.

m: the last minim is often curved inwards at the end of a line; the uncial letter occurs at the beginning of words (73[66]v18 and 19).

q: the descender is usually straight, but sometimes curves sharply to the left at the bottom (62v23 and 25 and 63r in § 2; 64v11 in § 3; 67[71]v11 and 12 in § 5; and 73[66]v5 and 75[68]v9 and 15 in § 7).

r: the minuscule form is always sharply angular towards the end; the '2'-like form is sometimes used after *o*, independently of the -*orum* abbreviation (65rb27).

s: a near-cursive minuscule *s* is not uncommon near the ends of lines (62r12, 15 and 22 in § 1; 63r17 in § 2; 64v6 in § 3; 65rb25 in § 4; 67[71]v25 in § 5; 68[72]v32 in § 6; and 72[76]v9 and 74[67]v11 in § 7); high *s* occurs (62v13), especially before *t* (65v4 and 11 and 74[67]v25).

t: the bow is often curled inwards and the crossbar often has a triangular serif, in majuscule and minuscule alike; at the beginning of a line the crossbar is sometimes flourished (64v10, here in *g*, in § 3; 65v14 in § 4; 68[72]v14 and 70[74]v25 in § 6; and 71[75]r13 and 75[68]v11 in § 7).

u: a splayed form (65r31 and 74[67]r10, 12 and 13), like the one used in the original collectar by scribe O,[1] and *v* (70[74]v20) occur from time to time.

x: generally ugly, with the tail seriffed to the right.

y: see 65v1 margin.

z: see 65v22.

Unusual forms of the abbreviation stroke[2] occur at 62r16 and 62v3 and 4. In *pre-* the stroke is generally a shallow curve, without serifs (65rb19 in § 4; 67[71]v20 in § 5; and 68[72]v6 and 28 and 69[73]r2 and 12 in § 6).

The ligatures *em, en, er, es, et* and *ex* are all common and the head of *e* is generally rather high (61v); *ep* occurs (73[66]v15 and 17); others are *æt* (63r1) and *tt* (63r16). The shape of *ex* is characteristic (61v4, 68[72]v7, 73[66]v3 and 76[69]r2).

Punctuation etc. Punctuation at the end of a paragraph is generally by the 'colon' and dash, sometimes by a mere point, or by a triangular arrangement of two points and a large 'comma';[3] within paragraphs major pauses are marked by a point or by a 'semicolon', minor pauses by the *punctus elevatus*; the question mark occurs at 74[67]v15. Acute accents occur over monosyllables and long vowels; in the latter case they sometimes look as if they were meant for circumflex accents (69[73]r11 and 69[73]v5 and 9). Runovers are marked with two thin strokes (61v12 and 15) or with one (69[73]v19 and 71[75]v12). Double *s* occurs for single *s* (*issaac, quessimus* and *ecclessiae*); in §§ 6 and 7 *mærtyr* is common (69[73]v29 and 74[67]v19 and 22). Corrections involving expunctuation (62v1 and 15) and the caret mark (68[72]v21) occur; and on 70[74]r and v a special mark is used to close up *-que*. For corrections by Aldred and scribe M3, see above, p. 29, and below, p. 35.

1. See above, p. 19.
2. See above, p. 30.
3. See above, p. 30.

Abbreviations. The following symbols for syllables: *b;* for *-bus*; *c̄* for *con-*; the usual symbol for *-orum*, and *ar̄* for *-arum*; *r̄t* for *-runt*; the '2'-symbol for *-ur* in *-mur* and *-tur*; a high 'comma' for *-us*. For words: *autem*, the Insular *h*-symbol; *bene*, *b̄*; *esse*, *.ē̄.*; *est*, the Insular symbol; *et*, either the Insular symbol or the Insular form of *et* ligature; *frater, mater, pater* etc., *fr̄s, mr̄is, pr̄, pr̄em* and *pr̄e*; *gloria* etc., *gloā̄*; *ille* etc., *il̄.*; *misericordia, mis̄edia*; *nobis, nob̄*; *nomen* etc., *noā̄*; *non, n̄*; *noster* etc., *n̄r* and *nr̄i*; *omnis* etc., *om̄s (omnes), om̄ia, om̄ium, om̄ib;* and *oīb;*; *per*, either the Insular or the continental symbol; *pre-*, *p̄* (for the form of the bar, see above); *pro*, *ꝓ*; *quam*, *q* with a straight bar across the descender (70[74]v14); *quia*, *q* with a straight bar across the descender; *quod*, either *q* with a sinuous bar across the descender or *q̄d*; *quoque*, *q̄q̄*; *quoniam*, *q̄m* and (once) *qūo* (74[67]v8 and 17); *saeculum* etc., *scl̄i*; *secundum*, *sc̄dm*; *sunt*, *s̄t*; *uel*, either *ł* or *uł*. *Nomina sacra* are treated in the normal way.

Decoration. Scribe C's initials are mostly enlarged text-letters, but some capitals occur (*A*, 65r; *B*, 75[68]r; *D*, 72[76]r; and *F*, 71[75]r). The shape of the capitals and the simple decoration added to some letters recall Aldred's initials: note *F* (71[75]r; cf. 1r); trumpet pattern (cf. 1r) in *D* (61v and 75[68]r), *C* (at 70[74]r10) and *P* (at 74[67]r); spirals in *a* (70[74]v26), *d* (62v6) and *b* (72[76]r and 74[67]v). A monogram of *be* occurs at 68[72]r. The *d* with internal contour and bosses at 62r1 seems to derive from some of scribe O's initials in the original collectar (cf. 35v14 and 37v13). A red pigment, not a thin red ink like Aldred's, was used to draw, or fill, initials and for rubrics in §§ 5 and 6 and in part of § 7 (67[71]v6–74[67]v6), and in § 8 (76[69]r).

C also wrote the Latin sequence for St Cuthbert, with musical notation, in Cambridge, Corpus Christi College 183, 96v1–16.[1] Note the cross and *p̄* for *prae*, with his characteristic abbreviation stroke, in line 1; *q* with the descender curving to the left in lines 4 and 8; the final punctuation in line 16; and initial *A*, *ę*, *x* and the abbreviation stroke, *passim*. In general appearance the sequence is close to 76[69]r in the 'Ritual'. The Corpus manuscript contains Bede's prose and verse Lives of St Cuthbert and other items, including a hymn and a mass for St Cuthbert (92v–95v), all in the original hand. It was apparently commissioned for Chester-le-Street after 934 by King Athelstan, who visited St Cuthbert's shrine in 934 and 937[2] and died in 939.[3]

Scribe D

Scribe D (63v6–64r8) wrote a bold, if rather disjointed, script which is always more majuscule than minuscule, but which verges on minuscule from 63v13 onwards, after which minuscule *s* often replaces round (uncial) *s* and 'square' *a* sometimes replaces majuscule *a*. A tall *a* occurs at 63v23. For *ae*, *æ* is usual, but sometimes *ę* occurs. The letter *c* may be 'horned', and *e* sometimes approximates to the 'horned' form. A rather tall uncial *d* is usual, but the half-uncial letter occurs at 63v6 and 64r1 and 3. The letters *g*, *n* and *r* are always minuscule, and *s* is either round (uncial) or minuscule. The abbreviation stroke is straight, but hooks down on the right at the end of a word. Ligatures are *eg, em, en, er, es, et* and *ex*. Abbreviations are *b* and *q* followed by a pair of large 'commas' (once by a 'semicolon') for *-bus* and *-que*; *or̄* for *-orum*; a high 'comma' for *-us*; either the Insular or the continental symbol for *per*; *ł* for *uel*; and *urā* for *uestram*. A runover is marked with two points and two dashes at 63v19. A point and a large 'comma' are used to

1. Mynors, *op. cit.*, no. 16; Ker, *Catalogue*, no. 42. The 'Ritual' and this passage in the Corpus manuscript are cited as belated examples of majuscule by F. Wormald, 'The Insular Script in Late Tenth Century English Latin Manuscripts', *Atti del X congresso di scienze storiche* (Rome, 1955), pp. 160–4.

2. For Athelstan at Chester-le-Street, see J. Armitage Robinson, *The Times of Saint Dunstan* (Oxford, 1923), pp. 51–5.

3. For scribe M3's additions to the same manuscript and for other additions to it made at Chester-le-Street or Durham in the tenth and eleventh centuries, see below, pp. 36 and 42, n. 10.

punctuate the end of a paragraph. Points stand at either side of the numeral in 63v14. Note *ussum* for *usum*. A *signe de renvoi* of point and dash is used with an insertion at 64r8. The rubric at 63v5 is in red pigment, and enlarged text-letters are used for initials.

Scribe E

Scribe E, it seems, wrote both 64r9–17 and 53v (over erasure of the original collectar) in Caroline minuscule of the fine, bold type used for liturgical manuscripts, and 84v (in the middle of Aldred's gathering XI) in a less imposing hand which is chiefly Caroline, but which exhibits some Insular letter forms as replacements for, or alternatives to, the Caroline forms. The following features are common to all three passages: (1) The typical Insular wedge is absent from the tops of minims and ascenders. (2) Ascenders and minims ending on the base-line are usually provided with heavy feet (note the large *m* used as an initial at 84v30, for comparison with 53v and 64r). (3) Punctuation is mostly by a median point (note triangles of points at 64r12 and 17). (4) The abbreviation stroke is sinuous (53v2, 4, 5, 14 and 16, 64r15 and 17 and 84v *passim*). (5) Note the appearance of & at 53v3, 64r11, 15 and 16 and 84v9 and 20. (6) Compare the following capital and uncial letters used as initials: *E*, 64r13 and 84v23; *N*, 53v7, 64r12 and 84v11, 22 and 34; *P*, 53v13 and 64r9; and *Q*, 53v10 and 84v2 and 27. (7) Note the appearance of *c* and *e* in all three passages. (8) Compare the pointed Anglo-Saxon *a* usual in 84v with 53v12, and the low-headed Caroline *a* of 84v4 and 20 with 53v5, 7 and 8; also the Anglo-Saxon *r* of 84v7, 8 and 12 with 53v10. (9) Note *amen* at 53v16 and 64r12 and 17.

In 53v and 64r the following Insular forms intrude into the Caroline minuscule: Insular majuscule *a* at 53v2 and 13 and 64r10 and 15; pointed Insular minuscule *a* at 53v12 (note the low-headed Caroline form at 53v5, 7 and 8); Insular round *d* at 64r15; 'horned' *e* at 53v15; and Insular minuscule *r* at 53v10. The alphabet of 84v is mostly Caroline; but pointed Insular minuscule *a* is the usual form, except for some examples of low-headed Caroline *a* (84v4 and 20); *d* is always the round Anglo-Saxon letter; Anglo-Saxon minuscule *g* occurs at 84v4 and Anglo-Saxon minuscule *r* occurs at 84v7, 8 and 12 (note the hybrid *r* at the end of 84v16); round *s* drawn out in the Insular way occurs at 84v1, 8 and 20, and a tall form of the same letter at 84v19 and 29. Other points to notice are the *st* ligature (at 53v6 and 14 and 84v30); the use of *æ* (84v2) and of a handsome *ę* (at 64r13 and 17); '2'-shaped *r* after *o* at 64r15 and 17 and at 84v14, 20 and 33. In 53v and 64r only rustic capital and uncial letters are used for initials; in 84v the same two sorts are joined by enlarged text-letters, both Insular (*a*, line 7) and Caroline (*m*, line 30).

Although he had obviously been reared in the tradition of Insular script, E wrote Caroline minuscule with real skill. The Insular intrusions in 53v and 64r look as if they happened in spite of a firm resolve to write pure Caroline; at 84v, a much less imposing—and rather crowded—passage, his choice of pointed *a* and round *d* was probably deliberate, since the pure Caroline forms of the two letters are not to be found on the page.

E used few abbreviations. *Nomina sacra* are generally normal; but he wrote out in full *deus* and *dominus* on 64r and *Ierusalem* and *Israhel* on 84v (note *isrl* at 84v2). His other abbreviations include: *q:* for *-que*; *glām* for *gloriam*; *gr̄a* for *gratia*; *nr̄ae* for *nostrae*; *om̄s* and *om̄a* for *omnes* and *omnia*; ꝑ; and *scli* for *saeculi*.

Scribe F

Of scribe F's two passages (64v17–65rb17 and 76[69]v) the second is practically illegible due to prolonged rubbing (it may once have stood at the end of the manuscript[1]); but the initials that can be seen in the middle of 76[69]v, along with *a*, *e*, *d*, *r*, *s* or *t* followed by descending

1. See above, p. 16.

i, and the abbreviation stroke are enough to establish that one man wrote both passages, the contents of which are in any case similar.[1] The following description is based on the earlier passage only.

F's business-like but inelegant handwriting is Caroline in most respects; but—like scribe E—he was deeply imbued with Insular habits; *a* is always the pointed, Insular minuscule kind;[2] *b, d* and *l* are apt to begin with Insular wedges; *e* is always 'horned', and so is *c* at 65ra31; *i* descends after *t* (65ra2), and *i-longa* (with wedge) occurs at 65ra7; Insular minuscule *s* occurs unequivocally at 65ra10, and many Caroline *ss* descend further than usual; at 64va20 and b26 *t* has the Insular triangular serif at the left end of the cross-bar. On the other hand, *y* is straight (65ra10); the only ligature is *st* (65ra3); and *&* is always Caroline in form (65ra1). Both passages have rubrics in red pigment. F's initials are all pure capital or uncial, excepting an odd *F* at 64va24 which looks like a cross between the two.

F treats *nomina sacra* in the usual way (but note *hirlm* for *hierusalem*); *b;* and *q:* stand for *-bus* and *-que*; a bar over *m* stands for *-en-*; *r̄t* for *-runt*; a high 'comma' for *-us*; *oꝝ* for *-orum*; *āut* for *autem*; the Insular symbol for *est*; *miscđam* for *misericordiam*; *n̄c* for *nunc*; *om̄i* for *omni*; *p̄rib;* for *patribus*; *ꝑ* for *per*; *q<* for *quia*; and *q̄m̄* for *quoniam.*

So much for Aldred the Provost and scribes B to F, who wrote the additions to the main text of the original collectar, about the year 970. Scribes M1 to M3, who wrote the most important of the subsequent additions, mainly in the margins of the 'Ritual', seem to have done their work at various times between 990 and the middle of the eleventh century.

1. See below, pp. 43–4, 48 and 49.

2. Caroline scribes used pointed *a* in their glosses from at least the tenth century. See B. Bischoff in *Nomenclature des écritures livresques du IXe au XVIe siècle* (C.N.R.S., Paris, 1954), p. 8, fig. 2.

Scribe M1

The sentence invoking God's protection for Bishop Ealdhun (990–1018) in the wide lower margin of 75[68]v—*Dominus saluet. honoret. amet. aldhunum antistitem.*—is written in large Caroline minuscule of perfect purity, by an expert writer who was not in the least backward. The bows of *m* and *n* are slightly angular; the feet given to some minims are lightly made. The second stroke of *h* is pointed at the bottom and turns inwards, and *e* is plain and not 'horned': which suggests that M1 was familiar with the distinctions between the forms of those two letters in Latin and Anglo-Saxon which scribes normally observed in the later tenth century,[3] to which period his handwriting apparently belongs. This entry may have been made at any time in Ealdhun's episcopate.

Scribe M2

The entries in the gap left by Aldred at the bottom of 77v (lines 19–25), when he changed over from hymns written in one column to capitula written in two, are in a somewhat idiosyncratic Anglo-Saxon minuscule. The typical Insular wedges have been abandoned for the simpler Caroline approach stroke; Caroline *a* and *d* occur (lines 20 and 24), and *ę* (line 20) has a zigzag Caroline appendage, not the Insular loop. The letters *c* and *e* are 'horned'; round *d* is very squat; in ligatures *(em, en, er, en* and *et) e* is very high indeed; *s* is often round, and tall *s* occurs at line 20. Punctuation is by *punctus elevatus* (line 19) or by a median point. Abbreviations include: *-oꝝ*; *nob̄* for *nobis*; *om̄a* for *omnia*; *om̄p̄s* for *omnipotens*; *ꝑ* for *per*; *p̄* for *pre-*; *q̇* for *qui*; *qđ* for *quod*; *sclꝍ* for *seculorum*; and *ur̄os* for *uestros.* Two of the capitals used as initials are decorated with internal bosses which suggest the influence of scribe O's work in the original collectar. *Amen* in lines 20 and 22 is in a mixture of rustic capital and uncial letters.

M2 was apparently the writer of part of a

3. See Ker, *Catalogue,* pp. xxv–xxvi and xxix–xxx.

memorandum in Anglo-Saxon, recording two grants of land to St Cuthbert's, in the *Liber vitae* of Lindisfarne and Durham, B.M. Cotton Domitian vii, 47v, which Ker[1] describes as 'in a script of mid-eleventh-century type'. The last two-and-a-half lines of the memorandum, beginning 7 *all þ ðer into hyreð,* were written with a pen cut quite differently from the pen used for the previous lines, and are apparently by another hand.[2] The most recent edition of the memorandum is by A.J.Robertson.[3] She suggests that the first of the two grants, in which Earl Northman hands over Escomb and land at Ferryhill, both in Co. Durham, to the community, may mark the restoration of part of the estates which Bishop Ealdhun leased to Earls Ethred, Northman and Uhtred, according to Simeon of Durham, *Historia ecclesiae Dunelmensis,* and to the *Historia de Sancto Cuthberto*.[4] Neither Earl Northman nor *ulfcytel osulfes sunu,* the author of the second grant in the memorandum, can be securely identified or dated from other sources; but the memorandum was presumably written during, or not very long after, Ealdhun's episcopacy.

The memorandum is reproduced in the facsimile of the *Liber vitae,* edited by A.H. Thompson.[5] The letters *þ* and *ð* and the symbol 7 in the memorandum give it a very different general appearance from M2's Latin text at 77v19–25, but the following details of the memorandum seem to justify the attribution of both texts to one hand: (1) the pen was cut and held in the same way; (2) Insular wedges are absent; (3) round *d* is very squat; (4) *e,* but not *c,* is 'horned'; (5) a rather high *e* occurs in the ligatures *en* and *et* (lines 3 and 5); (6) round *s* and tall *s* occur (lines 1 and 4); and (7) the appearances of *f, r* and the usual Insular minuscule *s* are very similar indeed in both texts.

1. *Ibid.,* no. 147, p. 186.
2. See below.
3. *Anglo-Saxon Charters,* 2nd edn. (Cambridge, 1956), no. LXVIII, pp. 140 and 383–4.
4. *Symeonis monachi opera omnia,* ed. T.Arnold, I, 83 and 213.
5. Surtees Society, CXXXVI (1923).

Scribe M3

Scribe M3 added liturgical texts in the margins of 47v and 68[72]v. The former reads:

> Ærest halga water 7 salt. 7 siðþan sing þonne. A'. Asperges me d' [noted] mid þæm sealme. Miserere mei. 7 þisne coll' [i.e. *Adesto domine,* line 12]. 7. Pax huic domui [noted]. 7 ds' misereat*ur*. 7 þisne coll' [i.e. *Benedic domine,* line 18; indicated by a *signe de renvoi* of three points]. Siðþan þisne. A'. Benedic dne' domum istam et omnes habitantes in eo quia dne' dixisti pax huic domui benedic dne' timentes te pusillos cu*m* maioribu*s* benedicti uos a dno' qui fecit celum et terra*m* [noted] ụ*el* Ḅ...dị ṇos dnẹ' .... xii ...

The latter reads: 'A'. P*er* signu*m* crucis. V'. Adoramu*s* te xpe' *et* benedicimu*s* tebi *quia per* cruce*m* tua*m* redemisti mundum. V'. Dicite in nationibu*s* dns' regnaụịṭ a ligno.' The same hand has made changes in the Latin text at: 47v23, 'maneat p*er*'; 68[72]r20–27 *passim*; 68[72]r28, 'clem*en*ti miseratione repelle. p*er*'; 68[72]v4, 15 and 23–7 *passim*; 69[73]r, at top, 'p*re*dicam*us*'; 69[73]r7 and 24; 69[73]v11 and 32; 69[73]v17, '*ue*l memoriam', 28 'cuthberhti' and 29, 'quesumus'; 70[74]r4, 18 and 24; 70[74]v 24; 71[75]r6; and 72[76]v16.

M3's hand is both expert and elegant, with nothing provincial about it. He wrote different forms of *a, d, e, g, r, s* and *&* in Latin and in Anglo-Saxon, in accordance with normal eleventh-century practice. In Latin he used Caroline *f;* but he missed the opportunity to distinguish *h,* where he always uses the 'Latin' form.[6] His initials are good rustic capitals. M3's hand is similar in date, type and quality to the hand of the last two-and-a-half lines of the memorandum in Domitian vii, 47v, the rest of which I attribute to scribe M2; but in spite of several similarities in the treatment of letters, there seem to be no adequate grounds for an identification. To judge by the style and

6. See Ker, *Catalogue,* pp. xxv–xxvii and ff.

apparent date, together with the black ink, of the later drawings at 45r and 59r,[1] they could well have been done by M3.

M3's addition of *cuthberhti* at 69[73]v28 has already been cited[2] as evidence that he was writing at Durham. In his few words of Anglo-Saxon the form *sealme* indicates that his language was 'Southern (Saxon)'.[3] His handwriting suggests an eleventh-century date, before, or at most not long after, the Norman Conquest.[4] His musical notation appears to belong to the middle of the eleventh century.[5]

In Cambridge, Corpus Christi College 183,[6] the Bede etc., given to Chester-le-Street by Athelstan, M3 apparently added some musical notation in the main text of 93v and two short noted passages, in Latin, in the margins of 93r and 93v. The first marginal addition is certainly by M3 (note, for example, *g*, *p* and *&*, and compare 'Ritual', 47v); and the second addition seems to be by the same hand as that of the first, although the writing is larger and rougher than any of M3's work in the 'Ritual'.

Minor Tenth- and Eleventh-Century Additions

Most of the *probationes pennae,* scribblings etc. in the 'Ritual' seem to have been written between the making of the main additions, *c.* 970, and the Norman Conquest. None of them, apparently, can be ascribed to the period before the manuscript reached Chester-le-Street; and in view of the provincial character of the community's scriptorium as late as 970, it seems safer not to date in the tenth century even specimens which in southern England could be so dated with full confidence. Minor additions in 61v–89v must, of course, have been made after about 970. In listing these earlier additions I indicate which of them are in Caroline minuscule. They are: 9v top, *r, ab*; 11v1 left, *xƀ* (perhaps by O[7]); 14v1 left, *a*; 16r top, *qui* plus 16v top, *magnus dns'* plus 17r14 right, *amen* (these three are by the same hand, which could be Aldred's); 17v bottom, *om* (Car.); 33v6 left, *pr* (Car.); 44v14, *ab* (Car.); 47v1–3 left, *ƀ xƀ sc.. a a*: 49v11 left, *abcd*; 51r19 left, *tḥe ṇ*; 51v10 left, *abcdefghikl pqrs*; 56r13 right, *hal*; 57r4 left, *p*; 58v16 left, *x*; 60v bottom, *omips* (Car.; reminiscent of scribe E[8]); 60v bottom, *o o o arcus ris ros arcus ris ṛọ*. (Car.; but note length of *r*); 68[72]v top, *....homo*; 71[75]v top, *ịṇ ṇomine dne' am'* (in red); 73[66]v top, *Dni' c* (capital and uncial); 74[67]r bottom, *ạbcd* (Car.); 74[67]v top, *gloriabitur* (Car.; reminiscent of E again); 75[68]r23 *cod* (Car.); 75[68]r bottom, *ihc'. xpc'* (Car.); 75[68]v13 left, *Dn* (Car.); 76[69]r26, *abcdefghiklṃṇọp* (erased towards the end);[9] 76[69]r bottom, *Dne'*; 76[69]v left, *ịṇ te sperau*[*i*] (Car.); 83v17 left, *ðat*;[10] 87vb, *ce*; 89r top, *ab ab.*; 89r top, *Dns' sal..ṭ hon* (Car.); and 89v top, *a tres. spẹcịẹ ðrịẹ megulitạṣ æ abcdefg æ æ æ.*[11]

Minor Additions after c. *1066*

All in Caroline minuscule, unless otherwise described: 47v7 left, *bloetsa drihtin* (eleventh- or twelfth-century; copied from the gloss); 78r bottom, *Ricardus* (twelfth-century); corrections to 83va7 and b5, changing the incipits of psalms 70 and 55 from the Gallican to the Roman version (twelfth-century); 9r12 right, *I. M.* ('secretary hand', sixteenth-to-seventeenth-century); and 54r right and 73[66]r bottom, a few dim letters which may be modern.

1. See above, p. 23.
2. See above, p. 17.
3. See below, p. 54.
4. Ker, *Catalogue,* p. 145, dates M3's hand in the first half of the eleventh century.
5. So Professor Wormald and Mr D. H. Turner have kindly informed me.
6. See above, p. 32, n. 1.
7. See above, p. 13.
8. See above, p. 33.
9. In the photograph made for this facsimile, it looks as if some rough writing in Anglo-Saxon minuscule has been erased in and around the bottom right hand corner of 76[69]r; but only a few letters are, or seem to be, legible.
10. Signs of erased writing similar to those on 76[69]r can be seen in the photograph of 83v, notably in the left margin opposite line 7.
11. Ker, *Catalogue,* p. 145, dates this entry 's.x?'.

THE END-LEAF

The end-leaf (fol. 89) is a fragment of a lectionary of Epistles and Gospels, containing fifteen long lines on each side (89v1 is illegible). The contents are:

89r1–2: et prosiliti ... magnalia dei (*Acts,* II. 11), being the end of the Epistle for Whit Sunday, *Acts,* II. 1–11, no. LXXXVII (p. 12) in W.H. Frere, *Studies in Early Roman Liturgy, III: The Roman Epistle-Lectionary,* Alcuin Club Collections, XXXII (1935).

89r3–v5: *die dominico pentico[stes lectio] euang' secun[dum ioh']*. Si quis diligit (*John,* XIV. 23) ... pacem relinquo uobis, pacem (27); multa loquor (30)... sic facio (31). The beginning and end of the Gospel for Whit Sunday, *John,* XIV. 23–31, no. 137 (p. 43) in the Standard Series of Frere, *Studies II: The Roman Lectionary,* Alcuin Club Collections, XXX (1934).

89v5–15: *lectio libri sapien' solam'*. In omnibus requiem (*Ecclus.,* XXIV.11)... plenitudine (16). Compare the Epistle for the Assumption of the B.V. Mary, *Ecclus.,* XXIV. 11–13 and 15–20, no. CXVIII (p. 16) in Frere, *Roman Epistle-Lectionary.*

The fragment, consisting of a single leaf from which up to seven lines have been cut away at the bottom, is described by E.A. Lowe in *CLA,* II, no. 151. Three different hands seem to be distinguishable, one of which wrote only the rubrics in red at r3 and v5. The first text-hand (89r) wrote a bold, ornamental script strongly reminiscent of the Anglo-Saxon 'decorative minuscule' used for the prefaces in the Echternach Gospels, Paris, B.N. lat. 9389, and for the last lines of some pages in Durham Cathedral Library, A.II.17, part I.[1] These two manuscripts were apparently written at Lindisfarne, *c.* 700, by the same scribe.[2] The second text-hand (89v) wrote a plain but expert Anglo-Saxon majuscule of a type found in several eighth-century manuscripts from Northumbria, of which the closest is perhaps the fragment of Leviticus in Durham Cathedral Library, C.IV.7.[3] While supporting Lowe's attribution to Northumbria, these comparisons suggest that 'saec. VIII–IX', his date for the fragment in the 'Ritual', may be unnecessarily late. 'Saec. VIII' seems preferable.

1. *CLA,* v, no. 578, and *CLA,* II, no. 149.
2. Brown in *Cod. Lind.,* bk I, pp. 92–106 and pls. 2–14.

CONCLUSIONS

Scribe O, to judge by the general appearance of his work, wrote the original collectar during the first quarter of the tenth century. His writing is more advanced than the writing of the Worcester copy of King Alfred's translation of the *Pastoral Care*[4] (890–7), or of the annals up to 891 in the Parker Chronicle and Laws;[5] but it is not in the 'square' style of Anglo-Saxon minuscule used by the scribe who wrote the Parker annals for the years 891 (added entry) to 924[6] and the Tollemache manuscript of the Alfredian translation of Orosius.[7] O wrote a basically set hand, like the scribes to whom he has just been compared; but the few cursive letters that he allows[8] suggest that he was equally familiar with the cursive variety of Anglo-Saxon minuscule found in charters such as B.M. Add. Ch. 19791 (Werferth, bishop of Worcester, 904).[9] The scanty but unmistakable traces in his work of the influence of ninth-century manuscripts written in Caroline minuscule —Caroline *g* at 6r5[10] and an admixture of capital and uncial forms in his display script[11]—may

3. *CLA,* II, no. 154. For the group of manuscripts, see Brown in *Cod. Lind.,* bk I, p. 91.
4. Oxford, Bodleian Library, Hatton 20. Facsimile ed. N.R. Ker, *Early English Manuscripts in Facsimile,* VI (Copenhagen, 1956). Ker, *Catalogue,* no. 324.
5. Cambridge, Corpus Christi College 173, 1–16r. Facsimile ed. R. Flower and H. Smith, Early English Text Society (1941). Ker, *Catalogue,* no. 39.
6. *Ibid.,* 16v–25v.
7. B.M. Add. 47967. Facsimile ed. A. Campbell, *Early English Manuscripts in Facsimile,* III (Copenhagen, 1953). Ker, *Catalogue,* no. 133.
8. See above, p. 18.
9. *Pal. Soc.,* ser. I, pl. 13.
10. See above, p. 19.
11. See above, p. 19.

have been derived from his probably continental exemplar.[1] The material at present available for comparison with O's abbreviations is too limited to justify anything but the most general conclusions.[2] He used a mixture of the older Insular abbreviations with continental abbreviations which seems to be typical of his period in England. The most striking of his abbreviations is *v̇* for *ut*,[3] which is of Welsh origin,[4] but which in O's period was used in Ireland and Cornwall as well as in Wales and has been noted in one other English manuscript.[5]

The decorative motifs used by O in his initials[6] are typical of the last years of the ninth century and the first half of the tenth—biting dog heads, sometimes with lappets or foliate tongues; masks, often with double tongues; an occasional human head wearing a pointed cap; human faces in letters such as *O*; and inner contours to letters forming a debased trumpet pattern or bosses. The source of most of these motifs has long been recognized as English manuscripts of the late eighth and early ninth centuries.[7] Five are particularly relevant: (1) B.M. Royal 1 E. vi, a fragmentary manuscript of which the remainder contains the gospels, late-eighth-century (or even early-ninth), from Canterbury;[8] (2) B.M. Cotton Tiberius C. ii, Bede, *Historia ecclesiastica*, late-eighth-century;[9] (3) Paris, B.N. lat. 10861, *Vitae sanctorum*, eighth-to-ninth-century;[10] (4) Rome, Vatican Library, Barberini lat. 570, a gospel book, late-eighth-century;[11] and (5) Cambridge, University Library, Ll. 1. 10, the Book of Cerne, early-ninth-century, perhaps from Lichfield.[12]

Of the later, contemporary manuscripts the one that has the range of motifs closest to O's range in the 'Ritual' seems to be the Worcester manuscript of the *Pastoral Care* (890–7);[13] and a rather less wide range is found in B.M. Royal 5 F. iii, Aldhelm, *De laude virginitatis*, ninth-to-tenth-century, from Worcester.[14] O's drawings are more accomplished than the drawings in either of these manuscripts and they approach, in quality and style, if not in complexity, those in the Tollemache Orosius.[15] The 'long and short' acanthus leaf, which apparently makes its first manuscript appearance in the 'Ritual',[16] also occurs in the embroidered stole and maniples, now among the relics of St Cuthbert at Durham, that were made for Bishop Frithestan of Winchester, to the order of Queen Ælflæd, between 909 and 916.[17] As a decorator, O was ambitious and, it seems, well abreast of the times: which suggests that he worked in an important centre. His less ambitious initials—those with a few dog heads, or with an internal contour making trumpet pattern or bosses—can be matched in several manuscripts of the first

1. See below, p. 43.

2. The evidence is in W.M.Lindsay, *Notae latinae* (Cambridge, 1915) and D.Bains, *A Supplement to Notae latinae* (Cambridge, 1936).

3. See above, p. 20.

4. Lindsay, *op. cit.*, pp. 320–1, and *Early Welsh Script* (Oxford, 1912), p. 40.

5. Bains, *op. cit.*, p. 51. On Welsh influence in tenth-century English scriptoria, see T. A. M. Bishop, 'The Corpus Martianus Capella', *Transactions of the Cambridge Bibliographical Society*, IV, 4 (1967), 257–75.

6. See above, pp. 21–3.

7. J.Brøndsted, *Early English Ornament* (London and Copenhagen, 1924), pp. 241–69; T. D. Kendrick, *Anglo-Saxon Art to A.D. 900* (London, 1938), pp. 211–22, and *Late Saxon and Viking Art* (London, 1949), pp. 27–38; F.Wormald, 'Decorated Initials in English Manuscripts from A.D. 900 to 1100', *Archaeologia*, XCI (1945 for 1941), 107–35.

8. *CLA*, II, no. 214; E.H.Zimmermann, *Vorkarolingische Miniaturen* (Berlin, 1916), pls. 289–92.

9. *CLA*, II, no. 191; Zimmermann, *op. cit.*, pls. 291–2; Ker, *Catalogue*, no. 198.

10. G.L.Micheli, *L'Enluminure du haut moyen âge et les influences irlandaises* (Brussels, 1939), p. 51, fig. 86 (2r); *Cat. Codd. Hagg. Latt. Biblioth. Nat. Parisiensis*, edd. Hagiographi Bollandiani, vol. II (1890), no. DXIV, pp. 605–6. Perhaps written in France.

11. *CLA*, I, no. 63; Zimmermann, *op. cit.*, pls. 313–17.

12. Zimmermann, *ibid.*, pls. 293–6; Ker, *Catalogue*, no. 27.

13. See above, p. 37, n. 4.

14. Sir G.F.Warner and J.P.Gilson, *Catalogue of Western Manuscripts in the Old Royal and King's Collections* (1921), I, 120, vol. IV, pl. 44; Ker, *Catalogue*, no. 253. Compare also the late-ninth-century Ovid from Wales in Oxford, Bodleian Library, Auct. F.4.32, fols. 37–46; Wormald, *loc. cit.*, pp. 112–13; Ker, *Catalogue*, no. 297; R.W.Hunt, *Saint Dunstan's Classbook from Glastonbury*.

15. See above, p. 37, n. 7.

16. See above, n. 7.

17. Wormald, *loc. cit.*, pp. 114–15; R.Freyhan, 'The Place of the Stole and Maniples in Anglo-Saxon Art of the Tenth Century', *The Relics of St Cuthbert*, ed. C.F.Battiscombe (Oxford, 1956), pp. 409–32, pls. XXIV–XL.

half of the tenth century, among them the Laws (33r–52v) in the Parker Chronicle and Laws, by a writer slightly later in date than the one who wrote the annals for the years 891 (added entry) to 924;[1] Bald's Leechbook, B.M. Royal 12 D. xvii, by the writer of the Parker annals for the years 925 to 955;[2] and the Exeter Book, Exeter, Cathedral Library, 3501.[3] Ker[4] has pointed out the likeness between O's scroll-like runover signs and those in the Exeter Book, and one may also compare O's two-barred initial *H,* with key-pattern filling, at 29v11 with a very similar letter in the Exeter Book at 65v (see also 67r and 97v).

The dialect of the Anglo-Saxon texts in O's handwriting[5] shows that he was a West Saxon; the manuscripts with which his initials can be compared all seem to come from the south-west; and four of them—the Worcester manuscript of the *Pastoral Care,* the Parker Chronicle and Laws (the second hand), the Tollemache Orosius, and Bald's Leechbook—are probably from Winchester, like the stole and maniples made for Bishop Frithestan.[6]

Of the scribes who made the main additions to the original collectar at Chester-le-Street, about 970, Aldred the Provost[7] was the most accomplished: he was a fluent writer, with a strong sense of style, who could vary his handwriting very widely to suit the matter in hand. His glosses, in the Lindisfarne Gospels and in Bodley 819 as well as in the 'Ritual' itself, are not in the 'square' style of Anglo-Saxon minuscule found in glossed manuscripts that are more or less contemporary with his own, such as the psalter, Oxford, Bodleian Library, Junius 27;[8] the psalter, B.M. Royal 2 B. v;[9] and the Aldhelm, B.M. Royal 7 D. xxiv.[10] They have far more in common with the ninth-century glosses in the psalter, B.M. Cotton Vespasian A. i;[11] and it is not surprising that Wanley and Lowe, two of the supreme authorities on Anglo-Saxon scripts, have dated his work to the age of King Alfred.[12] Aldred's decorative minuscule, in which he wrote the main text of the 'Ritual', 77r–84ra2 and 85r–88v, also harks back to the ninth century. It has something in common with the first hand in the Aldhelm, B.M. Royal 5 F. iii,[13] ninth-to-tenth-century, but much more with the writing of the Book of Cerne,[14] which can hardly be later than the first half of the ninth century. Note, in Cerne, the deep splitting of letters such as *f, p, r* and *s*; the flourishes in half-uncial *d* and in *q*; the compromise form of *r*; the appearance of the *pro* symbol (Cerne, 32r 11 and 12; *pro* in the 'Ritual', 81va6, and cf. *p*, 83ra14). Even Aldred's majuscule (66[70]r–67[71]v5), written with a pen that was not quite thick enough for the size of letter, suggests the majuscule in Cerne at 3r, 22r4 and 43r3; only 3r4 and 43r3 are written with a thick pen, and in 3r15 the Cerne script descends from majuscule to minuscule in just the same way as Aldred's.

In Aldred's Latin abbreviations, found in the 'Ritual' and Bodley 819,[15] which in general are a mixture of early Insular with continental forms that is probably typical of England in

1. See above, p. 37, n. 5.

2. Facsimile ed. C.E.Wright, *Early English Manuscripts in Facsimile,* v (Copenhagen, 1955); Ker, *Catalogue,* no. 264.

3. Facsimile ed. R.W.Chambers, M.Förster and R.Flower (London, 1933); Ker, *Catalogue,* no. 116. A rather later manuscript with similar modest initials is the Blickling Homilies, facsimile ed. R.Willard, *Early English Manuscript in Facsimile,* x (Copenhagen. 1960); Ker, *Catalogue,* no. 382.

4. *Ibid.,* p. 145.

5. See above, p. 12, and below, pp. 53–4.

6. For the Winchester manuscripts, see above, p. 37, nn. 4, 5 and 7, and above, n. 2; for the stole and maniples, see above, p. 38, n. 17.

7. See above, pp. 23–9.

8. Ker, *Catalogue,* no. 335; *New Pal. Soc.,* ser. II, pl. 62.

9. Ker, *Catalogue,* no. 249; Warner and Gilson, *op. cit.,* pl. 22.

10. Ker, *Catalogue,* no. 259; Warner and Gilson, *op. cit.,* pl. 54a.

11. Facsimile ed. D.H.Wright, *Early English Manuscripts in Facsimile,* XIV (Copenhagen, 1967); *CLA,* II, no. 193; Ker, *Catalogue,* no. 203; *Pal. Soc.,* ser. I, pl. 18.

12. Wanley, *op. cit.,* pp. 295–8 on the Lindisfarne and 'Ritual' glosses (see above, p. 23); Lowe, *CLA,* II, no. 235 on the glosses in Bodley 819 ('saec. ix–x').

13. See above, p. 38, n. 14. The first hand is shown in Warner and Gilson, *op. cit.,* pl. 44a.

14. See above, p. 38, n. 12. For the script, see Zimmermann, *op. cit.,* pls. 293–4.

15. See above, pp. 28–9.

the tenth century, there is a small but notable element which—as far as one can tell from the available evidence[1]—suggests survival from eighth-century Northumbria. He uses four abbreviations of Irish origin (*hs̄* for *huius*, *s̊* for *sicut*, *s̄r* for *super* and *s̄ra* for *supra*) which occur in a number of Irish manuscripts of the eighth, ninth and tenth centuries, and are not unknown in manuscripts in Anglo-Saxon script written on the continent in the eighth and early ninth centuries, but which have been noticed in only two native English manuscripts other than Aldred's.[2] The two native manuscripts are both of the eighth century and both are of Northumbrian origin, namely the Pauline Epistles, glossed, etc., Cambridge, Trinity College B. 10. 5,[3] and the psalter, glossed, Vatican Library, Pal. lat. 68.[4] Another abbreviation with a Celtic flavour is *-ra-* in which the commas over *t* or *g* standing for suprascript *a* resemble a cursively written *n*.[5]

Aldred's initials are apparently influenced by O's work in the 'Ritual' itself;[6] and he may have picked up reversed *e* in ligatures from the same source.[7] His work on the Lindisfarne gloss will have familiarized him with Anglo-Saxon majuscule of excellent quality,[8] and in Bodley 819 he had before him a good example of the minuscule written at Wearmouth-Jarrow in the eighth century.[9] His majuscule, unlike scribe C's,[10] looks artificial, the result of imitation, not of training.[11] His decorative minuscule may also be the result of imitation: flourished half-uncial *d* and *q* appear in Bodley 819, but not in Lindisfarne;[12] but his most formal script in Lindisfarne (3r and the five sentences on the gospels in the colophon group on 259r) suggest that he was already familiar with the old-fashioned type of decorative minuscule he used in the 'Ritual', 77r–84ra2 and 85r–88v. He writes the script so confidently that he may well have been taught it, along with the rare abbreviations mentioned above, in the centre in which he was educated. That centre was apparently a backward one, somewhere in Northumbria, to which the style of writing current in southern England from the second quarter of the tenth century onwards had not yet penetrated. Whether or not Aldred was educated in the community of St Cuthbert at Chester-le-Street is uncertain. His writing makes a very different effect from that of his fellow-workers in the 'Ritual' and from the other fragments of tenth-century writing from Durham.[13] It may only be that he was more enterprising than the others and evolved a personal style of his own; but it seems more likely that he was a stranger, since his colophon in the Lindisfarne Gospels (259r)[14] tells how he bought his way into the community *(hine gihamadi)* as a man old enough to be in priest's orders *(presbiter indignus et miserrimus)*, by glossing Matthew, Mark and Luke and paying eight ores of silver for his induction *(tó inláde)*. Wherever Aldred came from, the possibility remains that he was to some extent self-taught. He rose to be provost, which probably meant that he was second in the community after Bishop Ælfsige.[15] As such he may have been

1. See above, p. 38, n. 2.

2. Lindsay, *Notae latinae*, pp. 37, 288, 298 and 300; Bains, *op. cit.*, pp. 8, 46 and 48. The references to Vitellius C. viii, fols. 86–90, in the latter book may be discounted, since those leaves are in fact part of Cambridge, Trinity College B.10.5 (see below). See too Lindsay, p. 9, and Bains, p. 2, on *ap̄* for *apud*.

3. *CLA*, II, no. 133; Ker, *Catalogue*, no. 83; Mynors, *op. cit.*, no. 8 (at Durham in 1391); T.A.M. Bishop, 'Notes on Cambridge Manuscripts. Part VII: Pelagius in Trinity College B.10.5', *Transactions of the Cambridge Bibliographical Society*, IV, 1 (1964), 70–7, pls. IX and X. B.M. Cotton Vitellius C. viii, fols. 86–90 are part of B.10.5.

4. *CLA*, I, no. 78; Ker, *Catalogue*, no. 388; W.M. Lindsay, *Early Irish Minuscule Script* (Oxford, 1910), pp. 67–70 and pl. XII.

5. Lindsay, *Notae latinae*, pp. 354–7; Bains, *op. cit.*, pp. 58–9.

6. See above, p. 29.

7. See above, pp. 20 and 27.

8. See above, p. 23.

9. See above, p. 27, n. 2.

10. See below, p. 41.

11. See above, p. 28.

12. See above, p. 27, and *Cod. Lind.*, bk II, p. 33.

13. See above, pp. 29–36, and below, p. 42, n. 10.

14. See above, p. 25, and *Cod. Lind.*, bk II, pp. 5–11.

15. See *ibid.*, pp. 31–2.

in charge of the scriptorium, but he seems to have had no imitators. For all his skill, he was living in the past.

Scribe C,[1] whose dialect—like Aldred's—marks him out as a Northumbrian,[2] was less of a virtuoso than Aldred, and the natural, unforced quality of his handwriting raises no suspicion that he may have been self-taught. He was a relic from, if anything, an even more distant past than Aldred. His majuscule (71[75]r) is remarkably similar in style to the majuscule of several eighth-century manuscripts which are certainly or probably of Northumbrian origin, although he does not use all the letter forms that an eighth-century scribe might have used.[3] The closest parallels are the majuscule of 89v of the 'Ritual' itself;[4] of some fragments of Leviticus in Durham, Cathedral Library, C. IV. 7;[5] and of the gospel book, B. M. Royal 1 B. vii.[6] Other comparable hands are in the gospel book, Durham, Cathedral Library, A. II. 16, fols. 24–33 and 87–101;[7] in the fragments of gospel books in B. M. Cotton Tiberius B. v, fol. 75[8] and in Lincoln, Cathedral Library, 298 (1);[9] and in three fragments now in German libraries which are either of native Northumbrian origin or else derive from Northumbrian centres on the continent.[10] Scribe C's minuscule (70[74]v) is not like Aldred's, nor like the polished, pointed minuscule of the eighth and ninth centuries,[11] nor like the contemporary 'square' minuscule of southern England.[12] Although much more expert, C's minuscule has something of the spacious quality of the minuscule in the eighth-century Pauline Epistles, Cambridge, Trinity College B.10.5,[13] the abbreviations in which have been compared with Aldred's[14] and which was at Durham in the later Middle Ages. C's majuscule and minuscule both look like the products of an ancient and unbroken Northumbrian tradition, preserved in isolation from developments elsewhere in England. Scribe D's less expert majuscule (63v–64r)[15] makes the same impression.

Although we have no definite evidence, as we have with Aldred,[16] for thinking that C and D may have been educated elsewhere, we still cannot be sure that they were trained to write at Chester-le-Street; but the character of their work is perfectly in keeping with what we know of the often precarious history of the community of St Cuthbert since the end of the eighth century.[17]

The work of scribes E[18] and F,[19] who were both contemporary with Aldred and with scribes C and D,[20] shows that by about 970 the Caroline minuscule, which began to be accepted in England for Latin texts in the early days of the ecclesiastical reforms of Saints Dunstan, Æthelwold and Oswald,[21] had reached Chester-le-Street. E's best writing (53v and 64r) is a fine example of the large Caroline minuscule found in late-tenth-century liturgical manuscripts from the south of England, such as the Benedictional of St Æthelwold, B. M. Add. 49598.[22] The Insular intrusions in 53v and 64r, and the more frankly mixed character of E's writing at

1. See above, pp. 29–32.
2. See above, p. 29, and below, p. 54.
3. See above, pp. 29–30.
4. See above, p. 37.
5. *CLA*, II, no. 154; Mynors, *op. cit.*, no. 10 and pl. 11.
6. *CLA*, II, no. 213; Ker, *Catalogue*, no. 246.
7. *CLA*, II, no. 148b; Mynors, *op. cit.*, no. 7 and pls. 5–7.
8. *CLA*, II, no. 190; Ker, *Catalogue*, no. 194.
9. *CLA*, II, no. 160.
10. *Ibid.*, VIII, nos. 1045, 1165 and 1195, the last of which may have been written at Echternach. All but the 'Ritual' fragment and those in Germany were listed as a group in a review of Northumbrian majuscule in *Cod. Lind.*, bk I, pp. 89–92.
11. Compare Bodley 819 (see above, p. 27, n. 2) and the Book of Cerne (see above, p. 38, n. 12).
12. Compare the main texts and glosses of Junius 27, Royal 2 B. v and Royal 7 D. xxiv (see above, p, 39, nn. 8–10).
13. See above, p. 40, n. 3.
14. Above, p. 40.
15. See above, pp. 32–3.
16. See above, p. 40.
17. See, for example, *Cod. Lind.*, bk I, pp. 20–3.
18. See above, p. 33.
19. See above, pp. 33–4.
20. See above, pp. 15–17.
21. See Wormald, 'The Insular Script', and Ker, *Catalogue*, pp. xxv–xxvii.
22. Sir G. F. Warner and H. A. Wilson, *The Benedictional of St Æthelwold* (Roxburghe Club, 1910); F. Wormald, *The Benedictional of St Ethelwold* (London, 1959).

84v show that he had, like most of his contemporaries, originally been taught to write in the Anglo-Saxon way. The majuscule *a* at 64r suggests that he practised both the majuscule and the minuscule scripts. F's modest hand (64v–65r) is another frank mixture of the Caroline and Insular scripts and recalls the passages in Oxford, Bodleian Library, Auct. F.4.32, 1r and v, 20r, 36r and 47r which appear to have been written by St Dunstan himself before he left Glastonbury in 957;[1] it has none of the polish of the 'Anglo-Caroline' script written in some important southern scriptoria in the second half of the tenth century, among them St Augustine's and Christ Church, Canterbury.[2]

The work of scribes M1 (75[68]v), M2 (77v) and M3 (47v), all of which seems to belong to the episcopate of Bishop Ealdhun (990–1018) or the generation that followed it, marks an important stage in the modernization of the community's scriptorium. M1's inscription[3] is in perfectly pure Caroline minuscule of the best quality; and unless it was written by a southern visitor merely giving a demonstration of the new fashion, it argues for close contact between the community and more advanced centres. The handwriting of M2,[4] whose presence in the *Liber vitae* as well as in the 'Ritual' seems to prove that he belonged to Durham, is a little eccentric, but none the less recognizably of the first half of the eleventh century. M3,[5] whose dialect is southern in character, wrote a polished script in which Latin and Anglo-Saxon were carefully distinguished and which would have passed without comment in any southern scriptorium. The beheaded entry at the bottom of 47r of the *Liber vitae*,[6] which seems to be more or less contemporary with the work of M3, is hardly less up-to-date.

Scribe B (61r)[7] and the writers of the tenth-to-eleventh-century marginal entries in the 'Ritual',[8] together with the writers of more or less contemporary entries, not so far mentioned, in the *Liber vitae*[9] and in four other manuscripts from Chester-le-Street,[10] present a somewhat confused picture. Their performances confirm the impression, conveyed even by the better writers, of a centre with no single dominant tradition and suggest that the general standard of writing was distinctly low.

1. See above, p. 17, n. 4.

2. T. A. M. Bishop, *Aethici Istrici Cosmographia, Cod. Leid. Scal. 69, Umbrae codicum occidentalium,* x (1966). See also Bishop in *Transactions of the Cambridge Bibliographical Society,* II, 4 (1957), 323–36; III, 1 (1959), 93–5; III, 5 (1963), 412–23.

3. See above, p. 34.

4. See above, pp. 34–5.

5. See above, pp. 35–6.

6. See above, p. 35, nn. 1, 3 and 5.

7. See above, p. 29.

8. See above, p. 36.

9. B. M. Cotton Domitian vii, 15r, 19v, 20v, 24r, 24v, 26r, 36r and 47v1–10. About half a dozen different hands seem to have been responsible.

10. (1) Durham, Cathedral Library, A. II. 17, 79r, 80r and v, 104r and 106r; Mynors, *op. cit.,* nos. 3 and 4, frontispiece and pls. 2 and 3; Ker, *Catalogue,* no. 105; some of these refer to Bishop Aldred of Chester-le-Street (944–68). (2) Durham, Cathedral Library, B. II. 30, 2v, ninth-to-tenth-century; Mynors, *op. cit.,* no. 9, and pls. 8–10. (3) B. M. Cotton Otho B. ix, 1v, a liturgical passage for St Cuthbert, in Latin, apparently in pure minuscule (the manuscript was severely damaged in the fire of 1731); Mynors, *op. cit.,* no. 15; Ker, *Catalogue,* no. 176. (4) Cambridge, Corpus Christi College 183, 96v17–22, a list of chalices etc., in Anglo-Saxon, dated by Ker to the tenth century (see above, p. 32, n. 1). The Anglo-Saxon document of Walcher, bishop of Durham (1071–80), at 96v23–6 is in a perfectly up-to-date hand of the second half of the eleventh century. For comments on the tenth-century writers in the community, see Ker, 'Aldred the Scribe', pp. 11–12.

THE LITURGICAL CONTENTS OF THE MANUSCRIPT

BY F. WORMALD

In the following section which is devoted to the liturgical portion of the 'Durham Ritual' not very much can be attempted except to try to indicate what the contents of the manuscript are. Anyone who has used the edition published by the Surtees Society in 1927 *(Rit.)* will have found that the rubrics which are attached to the various prayers are not at all reliable guides to the contents. In some cases prayers which at first sight appear to be under a particular heading are on closer examination found merely to follow a prayer which has a connexion with the rubric. Thus on 60r–v the prayers to be said at the times of the canonical hours belong at first sight to the group of prayers for the blessing of a house which immediately precedes them. This confusion is particularly noticeable in the last part of the book. It is hoped that this list of contents will enable the users of the facsimile to identify the contents without too much difficulty.

As has often been pointed out the name 'Ritual' for this manuscript is incorrect, since a large part of it consists of a collectar. Actually the liturgical portion divides into three separate parts, the first (1–45r21) being the collectar, the second (45r21–53r and 54r–61r10, the original contents of 53v having been erased) being mainly a long series of benedictions including the blessing of a nun and a nuptial mass, and the third (61r11–84v) being miscellaneous. The first two of these sections were written in southern England by the original hand, called by Professor Brown Hand O. From the contents of the collectar it is not possible to suggest where it was written; there are no English saints in the sanctorale to guide us. On the other hand the fact that a collect for St Quentin (35r) is provided suggests that the archetype may have had a connexion with St Quentin in Vermandois. Attention should also be drawn to the importance given to St Martin by providing him with a collect for his translation on 4 July and seven collects for his deposition on 11 November. In view, however, of the very widespread nature of his cult it would be unwise to press this point. No attempt has been made here to track down the sources of the capitula and collects in the collectar as this would require an investigation into a large amount of unprinted material. As far as the second section is concerned a number of the formulae can be found in the Gregorian and Gelasian Sacramentaries. In the cases of the formulae for the ordeal, references have been given to comparable texts printed by K. Zeumer in the *Monumenta Germaniae historica,* Legum, sectio v (Hanover, 1886).

In many ways the most interesting part of the manuscript is the third section which contains the additions which have been shown by Professor Brown, above, pp. 15–17, to have been made within the community of St Cuthbert by the provost Aldred and his companions in the second half of the tenth century. Though these do contain some benedictions, as those written by Aldred on 66[70]r–67[71]v, they mainly have nothing to do with the first two sections. They were written chiefly by scribe C and Aldred. C added memoriae to be said at lauds and masses for the commune sanctorum, while Aldred provided a group of hymns and a series of suffrages and collects to be said at prime, terce, none, vespers and compline, known as the Gallican and Celtic Capitella. An interesting addition is that made by scribe F on 64v17–65rb17 and 76[69]v, consisting of antiphons, versicles and responds to be said at matins in connexion with lessons from various books of the bible. The importance of this section is that it is among the earliest documents showing what portions of the daily office in England were like. It is of course extremely incomplete, since much is omitted which would be found in such books as homiliaries and antiphoners. What is there suggests that what we have may be an attempt to bring certain elements in the daily office into reasonably convenient groups rather in the same way as in the collectar. Much of the material would be said by the priest or at any rate have to be at hand for his use. The collectar is fundamentally a priest's book and the additions made in the community of St Cuthbert suggest that it remained one.

The following list of the liturgical contents is divided according to the scheme of the summary description, above, pp. 14–15. In each case the manuscript folio reference is followed by the relevant page reference to *Rit.*, this page reference being placed within round brackets. Rubrics have not been transcribed in all cases. I am indebted to Professor H. Gneuss for information concerning the hymns.

α. THE ORIGINAL COLLECTAR

1. *The Temporale (1r–21r)*

1r1–14 (1): Capitula (7), the first imperfect, for Epiphanytide. Preceding leaves containing the beginning of the temporale have been lost.

1r16–v22 (2–3): *item collecta in epiphania.* Collects (8) for Epiphanytide.

2r1–21 (3–4): *.iiii. non. febr. purificatio sancte mariæ.* Capitula (7) for the Purification of the B.V. Mary.

2r21–v11 (4): *item collectiones.* Collects (3) for the Purification of the B.V. Mary.

2v13–3r7 (5): *item capitula IN CAPVT IEIVNII.* Capitula (5) for Ash Wednesday.

3r7–18 (5–6): *INCIP' CAPITVLA IN LXX[a].* Capitula (3) for Septuagesima.

3r18–v9 (6): *IN LX.* Capitula (6) for Sexagesima.

3v10–4r14 (6–8): *Hae sunt collectiones in septuagessima vsque caput ieunii.* Collects (9) from Septuagesima to Ash Wednesday.

4r15–v21 (8–9): *feria .iiii. caput ieiunivm.* Collects (10) for Ash Wednesday.

5r1–7r2 (9–14): *capit' IN quadragessima .i.* Capitula (34) for Lent.

7r3–9r13 (14–18): *collectiones unde supra.* Collects (33) for Lent.

9r15–10r17 (18–21): *item capitula ex profetis de passione domini.* Capitula (15) for Passiontide.

10r19–11r4 (21–2): *item capitule ex apostolorum* (i.e. Epistles). Capitula (9) for Passiontide.

11r5–12r3 (22–4): *item collecta.* Collects (13) for Passiontide.

12r4–14v3 (24–9): *capitula de resurrectione domini.* Capitula (32) for Eastertide.

14v4–17v10 (29–36): *collecta in sabato sancto pascha.* Collects (41), the twentieth imperfect, for Eastertide. A leaf after fol. 15 has been lost.

17v11–23 (36): *Hæ sunt capitulæ in lætania maiore.* Capitula (3) for Rogationtide. Leaves containing the remainder of the temporale and the beginning of the next series of collects have been lost.

18r1–19r23 (36–9): Collects (23), the first and seventeenth imperfect, of a general nature, some agreeing with the *Orationes ad matutinas* found in *The Gelasian Sacramentary*, ed. H.A. Wilson (Oxford, 1894), pp. 291–2. Leaves have been lost between fols. 18 and 19.

19r24–21r12 (39–43): *item alia oratio pro peccatis.* Collects (28), many agreeing with the *Orationes pro peccatis* in *The Gregorian Sacramentary*, ed. H.A. Wilson, Henry Bradshaw Society, XLIX (1915), 122–6.

2. *The Sanctorale (21r–38v)*

21r14 (43): Rubric, *item alia. incipiunt capitula maiorum solemnitatum.*

21r15–v9 (43–4): Capitula (5) for St Stephen, protomartyr (26 Dec.).

21v14–22r11 (44–5): Collects (5) for St Stephen, protomartyr (26 Dec.).

22r12–v7 (45–6): Capitula (6) for St John, ap. and evang. (27 Dec.).

22v12–23r9 (46–7): Collects (6) for St John, ap. and evang. (27 Dec.).

23r10–v7 (47–8): Capitula (5) for the Holy Innocents, mm. (28 Dec.).

23v7–24r2 (48): Collects (5) for the Holy Innocents, mm. (28 Dec.).

24r3–6 (49): Collect for St Silvester, p. and conf. (31 Dec.).

24r6–9 (49): Collect for S. Felix in Pincis (14 Jan.). Wrongly dated *xviii* instead of *xix kl.*

24r9–12 (49): *xvi kl.* Collect for St Marcellus, p. and m. (16 Jan.). Wrongly dated *xvi* instead of *xvii.*

24r13–16 (49): *xv kl februarii.* Collect for St Prisca, v. and m. (18 Jan.). The heading gives the date wrongly.

24r17–21 (49): Collect for St Fabian, p. and m. (20 Jan.).

24r21–v2 (50): Collect for St Sebastian, m. (20 Jan.).

24v3–11 (50): Collects (2) for St Agnes, v. and m. (21 Jan.).

24v12–15 (50): Collect for St Vincent, m. (22 Jan.).

24v16–19 (50–1): Collect for the octaves of St Agnes, v. and m. (28 Jan.).

24v20–25r1 (51): Collect for St Agatha, v. and m. (5 Feb.).

25r2–5 (51): Collect for St Valentine, priest and m. (14 Feb.).

25r5–9 (51): Collect for St Gregory, p., conf. and doctor (12 Mar.).

25r9–14 (51): Collect for the Annunciation of the B. V. Mary (25 Mar.).

25r14–17 (51–2): Collect for Saints Tiburtius, Valerian and Maximus, mm. (14 Apr.).

25r18–21 (52): Collect for St George, m. (23 Apr.).

25v1–4 (52): Collect for St Mark, evang. (25 Apr.).

25v4–8 (52): Collect for St Vitalis, m. (28 Apr.).

25v8–11 (52): Collect for Saints Philip and James, app. (1 May).

25v12–16 (52–3): Collect for Saints Alexander, p., Eventius and Theodolus, mm. (*Theodorus* in title) (3 May).

25v16–19 (53): Collect for St John, ap. and evang., ante portam latinam (6 May).

25v19–26r1 (53): Collect for Saints Gordian and Epimachus, mm. (10 May).

26r2–5 (53): Collect for Saints Nereus, Achilleus and Pancras, mm. (12 May).

26r7–9 (53): Collect for Natale S. Mariae ad Martyres (13 May). No rubric.

26r9–12 (53): Collect for St Urban, p. and m. (25 May).

26r12–15 (54): Collect for Saints Marcellinus and Peter, mm. (2 June).

26r16–19 (54): Collect for Saints Primus and Felician, mm. (9 June).

26r19–v2 (54): Collect for Saints Basilides, Cyrinus, Nabor and Nazarius, mm. (12 June).

26v2–5 (54): Collect for Saints Mark and Marcellian, mm. (18 June). Wrongly headed *iiii. kl. iuli.*

26v5–9 (54): Collect for Saints Gervase and Protase, mm. (19 June). Wrongly headed *iii. kl. iuli.*

26v9–27r9 (55): Capitula (6) for St John the Baptist (24 June).

27r10–v8 (56): Collects (6) for St John the Baptist (24 June).

27v8–13 (57): Collect for Saints John and Paul, mm. (26 June).

27v13–17 (57): Collect for St Leo, p. (28 June).

27v17–28r19 (57–8): Capitula (7) for St Peter, ap. (29 June).

28r20–29r3 (58–9): Collects (7) for Saints Peter and Paul, app. (29 June).

29r3–21 (59–60): Capitula (4) for the Commemoration of St Paul, ap. (30 June).

29r21–v9 (60–1): Collects (3) for the Commemoration of St Paul, ap. (30 June).

29v10–19 (61): Capitula (2) for the octave of the apostles (6 July).

29v19–30r8 (61–2): Collects (3) for the octave of the apostles (6 July).

30r8–11 (62): Collect for Saints Processus and Martinian, mm. (2 July).

30r11–16 (62): Collect for the Translation of St Martin, b. and conf. (4 July).

30r17–20 (62): Collect for the Septem Fratres, mm. (10 July).

30r21–v2 (62–3): Collect for St Benedict, ab. (11 July).

30v3–6 (63): Collect for St James, ap. (25 July).

30v6–11 (63): Collect for Saints Felix, p., Simplicius, Faustinus and Beatrice, mm. (29 July).

30v12–17 (63): Collect for Saints Abdon and Sennen, mm. (30 July).

30v17–21 (63): Collect for the Holy Maccabees, mm. (1. Aug.). There follows the rubric for St Stephen, p. and m. (2 Aug.), but no collect. A leaf has been lost.

31r1–14 (64): Collects (4), the first imperfect, for St Laurence, m. (10 Aug.).

31r14–17 (64): Collect for St Tiburtius, m. (11 Aug.).

31r17–20 (64–5): Collect for St Hippolytus, m. (13 Aug.).

31r20–v1 (65): Collect for St Eusebius, conf. (14 Aug.).

31v2–20 (65): Capitula (4) for the Assumption of the B. V. Mary (15 Aug.).

31v20–32r23 (66–7): Collects (7) for the Assumption of the B. V. Mary (15 Aug.).

32v1–4 (67): Collect for the octave of St Laurence, m. (17 Aug.).

32v4–7 (67): Collect for St Agapitus, m. (18 Aug.).

32v8–11 (67): Collect for St Timothy, m. (23 (Aug.).

32v12–16 (67): Collect for St Bartholomew, ap. (24 Aug.).

32v17–19 (67–8): Collect for the Beheading of St John the Baptist (29 Aug.).

32v20–3 (68): Collect for Saints Felix and Adauctus, mm. (30 Aug.).

33r1–19 (68–9): Capitula (5) for the Nativity of the B. V. Mary (8 Sept.).

33r19–v23 (69–70): Collects (8), the last imperfect, for the Nativity of the B. V. Mary (8 Sept.). A leaf has been lost.

34r1–15 (70–1): Capitula (5), the first imperfect, for the Dedication of St Michael the Archangel (29 Sept.).

34r16–v13 (71–2): Collects (6) for the Dedication of St Michael the Archangel (29 Sept.). No rubric.

34v13–16 (72): Collect for St Mark, p. and conf. (7 Oct.).

34v17–21 (72): Collect for S. Dionisius cum sociis, mm. (9 Oct.).

34v21–35r2 (72): Collect for St Callistus, p. and m. (14 Oct.).

35r2–5 (72): Collect for St Luke, evang. (18 Oct.).

35r6–10 (72–3): Collect for Saints Simon and Jude, app. (28 Oct.).

35r10–13 (73): Collect for St Quentin, m. (31 Oct.).

35r13–16 (73): Collect for the vigil of All Saints (31 Oct.).

35r16–v9 (73–4): Collects (4) for All Saints (1 Nov.).

35v10–19 (74): *item collectiones in cotidianis diebus.* Collects (3) for the daily office of All Saints.

35v20–36r19 (74–5): *item in cotidianis diebus ut supra.* Collects (5) for the daily office of All Saints.

36r19–v2 (75): Collect for the Quattuor Coronati, mm. (8 Nov.). Wrongly dated *vi idus octobris.*

36v2–5 (75–6): Collect for St Theodore, m. (9 Nov.).

36v5–37r16 (76–7): Collects (7) for St Martin, b. and conf. (11 Nov.).

37r16–v5 (77–8): Collects (2) for St Cecilia, v. and m. (22 Nov.).

37v5–9 (78): Collect for St Clement, p. and m. (23 Nov.).

37v9–12 (78): Collect for St Chrysogonus, m. (24 Nov.).

37v12–15 (78): Collect for St Saturninus, m. (29 Nov.).

37v15–38r6 (78–9): Capitula (5) for St Andrew, ap. (30 Nov.).

38r6–v8 (79–80): Collects (7) for St Andrew, ap. (30 Nov.).

38v9–12 (80): Collect for St Lucy, v. and m. (13 Dec.).

38v12–15 (80): Collect for St Thomas, ap. (21 Dec.).

3. *The Commune Sanctorum (38v–45r21)*

38v16–22: Rubric announcing apparently the end of the sanctorale and the beginning of the commune sanctorum.

39r1–14 (81): *capitula in uigilia unius apostoli.* Capitula (5) for the vigil of an apostle.

39r14–v12 (81–2): *Secuntur collectiones ad uigilias apostolorum.* Collects (7) for the vigil of an apostle.

39v13–40r7 (82–3): *item in uigiliis apostolorum.* Capitula (5) for several apostles.

40r8–v5 (83–4): *item collectiones apostolorum.* Collects (7) for several apostles.

40v5–41r4 (84–5): *in uigilia unius martiris.* Capitula (6) for the common of a martyr.

41r5–19 (85–6): Collects (5) for the common of a martyr. No rubric.

41r19–v11 (86): *in uigilia martirum.* Capitula (4) for the common of martyrs.

41v11–42r10 (87–8): *secuntur collectiones ad uigilias.* Collects (6) for the common of martyrs.

42r10–v8 (88): *in natale unius confessores.* Capitula (5) for the common of a confessor.

42v9–43r14 (88–90): Collects (7) for the common of a confessor. No rubric.

43r15–v2 (90): *in ecclesia cuiuslibet sancti martiris siue confessoris.* Collects (2) for the common of a martyr or confessor.

43v3–18 (90–1): Capitula (4) for the common of saints. ?Confessors. No rubric.

43v19–44r14 (91–2): Collects (6) for the common of confessors. No rubric.

44r14–v7 (92): Capitula (6) for the common of confessor saints. Headed *in natalibus plurimorum martirum.*

44v8–22 (93): Collects (5), the last imperfect, for the common of confessors. No rubric at the beginning. Two leaves containing more of the common of saints have been lost.

45r1–21 (93–4): *ad crucem salutandam.* Collects (6) to the Holy Cross.

4. *Benedictions etc. (45r21–61r10)*

45r21–v14 (95): Blessings (2) of palms on Palm Sunday.

45v15–46v4 (95–7): Prayers (5) for those receiving the tonsure. No rubric at the beginning.

46v5–47r10 (97–8): Blessings of vessels (3) including two *super uasa reperta in locis antiquis.*

47r10–15 (98): Blessing of fruit trees.

47r15–17 (99): Blessing of apples.

47r17–22 (99): Blessing of new bread.

47r22–v11 (99): Blessings (2) of food.

47v11–23 (99–100): Blessings (2) of a house. In the margin against the first prayer, beginning *Adesto domine,* scribe M3 has added (and provided with neums where appropriate):

> Ærest halga water ⁊ salt. ⁊ siðþan sing þonne. Antiphona. Asperges me domine mid þæm sealme. Miserere mei. ⁊ þisne collectan [i.e. *Adesto domine*]. ⁊. Pax huic domui. ⁊ deus misereatur. ⁊ þisne collectan [i.e. *Benedic domine*].

And lower down:

> Siðþan þisne. Antiphona. Benedic domine domum istam et omnes habitantes in eo quia domine dixisti pax huic domui benedic domine timentes te pusillos cum maioribus benedicti uos a domino qui fecit celum et terram....

48r1–49v4 (100–3): Prayers and exorcisms (6) for the ordeal by boiling water. Cf. *M.G.H.,* Legum, sectio v, pp. 610–11.

49v4–50v6 (103–5): Blessings (6) of a nun.

50v7–51r4 (105–6): Mass for the blessing of a nun.

51r4–53r23 (106–11): Nuptial mass with blessings.

(For an addition by scribe E on 53v, see below, under β. 4 *(b).*)

54r1–55r20 (112–14): Prayers and exorcisms (3) for the ordeal by hot iron. For a Latin version similar to the Old English prayer on 55r, see *M.G.H.*, Legum, sectio v, p. 710.

55r20–59v12 (114–22): Miscellaneous blessings (19) of nets etc.

59v13–60r6 (122–3): Prayers (3) for the blessing of a house.

60r7–61r10 (123–5): Miscellaneous collects and prayers (11), including a group to be said at the canonical hours throughout the day. No rubric.

β. THE ADDITIONS

1. *Texts Written by Several Hands (61r11–65v)*

61r11–22 (125): Prayer against poison. No rubric. Scribe B.

61v1–62v18 (126–9): *Incipiunt benedixiones ad lectionem*. Blessings over lessons for Christmas, Epiphany, Easter, Ascension, Whitsun and Advent, the Virgin, peace, the Trinity, apostles, martyrs, confessors and All Saints. Scribe C.

62v18–63v4 (129–30): *benedictio lac et mel*. Scribe C.

63v5–23 (130): Blessing of grapes (63v5–11), blessing of new bread (63v12–19) and blessing of fruits, apples and nuts (63v20–3). Scribe D.

63v23–64r8 (130–1): *benedictio putei*. Scribe D.

64r9–17 (131): General prayers (2). No rubric. Scribe E.

64v1–16 (131–2): Hymn for Passiontide beginning *Auctor salutis unicus*.... No rubric. Scribe C.

64v17–65rb17 (132–5): Antiphons, versicles and responds for lections from the Books of Tobit, Judith, Maccabees and the Minor Prophets. Scribe F.

65rb18–32 (135–6): Hymn for Lent beginning *Audi benigne conditor*.... No rubric. Scribe C.

65v1–16 (136–7): *ymnus infra xlma*. Hymn for Passiontide beginning *Vexilla regis prodeunt*.... Scribe C.

65v17–29 (137–8): Hymn for Eastertide beginning *Ad cenam agni prouidi*.... No rubric. Scribe C.

2. *Texts Written by Scribe C Unless Otherwise Stated (66[70]r–76[69]v)*

66[70]r1–67[71]v5 (145–7): Prayers (5) for the protection of crops against depredations of birds etc. Written by Aldred.

67[71]v6–22 (147–8): Prayer over salt and water to be used against demoniac possession.

67[71]v23–68[72]r16 (148): Prayers (4) for the blessing of a house.

68[72]r17–28 (148–9): Evening prayers (3). No rubric.

68[72]v1–10 (149–50): Memoriae (2) of the Holy Cross. No rubric at the beginning. In the margin scribe M3 has added: *Antiphona. Per signum crucis. Versiculus. Adoramus te christe et benedicamus tebi quia per crucem tuam redemisti mundum. Versiculus. Dicite in nationibus dominus regnauit a ligno*. There is an error at *Rit.*, p. 150, where the versicle *Dicite in nationibus* is misplaced.

68[72]v8–16 (150): Evening prayers (3). Cf. *Orationes vespertinales, The Gregorian Sacramentary*, ed. Wilson, pp. 227–8.

68[72]v17–30 (150–1): Memoriae (3) of the Holy Cross.

68[72]v31–70[74]r14 (151–5): Memoriae of St Michael the Archangel, the B.V. Mary (2), St Michael and All Angels, St John the Baptist, St Peter, St Andrew, Saints Peter, Paul and Andrew, All Saints, St Paul, St John the Evangelist, confessors (scribe M3 has added the name *Cuthbert* between the lines), a martyr, apostles, martyrs and all saints (2).

70[74]r15–71[75]r7 (155–8): Memoriae for the dead.

71[75]r8–71[75]v6 (158–9): Missa de Sanctæ *(sic)* Trinitate.

71[75]v7–72[76]r16 (159–60): *In natale unius confessoris*. Mass for a confessor.

72[76]r17–72[76]v20 (161–2): Mass for a martyr.

72[76]v21–73[66]r22 (162 and 138–9): Mass for several martyrs.

73[66]r22–74[67]r10 (139–40): Mass for the common of a virgin martyr.

74[67]r11–74[67]v21 (140–1): Mass for the vigil of an apostle.

74[67]v22–75[68]v23 (142–3): Mass for the common of an apostle.

75[68]v24–5 (143): Note, *Dominus saluet. honoret. amet. aldhunum antistitem.* Added by scribe M1.

76[69]r1–26 (143–5): Collects (8) for the canonical hours. No rubric.

76[69]v1–29: Antiphons, versicles and responds for lections from the Books of Kings, Wisdom and Job, similar in arrangement to the list on 64v–65r. Scribe F.

3. *Texts Written by Aldred Unless Otherwise Stated (77r–84v)*

77r1–11 (162–3): *Incipit ymnus ad primam horam* (daily throughout the year), beginning *Iam lucis orto sidere....*

77r12–18 (163–4): *Incipit ad tertiam horam ymnus* (daily throughout the year), beginning *Nunc sancte nobis spiritus....*

77r19–24 (164): *Incipit ymnus ad sextam horam* (daily throughout the year), beginning *Rector potens uerax deus....*

77v1–8 (164–5): *Incipit ymnus ad nonam horam* (daily throughout the year), beginning *Rerum deus tenax uigor....*

77v9–13 (165): *Ymnus de resurrectione iesu christi domini nostri.* Stanza 11, beginning *Rex christe clementissime. Tu corda nostra posside...,* and the doxology of the Eastertide hymn which begins *Aurora lucis rutilat...* (*Analecta hymnica medii aevi,* 51. 89).

77v14–18 (165–6): *Ymnus ad uesperum in dominica nocte.* Hymn for the first vespers of Sunday (i.e. sung on Saturday) during winter (see *Regularis concordia,* ed. Dom Thomas Symons [London etc., 1953], p. 25), beginning *O lux beata trinitas....*

77v19–25 (166): Episcopal benediction. No rubric. Added by scribe M2. The first two clauses correspond to those provided for the fifth Sunday after Pentecost in the Benedictional of St Æthelwold.

78r1–79va5 (166–71): *Incipiunt capitulæ ad primam.* A series of suffrages to be said at prime known as the Gallican Capitella; see *The Monastic Breviary of Hyde Abbey, Winchester,* ed. J.B.L. Tolhurst, VI, Henry Bradshaw Society, LXXX (1942), 30–6.

79va6–b2 (171–2): *postea sequitur oratio ad primam.* Collects (2) for prime on weekdays.

79vb3–14 (172): *Oratio in die dominica ad primam.* Collect.

79vb15–80va9 (172–4): *Incipiunt capitulæ ad tertiam et sextam et nonam horam.* A series of suffrages rather similar in pattern to those for prime on 78r–79v. They include two groups, one *pro fidelibus defunctis,* 80rb11 (173), and a second *pro fratribus nostris absentibus,* 80rb15 (174). These also form part of the Gallican Capitella; see Tolhurst, *ibid.,* pp. 39–42.

80va10–11 (174): Rubric, *require infra collectiones tres.* It is possible that this refers to the three prayers provided for prime on 79v.

80va12–22 (174): *Oratio secreta ante initium uespertinæ laudis.* Collect beginning. *Actus nostros hodiernos quesumus in beneplacito....*

80va23–82ra5 (175–9): A series of suffrages to be used at vespers similar in pattern to those for prime on 78r–79v and for tierce, sext and none on 79v–80v. No rubric at the beginning. They include a number under individual headings, including *pro rege nostro, pro æpiscopo nostro* and *pro fratribus nostris absentibus.* These are known as the Celtic Capitella; see Tolhurst, *ibid.,* pp. 19–27.

82ra6–b11 (179–80): Collects (2).

82rb12–va3 (180): *ymnus ad complendum* (daily during summer, or here possibly throughout the year), beginning *Te lucis ante terminum....*

82va4–83rb10 (180–2): Suffrages with collects (2) for compline. No rubric at the beginning.

These are the Gallican Capitella; see Tolhurst, *ibid.*, pp. 36–9.

83rb11–21 (183): Rubric, *hii sunt .vii. psalmi poenitentiales ad primam horam*. Incipits of the Seven Penitential Psalms.

83rb22–84ra2 (183–4): Incipits of special psalms to be said at tierce (8), sext (5), none (8) and vespers (3). In the case of those at tierce they are called the *psalmi orationum*.

84ra4–b18 (185): Four collects to St Cuthbert; see notes immediately below them. See C. Hohler, 'Durham Services in Honour of St Cuthbert', *The Relics of St Cuthbert,* ed. C. F. Battiscombe, pp. 157–8.

84v1–35 (185–7): Antiphons, versicles and responds for the first four Sundays in Advent. Scribe E.

4(*b*) *Addition by Scribe E Within the Original Collectar*

53v1–16 (111–12): Hymn for Passiontide beginning *Auctor salutis unicus...*, as on 64v1–16. No rubric.

(For additions by scribes M1–3, see above, at 47v11, 68[72]v1, 75[68]v24 and 77v19.)

ALDRED'S EDUCATIONAL ADDITIONS

The last four leaves of the additions (fols. 85–8) contain a series of educational memoranda written by Aldred continuously, except for a gap of ten lines (87vb16–25), and apparently all at the same time. The description which follows is based on *Rit.*, pp. xi and xix–xx.

85ra1–86rb9 (187–92): *hæ sunt notas predistinatas.* Ap̄. aput. ā. aut. at̄. autem. ac̄o. auctio. ... ut̄. utilis. xīo. existimo. zl̄. zabulus. z̄e. zelus. zoe. zeloes. An alphabetical list of some 225 *notae juris,* of which about one quarter are legal terms. Of the *notarum laterculi* printed by Th. Mommsen in H. Keil, *Grammatici latini,* IV (Leipzig, 1864), 265–352, the closest seems to be the *Notae lindenbrogianae* (pp. 285–300), which, like this list, has *notae* for the ecclesiastical words *beatus, lapsus, omnipotens, salus* and *spes* (cf. p. 287), and for *affectus, egressus* and *lapis.* The only other ecclesiastical words in our list are *zabulus, zelus* and *zeloes.*

86rb10–86va16 (192): *De octo pondera de quibus factus est adam.* Octo pondera de quibus factus est adam. Pondus limi. inde factus est caro. ... pondus gratiæ inde est sensus hominis (86va5). A similar passage on the eight pounds of different materials from which Adam was made occurs in the 'Dialogue of Solomon and Saturn', in Anglo-Saxon prose, found in B.M. Cotton Vitellius A. xv, 86v–93v, saec. xii med. (Ker, *Catalogue,* no. 215); see B. Thorpe, *Analecta Anglo-Saxonica* (London, 1834), pp. 93–4; J. M. Kemble, *The Dialogue of Solomon and Saturn* (Ælfric Society, 1848), p. 180. Followed immediately by two questions, *Dic mihi cur non æquales sunt duæ anhelæ* and *Dic mihi unde flauescat uentus* (86va 5–16).

86va16–87ra10 (192–3): *De dignitatibus romanorum.* Imperator qui imperium tenet multorum populorum. ... Princeps super decem (86vb16). Explanations of eleven Roman imperial offices. Followed immediately by notes on the names given to kings by the Hebrews and others (86vb17–23), and on *magistratus sive tristatus* in Egypt (87ra1–10). The last note is based on Jerome, *Commentaria in Ezechielem,* VII, xxiii (*Pat. lat.,* xxv, 219).

87ra11–87va15 (193–4): *De gradibus æcclessiæ.* i. Hostiarius qui in ueteri testamento. ... Papa qui et pater patruum uel pater patriæ. Explanations of ecclesiastical offices. Those of *subdiaconus* and *chorepiscopus* are based on Isidore, *De ecclesiasticis officiis,* II, x and vi (*Pat. lat.,* LXXXIII, 790 and 786); that of *exorcista* on Rhabanus Maurus, *De clericorum institutione,* I, x (*Pat. lat.,* CVII, 304).

87va16–b15 (195): *Interpretatio nominis sacerdotum.* Sacerdos huic nomine functus.... Followed immediately (87vb2) by explanations of eight Greek words: *Patriarha* ... *Ypapante.*

88ra1–b24 (195–7): *Nomina locorum in quo apostoli requiescunt.* Beatus matheus apostolus et euangelista requieuit in terra armenia in terra amanitorum ... Beatus stephanus primus martyr requiescit hierusalem in prouincia syria. A list of the burial places of the apostles and of St Stephen.

88va1–24 and b1–21 (197–9): [a.] Adam primus homo factus est a domino de prima littera id est de .iiii. litteris. de quibus nominatum est nomen eius. b. Bonus filius id est abel qui pietatem prestabat parentibus suis. ... y. Finis sæculi id est dies iudicii. z. Zezania in medio triticorum id est peccatores in medio iustorum. An alphabet of words, 'of which the general theme is sin and redemption' (*Rit.,* p. xx).

88vb22–6 and a25–6 (199): Matheus habet testimonia xxx.iii. canones. cc. lv. .... A table of the *testimonia* (citations from the Old Testament) and *canones* (Ammonian sections) in the four gospels. Compare the lists of *testimonia* printed by [D. de Bruyne], *Préfaces de la bible latine* (Namur, 1920), pp. 186–8, from Paris, B.N. lat. 6 and Paris, B.N. lat. 268.

GLOSSARY TO ALDRED'S GLOSS

BY A.S.C. ROSS AND E.G. STANLEY

FOUNDED ON WORK DONE BY CONSTANCE O. ELLIOTT

The Anglo-Saxon material of the 'Durham Ritual' consists almost entirely of Aldred's gloss to most of the original collectar (1r–53r and 54v–61r10), as well as to much of the later additions (61r11–61v10, 66[70]r–67[71]v5, 77r–83v and 85r–88v).[1] As well as this major Anglo-Saxon item, there are the following minor ones: the passage with the rubric *halsuncge* (55r), which was called 'Durham Admonition' by H. Sweet, *The Oldest English Texts* (EETS, 1885), pp. 175–6, and the eight rubrics at 55r20, 55v15, 56r4, 56v4 and 15, 57r10 and 57v1 and 19;[2] the sentence at 72[76]r3;[3] Aldred's colophon (84r) and the word *gilanid'* (= *gilanidon)*[4] in his memorandum (84r); the Anglo-Saxon elements in the liturgical additions in the margins of 47v;[5] *ðat* in the left hand margin against 83v17 and *ðrie megulitas* at the top of 89v;[6] and *bloetsa drihtin* in the left hand margin against 47v7.[7]

As has been stated,[8] Aldred wrote the 'Ritual' gloss about 970 and the Lindisfarne gloss earlier. Linguistically, the two glosses are very similar, but not identical. The dialect of both is, of course, 'North Northumbrian'. The phonology of this dialect is, today, perhaps best ascertained from a perusal of A. Campbell, *Old English Grammar* (Oxford, 1959). But, despite its age and the fact that it was based on Stevenson's edition—which is often inaccurate—U. Lindelöf, *Die Sprache des Rituals von Durham* (Helsingfors, 1890) is still useful. The grammar of the dialect—very different from that of West Saxon—is set out in the 'Standard Paradigms' in *Cod. Lind.*, bk II, pp. 37–42. In the main, these paradigms are valid for the 'Ritual' gloss also, though the grammar of the latter shows less of the abundant variation to be observed in the Lindisfarne gloss. The grammar of the Lindisfarne gloss is also set out in H. C. A. Carpenter, *Die Deklination in der nordhumbrischen Evangelienübersetzung der Lindisfarner Handschrift* (Bonn, 1910), and T. Kolbe, *Die Konjugation der Lindisfarner Evangelien* (Bonn, 1912) (compare, further, A. S. C. Ross, *Studies in the Accidence of the Lindisfarne Gospels* [Leeds, 1937]), that of the 'Ritual' gloss in the work of Lindelöf just mentioned. Some work has been done on the vocabulary of the two glosses; much of this can be extracted from the relevant entries in F. Holthausen, *Altenglisches etymologisches Wörterbuch* (Heidelberg, 1934). Mention should also be made of the 'Aldrediana' series of articles and monographs, in which various points concerning Aldred's two great glosses are discussed. A list of the publications of the series will be found in *English Philological Studies,* x (1967), 1, n. 1; further ones are in course of preparation.

Of the *halsuncge,* Lindelöf says:[9] 'There is

1. The Latin of most of the glossed additions was written by Aldred. For an account of the Latin texts, see above, pp. 48–50.

2. The *halsuncge* and the rubrics, like the rest of the original collectar, were written by scribe O; see above, p. 18.

3. Written by scribe C; see above, pp. 29–30.

4. See above, p. 24.

5. Written by scribe M3; see above, p. 35.

6. These scribbles are among minor tenth- and eleventh-century additions; see above, p. 36.

7. An eleventh- or twelfth-century addition; see above, p. 36. This seems to be the scribble to which Lindelöf refers, *Rit.,* p. xlviii, though he assigns it to 'p. 132', i.e. 73[66]v.

8. Above, pp. 17 and 26.

9. *Rit.,* p. l.

nothing in it which militates against its being Southern (Saxon) of the (perhaps early) tenth century.' And of the eight rubrics, he says:[1] 'These rubrics ... are somewhat puzzling from the point of view of dialect. Their language cannot be identified with that of the "halsuncge", but shows curious features of a mixed dialect. The first of the rubrics has some distinctly non-Northumbrian characteristics..., whereas the rubrics on MS. pp. 111–114 [56r–57v] have certain features of a decidedly Northumbrian (or at any rate Anglian) character....' We are in agreement with these two statements.

The short item at 72[76]r3 shows one distinctively Northumbrian form, namely *nioða*. As might be expected, Aldred's so-called colophon essentially shows his own dialect; indeed the form *daegi, dægi* is very characteristic of it. Nevertheless, the final *-n* of *wudigan gæte* would be abnormal in it;[2] the West Saxon form of the place-name has probably had an influence. The language of the vernacular parts of the liturgical additions on 47v can be described aptly by Lindelöf's term 'Southern (Saxon)'. The short item in the margin opposite 47v7, with its distinctively Northumbrian form, *bloetsa,* was probably copied from Aldred's gloss.

The conventions of this glossary (which includes the minor Anglo-Saxon items, as well as Aldred's gloss, in its scope) are those of the *Index verborum glossematicus* to Aldred's gloss to the Lindisfarne Gospels, published in *Cod. Lind.*, bk II, pp. 43–176. They are set out in detail there. Here a summary will suffice.

The *Glossary* comprises the linguistic forms of the Anglo-Saxon text and the Latin words[3] (where they exist[4]) which are glossed by these forms. But, whereas the *Index* records every occurrence of every form, the *Glossary* records every glossematic relationship of every form but no more than two or three occurrences of each glossematic relationship.[5]

In the *Glossary* the typical entry has six parts: the head-word, the glossemes, the formal indicators, the forms, the references and the glossematic indicators. Most of this is self-evident and only the following comments are required.

The head-word. The head-word is ideal; a nomen is entered in the non-genitive singular, a verb in an ideal third singular present indicative. Brackets indicate a variant form. A question mark following a head-word means that the ideal form is uncertain. The head-words—brackets and unhyphened prefixes being ignored—are alphabeticized as follows:

a æ b c d e f g h i l m n o p r s t ð u x y z.

A nominal or verbal compound appears under its second element, and the prefixes *ge-*,[6] *a-* and *un-* (which appear in this order) are unhyphened. Very few cross-references are given.

The glossemes and glossematic indicators. The latter (which are small *italic* letters of the English alphabet) occur twice: first preceding the glossemes and secondly, printed suprascript, after the references. Two classes of glossemes (expressed in a standard Latin orthography) are distinguished: those printed in SMALL CAPITALS represent the usual meaning of the Anglo-Saxon words and those printed in small roman the less usual meanings; the distinction between these two classes is, naturally, somewhat subjective. There are a few 'wrong' glosses, but these are not distinguished from the normal ones. There are many cases in which an Anglo-Saxon word has no glosseme—the whole of the West Saxon material belongs here; a reference to a word of this kind therefore appears without

1. *Ibid.*, n. 1.

2. But compare *ðirddan,* five times in the Lindisfarne gloss.

3. We have called these the *glossemes;* the derived adjective is *glossematic.*

4. The West Saxon material, which is not a gloss, is entered in a self-evident manner.

5. There are also two minor differences between *Index* and *Gloss.* In the latter (1) an asterisk indicates that a form is not entirely legible—in some cases a footnote is added stating in what the illegibility consists—and (2) most proper names are not entered.

6. A past participle with *ge-* is entered under the main verb.

a glossematic indicator. If two Anglo-Saxon words together gloss one Latin word, the glosseme and its indicator are placed in brackets.[1] If an Anglo-Saxon word in some instances by itself glosses a Latin word and in other instances does so in conjunction with another Anglo-Saxon word, the glosseme is not bracketed, but its indicator is bracketed in the reference of an occurrence of the second kind. If, at its every occurrence, an Anglo-Saxon word has one and the same glosseme, no glossematic indicator is used. If at every occurrence an Anglo-Saxon word either has a glosseme and always the same glosseme or has no glosseme, no glossematic indicator is used with reference to an occurrence of the first kind and a suprascript hyphen is used instead of a glossematic indicator with reference to an occurrence of the second kind. If at every occurrence an Anglo-Saxon word has the same glosseme but in some instances by itself glosses that word and in other instances does so in conjunction with another Anglo-Saxon word, no glossematic indicator is used with reference to an occurrence of the first kind and a suprascript pair of empty brackets is used instead of a glossematic indicator with reference to an occurrence of the second kind.[2]

The formal indicators. These parse the forms and are abbreviated in an obvious way.[3]

The references. In a reference to a folio which is misbound in the manuscript but is in its correct place in the facsimile,[4] only the correct number is used.

1. But certain cases form exceptions to this rule: (1) definite article + nomen glossing a Latin nomen; (2) preposition + nomen (or pronoun) glossing a Latin oblique case; (3) *to* + verb-form glossing a Latin verb; (4) *la* + nomen glossing a Latin vocative; (5) personal pronoun + verb glossing a Latin verb; and (6) verb + auxiliary glossing a Latin verb. In any of these six cases neither the glosseme nor its indicator is placed in brackets in the entry in which the main Anglo-Saxon word is the head-word, but in the entry in which the secondary Anglo-Saxon word is the head-word there is an explanatory comment which follows the glosseme(s) and is preceded by an italic *CAPITAL* letter.

2. Forms with *n*-synalœphe present difficulties; an examination of the entry **(n)ænig** will inform the reader as to the nature of our treatment of them (and the use of the plus sign).

3. The formal indicator *pl.* (= plural) is omitted in the case of plural Anglo-Saxon nouns glossing Latin plurals.

4. See above, p. 11, n. 1.

GLOSSARY

abbud: ABBAS ‖ *sg. gen.* abbudes 30r 22.

adl: *a* LANGUOR *b* MORBUS ‖ *pl. nom.* + *acc.* adlo 59r10[b]; 78vb7[a].

adligað: PESTILENS ‖ *pres. part.* adliende 59r14.

agenlic: *a* PROPRIUS *b* debere ‖ agenlic 51r1[b]; *agenligc 10r22[a]. *sg. gen.* agenlices 24r19[a].

under-agenlic: subniti ‖ *pl. dat.* underagenlicum 83rb4–5.

giagnað: POSSIDERE ‖ *pres. subj.* + *inf.* giagnige 10r15.

agnung: POSSESSIO ‖ agnung 85vb17.

ah: *a* AN *b* SED *A—insertion* ‖ ah 3r9[b]; 51r8[A]; 51r15[a].

ald: *a* ANTIQUUS *b* SENIOR *c* UETUS *d* PRISTINUS *e* parens ‖ *sg. gen.* aldes 45v6[a]; 54v8[c]. *sg. dat.* aldum 87ra13[c]. *sg. acc. masc.* aldne 16r6[c]. *sg. weak* alda 12v22[c]. halda 50v2[c]. *pl. nom.* + *acc.* aldo 23r20[b]; 87vb15[a]. alde 12r20[c]. *pl. gen.* aldra 81va21[a]. *pl. dat.* aldum 5v12[d]; 12r22[c] [*alt.f.* aldes]; 17v16[a]. *comp. pl. nom.* + *acc.* aeldro 87rb12[b]. *pl. dat.* *aeldrum 88va6[e].

gialdað: SENESCERE ‖ *pres. subj.* + *inf.* gialdia 53r11; 53r17.

aldor: PARENS ‖ *sg. gen.* aldores 16v5.

aldordom: MAGISTRATUS ‖ aldordom 87ra1.

aldorlic: *a* PRINCIPALIS *b* PRINCIPALITER ‖ *sg. dat.* aldorlic' 78va6[a]. *adv.* aldorlice 4v12[b]; 52v4[b]. *sg. weak* aldorlic' 77v15[a].

all: *a* CUNCTUS *b* OMNIS *c* TOTUS *d* UNIUERSUS (*e* arridus) (*f* exercitus) (*g* pharao), (*h* sabaoth), *i* uniuersitas ‖ all 6v23[b]; 19v10[c]. *sg. fem.* allo 7v21[a]. *sg. gen.* alles 1r6[(h)]; 2r5[b]; 17v20[(f)]; 18r18[c]; 52r19[i]. *sg. dat.* allum 19r10[c]; 28r20[b]; 66v16[d] [*alt. f.* allne]. *sg. acc. masc.* allne 28r6[d]; 59r1[b]. alne 60r8[c]. ealne 55r13[-]. *sg. acc.* + *dat. fem.* alle 5v3[b]. *sg. dat. fem.* allra 61r7[c]. allre 2v13[c]; 43v2[c]. alra 43v1[c]. *pl. nom.* + *acc.* allo 2r13[b]; 7r20[a]; 26v15[d]; 86vb 19[(g)]. alle 2r7[b]; 86vb22[(e)]. al' 49r22[b]. ealle 55r12[-]; 55r14[-]. *pl. gen.* allra 1r20[b]; 11r20[a]. alra 5v1[b]; 35v3[b]. *pl. dat.* allum 3r11[b]; 4v10[a].

aloð: CERUISIA ‖ *sg. gen.* alðes 56v13.

an, enne: *a* SEMEL *b* SOLUS *c* TANTUM *d* UNUS (*e* UNUSQUISQUE) ‖ an 3r9[d]; 6v4[(e)]; 14r16[(c)]. enne 81va5[d]. *sg. fem.* ana 52v5[b]. an'a 15v15[d]. *sg. dat.* anum 36v16[b]; 39v20[(e)]; 51r12[d]. *sg. dat. fem.* anra 8r21[b]. *adv.* aene 10v1[a]; 10v10[a].

anni(s)s(e: UNITAS ‖ annisse 40r5; 58r18. annise 49r21; 82rb9. annis' 45r22.

apostol: APOSTOLUS ‖ apost' 28v11. *sg. gen.* apost' 32v14. apl' 25v18; 28v3. *pl. nom.* + *acc.* ap'las 66v21. *pl. gen.* apostol' 15r5; 15r9. aposto' 25v9; 29r6. ap'la 35r7; 36r5. apl'a 35v21.

ap' 28v6; 28v21. *pl. dat.* apostolum 55v7.
efne-apostol: COAPOSTOLUS ‖ efneap' 29v21.
apostolic: APOSTOLICUS ‖ apost' 39v 10. ap' 28v9; 28v14. *sg. gen.* apost' 40r11. *pl. dat.* ap'cum 28v18.
arfæst: PIUS ‖ arfæst 38r18. *sg. gen.* arfæst' 24v18. *sg. dat.* arfæstum 33v17; *53r1. *sg. dat. fem.* arfæst' 4r2; 43r19. *sg. weak* arfæsta 77r24. arfeasta 77v6. *pl. nom.* + *acc.* arfæsto 30r19. arfeasto 36v1. *pl. dat.* arfæstum 37r15.
arfæstlic: PIUS ‖ *sg. fem.* arfæstlic' 43v20. *sg. dat.* arfæstlicum 19r17. *adv.* arfæstlice 19v11; 37r6.
arfæstni(s)s(e: *a* PIETAS *b* piaculum ‖ arfæstnisse 58v16[a]; 88va6[a]. arfæstnise 9r9[a]; 18v9[a]. arfæstn' 8r20[a]; 57v 16[a]. arfæst' 4r20[a]; 12r1[b]. arfæst 15v 15[a]. arfeastnis' 17r20[a]. *sg. gen.* arfæstnise' 20v13[a]. arfæstnis' 17r16[a]; 19v18[a]. arfæst' 20r14[a]; 20v9[a].
arleas: IMPIUS ‖ *sg. weak* arleasa 5r17; 5r22.
arleasni(s)s(e: INIQUITAS ‖ arleasnisse 5r16.
arlic: (*a* AURORA) *b* DILUCULO *c* MANE *d* MATUTINUS ‖ arlic 33r17[(a)]; 77r21[c]. *sg. fem.* arlica 79va16[d]. *adv.* arlice 40v14[b]; 77v17[c].
arm: *see* **(e)arm.**
asald: ASINUS ‖ *sg. dat.* assalde 45v2.
ata: ZIZANIA ‖ hata 88vb19.
attor: UIRUS ‖ attor 61r19.
æ: LEX ‖ æ 3v5; 51v23. ae 14r17; 16r 10. *sg. gen.* æes 3v9. aes 47v21.
syndir-æ: PRIUILEGIUM ‖ syndurae 85vb20.
æc: *a* ATQUE *b* ET (*c* NEC) (*d* NEQUE) *e* -QUE *f* QUOQUE ‖ æc 2v10[b]; 3r6[(d)]; 3v17[a]; 4v20[e]; 8r1[(e)]; 9r1[f]; 13v8[(a)]; 13v20[(c)].
æc-to-ðon: QUOQUE ‖ æctoðon 37v8.
æc-ðon: QUOQUE ‖ æcðon 8r11; 45r9.
æc(c)cer: SEGES ‖ æccer 67v1. *pl. nom.* + *acc.* acras 66v1. accras 57v4. *pl. dat.* acrum 66r9; 67r8.
æce: *see* **ece.**
æd(-: *see* **æt(-.**
æfæstni(s)s(e: RELIGIO ‖ æfæstnis' 14r20. *sg. gen.* æfeastnis' 46r2.
æfist(a: *a* INUIDIA (*b* Zabulus) ‖ æfest 86rb8[(b)]. *pl. nom.* + *acc.* aefisto 12v2[a].
giæfistað: INUIDERE ‖ giæfistiað 59r 16.
aefne: *see* **efne.**
æfter: *a* ITERUM *b* POST *c* SECUNDUM *d* SECUNDUS ‖ æft' 10r3*c*; 46v13[b]. aeft' 78rb10[c]; 83vb9[b]. eft' 5v12[a]. *comp.* æft'ra 79va17[d]; 86va21[d].
æfter-ðon: *a* DEIN *b* POST *c* POSTEA ‖ æft'ðon 79va6[c]; 85ra21[a]; 85vb12[b].

æht: res ‖ aeht 86ra14.
æhta, -o: OCTO ‖ æhta 86rb10. aehto 86rb12.
ælc: *a* OMNIS (*b* Antiochus) ‖ ælc 2r6[a]; 3r11[a]. aelc 6r19[a]; 12v3 (2)[a,a]. ælce 86vb21[(b)]. *sg. gen.* ælces 10v16[a]; 37v 18[a]. *sg. dat.* ælcum 16v16[a]; 47r7[a]. aelcum 37v23[a]; 60v6[a].
æld-: *see* **ald-.**
ældo: *a* AETAS *b* SENECTUS ‖ ældo 52v 22[b]; 87rb12[a]. *sg. gen.* ældes 40r7[a]; 79ra8[a]. ældo' 46r22[a].
æ(l)lmi(s)sa: *a* ELEEMOSYNA *b* eleemosynarius ‖ aellmisa 27v19[a]. *pl. dat.* ælmissum 61r5[b]. aelmisum 81rb18[a].
(n)ænig: *a* ALIQUIS *b* NEMO *c* NULLUS (*d* QUIS) *e* QUISQUAM *f* ULLUS ‖ ænig 6v12[(b)]; 13r8[(b)]. aenig 6r2[(d)]. nænig 13r8[b]; 23r20[(b)]. *sg. fem.* nængo 4r23[c]; 48v18[c]. *sg. dat.* ænigum 3v3[e]. aenigum 85vb6[b]. ængum 6r2[a]; 54v16[f]. nængum 3v14[c]; 5v20[(b)]; 79va10[c]. *pl. nom.* + *acc.* nængo 24v2[c]; 28v17[c]. *pl. dat.* nængum 16v1[c]; 18v19[c].
æ(p)pel: POMUM ‖ *pl. gen.* æpilra' 47r16.
ær: *a* ANTE (*b* PRAE) *c* PRIMUS *d* PRIOR PRIUS *A—insertion* ‖ ær 33r5[a]; 85vb 14[(b)]; 88va13[A]. aer 5v14[a]; 22r9[a]. *sup.* ærist 43v10[d]; 87va19[c]. aerist 23v19[d]. *pl. dat.* æristum 46v1[c].
ær-ðæt: *a* ANTEQUAM *b* PRIUSQUAM ‖ ærþ 2v9[b]; 26v11–12[a]. aerþ 26v11[b].
ærca: ARCA ‖ aerce 87rb10.
æt, æd: *a* APUD (*b* DEMUM) *A—insertion* ‖ æt 26r1[a]; 85ra23[(b)]; 88rb13[A]. æd 13v20[a]; 14r20[a].
æt-(æd-)geadre: *a* SIMUL *b* pariter ‖ ædgeadre 19v5[b]. ætgeadre 36r7[b]; 36r8[b]. ædgeadre 13r4[a].
ættern: *a* UENENARI *b* UENENOSUS *c* UIPERA *d* UIRUS ‖ *sg. gen.* ætt'nes 59v10[b]. *sg. weak* ætt'ne 61r15; 61r19[a]. hætt'ne 61r14[c]. *pl. nom.* + *acc.* aetterno 66r8[b]. ætt'na 61r16[a]. ætt'no 61r20[d].
bal(d)lice: FIDUCIALITER ‖ ballice 32r5.
ban: OS ‖ *pl. nom.* + *acc.* bano 81va4.
basnung: EXSPECTATIO ‖ *sg. acc.* + *dat.* basnunge 28r20.
on-basnung: EXSPECTATIO ‖ onbasnung 2v8.
bæcere: BAPTISTA ‖ bæcere 27r17; 27v4. bæchere 27r14. bæc' 88ra18. *sg. gen.* bæcere' 27v2. bæcer' 32v17.
bæcling: (RETRORSUM) ‖ bæcling 9v1.
bældo: FIDUCIA ‖ bældo 44v16. baeldo 42v11.
beadeð: EDICERE ‖ *pret. part. pl. nom.* + *acc.* giboden' 85rb4.
bi-beadeð: *a* COMMITTERE *b* MANDARE ‖ *pres. subj.* + *inf.* bibeade 26v15[b]. *pret. part.* beboden 85rb12[a].

for-beadeð: PROHIBERE ‖ *pret. part. pl. nom.* + *acc.* f'bodeno 43v4.
oele-beam: OLIUA ‖ oelebeam 31v16.
b(e)arm: SINUS ‖ *sg. dat.* bearme 48r 19.
b(e)arn: FILIUS ‖ bearn 5r13; 13v17. bearn' 45r12. *sg. gen.* bearnes 5r16; 11v14. bearn' 45r6; 48r6. *sg. dat.* bearne 11r1; 23v15. *pl. nom.* + *acc.* bearnas 52v21. bearno 14r4 [*alt. f.* bearnas]; 14r4. beorno 6r12. *pl. gen.* bearna 52v21. *pl. dat.* bearnum 52r4.
gibearscip(e: continuus ‖ *pl. nom.* + *acc.* gibearsciopo 15r13.
becnað: SIGNIFICARE ‖ *pres. part. pl. nom.* + *acc.* becnendo 49v8.
becon: SIGNUM ‖ becon 9r15; 58r7. *sg. gen.* becon' 45r17. *pl. nom.* + *acc.* beceno 21r16.
bed(d: *a* PREX *b* praecipue ‖ *pl. nom.* + *acc.* beado 3v11[a]; 4v1[a]. beodo 21r10a; 34v14[a]. *pl. dat.* beadum 15r6[a]; 42v19[b]. beodum 28v19[a]; 34v20[a]. beaddum 44r7[a].
gibed(d: *a* DEPRECATIO *b* OBSECRATIO *c* ORATIO *d* PREX *e* SUPPLICATIO ‖ gibed 20r9[a]; 43r12[c]; 47r2[b]. gibedd 79ra17[c]; 79va3[c]. gebed 80va6[c]; 80va12[c]. gebedd 83ra20[c]; 83rb17[c]. *sg. gen.* gibedes 4v16[b]. *sg. dat.* gibede 22r6[a]; 36v5[c]. *pl. nom.* + *acc.* gibeado 3v17[d]. gibeodo 7r19[d]; 20r15[c]. *pl. dat.* gibeadum 4v19[e]; 28v2[c].
gibedda: *a* CONIUNX *b* UXOR ‖ gibedde 37r22[a]. gibedd 86rb7[b].
sig-beg: CORONA ‖ sigbeg 1r6; 3r12. *pl. nom.* + *acc.* sigbego 37v3.
suir-beg: MONILE ‖ *pl. nom.* + *acc.* suirbeg 2r15.
begeð: *a* CASTIGARE *b* COMPUNGERE *c* REDIGERE ‖ *pres. ind. sg. 1* bego 3r16[a]; 3r16[c]. *pret. part. sg. dat.* gebegdum 83va20[b].
gibegeð: *a* CASTIGARE *b* DECLINARE *c* INCLINARE ‖ *pres. subj.* + *inf.* gibega 7r18[a]; 79va11[b]. *imp. sg.* gibeg 20v9[c]; 47r3[c]. *pres. part.* *gibegende 19r3[c].
under-begeð: SUBICERE ‖ *pret. part.* underbeged 61r13.
i(n)n-belgeð: ASPIRARE ‖ *pret. part. pl. nom.* + *acc.* inbolgeno 7v20.
bema: TUBA ‖ bema 2v19.
bend: UINCULUM ‖ *sg. dat.* bende 52r3. *pl. dat.* bendum 3v18.
giberbed: UERMICULATUS ‖ *pl. nom.* + *acc.* giberbedo 2r16.
æ(p)pel-berende: POMIFER ‖ æppilberende 47r11.
deað-berende: MORTIFER ‖ *pl. nom.* + *acc.* deaðberendo 61r19.
uæst(e)m-berende: FRUCTIFER wæstimberende 16v15.

berendlicni(s)s(e: FECUNDITAS ‖ berendlic'e 15v22. **berendni(s)s(e:** *a* FECUNDITAS *b* FETUS ‖ berendnise 14v22[b]. berendnis' 52r5[a]. **unberendni(s)s(e:** STERILITAS ‖ unberendnise 57r13; 58v4. **bereð:** *a* FECUNDUS *b* FETARE *c* NASCI *d* PORTARE ‖ bereð 5r13[d]. bearað 13r14[d]; 51r18[d]. beres 5r15[d]. *infl.inf.* berenne 57r10–11. *pres.part.* berende 52v18[a]; 85rb9[b]. *pret.part.* *geboren 88va15[c]. *sg.dat.* giboren' 48v11[d]. **gibereð:** *a* GESTARE *b* INGERERE *c* PORTARE ‖ *pres.subj.* + *inf.* gibeara 77r14[b]. *pret.ind.sg.1,3* gibær 35r5[c]. gebær *88vb5[c]; 88vb13[c]. *pret.pl.* geberon 87rb10[a]. **abereð:** *a* BAIULARE *b* SUFFERRE ‖ abereð 41r2[b]. *pret.part.* aboren 54v18[a]. **under-bereð:** *a* SUPPORTARE *b* SUSTINERE *c* subsistere ‖ underbearað 6v18[a]. *pres.subj.* + *inf.* underbeara 4r7[c]. *pret.sg.ind.1,3* underbær 13v7[b]. **berht, breht:** *a* CLARUS *b* CONSPICUUS ‖ breht 31r13[b]; 77v4[a]. *pl.dat.* breht'um 10r8[a]. **berhtað, brehtað:** DECLARARE ‖ *pret.part.* giberhtad 1v14. **giberhtað, -brehtað:** *a* CLARIFICARE *b* DECLARARE ‖ *pres.subj.* + *inf.* giberhta 49r15[b]. *infl.inf.* gibrehta' 18r15[a]; 48r13[b]. **berht- (breht-)ni(s)s(e:** *a* CLARITAS *b* SPLENDOR ‖ berhtnisse 1v5[b]; 1v8[a]. brehtnise 33r2[a]. *sg.gen.* brihtnises 7v3[a]. **bereð:** *a* ACCENDERE *b* ARDERE *c* INCENDERE ‖ *pres.part.* bernende 67r17[b]. *pret.part.* giberned 18v18[a]; 26v8[a]. *pl.nom.* + *acc.* gebernedo 66r6[c]. *pl.dat.* gibernedum 49r8[a]. **giberneð:** *a* ACCENDERE *b* EXURERE ‖ *pres.ind.sg.2* gibernes 44v9[a]. *pres. subj.* + *inf.* giberne 48r3[b]. *imp.sg.* gibern 18v8[a]. **bia:** *see* **bio.** **bi(d)deð:** *a* DEPRECARI *b* EXORARE *c* IMPLORARE *d* OBSECRARE *e* ORARE *f* POSCERE *g* PRECARI *h* QUAERERE *i* ROGARE *j* SUPPLICARE *k* competere, *l* deponere ‖ biddað 2v3[b]; 5v24[i]; 15v4[h] [*alt.f.* bidað]; 40r12[a]; *57v2[e]; 58v13[c]. biddas 1v2[h]; 20r6[g]; 32v21[a]; 44v19[b] [*alt.f.* bidas]; 82rb14[f]; bidd' 2v7[h]; 47r13[g]. bid' 1v13[h]; 18r13[a]; 46r12[l]; 49v7[b]. *pres.ind.sg.1* biddo 5v4[d]. bido 56r6[i]; 78vb23[g]. *pres.sub.* + *inf.* bidde 56v7[i]; 77r2[g]. bidda 82ra22[i]. *pres. part.sg.gen.* biddendes 4v2[j]; 23r4[k]. *pl.dat.* biddendum 59v12[f]. **gibi(d)deð:** *a* DEPRECARI *b* EXORARE *c* IMPLORARE *d* ORARE *e* PRECARI *f* ROGARE *g* SUPPLICARE ‖ gibiddað 40v17[a]; 83rb5[b]. gibiddas 34r21[a]. gibi[d]dad 6r4[d]. *pres.subj.* + *inf.* gibidde 5v11[e]; 32r19[d] [*alt.f.* gibide]; 38r11[c]. gibidda 5v12[a]; 21v14[b]; 42r5[g]. *imp.sg.* gibid[d] 78vb23[d]. *pret.ind.sg.1,3* gibæd 21v18[b]; 27v19[f]. **abi(d)deð:** EXORARE ‖ *infl.inf.* abiddanne 42r4. **bideð:** EXSPECTARE ‖ *pres.ind.sg.1* bid'o 9v22. **bifað:** TREMERE ‖ *pres.part.* bibgiende 59v5. **bi-fora(n:** *a* ANTE *b* CORAM ‖ bif'a 9v13[b]; 23r20[a]. bif'an 6v3[a]; 34r7[a]. **bindeð:** *a* LIGARE *b* UINCERE ‖ *pret. part. pl. nom.* + *acc.* gibundeno 10r16[b]. *pl. dat.* gibundenum 51v19[a]. **unbindeð:** *a* ABSOLUERE *b* EXSOLUERE ‖ unbindeð [*alt. f.* onbindeð] 60v5[b]. *pret. part. pl. nom.* + *acc.* unbundeno 3v18[a]; 38r11[a]. **bi-nioða:** INFRA ‖ benioða 80va10. **bio, bia:** APIS ‖ *pl. nom.* + *acc.* bia 58r6. **bi(o)nna:** *a* INTERIUS *b* INTRA *c* INTRINSECUS ‖ bionna 45v13[c]; 60r21[b]. bin'a 7v23[a]. **biorneð, beorneð:** *a* ARDERE (*b* cerarius) *c* edax ‖ *pres. part.* biornende 87vb7[(b)]. *sg. gen.* biornendes 48v9[a]. *pl. nom.* + *acc.* biornendo 31r8[c]. **gibiorneð, -beorneð:** *a* FLAMMESCERE *b* SUCCENDERE ‖ *pres. subj.* + *inf.* gibeorna 77r16[a]. *pret. sg. ind. 1, 3* gibarrn 51v9[b]. **i(n)n-biorneð, -beorneð:** INARDESCERE ‖ *pres. subj.* + *inf.* inbiorne 45v14. **on-biotað:** IMMINERE ‖ *pres. part. pl. dat.* onbiotendum 8v4; 25v15. **grist-bio(t)tung:** STRIDOR ‖ gristbiotung 51v21. **gibirg:** GUSTUS ‖ *sg. dat.* gibirge 56r13. **birgeð:** GUSTARE ‖ *pres. part.* birgende 47r20. **gibirgeð:** GUSTARE ‖ gibirgað 47v5. **biscop, biscob:** *a* EPISCOPUS *b* PONTIFEX ‖ biscop 17r6[b]. bisco' 81ra5[a]; 87rb18[a]. bisc' 10r19[b]; 87rb14[a]. bis' 87va12[a]. **heh-biscop, -biscob:** *a* ARCHIEPISCOPUS *b* PONTIFEX ‖ hehbisco' 24r11[b]; 24r20[b]. hehbisc' 27v14[b]; 42v6[b]; 87rb20[a]. ‖ hehbis 36v11[b]. *sg. gen.* hehbiscopes 24r5[b]. hehbiscob' 36v7[b]. *sg. dat.* hehbiscop' 34v15[b]. **liod-biscop, -biscob:** CHOREPISCOPUS ‖ *pl. nom.* + *acc.* liodbisco' 87va5. **biscophad:** PONTIFICIUM ‖ biscophad 28v12; 44r14. **bisin:** *a* EXEMPLUM *b* FORMA (*c* IMITARI) *d* IMITATIO *e* PARABOLA *f* substantia ‖ bisen 24r9[(c)]; 27v17[(c)]. bisin 11r10[a]; 37v9[(c)]. *sg. acc.* + *dat.* bisene 2v4[f]; 23v18[a]. bissene 30r11[d]. bisine 10v2[b]; 36r3[a]. *pl. nom.* + *acc.* biseno 24r8[a]; 30r16[(c)]. bisino 35r2[a]. *pl. dat.* bisenum 25v11[a]; 51r21[e]. bisinum 31v1[a] [*alt. f.* bisino]; 38v8[a]. **gilic-bisin:** *a* IMITATIO *b* imitator ‖ gilicbisin 44r9[a]. *sg. acc.* + *dat.* gilicbisene 24v1[a]. *pl. nom.* + *acc.* gilicbiseno 6r7[b]. **bisnað:** FORMARE ‖ *pret. sg.* bisinde 27r5. **gibisnað:** *a* IMITARI *b* INFORMARE ‖ *pres. subj.* + *inf.* gibisnia 25r17[a]. *pres. part. sg. fem.* gibisnendo 49v9[b]. **gibisnere:** IMITATOR ‖ gibisnere 22r9. **gilic-bisnung:** IMITATIO ‖ gilicbisnung 36v5. **bitterni(s)s(e:** AMARITUDO ‖ bitternisse 6r19. bitternise 55v5. **bi-tuih, -tui(e)n:** *a* INTER *b* INUICEM *c* interius ‖ bituih 7v18[a]; 7v23[c]. betuien 85va7[a]. bituien 6r22[b]; 7v19[a]. bitwien 3v3–4[b]. bituen 2r20[a]; 6r3[b]. **bi-ðon:** UNDE ‖ biðon 45r16; 48r9. **giblaueð:** FLAUESCERE ‖ geblawað 86va13. **ablaueð:** ASPIRARE ‖ *pret. sg. subj.* + *ind. 2* ableawe 1r23. **eft-blaueð:** RESPIRARE ‖ *pres. subj.* + *inf.* eftblawa 20r18. **eft-giblaueð:** RESPIRARE ‖ *pres. subj.* + *inf.* eft...giblaue 21r12. **in-blaueð:** INSPIRARE ‖ *pres. part.* inblauende 49v11. **on-blaueð:** INSPIRARE ‖ *pres. part.* onblauende 50r9. onblawende 16r20. **to-blaueð:** ASPIRARE ‖ *pres. ind. sg. 2* to...blawas 14v11. **ablendeð:** CAECARE ‖ *pret. part.* ablendad 88va8. **blind:** CAECUS ‖ *sg. dat.* blindum 48v10. *pl. gen.* blinda 56r2. **blind-(blend-)ni(s)s(e:** CAECITAS ‖ blendnise 18v11. blinnis'e 46r5. **unablinnendlice:** INCESSANTER ‖ unablinnendlice 1v21. unablinnenlice 11v6–7. **blinneð:** *a* CESSARE *b* DESINERE ‖ *pres. ind. sg. 1* blinno 33r6[b]. *pres. ind. sg. 2* blinnes 31r16[b]. *pres. subj.* + *inf.* blin' 2v19[a]. **giblinneð:** CESSARE ‖ *pres. subj.* + *inf.* geblinne 87a21. giblinna 8r11. **bituih-blinni(s)s(e:** INTERMISSIO ‖ bituihblinnisse 6r4. **unbliðe:** INQUIETUS ‖ *pl. nom.* + *acc.* unbliðo 5v24. **bliðelic:** *a* BLANDUS *b* PROPENSE *c* PROPITIUS *d* SERENUS *e* SINCERUS ‖ *sg. dat.* bliðelicum 52r2[a]. *adv.* bliðelice 31r1[e]. *sg. acc.* + *dat. fem.* bliðelic'

23v18[e]. *pl. dat.* bliðelicum 59v20[d]. *comp. adv.* bliðelicor 17r1[b].

bliðni(s)s(e: HILARITAS ‖ bliðnisse 56v13.

blod: *a* SANGUIS *b* filius ‖ blod 10r21[a]; 54v7[a]. *blód 10r22[a]. *sg. gen.* blodes 45r19[b]. *sg. dat.* blode 12r12[a]; 13v10[a]. *pl. gen.* bloda' 78va13[a].

bloedsað, bloetsað: BENEDICERE ‖ bloedsiað 55v17. *pres. subj. + inf.* bloedsia 58v15. bloetsia 57v16. bloedsiga 82vb15. bloetsiga 56v8. *imp. sg.* bloedsa 80ra24; 83ra18. bloetsa 47v7; 47v18. *pret. part.* gibloedsad 12r5; 22r23. gebloedsad 82vb10. *pl. nom. + acc.* gibloedsado 55r5; gibloed' 58r20.

gibloedsað, -bloetsað: BENEDICERE ‖ gebloedsiað 67v3. *gibloedsað 55v21. gibloetsas 55v12. *pres. subj. + inf.* gebloedsia 67v1. gibloedsia 40r13; 45v3. gibloedsiga 80ra19; 82vb19. gibloetsia 47r13. *imp. sg.* gebloedsa 81ra11; 82ra1. gibloedsa 47r16; 47r18. gibloetsa 53r10. *pret. sg.* gibloedsade 22v1; 55v7. *pret. sg. ind. 2* gibloedsadest 47r19; 53r15. gibloetsadest 56v10.

bloedsung, bloetsung: BENEDICTIO ‖ bloedsung 42r16; 46r9. bloed' 56r19. bloetsung 37v16; 38r14. *sg. gen.* bloeds' 59r9. bloetsunges 44r11; 45v5. bloets' 57v2. *sg. acc. + dat.* bloedsunge 36v17; 51r6. bloetsunge 56r15. *pl. nom. + acc.* bloedsungas 61v1. bloets' 57v12. *pl. gen.* bloedsunga 49v13. *pl. dat.* bloedsungum 42r18.

gibloedsung, -bloetsung: BENEDICTIO ‖ *sg. acc. + dat.* gibloedsunge 22v1; 56v16.

unblonden: NON MIXTUS ‖ unblonden 33r11.

blostma: *a* FLOS *b* ros ‖ blostme 39r14[b]. *sg. gen.* blostmes 86rb21[a]. *pl. nom. + acc.* blostmo 2r3[a]. *pl. gen.* blostmana 37v2[a].

boc: *a* LIBER (*b* Exodus) ‖ boc 87ra5[(b)]. bóc 14v1[a]. *pl. nom. + acc.* boec 54v8[a].

bod: PRAECEPTUM ‖ *pl. nom. + acc.* bodo 37v23. *pl. gen.* bodana 45v19; 46r19. *pl. dat.* bodum 43v1.

gibod: MANDATUM ‖ gebod 85va23.

bi-bod: *a* MANDATUM *b* PRAECEPTUM ‖ bibod 3v6[a]. *pl. gen.* bibodana [*alt f.* bibodum] 18v13[b]. biboda' 79rb14[a]. *pl. dat.* bibodum 5r11[b]; 20v19[a]. bebodum 85va16[a]; 85va23[a].

bodað: *a* PRAEDICARE (*b* euangelizare) ‖ *pres. subj. + inf.* bodia 23r9[a]; 32v16[a]. *infl. inf.* bodian' 28v4[a]. *pres. part.* bodende 21v9[(b)]. *pret. sg.* bodade 29r4[a]. *pret. pl.* bodadon 33r15[a].

bodere: PRAEDICATOR ‖ bodere 38r19.

fore-(fora-)bodere: *a* PRAECO *b* praeconium ‖ f'ebodere 23v8[b]. *pl. nom. + acc.* f'eboderas [*alt. f.* f'eboderes] 87ra18[a].

bodung: PRAEDICATIO ‖ *sg. acc. + dat.* bodunge 29r22.

fore-(fora-)bodung: PRAEDICATIO ‖ f'ebodung 29r16.

boege: (*a* ALTERUTER) *b* AMBO (*c* UTERQUE) ‖ ba 14r13[a]; 52r6[(c)]. *gen.* boegera 30r1[b].

boen: *a* DEPRECATIO *b* SUPPLICARE *c* SUPPLICATIO ‖ *sg. acc. + dat.* boene 19v16[a]; 22v12[c]; 38r17[b]. boen' 39v2[c]. *pl. nom. + acc.* boeno 19v20[c]; 34v15[c]. *pl. dat.* boenum 24v13[c]; 36r10[c].

giboen: SUPPLICATIO ‖ *sg. acc. + dat.* giboene 35v4; 35v12.

boenlic: *a* DEPRECABILIS *b* SUPPLICITER ‖ boenlic 80ra8[a]. boen' 81rb17 mg[a]. *adv.* boenlice 49v7[b].

boensað: *a* DEPRECARI *b* SUPPLEX *c* SUPPLICARE ‖ *pres. part.* boensande 22v19[c]; 40v15[a]. *sg. gen.* boensendes [*alt. f.* beoensendes] 20r10[c]. *pl. nom. + acc.* boensando 32v21[b]; 34r21[b]. boensendo *35r18[c]; 77r2[b]. *pl. gen.* boensandra 19v9[c]; 20r15[b]. boensendra 19v4[b]; 34v5[b]. *pl. dat.* boensandum 20v5[c].

giboensað: SUPPLEX ‖ *pres. part. pl. dat.* giboensandum 25r12.

boensum(m: SUPPLEX ‖ boensu' 34v12.

boeteð: iterare ‖ *pret. part. sg. fem.* giboetado 30r7. *sg. dat.* giboetadum 32v2.

eft-boeteð: *a* REPARARE *b* INSTAURARE *c* RESTAURARE ‖ *pres. ind. sg. 2* eftboetest 17r15[a]. *imp. sg.* eftboet 35r2[c]. *pret. part.* eft...giboeted 3v6–7[b].

eft-giboeteð: INSTAURARE ‖ *pres. subj. + inf.* eftgiboeta 11r18.

boeting: cubile ‖ *pl. dat.* boetingum 18r10.

eft-bot: REPARATIO ‖ *sg. gen.* eftbot' 16r19.

bræding: STRATUS ‖ *sg. gen.* brædinges 82va16.

bio-bread: FAUUS ‖ biobread 2r9.

bre(c)ceð: CONTERERE ‖ *pret. part.* gebrocen 81va5.

breht(-: *see* **berht(-.**

stenc-brengende: ODORIFER ‖ *pl. gen.* stengcbrengendra 37v2.

brengeð: *a* CONFERRE *b* DEFERRE *c* FERRE *d* OFFERRE ‖ brengeð 50r13[d]; 50v17[d]. *pres. subj. + inf.* brenge 49v20[d]. *pres. part.* brengende 37v2[b]; 45v4[c]. *pret. pl.* brohton 52r9[d]. brohten 45v12[c]. *pret. part. pl. nom. + acc.* gibrohto 44r5[a]. *pl. dat.* gibrohtum 50v12[d].

gibrengeð: *a* CONFERRE *b* OFFERRE *c* REFERRE *d* exhibere ‖ *pres. subj. + inf.* gibrenge 50v10[b]. gibrenga 6v4[c]; 15v6[a]; 42v4[b]. ^{gi}brenga 14v8[d]. *imp. sg.* gibreng 5v6[b]; *77r23[a]. *pret. sg.* gibrohte 26v1[a]; 42v7[b]. *pret. sg. ind. 2* gibrohtest 24v22[a]; 25r7[a]. gibrohtes 15r16[a].

eft-brengeð: REFERRE ‖ *pres. subj. + inf.* eftbrenga 57v3. eft...brenga 18r9.

eft-gibrengeð: REFERRE ‖ *pres. subj. + inf.* eftgibrenga 44r13. eftgebrenga 80va19.

ofer-brengeð: TRANSFERRE ‖ *pret. sg. ind. 2* of'brohtes 16r9. *pret. part.* of'...broht 16v6.

briost: PECTUS ‖ *sg. gen.* briostes 45v13. *sg. dat.* brioste 77r14.

brogna: FRONS ‖ *pl. gen.* brognena 45v4.

gibrogna: UIRGULTUM ‖ gibrogne 9v13.

broðer: *a* FRATER *b* affinis ‖ broðer 37r22[b]; 78vb17[a]. broðor 79ra1[a]. *pl. nom. + acc.* broðro 3r8[a]; 3r11[a]. broð' 3r19[a]; 3r20[a]. broð 6r4[a]; 13r8[a]. bro' 12r14[a]; 12r17[a]. br' 12v14[a]. *pl. gen.* broðra 34r11[a]. *pl. dat.* broðrum 80rb15[a]; 81ra20[a].

broðerscip(e: fraternus ‖ broðerscip 30v18.

reht-gibroðro, -a: GERMANI ‖ rehtgibroðro 27v13.

bru: PALPEBRA ‖ *pl. dat.* bruum 82va18.

bru(c)ceð, bry(c)cað: UTI ‖ *pres. part. pl. dat.* bruccendum 46v21.

gibru(c)ceð, -bry(c)cað: *a* FUNGI *b* PERFRUI *c* UTI ‖ gibrucað 47r17[c]. *pres. subj. + inf.* gebruc' 87va2[c]. gibruca 27r18[b]. *pres. part.* gibrycgende 46v9[c]. *pret. sg. subj. + ind. 2* gibrece 42v3[a].

ðerh-bru(c)ceð, -bry(c)cað: PERFRUI ‖ *pres. subj. + inf.* ðerhbruca 30v10; 33v10.

lif-bru(c)cung, -bry(c)cung: conuersatio ‖ lifbrycgung 4r3.

brycg: PONS ‖ brycge 87va3.

gibrycsað: *a* FUNGI *b* UTI ‖ gibrycsiað 57v12[b]. *pret. sg.* gebrycsade 87va18[a].

brymm: PELAGUS ‖ *sg. gen.* brymmes 29v22.

bufa: SUPRA ‖ bufa 17r15; 23r11.

bul: MURENULA ‖ *pl. nom. + acc.* bulas 2r15.

gibunde(n)ni(s)s(e: LIGARE ‖ *sg. gen.* gibundennises 28v10.

bryd-bur: THALAMUS ‖ brydbur 53r10.

bur(u)g: *a* URBS *A—glossing a Latin town-name* ‖ burg 87vb6[a]. *sg. dat.* byrig 88ra9[A]; 88ra12[A]. byr' 88rb11[A]; 88rb16[A].

butan: *a* ABSQUE *b* EXTRA *c* NISI *d*

PRAETER *e* SINE *f* exterius (*g* uidelicet) ‖ butan 1r12[e]; 3v3[c]; 8r1[f]; 43v18[a]; 50r16[b]; 66v18[d]; 86rb6[(g)].
by(c)geð: EMERE ‖ *pret. part.* giboht 13r13; 51r17. *pl. nom.* + *acc.* gibohto 23r22.
byend: *a* HABITANS *b* HABITATOR ‖ byend 46v18[b]. *pl. nom.* + *acc.* byende 47v14[a]. byendo 47v23[a]; 53r10[a]. *pl. gen.* byendra 59r16[a].
i(n)n-byend: INHABITATOR ‖ inbyend 50r11.
byeð: HABITARE ‖ *pres. ind. sg. 1* bya 17v21.
gibyeð: *a* HABITARE *b* POSSIDERE ‖ gibyað 34r13[a]. *pres. subj.* + *inf.* gibye 6v22[a]; 77v10[b].
i(n)n-byeð: INHABITARE ‖ *pres. subj.* + *inf.* inbye 3r18.
gi-i(n)n-byeð: INHABITARE ‖ *imp. sg.* giinbya 31v6.
bying: HABITACULUM ‖ *pl. dat.* byencgum 60r2.
unbying: SOLITUDO ‖ *pl. nom.* + *acc.* unbyengo 1r8.
gibyredlic: *a* CONGRUUS *b* CONUENIENTER *c* DEBERE *d* opportunitas ‖ *sg. gen.* gibyredlices 6r15[d]. *sg. dat.* gibyredlicum 4r20[a]; 39r16[a]. gibyredlic' 36v8[a]. *adv.* gibyredlice 4v8[b]; 8r13[b]. *pl. nom.* + *acc.* gibyredlico 77v11[c].
ungibyredlic: INCONGRUUS ‖ ungebyredlic 82ra20.
gibyreð: DECET ‖ *pret. sg.* gibyrede 43v7.
ðerh-gibyreð: PERTINERE ‖ *pres. subj.* + *inf.* ðerhgibyre 19r7.
byrgen(n: MONUMENTUM ‖ *sg. acc.* + *dat.* byrgenne 48v11.
byrgeð: CONSEPELIRE ‖ *pret. part. pl. nem.* + *acc.* *gibyrgedo 12v18.
bi-byrgeð: SEPELIRE ‖ *pret. part. pl. nom.* + *acc.* bibyrgedo 29v16.
byrn: *a* ARDOR *b* COMBUSTIO *c* INCENDIUM *d* INCENSUM ‖ *sg. acc.* + *dat.* byrne 31r7[a]; 54v19[b]. *pl. nom.* + *acc.* byrno 31r8[c]. byrno' 34r5[d]. *pl. dat.* byrnum 31r3[c].
i(n)n-byrn: INCENDIUM ‖ *pl. nom.* + *acc.* inbyrno 31r6.
byrna: *a* LORICA *b* THORAX ‖ byrne 14r7[a]; 44r20[b].
byrsteð: RUGIRE ‖ *pres. part. sg. gen.* byrstende 59v4.
byrðen(n: PONDUS ‖ byrðen 24r18.
cald: FRIGIDUS ‖ cald 86va3; *86va8.
calf: UITULUS ‖ *pl. nom.* + *acc.* calfero 58r6. *pl. gen.* calfra 10r22.
calic: CALIX ‖ *sg. gen.* calic' 55v7.
carcern: CARCER ‖ *sg. gen.* carce' 28r9. *sg. dat.* carc' 28r7.
stan-carr: PETRA ‖ stancarr 9v6.
Caser: *a* CAESAR *b* Augustus ‖ caser 85ra6[b]. *sg. gen.* caseres 85ra6[b]. *pl. nom.* + *acc.* caseras 86vb20[a].
caserdom: respublica ‖ caserdom 86ra10–11.
cæfertun: PRAETORIUM ‖ cæfertun' 85vb18.
cæg(a: CLAUIS ‖ *pl. dat.* cægum 28v11.
cearfeð: CAEDERE ‖ *pret. part.* corfen 33r10.
ceaseð: *a* ELIGERE *b* adoptio *c* aptare *d* Christus *e* optare *f* optimus ‖ *pret. part.* gicoren 2v9[d]; 12v6[a]; 13v18[f]; 52r4[b]. *sg. dat.* gicorenum 52v22[e]. *sg. weak* gicorene 39v17[d]. *pl. nom.* + *acc.* coreno 4v9[c]. gecoreno 86vb17[d]; 87ra 6[a]. gicoreno 6v16[a]; 51v22[a]. *pl. gen.* gicorenra 50v5[a]. *pl. dat.* gicorenum 31v7[a].
giceaseð: *a* ELIGERE *b* aptare ‖ *pres. ind. sg. 2* giceas' 9r11[a]; 24v4[a]. *pres. subj.* + *inf.* gicease 13v11[b]; 31v20[a]. *pret. sg. ind. 1, 3* giceas 27r9[a]; 37v22[a].
ceastra: CIUITAS ‖ ceastre 5v5; 31v8. ceast' 51v8; 87vb6. ceast'a 88ra19.
cedrisc: cedrus ‖ cedrisc 31v13.
cefis: CONCUBINA ‖ *pl. nom.* + *acc.* cefissa 33r16.
ceigere: CLAMATOR ‖ *pl. nom.* + *acc.* ceigeras 87ra19.
ceigeð: *a* APPELLARE *b* CLAMARE *c* INUOCARE *d* UOCARE ‖ ceigað 51v12[d]. *imp. sg.* ceig 2v19[b]; 87ra21[b]. *pres. part.* ceigende 21r12[b]. *pret. part.* giceiged 57v10[c]. geceiged 87rb5[d]. *pl. nom.* + *acc.* giceigdo 6v21[d]; 44v7[d]. geceigdo 86vb18[d]. giceigido 51v22[d]. giceido 45v2[a].
giceigeð: *a* CLAMARE *b* INUOCARE *c* PROUOCARE *d* UOCARE ‖ giceigað 80ra 22[b]. geceigað 81ra4[b]; 87rb13[d]. gicegað 26r14[c]. *pres. subj.* + *inf.* giceiga 45v17[d]; 51r23[d]. giceia 46r17[d]. *pret. sg.* giceigde 78ra14[a]. geceigde 83rb19[a]. giceide 21v4[a]; 27r3[d]. *pret. pl.* geceigdon 81rb25[a].
aceigeð: UOCARE ‖ *pret. part. pl. nom.* + *acc.* aceigido 34r9.
eft-giceigeð: REUOCARE ‖ *pret. sg. ind. 2* eftgiceidest 18v12.
i(n)n-ceigeð: INUOCARE ‖ *pres. ind. sg. 1* inceigo 57v15.
gi-i(n)n-ceigeð: INUOCARE ‖ *pres. ind. sg. 1* gii'cege 10r9.
on-ceigeð: INUOCARE ‖ onceigas 49v 22.
giceiging, -ceigung: INUOCATIO ‖ *pl. dat.* giceigingcum 46v12.
i(n)n-ceiging, -ceigung: INUOCATIO ‖ *sg. acc.* + *dat.* inceigincge 66v4. in'ceiginge 59v9. inceigence 79vb8. *pl. dat.* innceigungum 59r7.
on-ceiging, -ceigung: INUOCATIO ‖ *sg. acc.* + *dat.* onceigunge 59r18–19. onceigince 67v4.
on-giceiging, -ceigung: INUOCATIO ‖ ongiceiging 47v9.
on-ceigni(s)s(e: INUOCATIO ‖ onceignise 54v22.
ceir: CLAMOR ‖ ceir 6r19; 79ra18.
cempa: MILES ‖ *pl. dat.* cempum 86vb10; 86vb14.
an-cenda: *a* UNIGENITUS *b* unicus ‖ ancende 1r16[a]; 1v1[a]. ancend' 14v9[a]; 49r20[a]. ancend 45r12[b]. ancen' 2v3[a]. *sg. gen.* ancendes 21v19[a]; 80va17[a]. ancendes' 11r16[a]. ancend' 45r6[a]; 56v7[a]. ancen' 45r2[a].
frum-cenda: *a* PRIMOGENITUS *b* origo *c* primitiae ‖ frumcend' 13r15[c]. *sg. fem.* frumcendo 33r9[a]. *sg. gen.* frumcend' 17r15[b]. *pl. nom.* + *acc.* frumcendo 1v6[c]; 21v15[c].
cenneð: *a* GIGNERE *b* NASCI ‖ *pret. part.* gicenned 61v2[b]. gecenned 88va13[b]. *pl. nom.* + *acc.* gicendo 12v4[a].
gicenneð: *a* EDERE *b* GIGNERE ‖ *pret. sg.* gicende 13v21[b]; 52r7[a].
a(c)cenneð: *a* NASCI *b* PARENS ‖ *pres. part. pl. dat.* acennendum 88va7[b]. *pret. part.* acenned 61v4[a]; 61v5[a]. acenn' 13v14[a]; 61v7[a]. accenn' 61v10[a].
eft-cenneð: REGENERARE ‖ *pres. subj.* + *inf.* eftcenne 58r9.
eft-gicenneð: REGENERARE ‖ *pret. sg.* eftgicende 12r6.
eft-a(c)cenneð: *a* REGENERARE *b* RENASCI ‖ *pret. part. pl. nom.* + *acc.* eft...acennedo 16r16[a]. *pl. dat.* eftacennedum 15v14[b]. eftac'endum 16r 21[b].
gicennicg(e: GENETRIX ‖ gicennice 33r14.
a(c)cennicg(e: GENETRIX ‖ acennic 25r12. *sg. gen.* acennic' 33r21.
b(e)arn-cennicg(e: GENETRIX ‖ bearncen' 32r17. *sg. gen.* bearncennices 33v22.
sunu-cennicg(e: GENETRIX ‖ sunucennic 32r3. sunucenn' 32r9. sunucen' 32r15. *sg. gen.* sunucennices 32r7.
a(c)cenni(s)s(e: *a* NATIUITAS *b* PARTUS *c* natalicia *d* natalis ‖ accennisse 23v23[a]. accennis' 55v7[d]. acennisse 1v18[a]; 33v2[b]. acennise 33r19–21[a]; 33v6[a]. acen' 40r9[c]. *sg. gen.* acennis'es 33v3[a]. acennise' 50v17[d].
eft-a(c)cenni(s)s(e: REGENERATIO ‖ *sg. gen.* eftacennisses 17r17.
symbel-cenni(s)s(e: *a* NATALICIA *b* NATALICIUM *c* NATALIS ‖ symbelcennise 26v4[a]; 31r23[a]. symbelcenn' 35r8[a]; 38v7[b]. symbelcen' 27r18[a]; 37v14[b]. symb'cennis' 41r10[c]. *pl. dat.* symbelcenn' 44v20[a].

ceping: NEGOTIATIO ‖ *sg. acc.* + *dat.* cepinge 39r8; 51v5.

ym(b)-cerr: uersutia ‖ *pl. nom.* + *acc.* ymbcerro 58v9.

gicerreð: *a* CONUERTERE *b* REUERTERE ‖ gicerreð 2v13[a]. gicerrað 2v16[a]. *pres. subj.* + *inf.* gicerre 10r5[b]. *imp. sg.* gicerr 5v10[a]; 7r13[a].

from-cerreð: AUERTERE ‖ *imp. sg.* from cerr 78rb23; 79ra16.

ym(b)-cerreð: AUERTERE ‖ *pret. sg.* ymbcerd 9v3.

gicid: LIS ‖ giciid 77r4. *pl. gen.* giciidana 77r22.

cild: INFANS ‖ *pl. nom.* + *acc.* cildo 12v4. *pl. gen.* cildra 23v17. cildena 50r3.

steap-cild: PUPILLUS ‖ *pl. nom.* + *acc.* steapcildo 14r21.

cildhad: INFANTIA ‖ cildhad 1v14.

cirica: ECCLESIA ‖ cirica 7r4; 9r5. ciricæ 38v6. ciricae 23r8. *sg. gen.* cirices 52r8. cirica' 15r8. *pl. nom.* + *acc.* ciricean 55r15⁻.

ciriclic: ECCLESIASTICUS ‖ *sg. dat.* ciricelica 80vb17.

clæne: *a* CASTUS *b* MUNDUS *c* PURUS (*d* sacramentum) ‖ clæne 14r20[b]; 14v8[c]; 52v2[(d)]. clene 78va1[b]. *sg. dat.* clænum 17v5[c]; 50r2[b]. *pl. nom.* + *acc.* clæno 15r9[(d)]; *77r5[c]. clæne 15v5[(d)]; 16r 15[(d)]. *pl. gen.* clænra 50r11[a]. *pl. dat.* clænum 4r5[c]. *sup.* clæneste 39r9[c].

unclæne: IMMUNDUS ‖ unclæne 57v17; 58v10. *sg. gen.* unclænes 59v10.

unclænlic: illicitus ‖ *pl. nom.* + *acc.* unclænlico 52v15.

clænni(s)s(e: *a* CASTITAS *b* PURITAS ‖ clænnisse 24r1[b]. clænnis' 49v10[a]; 53r23[a]. clæn'se 47v17[a]. clæn' 37r21[a].

unclænni(s)s(e,: IMMUNDITIA ‖ unclænnisse 58v18. unclænnise 46v8. unclænnis' 59r13.

clænsað: *a* MUNDARE *b* PURGARE *c* PURIFICARE *d* castigare *e* mundus ‖ *pres. ind. sg. 1* clænsigo 3r16[d]. *pres. subj.* + *inf.* clænsia 46v22[e]. *pret. part.* giclænsad 44r3[a]. *sg. gen.* giclænsades 17v1[c]. *pl. nom.* + *acc.* giclænsado 8r3[a]; 25v7[a]. giclæns... 16r23[b]. *pl. dat.* giclænsadum 2v5[c].

giclænsað: *a* EMUNDARE *b* EXPURGARE *c* MUNDARE *d* PURIFICARE *e* SANARE *f* castigare ‖ giclænsað 12r20[b]. *pres. ind. sg. 2* giclænsas 7r5[d]. *pres. subj.* + *inf.* giclænsiga 46v7[a]; 50v3[b]. giclænsigo 9r1[f]. giclænsia 46v18[e]. *imp. sg.* giclænsa 46v15[a]; 78rb21[c]. giclænsig 3v22[d]; 4r23[a]. *pret. ind. sg. 2* giclænsadest 46v11[c].

clænsung: *a* PURIFICATIO *b* castigatio ‖ *sg. acc.* + *dat.* clænsunge 4v9[b]; 8r17[b]. *pl. dat.* clænsungum 59r8[a].

giclænsung: PURIFICARE ‖ *sg. acc.* + *dat.* giclænsunge 8r15.

cleafeð: SCINDERE ‖ cleafað 2v14.

clio(p)pað: *a* APPELLARE *b* CLAMARE (*c* INUOCARE) *d* UOCARE ‖ cliopað 5r20[(c)]. *pres. part.* clioppende 21r5[b]. *sg. gen.* clioppendes 27v3[b]. *pl. gen.* clioppendra 56r2[b]. *pret. part.* gicliop-pad 21r17[a]. gicliopad [*alt. f.* giclioped] 29r7[d].

giclio(p)pað: *a* PROUOCARE *b* UOCARE ‖ *pres. subj.* + *inf.* gicliopia 24r8[a]. *pret. sg.* gicliopade 10v16[b]; 12v8[b].

soð-clio(p)pað: PROUOCARE ‖ soð...cliopiað 20v8.

on-cnaueð: INTELLIGERE ‖ oncnaueð 80vb22.

cnæht, cneht: PUER ‖ cnæht 1r13; 26v14. *cneht 88vb2. *pl. nom.* + *acc.* cnæhtas 48v8. cnaihtas 49r6. *pl. gen.* cnehtana 83vb18. *pl. dat.* cnehtum 48r2.

cne(o)u: GENU ‖ *pl. dat.* cneum 21v4.

gicnycc: NEXUS ‖ *pl. dat.* gicnyccum 28v13; 32r11. gicnycgum 45r5.

unacny(c)cendlic: INSOLUBILIS ‖ *sg. dat.* unacnycendlic' 52r3.

cny(c)ceð: NECTERE ‖ *pret. part.* gicnyht 52v14.

gicny(c)ceð: NECTERE ‖ *pret. sg. ind. 2* gicnyhtest 52r3.

acny(c)ceð: CONNECTERE ‖ *pret. part.* *pl. dat.* *acnyhtum 53r2.

coelni(s)s(e: REFRIGERIUM ‖ coelnisse 17v19.

compað: MILITARE ‖ *pres. part.* compigende 29r10.

compdom: MILITIA ‖ *sg. gen.* compdomes 4r16.

to-gicore(n)ni(s)s(e: adoptio ‖ *sg. gen.* togicorenis' 14v7.

gicorenscip(e: *a* ELECTIO *b* EXCELLENTIA ‖ gicorenscipe 26v1[b]. *sg. gen.* gicorenscipes 1v6[a].

cost: MODUS ‖ *sg. dat.* coste 54v16. *pl. dat.* costum 52r6.

costað: *a* PROBARE *b* TENTARE *c* TRIBULARE *d* niti ‖ *pres. part. pl. dat.* costendum 21r5[c]. *pret. part.* gicosted 41r2[a]; 43v17[b]. gicostad 7r6[d]. gecost' 81rb25[c]. *sg. fem.* costedo 52v19[a].

gicostað: *a* COMPROBARE *b* PROBARE *c* TENTARE ‖ *pres. subj.* + *inf.* gicostia 48v5[a]. *pret. sg.* gicostade 29r11[b]; 41v4[c]; 41v6[b].

i(n)n-costað: inniti ‖ *pret. part.* inn...gicosted 8r21.

costung: *a* TENTAMENTUM *b* TENTATIO *c* TORMENTUM *d* TRIBULATIO ‖ costung 41r20[c]; 67r3[b]. *sg. acc.* + *dat.* costunge 14r22[d]; 41r2[b]; 66v3[b]. costuncge 21r 7[d]. cost' 79vb19[b]. *pl. nom.* + *acc.* costungo 57r20[b]; 81va1[d]. costung' 45v6[a]. *pl. dat.* costungum 18v19[b]; 83va10[d].

cræft: ARS ‖ *sg. dat.* cræfte 46v6.

cræftig: (OPIFEX) ‖ cræftig 88vb4.

tungul-cræftig: MAGUS ‖ *pl. gen.* tungelcræftigo 1r22.

Crecas: GRAECI ‖ crecas 87rb12. *dat.* crecum 87rb4.

Crec-(Creg-)isc: GRAECUS ‖ crecisc 87rb11; 87rb14. cregesc 87vb4. crec' 87va5; 87vb5.

Crist: CHRISTUS ‖ crist 6r8; 10r19. crist' 14r10; 47r9. c' 13v13; 58r17. *sg. gen.* cristes 3r18; 6v2. crist' 11r4; 12r5. cris' 58r15. cri' 58r7. *sg. dat.* criste 6r5; 6r22.

cristin: CHRISTIANUS ‖ cristin 30v7. *sg. gen.* cristin' 4r16. crist'es 15v11. *pl. gen.* cristenra 81ra8–9. *pl. dat.* cristinum 7v7.

cristinlic: CHRISTIANUS ‖ cristinlic 44r11.

cristni(s)s(e ‖ cristnesse 55r9.

cualm: UALETUDO ‖ cualm 67r3.

cuic: *a* UIUUS *b* holocaustum (*c* hostia) *d* uiuificus ‖ *sg. gen.* cuices 45r6[d]. *sg. dat.* cuicum 12r7[a]. *pl. nom.* + *acc.* cuico 41v7[b]; 43v11[(c)]; 58v11[a].

cuiclic: UITALIS ‖ cuiclic 45r17.

tean-cuidað: CALUMNIARI ‖ *pres. part. pl. dat.* teancuidendum 81rb9.

heafod-cuide: CAPITULUM ‖ *pl. nom.* + *acc.* heafudcuido 78r1.

somnung-cuide: COLLECTUM ‖ *pl. nom.* + *acc.* somnungcuido 1r15.

cuild: UALETUDO ‖ cuild 67r3.

culfra: COLUMBA ‖ culfra 33r13. *pl. gen.* culfra 2r18.

niue-cuma: ADUENA ‖ *pl. nom.* + *acc.* niuecumo 39v14.

un-for-cumen ‖ *pret. part. sg. gen.* unf'cumenes 59v1.

cunnað: inniti ‖ *pret. part.* gicunned 9v10.

a(c)cunnað: niti ‖ *pret. part.* acunned 28v20.

cunnung: conactus ‖ *pl. nom.* + *acc.* cunnunga 52v15.

acu(o)e(c)ceð: QUASSARE ‖ *pret. part.* acuoect 88vb7.

gicuoeme: PLACARE ‖ gicuoeme 22v 13.

cuoemeð: *a* DELECTARE *b* PLACARE *c* PLACERE ‖ *pres. part. pl. gen.* cuoemendra 44r7[c]. *pret. part.* gicuoemed 4v1[b]; 60r9[a].

gicuoemeð: *a* COMPLACERE *b* PLACARE *c* PLACERE ‖ *pres. ind. sg. 2* gicuoemes 4v1[b]. *pres. subj.* + *inf.* gicuoeme 29r11[c]; 30v6[c]. gicweme 13v12[c]. gicuoema 19r18[c]; 32r13[c]. *pret. sg.* gicuoemde 37r22[a]; 37v20[c]. *pret. pl.* gicuoemdon 35v12[c].

cuoemlic: *a* PLACABILIS *b* PLACARE *c* PLACERE *d* SUPPLICITER ‖ cuoemlic *20r22[b]; 39v2[b]; 43v2[c]; 60v19[a]. *adv.* *cuoemlice 44v18[d]. *pl. nom.* + *acc.* cuoemlico 19r10[c].
gicuoemlic: *a* COMPLACARE *b* PLACARE *c* PLACERE *d* SUPPLEX ‖ gicuoemlic 32v9[b]; 33r22[a]. gicuæmlic 77v18[d]. *sg. dat.* gicuoemlicum 9r20[c]. gicwoemlicum 10r13[c]. *pl. nom.* + *acc.* gicuoemlico 9r9[c].
cuoemlicni(s)s(e: sufficientia ‖ cuoemlic' 4r1.
gicuoemni(s)s(e: sufficientia ‖ gicuoemnise 6v7.
u(o)el-gicuoemni(s)s(e: BENEPLACITUM ‖ uelgicuoemnise 80rb4. uelgecuoemnise 80va16.
cuoen: REGINA ‖ *pl. nom.* + *acc.* cuoeno 33r15.
port-cu(o)ena: MERETRIX ‖ portcuoene 51r11. *sg. gen.* portcuoenes 51r10.
cu(o)eðeð: *a* AIT *b* DICERE *c* INQUIT ‖ cuoeðað 51v2[b]. *pres. ind. sg. 1* cuoeðo 78va14[b]. *pres. subj.* + *inf.* cuoeðe 10r16[b]. *pres. part.* cuoeðende 21v5[b]; 23v6[b]. *pl. gen.* cuoeðendra 56r3[b]. *pret. sg. ind. 1, 3* cuoeð 1r11[b]; 5r13[a]; 51r12[c]. cuoð 27v19[b]. cuæð 79rb21[b]. *pret. sg. subj.* + *ind. 2* cuoede 10r10[b]. *pret. part.* gecuoeden 85rb2[b]. gecuoed' 87ra 20[b]; 88rb19[b].
gicu(o)eðeð: DICERE ‖ *pres. subj.* + *inf.* gicuoeða 23r21. gicuæða 26v14. *pret. sg. ind. 1, 3* gecuoeð 85rb1. gicuoeð 21v6.
acu(o)eðeð: DICERE ‖ *pret. part.* acuoeden 61r14; 86va15.
fore-(fora-)cuoeðeð: PRAEDICERE ‖ *pret. sg. ind. 1, 3* f'ecuoeð 27r13.
uið-cu(o)eðeð: CONTRADICERE ‖ *pres. ind. sg. 1* wiðcuiðo 9r22.
cuð: *a* COGNITUS *b* NOTUS ‖ cuð 28r5[b]; 85ra14[a].
cuðlice: igitur ‖ cuðlice 3r14; 10v13.
fore-cyme: PRAEUENIRE ‖ *f'ecyme 39r22.
to-cyme: ADUENTUS ‖ tocyme 46v10; 49r3.
cy(m)með, cu(m)með: *a* PERUENIRE *b* UENIRE ‖ cymað 51v3[b]. *pres. subj.* + *inf.* cyme 11r19[b]; 79va4[a]. cume 45v2[b]. *pres. part.* cymende 45v9[b]; 50v20[b]. cymmende 36v8[b]; 39r17[b]. *sg. gen.* cymmendes 30v14[b]. *pret. sg. ind. 1, 3* cuom 34r4[b].
gicy(m)með, -cu(m)með: *a* CONUENIRE *b* PERUENIRE *c* PRAEUENIRE *d* UENIRE ‖ *pres. subj.* + *inf.* gicyme 17v4[c]; 28r22[b]. gicuma 51v1[d]. *pret. pl.* gicuomon 23v3[d]; 28v6[a].
for-cy(m)með, -cu(m)með: *a* DEUINCERE *b* UINCERE ‖ *pret. sg. ind. 1, 3* f'cuom 31r9[a]. *pret. sg. subj.* + *ind. 2* f'cuome 39r5[b]. *pret. part.* f'cummen 61r15b. *sg. dat.* f'cummenum 14v10[a].
fore- (fora-) cy(m)með, -cu(m)með: *a* PRAEUENIRE *b* PROCEDERE ‖ *pres. subj.* + *inf.* f'ecyme 39r16[a]; 79va14[b]. f'ecymo 35r10[a]; 41v14[a]. *imp. sg.* f'acym 7v20[a]. *pres. part.* f'acym' 14v11[a]. *pret. pl.* f'ecuomon 35r15[a]; 37r19[a]. f'ecuom' *39r18[a]; 41v13[a]. f'ecuome 35r8[a].
ofer-cy(m)með, -cu(m)með: DEUINCERE ‖ *pres. subj.* + *inf.* of'cyme 50v2.
soð-cy(m)með, -cu(m)með: PROCEDERE ‖ *pres. subj.* + *inf.* soðcyme 6r14. *pret. sg. ind. 1, 3* soðcuom 1v11; 27v12.
ofer-to-cy(m)með, -cu(m)með: SUPERUENIRE ‖ *pres. part. sg. gen.* of'tocymendes 83rb6.
to-cy(m)með, -cu(m)með: *a* ADUENIRE *b* UENIRE *c* adesse ‖ tocymeð 16r16[a]. tocymað 45r5[a]. *pres. subj.* + *inf.* tocyme 17r13[a]. *imp. sg.* tocym 4v19[c]; 7r10[c]. *pres. part.* tocymen' 57r21[b]. tocym' 58v10[b]. *pl. nom.* + *acc.* tocymendo 8r16[b]. *pret. sg. ind. 1, 3* tocuom 17r12[a].
ðerh-cy(m)með, -cu(m)með: PERUENIRE ‖ *pres. subj.* + *inf.* ðerhcyme 8r16; 15v2.
under-cy(m)með, -cu(m)með: *a* SUBUENIRE *b* SUCCEDERE ‖ *pres. subj.* + *inf.* undercyme 32r17[a]. undecyme [? *read* undercyme] 8v3[a]. *pres. part.* undercymende 18v3[b].
gicynd: NATURA ‖ gicynd 17r14.
cyne-: REGALIS ‖ cyne 12v6.
cyni(n)g, cini(n)g: *a* REX (*b* Antiochus) (*c* arridus) (*d* pharao) (*e* meus) ‖ cynig 2r19[a]; 45v2[a]. cyni'g 61v5[a]. cinig 77v10[a]. cyning 86v21[(b)]. *sg. gen.* cyniges 50v14[a]. cyninges 49r7[a]. cyn' 86vb23[(e)]. *sg. dat.* cynige 81ra1[a]. cynig' 51r22[a]. *pl. nom.* + *acc.* cyningas 27r8[a]; 86vb18[a]; 86vb19[(d)]; 86vb22[(c)]. *pl. gen.* cyninga 37v20[a]; 42r21[a].
cynn: *a* GENERATIO *b* GENS *c* GENUS *d* NATIO (*e* TRIBUNUS) ‖ cynn 12v6 (2)[c, b]; 45r3[c]; 85rb20[b]. *sg. gen.* cynnes 16r18[c]; 86vb11[(e)]. cynn' 47r4[c]; 59r5[c]. cyn' 45r15[c]. *sg. dat.* cynne 11r9[c]. *pl. nom.* + *acc.* cynno 26v20[b]; 41v10[d]. *pl. gen.* cynna 27r6[b]; 42r16[b]. cynno 1r20[b]; 1v6[b]. *pl. dat.* cynnum 1r16[b]; 2r7[a].
cynnam': CYNNAMOMUM ‖ cynnam' 31v18.
cyss: OSCULUM ‖ *sg. dat.* cysse 2r11.
gicysseð: OSCULARI ‖ *pres. subj.* + *inf.* gicysse 2r11.
for-cyðeð: REPROBUS ‖ *pret. part.* f'cyðed 3r17.
gicyðig: COGNITOR ‖ gicyðig 20r15.
cyðni(s)s(e: TESTAMENTUM ‖ cyðnisse 38r2. cyðnise 5v8; 42r16. *pl. dat.* cyðnissum 29v13.
gicyðni(s)s(e: *a* TESTAMENTUM *b* TESTIMONIUM ‖ gecyðnisse 86rb2[a]; 88vb22[b]. gecyðnise 87ra13[a]. gicyðnisse 23v16[b]; 34r12[b]. *sg. gen.* gicyðnisses 54v9[a]. gicyðniss' 13v10[a].
gidæf(n)að: *a* DEBERE *b* LICET *c* OPORTET ‖ gedæfnað 85vb7[c]. gidæfnað 3v3[a]; 6v3[c]; 85va10[b]. *pres. part.* gidæfende 52r23[b].
dæg: *a* DIES (*b* HODIERNUS) ‖ dæg 27v10[(b)]; 52r11[a]. Ħ 1r16[a]; 1v10[(b)]. *sg. gen.* dæges 14r7[a]; 18v2[a]. Ħes 23r6[a]; Ħges 32v13[a]. *sg. dat.* dægi 5r4[a]; 5r7[a]. *pl. nom.* + *acc.* dagas 50v22[a]. *pl. gen.* dagana 39r10[a]; 53r12[a]. *pl. dat.* dagum 17r1[a]; 21r15[a].
bæð-dæg: epiphania ‖ bæðdæg 1r15.
mid-dæg: MERIDIES ‖ midĦ 3r4.
sunna-dæg: SABBATUM ‖ *pl. gen.* sunnadaga 6v13.
symbel-dæg: *a* DIES FESTUS *b* natalicia ‖ symbelĦ 21v12[b]. *sg. gen.* dæges symbel' 6v13[a].
to-dæg(e: HODIE ‖ todæge 85rb22. toĦ 23v17; 24r2.
dæg-(gi-)huæmlice: *a* COTIDIANUS *b* COTIDIE ‖ dæggihuæmlice 36r1[a]. dægihuæmlice 35v15[b]; 35v16[a]. dæghuæmlice 36r8[b]. dæghuoæmlice 36r7[b].
dæg-gihu(o)elc: COTIDIE ‖ dægihuoelc 43v9.
dæg(i)lic: DIURNUS ‖ *pl. dat.* dægilicum 77r3.
mid-dæg(i)lic: MERIDIES ‖ *sg. dat.* middæglicum 77r21.
dæl: *a* PARS *b* PORTIO ‖ dæl 6v13[a]; 16r5[b]. *pl. nom.* + *acc.* dælo 31v10[a].
on-dælend: INFUSOR ‖ ondælend 49 v14.
dæleð: *a* EFFUNDERE *b* FUNDERE ‖ dæles 52r12[b]. *imp. sg.* dæl 20r6[a]. *pret. part.* gidæled 66v14[a].
gidæleð: *a* DIUIDERE *b* haurire ‖ *pres. subj.* + *inf.* gidæle 77r5[b]. *pret. sg.* gidælde 37v17[a].
bi-dæleð: PRIUARE ‖ *pret. part. pl. nom.* + *acc.* bidæledo 16v1.
eft-dæleð: REFUNDERE ‖ *pret. part.* eftgidæled 77r14.
i(n)n-dæleð: INFUNDERE ‖ *imp. sg.* indæl 1r22. *pret. sg.* indælde 23r4.
on-dæleð: *a* EFFUNDERE *b* INFUNDERE ‖ *pres. subj.* + *inf.* ondæle 41r12[b]. *imp. sg.* ondæl 8r23[b]; 59r9[a].

ðerh-dæleð: PERFUNDERE ‖ *imp. sg.* ðerhdæl 53r9.

dærst(a: *a* FERMENTUM *b* azyma ‖ *pl. nom.* + *acc.* dærsto [*alt. f.* dærsta] 12r20[a]. *pl. dat.* dærstum 12r22 (2)[a], [a]; 12v1[b].

dead: (*a* MORI) *b* MORTUUS ‖ dead 5r14[(a)]; 10v10[b]. *pl. nom.* + *acc.* deado 12r17[b]; 13r17[(a)]. deade 23v7[(a)]. *pl. gen.* deadra 13r12[b]; 13r17[b]. *pl. dat.* deadum 12r7[b]; 13r15[b].

deadað: MORI ‖ deadigað 13r10; 13r17. *pres. subj.* + *inf.* deadiga 13r9. deadia 13r10. *pret. part. pl. nom.* + *acc.* *deadedo 41r21.

deadlic: MORTALIS ‖ *sg. gen.* deadlices 19r22. *sg. dat.* deadlicum 6v2.

undeadlic: IMMORTALIS ‖ undeadlic 78va21.

undeadlicni(s)s(e: IMMORTALITAS ‖ undeadlicnise 33r3 (*alt. f.* undeadlicenise); 41v3.

gideapað: erumpere ‖ *pret. pl.* gideapedon 39r14.

dear: BESTIA ‖ *pl. dat.* dearum 81va15.

uil(de)-dear: BESTIA ‖ *pl. nom.* + *acc.* uildedearo 56v22. *pl. gen.* uildear 56v17.

dearf: AUDERE ‖ dearf 48r12.

deað: *a* MORI *b* MORS ‖ deað 2v9[b]; 5v8[b]. *sg. gen.* deaðes 32r11[b]; 77v5[b]. *sg. dat.* deaðe 10v9[b]; 23v9[a].

deau: ROS ‖ *sg. gen.* deawes 86rb19.

ded: *a* ACTIO *b* ACTUS *c* FACTUM (*d* proprius) ‖ ded 14r19[c]. déd 20v18[a]. *sg. gen.* dedes 24r19[a]. *sg. acc.* + *dat.* dede 3v14[a]. *pl. nom.* + *acc.* dedo 6v4[(d)]; 7v20[a]; 18r2[b]. *pl. gen.* dedana 15v16[a]. *pl. dat.* dedum 52v13[b]; 77r3[b].

u(o)erc-ded: OPERATIO ‖ *pl. nom.* + *acc.* uoercdedo 61r19.

degle: (*a* MYSTERIUM) *b* OCCULTUS *c* SECRETUS ‖ degle 55r2[b]; 80va12[c]. degla 1v13[(a)]. degle' 46v5[c]. *pl. dat.* deiglum 78rb21[b].

degleð: *a* ABSCONDERE *b* LATERE ‖ *pres. part. sg. gen.* deglendes 59r15[b]. *pret. part.* gideglad 12r17[a].

gideglo, -a: *a* ARCANUM *b* OCCULTUS ‖ gidegla 23r3[a]. *gen.* gideigla' 20r15[b].

degolni(s)s(e: OCCULTA ‖ *pl. dat.* degolnissum 80ra1.

demon: DAEMON ‖ *pl. dat.* demonum 66v2.

deðeð: MORTIFICARE ‖ *pret. part.* gideðed 10v11; 12v12.

deðing: MORTIFICATIO ‖ *sg. acc.* + *dat.* deðinge [*alt. f.* deðinges] 35r4.

diacon: *a* DIACONUS (*b* EPIDIACONUS) *c* leuita ‖ diacon' 22r8[c]; 87rb7[a]. diaco' 87va11[a]. *pl. nom.* + *acc.* diacon' 21v14[c]; 87rb5[(b)]. diaco' 87rb8[c].

under-diacon: SUBDIACONUS ‖ *underdiac' 87rb3.

gidilgað: DELERE ‖ *pres. ind. sg. 1* gidilga 9r18. *imp. sg.* gidilge 78rb24.

adilgað: DELERE ‖ *pres. subj.* + *inf.* adilga 60r12.

di(o)u(o)l, di(o)ubol, diobol: *a* DAEMON *b* DIABOLUS *c* diabolicus ‖ dioul 54v13[b]. diwl 88va10[b]; 88va14[b]. diul 56r11[b]; 67r5[a]. diobul 48r21[b]. diol 58r2[b]. *sg. gen.* dioules 47r5[b]; 55v20[b]. diuoles 48r8[b]. diobles 66v3[b]. diubles 58v9[c]; 67r18[b]. *sg. dat.* dioule 55r2[b]. *pl. nom.* + *acc.* diublas 66r7[a]. di[o]ules 59r10[a]. *pl. gen.* dioula 57r20[a]. *pl. dat.* dioblum 57v6[a]; 66v2[a].

di(o)u(o)lic, di(o)ubolic: *a* DIABOLICUS (*b* scelus) ‖ *pl. nom.* + *acc.* diowlica 17v9[a]. dioublica 49r18[a]. diublica 79ra6[(b)].

doema: IUDEX ‖ doeme 29r16; 48r16.

doemeð: IUDICARE ‖ *pres. ind. sg. 2* doemest 48v22. *pres. part.* doemend 17r12 (2). doem' 57r21.

gidoemeð: *a* ARBITRARI *b* IUDICARE ‖ gidoemað 41v10[b]. *pres. subj.* + *inf.* gidoeme 6v12[b]. gidoema 58v11[b]. *imp. sg.* gidoem 48v22[b]; 78rb12[b]. *pret. sg.* gidoemede 10v4[a]. *pret. sg. ind. 2* gidoemdest 10r11[b].

micil-doend: MAGNIFICUS ‖ micildoend 22r9; 59v2.

undo(e)ni(s)s(e: SOLUERE ‖ undoenise' 28v10.

u(o)el-do(e)ni(s)s(e: BENIGNITAS ‖ weldonis' 6v17.

doere: (OPIFEX) ‖ doere 88vb4.

doeð: *a* AGERE *b* FACERE *c* FACTOR *d* GERERE *e* festinare ‖ doeð 6r5[a]; 43r1[d]. doað 7r1[b]; 15v2[a]. doæð 24r9[a]. doas 81rb12[b]. *pres. ind. sg. 1* dom 5r8[b]; 29r4[b]. *pres. ind. sg. 2* doest 1r5[b]; 7v10[b]. *pres. subj.* + *inf.* doe 5v7[b]; 16v22[b]. *imp. sg.* do 4v11[b]; 9v19[b]. *pres. part.* doende 13v12[b]; 17v14[b]. *pl. nom.* + *acc.* doendo 7r1[a]; 8r8[b]; 14r15[c]. *pl. dat.* doendum 81rb1[a]; 81rb19[b]. *pret. sg.* dyde 6v4[d]; 11r11[b]. *pret. sg. ind. 2* dydest 16r16[b]; 78va20[e]. *pret. pl.* dydon 5v3[b]; 9r12[b]. *pret. part.* gidoen 54v15[a].

gidoeð: *a* AGERE *b* FACERE ‖ gidoeð 5r18[b]. gedoeð 5r10[b]. *pres. subj.* + *inf.* gidoe 2v5[b]; 5r12[b]; 18r5[a]. gidoa 6v7[b]; 7v5[a]. *imp. sg.* gido 16r17[b]. *pret. sg.* gidyde 21r16[b]; 37v1[b].

from-doeð: AUFERRE ‖ *imp. sg.* fromdo 77r22.

ofer-doeð: TRANSIGERE ‖ *pret. part. sg. dat.* oferdoene 18r6.

to-doeð: FACERE ‖ *pret. part. sg. dat.* todoenum 85rb7.

ðerh-doeð: PERAGERE ‖ *pres. subj.* + *inf.* ðerhdoa 11v4.

undoeð: ABSOLUERE ‖ *pres. subj. inf.* undoe 19v18. undoa 56v19. *imp. sg.* undo 20v1.

u(o)el-doeð: *a* BENEFACTOR *b* BENEFICIUM ‖ *pres. part. pl. dat.* ueldoendum 61r5[a]; 81vb7[a]. *pret. part. pl. nom.* + *acc.* welgidoeno 11r17[b].

dohter: FILIA ‖ dohter 53r16. *pl. nom.* + *acc.* dohtoro 33r15.

dom: IUDICIUM ‖ dom 5r10; 5r18. *sg. gen.* *domes 88vb18. *sg. dat.* dome 85va5. *pl. nom.* + *acc.* domas 5r11.

dor: OSTIUM ‖ dor 81vb23; 83ra15.

dræ(c)ca: DRACO ‖ dræcca 34r1; 61r14. dræcce 34r1.

on-dredeð: *a* EXPAUESCERE *b* TIMERE *c* TIMORATUS ‖ ondredes 22r13[b]; 61r7[b]. ondredað 61r13[a]; 81va9[b]. *pres. subj.* + *inf.* ondrede 10r10[b]. *imp. sg.* ondred 26v16[b]. *pres. part.* ondredende 9v8[b]; 21v7[c]. *pl. gen.* ondredenda' 81vb11[b].

drenc: *a* POTIO *b* POTUS ‖ *sg. gen.* drences 56r16[b]. drengces 56r8[a]. *sg. dat.* *drence 56r5.

drenceð: MERGERE ‖ *pres. part.* drencende 48v12.

gidrenceð: POTARE ‖ gidrenceð 22v7. *pret. sg.* gidrencde 40v10.

eft-adrifeð: REPELLERE ‖ *imp. sg.* eftadrif 16r10.

eft-for-drifeð: REPELLERE ‖ *imp. sg.* eftf'drif 18r19.

for-drifeð: *a* ABICERE *b* DEPELLERE *c* EXPELLERE *d* PELLERE *e* PROICERE *f* REPELLERE ‖ f'drifað 10r2[f]. *pres. subj.* + *inf.* f'drifa 78va3[e]. *infl. inf.* f'drifanne 57r19[c]. f'drifenne 59r10[a]. *pret. part.* f'drifen 59v11[d]. *sg. dat.* f'drifenum 18v10[b]. *pl. nom.* + *acc.* f'drifeno 46v8[b]; 88vb16[c].

from-adrifeð: ABICERE ‖ *pret. part. pl. nom.* + *acc.* fromadrifeno 67v3.

drihten: DOMINUS ‖ driht' 1r4; 1r6. driht 2v9; 4r4. drih' 3v11; 3v17; 18r20 [*alt. f.* drigh']. dr' 3v19; 3v23. d' 58v21. *sg. gen.* drihtnes 9v12; 13r10. *sg. dat.* drihtne 10r6; 10r7.

drihtenlic: DOMINICUS ‖ *sg. gen.* drihtenlices 11v3; 14v5. driht'lices 14v17; 14v19. driht' 56r18.

drinca: POTUS ‖ drince 6v12. *sg. gen.* drincæs 77r7.

scip-drincende: NAUFRAGANS ‖ scipdrincende 29v22.

drinceð: *a* BIBERE *b* MERGERE ‖ *infl. inf.* drinca' 56r13[a]. *pret. part.* gidruncen 29v21[b].

dryge: (arundo) ‖ dryge 41v9.

drygeð: ABSTERGERE ‖ *pret. part. sg. fem.* gidrygedo 47r6.

drync: POTUS ‖ *sg. gen.* drync' 56r13.

drysnað, -eð: EXSTINGUERE ‖ *pret. part.* gidrysnad 61r15.

gidrysnað, -eð: EXSTINGUERE ‖ *pres. subj.* + *inf.* gidrysne 31r4. *imp. sg.* gidrysne 61r18; 77r22.
adrysnað, -eð: EXSTINGUERE ‖ *pret. part.* adrysned 18v19.
unadrysnendlic: INEXSTINGUIBILIS ‖ unadrysnend' 50v20.
duola, duala: IGNORANTIA ‖ *sg. gen.* duoles 18v11.
giduola, -duala: *a* ERROR *b* IGNORANTIA ‖ *sg. gen.* giduoles 18r1[a]; 18v16[b]. giduoles' 16v21[a]. *pl. nom.* + *acc.* giduolo 19r21[a].
giduolað, -dualað: ERRARE ‖ *pret. sg.* giduolade 78ra6. *pret. pl.* gidwaladon 9v15.
duru: *a* IANUA *b* OSTIUM ‖ duru 80va1[b]. *pl. dat.* durum 50v14[a].
gidyrstgað: PRAESUMERE ‖ *pret. sg.* gidyrstgade 44v16.
dyrstig: AUDERE ‖ *pl. nom.* + *acc.* dyrstigo 82ra23.
fore-(fora-)dyrstig: PRAESUMPTUOSUS ‖ f'edyrstig' 48r11.
gieadgað: BEATIFICARE ‖ *pret. sg.* gieadgade 42v1; 42v3.
eadig: BEATUS ‖ eadig 14r19; 22v3. *sg. fem.* eadga 33v12; 37r21. eadgo 26r4. *sg. gen.* eadges 22r6; 22v9. eaðges 31r15. eadg' 35v20. ead' 41r6; 41r10. *sg. dat.* eadgum 21v15; 24r22. ead'um 43r11. *sg. weak* eadga 38r10; 88ra3. eadge 22r8; 27v4. eadg' 88rb1; 88rb4. eadig' 36v22. ead' 88rb7; 88rb10. *pl. nom.* + *acc.* eadgo 23v6; 34r8 [*alt. f.* eadges]. eadg' 39r15; 43r4. ead' 38r20; 39v5. ea 37v11. *pl. gen.* eadigra 15r6; 25v20. *pl. dat.* eadgum 44r1.
eadigni(s)s(e: *a* BEATITUDO *b* beatus ‖ eadignise 32v3[a]. eadignis' 25r6[a]. eadign' 16r17[b].
ealond: INSULA ‖ *sg. gen.* ealondes 27r2.
eara: AURIS ‖ eare 3r6; 9r22. eore 10r8. *pl. nom.* + *acc.* earo 20v9; 41v13. eara 61r21. *pl. dat.* earum 23r3; 83rb 21.
(e)arm: BRACHIUM ‖ arm 1r6. earm 9v12. *sg. gen.* armes 15r21. *sg. dat.* earme 44r18.
(e)arm: *a* EGENUS *b* MISER ‖ *sg. dat.* armum [*alt. f.* armne] 60v20[b]. *sg. acc. masc.* armne 80vb23[a]. *pl. gen.* armra 19v19[b].
(e)arn: AQUILA ‖ earn 78vb15.
(e)arnað: PROMERERI ‖ *pret. part. pl. nom.* + *acc.* giernado 35r9.
gi(e)arnað: MERERI ‖ giearniað 19v 13; 20r4. giearnigað 21r11. *pres. subj.* + *inf.* gearnia 50v21. giearnia 4v3; 19v3. giearniga 4r5; 7v18. giearnigo 1v4. *pret. sg.* giearnade 2v10.
fore-(fora-)(e)arnað: PROMERERI ‖ *pret. part. pl. nom.* + *acc.* foreearnado 40r10.
(e)arnung: MERITUM ‖ earnung 30v 16. *sg. acc.* + *dat.* earnunge 20v12; 43r19. *pl. nom.* + *acc.* earnungo 31r1; 35r11. earnunga 31r9; 35r21. *pl. gen.* earnunga 19v2. earnunge 8v19. *pl. dat.* earnungum 20v5; 25v11. eornungum 41r16.
earða: TERRA ‖ earðe 1r1; 1r12. eorðe 10r15; 12r16. eor' 79vb21. *sg. gen.* earðes 27r7; 57r15. eorðes 78va17. earðe' 46v14. *pl. dat.* earðum 34v3; 45v1. earðu [?*read* earðum] 31r13. eorðum 37r2.
earðcund: TERRENUS ‖ *sg. gen.* earðcundes 16v5.
earðlic: TERRENUS ‖ *pl. nom.* + *acc.* earðlico 16v18. *pl. dat.* earðlicum 9r1–2.
eastorlic: PASCHALIS ‖ eastorlic 15r 20; 15v17. eostorlic 15r5; 15r15. *sg. gen.* eastorlices 15v4. eostorlic' 15r9. *sg. dat.* eostorlicum [*alt. f.* eostorlico] 16r11. eostorlic' 16v10. *pl. nom.* + *acc.* eostorlico 15r12; 16v8. eastorlica 15v8. eostrolica 15r3. *pl. dat.* eastorlicum 4v8; 16v4. eostorlicum 16r8; 16v17. eastorlic' 4v17.
eastra: PASCHA ‖ eastro 12r21.
eaða: FACILE ‖ *comp.* eaðor 8v8; 9r2.
æd-(æt-)e(a)uað: *a* APPARERE *b* DEMONSTRARE *c* MANIFESTARE *d* OSTENDERE *e* PANDERE *f* REUELARE ‖ ædeawað 12r18[a]. *pres. ind. sg. 2* ædeawas 16r22[e]. *pres. subj.* + *inf.* ædeaua 48v5[c]; 48v19[a]. aedeaua 45v8[a]; 53r4[d]. *imp. sg.* ædeaua 5v2[d]. ædeawa 18v6[d]. aedeaua 1v8[a]; 78ra23[b]; 80rb9[d]. ædeau 80vb12[d]. *pret. sg.* ædeawde 1v2[a]. aedeaude 37v21[d]. ædeauade 39r2[d]. *pret. sg. ind. 2* aedeauades 1r17[f]. *pret. part.* ædeawad 5v9[b]. *pl. nom.* + *acc.* ædeawado 12r19[a].
eft-æd-(æt-)e(a)uað: REUELARE ‖ *pret. part. sg. fem.* eft...ædeawde 1v18.
e(a)udni(s)s(e: OSTENSIO ‖ eaudnise 54v20.
e(a)uislic: MANIFESTUS ‖ eauislice 54v22.
e(a)uislicað: MONSTRARE ‖ *imp. sg.* eauislica 37v19.
ebolsung: BLASPHEMIA ‖ ebolsung 6r20.
Ebrisc: *a* HEBRAEI *b* HEBRAICE ‖ *adv.* ebresc' 87vb3[b]. *pl. dat.* ebrescum 87rb6[a].
eca: AUGMENTUM ‖ éce 52r8. *pl. dat.* ecum 16v3.
ofer-eca: AUGMENTUM ‖ of'ece 30r8; 41r9.
ece, æce: *a* AETERNUS *b* PERENNIS *c* PERPETUUS *d* SEMPITERNUS (*e* hodiernus) *f* semita ‖ ece 1r21[c]; 1v5[d]; 1v10[(e)]; 2v11[a]; 27v2[f]; 77v5[b]. éce 7r8[a]; 79ra12[a]. *sg. fem.* eco [*alt. f.* ecnise] 10v16[a]. *sg. gen.* eces 25r6[a]; 38v1[c]. æces 13v10[a]; 46v4[a]. æc[r]es 66r15[a]. *sg. dat.* ecum 35v9[c] [*alt. f.* eco]; 45r14[c] [*alt. f.* ece]; *53r7[a]; 78ra9[a]. *pl. nom.* + *acc.* eco 15r14[c]; 15v3[a]; 19r23[d]. éco 10v1[a]. *pl. dat.* ecum 11v2[a]; 38r15[d]; 45r11[c].
ece-(æce-)lic: *a* AETERNUS *b* PERPETUUS *c* SEMPITERNUS *d* aeternitas *e* hodiernus ‖ ecelic 2v3[e]; 23v8[e]. *sg. gen.* ecelices 17r19[b]; 19r7[a]; 30r2[d] [*alt. f.* æcelices]. ecelices' 46r6[d]. *sg. dat.* ecelicum 16v8[e]; 19r3[b]; 30r4[b] [*alt. f.* ecelica]. ecelic' 27v10[(e)]. ecelice 14v 9[e]. *sg. weak* ecelice 16v11[b]. *pl. nom.* + *acc.* ecelica 22v14[c]; 80va15[e]. *pl. dat.* ecelicum 4r14[c]; 9r5[a]; 19r16[b].
gieceð: *a* ADICERE *b* AUGERE ‖ *pres. subj.* + *inf.* giece 5v12[a]; 24r6[b]. *imp. sg.* giec 18v7[b]. giéc 16r22[b]; 18v17[b].
ec-(æc-)ni(s)s(e: *a* AETERNITAS *b* AETERNUS *c* PERPETUUS *d* SEMPITERNUS ‖ ecnisse 10r2[d]; 44r15[c]; *80rb2[b]. ecnise 29v14[b]; 43v5[a]; 77r18[c]. ecnis' 41v11[c]. ecenis' 14v10[a].
ecnung: AUCTIO ‖ ecnung 85ra3.
ede: GREX ‖ ede 5r3; 17v7. *sg. gen.* edes 16r2.
efenlice: aequitas ‖ efennlice 44r21.
efe(r)n: UESPER ‖ efen' 77v4. *sg. dat.* eferne 18r8; 83vb11.
efe(r)nlic: *a* UESPER *b* UESPERTINUS ‖ efernlic 82ra9–10[b]. *sg. gen.* efernlices 80va13[b]. *adv.* efenlice 77v17[a]. *pl. dat.* efernlicum 80va21[b].
giefnað: COAEQUARE ‖ *pret. sg. ind. 2* giefendes 27v15.
efne: MATERIA ‖ aefne 56v12.
efne: AEQUALIS ‖ *pl. nom.* + *acc.* efno 86va6.
eft: ITEM ‖ eft 1r15; 66r12.
efter-sona: ITERUM ‖ *eft'sona 51v1.
eftmonað: *see* **eft-mynað**.
ega: OCULUS ‖ *pl. nom.* + *acc.* ego 2r17; 46r6. *pl. gen.* egna 55v15; 55v22. [*alt. f.* egna] 86rb22. *pl. dat.* egum 41r21; 42r20.
eg-hu(o)elc: *a* OMNIS (*b* UNUSQUISQUE) (*c* meus) ‖ eghuoelc 6v4[(b)]; 38r6[a]; 86vb23[(c)].
eg-hu(o)er: UBIQUE ‖ eghuoer 17v3; 33v16.
eg-huona: UNDIQUE ‖ eghuona 25v17; 27r19.
elnung: *a* ZELUS *b* Zelotes ‖ elnung 86rb9[a]. *sg. gen.* elnunges 86rb9[b].
embehtað, embihteð: MINISTRARE ‖ *pres. part. pl. dat.* embehtendum 34r18.
embehtere, embihtere: MINISTER ‖

pl. dat. embihtum' [? *read* embiht'um] 51v19.

endað: FINIRE ‖ *pret. part. pl. nom.* + *acc.* giendado 7v22.

giendað: *a* CONSUMMARE *b* CONSUMMATIO *c* PERFICERE ‖ *infl. inf.* giendanne 40r3[b]. *imp. sg.* giendig 78ra12[c]. *pret. sg.* giendade 29r13[a]; 31r12[a].

ðerh-endað: *a* PERFICERE *b* PERPETRARE ‖ *imp. sg.* ðerhenda 37r12*a*. ðerhendig 2v7[a]; 8r7[a]. *pret. sg.* ðerhendade 54v15[b]. *pret. pl.* ðerhendadon 54v16[b].

ðerh-giendað: PERFICERE ‖ *pres. subj.* + *inf.* ðerh[gi]endiga 10v18.

ende: FINIS ‖ ende 50r6; 50v11.

endebredað: ORDINARE ‖ *pret. part. sg. fem.* giendebredado 52v4. giendebredad' 33r19.

giendebredað: ORDINARE ‖ *pret. sg. ind. 2* giendebredades 52r16.

endebredlic: originalis ‖ *sg. gen.* endebredlices' 52v5.

endebredni(s)s(e: ORDO ‖ endebrednisse 19r13. endebred' 34r16; 85vb11.

endeleas: INFINITUS ‖ *pl. nom.* + *acc.* endeleaso 82rb11.

giendung: CONSUMMARE ‖ *sg. acc.* + *dat.* giendadunge [? *read* giendunge] 50v9.

engel, angel: ANGELUS ‖ engel 28r10; 28r13. *sg. gen.* engles 34r10. *sg. dat.* engle 25r11; 37v2. *pl. gen.* engla 34r16; 45r20. *pl. dat.* englum 34v6; 59r3.

heh-engel, -angel: ARCHANGELUS ‖ hehengel 66r6; 67r20. *sg. gen.* hehengles 34r20; [*alt. f.* hehengeles] 34v1. *sg. dat.* hehengele 66r22. *pl. gen.* hehangla 54v3.

enge(l)lic, ange(l)lic: ANGELICUS ‖ *sg. gen.* engelices 45r21. *pl. nom.* + *acc.* engellice 34v8.

erendure(c)ca, -ura(c)ca: APOSTOLUS ‖ erendwracca 29r7. erend' 38r10. *sg. gen.* erendurecæs 38r8.

erist: RESURRECTIO ‖ erist 13r16; 16r3. erest 12r7; 16r12. *sg. gen.* eristes 14v5; 14v16. erestes 11r13; 11v11. *sg. dat.* ereste 17r22.

ermðu: CALAMITAS ‖ *pl. dat.* ermðum 20r18.

erning: *a* CURSUS *b* agon ‖ erning 3r11[b]; 19r12[a]. [h]erning 29r13[a].

from-erning: EXCURSUS ‖ *sg. acc.* + *dat.* fromerninge 8v17.

on-erning: INCURSIO ‖ *sg. acc.* + *dat.* onerni'ge 17v9.

esne: *a* FAMULUS, *b* SERUUS ‖ esne 1r2[b]; 45v16[a]. *sg. gen.* esnes 9v8[b]; 60r6[a]. *pl. nom.* + *acc.* esnas 51r23[b]; 51v1[b]. esna 80ra9[b]. *pl. dat.* esnum 51v9[b]; 56v14[b].

efne-esne: CONSERUUS ‖ efneesne 34r11.

eðe: (ACCEPTABILIS) ‖ eð 5v19.

eðelice: FACILE ‖ *comp.* eðelicor 8v8.

eðni(s)s(e: PROSPERITAS ‖ eðnisse 83vb10. *sg. gen.* eðnisses 83vb16.

facon, -en: *a* DOLUS *b* FRAUS ‖ facon 12v3[a]; 47r5[b]. facen 50r4[a]. *sg. gen.* facnes 58v9[b]. *sg. dat.* facne 12v5[a].

fadorlic: *a* PATERNUS *b* PATROCINIUM ‖ *sg. gen.* fadorlices 12r11[a]. *pl. nom.* + *acc.* fadorlica 22r1[b]. fadorlico 24v7[(b)]; 30r4[(b)]. *pl. dat.* fadorlicum 33v20[(b)]; 40r13–14[(b)]; 41r6[(b)] [*alt. f.* fadorlico].

fagung: UARIETAS ‖ fagung 86rb22.

faldeð: FLECTERE ‖ *pret. part.* gifalden 40v10–11.

gifaldeð: IMPLICARE ‖ *pres. subj.* + *inf.* gifalde 29r10.

gifalleð: *a* CADERE *b* DECIDERE *c* RUERE ‖ *pret. sg. ind. 1, 3* gifeall 34r10[a]; 77v5[b]. gefeal [*alt f.* gefæl] 86ra9[c]. *pret. pl.* gifeallon 28r12[a].

infalleð ‖ infalled 56v4.

farmiga: *see* **fearmað**.

fæder, fader: PATER ‖ fæder 5r15; 12r5. faeder 18v13; 22r23. fader 36v17. fæd' 87vb2. faed' 77r24. *sg. gen.* fadores 5r15; 55r22. fador' 12v20; 23r13. fado' 67r21. fædor' 77r17. fæder' 13r22. *sg. dat.* feder [*alt. f.* fæder] 7r2; 13v19. *pl. gen.* fadora 82vb7. fædera 87va14. *pl. dat.* faedorum 17v22.

heh-fæder, -fader: PATRIARCHUS ‖ *hehfæder 87vb2.

hi(o)uisc-fæder, -fader: PATERFAMILIAS ‖ fæder hiwisc 85vb21.

gifælleð: PROSTERNERE ‖ *pres. subj.* + *inf.* gifælle 55v14.

fæmna ‖ *sg. gen.* faemnan 55r16.

fær: *a* ADITUS *b* EXCESSUS ‖ fær 14v10[a]. *pl. dat.* farum 11v6[b].

from-fær: EXCESSUS ‖ *pl. dat.* fromfarum 8v2.

færeð: *a* EXIRE *b* EXSILIRE ‖ faras 10r16[a]. *pres. part.* færende 28r2[b]; 28r14[a].

gifæreð: *a* ABSISTERE *b* PROGREDI *c* RECEDERE ‖ gifæres 33r17[b]. *pres. subj.* + *inf.* gifære 77r6[a]; 82rb18[c].

eft-færeð: RECEDERE ‖ eftfæreð *40v22; 77v16.

from-færeð: ABSCEDERE ‖ *pres. subj.* + *inf.* fromfære 77r8.

geond-færeð: illustrare ‖ *imp. sg.* gieondfær 7v4.

ofer-færeð: TRANSIRE ‖ oferfæreð 2r7. *pres. subj.* + *inf.* of'fara 18r8; 60r21.

færlice: *see* **ferlice**.

ende-fæstend: CONSUMMATOR ‖ endefæstend 13v6.

ðerh-ende-fæstend: profector ‖ ðerhendefæst' 15r8.

fæste(r)n, feaste(r)n: IEIUNIUM ‖ fæstin 4v19. fæst'n 7r14. *sg. dat.* fæst'ne 50r22. feast'ne 2v14. *pl. nom.* + *acc.* fæstino 4v14; 8v12. fæsteno 4v5. *pl. gen.* fæstinra 4r19. *pl. dat.* fæstinum 4r17; 4v8; 8r15 [*alt f.* gifæstinum]; 8r17 [*alt. f.* gifæstinum].

fæste(r)n-, feaste(r)n-lic: quadrigesimalis ‖ fæstin' 7r14. *sg. dat.* fæst'nlic' 7r4.

gifæsteð, -feastað: IEIUNARE ‖ *pres. subj.* + *inf.* gifeasta 8r6. gefæstæ 8v14.

fæstlice: QUIDEM ‖ fæstlice 28r7.

fæstnað: *a* MUNIRE *b* "fendere" *c* monumentum ‖ *pret. part.* gifæstnad 85rb11[b]; 85va22[c]. *pl. nom.* + *acc.* gifæstnado 30v5[a].

gifæstnað: *a* ACCOMODARE *b* COMMENDARE *c* CONSTRINGERE ‖ gifæstnað 19v17[c]. *pres. subj.* + *inf.* gifæstnia 30v1[b]. *imp. sg.* gifæstna 50v14[a].

afæstnað: *a* COMMENDARE *b* FIRMARE *c* MUNIRE ‖ *pres. subj.* + *inf.* afæstnia 52v16[c]. *pret. part.* afæstnad 33r7[b]; 37r20[a]. *pl. nom.* + *acc.* afæstnado 4r18[c].

ym(b)-fæstni(s)s(e: circumstantia ‖ ymbfæst' 80va1.

fæstnung: MUNIMENTUM ‖ fæstnung 57r8.

gifæstnung: MUNIMEN ‖ *sg. acc.* + *dat.* gifæstnunge 18r17.

heh-fæstnung: "POLIS" ‖ hehfæstn' 87vb5.

fæt(t: (*a* HYDRIA) *b* UAS *c* UASCULUM ‖ *pl. nom.* + *acc.* fato 46v6[c]; 46v22[b]; 56v10[(a)]. feta 56v4.

gifea: GAUDIUM ‖ gifea 13v7; 20r7. gefea 85rb19.

fearmað: prosperare ‖ *pres. subj.* + *inf.* *farmiga 81rb3.

f(e)arr: TAURUS ‖ *pl. nom.* + *acc.* farras 51v2.

fearr: (*a* ABESSE) *b* LONGE *c* PROCUL ‖ fearr 11r3[(a)] [*alt. f.* fearre]; 47r5[c]; 78va18[b]. farr 59v11[c].

fearra: (*a* ABESSE) *b* DE LONGE *c* PROCUL ‖ fearra [*alt. f.* ofearra] 27r3[b]. fearr [*alt. f.* fearre] 11r3[(a)]. fearre 47r3[c].

gifearrað: *a* ABSCEDERE *b* DISCEDERE ‖ *pres. subj.* + *inf.* gifearria 47r4[a]; 58v7[b].

gifeað: *a* CONGAUDERE *b* GAUDERE *c* LAETARI *d* gaudium ‖ gifeað 6v9[b]; 26r14[b]. gefeað 6r4[b]. *pres. subj.* + *inf.* gifeage 1r21[b]; 16v2[b]. gifeaga 4r14[b]. gifeagia 30v9[a]; 33v8[b]. gifeaia 30r6[b];

35v9[c]; 46r21[a]. gifea[1]ga 23v15[b]. gifeaiga 25v11[b]; 27r20[d]. gifea’ 44r10[b]. gifea 16v10[b] [*alt. f.* gifeaga]; 26r8[b]. *pres. part.* gefeande 83rb10[b]. gifeande 36v19[b]; 40r12[b]. *pl. nom. + acc.* gifeando 11r19[b]; 60v3[b].

feger: PULCHER ‖ feger 2r17 (2). *pl. nom. + acc.* fegro 39r11.

fegerni(s)s(e: *a* HONESTAS *b* pulcher ‖ fegernis’ 2r3[a]; 2r4[b].

feh: PECUNIA ‖ feh 85vb15.

gifeht: *a* ACIES *b* AGON *c* BELLUM *d* CERTAMEN ‖ gifeht 13v5[d]; 29r12[b]; 33r19[a]; 85ra12[c].

on-gifeht: IMPUGNATIO ‖ ongifeht 47r7; 58v19. *pl. dat.* ongifeht’ 59r20.

unafehtendlic: INEXPUGNABILIS ‖ unafehtendlic 44r21.

fehteð: PUGNARE ‖ *pres. ind. sg. 1* fehto 3r15.

gifehteð: *a* CERTARE *b* EXPUGNARE *c* PROELIARI *d* PUGNARE ‖ gifehtað 29r11[a]. *pres. subj. + inf.* gifehte 29r12[a]. *pres. part.* gifehtende 59v5[b]. *pl. nom. + acc.* gifehtendo 4r18[d]. *pret. sg. ind. 1, 3* gifæht 29r13[a]; 34r2[d]. *pret. pl.* gifuhton 34r1[c].

afehteð: EXPUGNARE ‖ *imp. sg.* afeht 78rb13.

of-gifehteð: EXPUGNARE ‖ *infl. inf.* ofgefehtanne 67r10.

on-fehteð: IMPUGNARE ‖ *pres. part. pl. nom. + acc.* onfehtendo 78rb13.

feld: CAMPUS ‖ *pl. dat.* feldum 1r10; 31v16.

æd- (æt-)feleð: ADHAERERE ‖ *pres. subj. + inf.* ætfela 43v1.

feng: captiuus ‖ feng 39v22.

gifeng: CAPTIUITAS ‖ *gifeng 39v22.

on(d)-fenge: *a* ACCEPTUS *b* ASSUMPTUS *c* SUSCEPTUS ‖ ondfenge 5v17[a]. *pl. nom. + acc.* ondfengo 41r12[a]. onfengo 4v9[c]. ondfoengo 8r18[b]. onfoengo 11r23[a].

on(d)-fengelic: (ACCEPTABILIS) ‖ ondfengelic 5v19.

feolo: (*a* QUANTUS), *b* TOT ‖ feolo 11r14[b]; 29v8[(a)].

feortig, feuo(e)rtig: QUADRAGINTA ‖ feortig 23r22. feouertig 23r12. feort’ 54v1. *dat.* feortigum 50r3. feourtigum 66v12.

feorða: QUARTUS ‖ feorða 52v21.

feou(e)r, feor: QUATTUOR ‖ feouer 23r12; *88va3[1]. feoer[o] 50r3. feour’ 66v11. feoro 23r20; 23r22 [*alt. f.* feorti]. feor’ 54v7. *feor[2] 54v2.

feou(e)rtene: QUATTUORDECIM ‖ *feouerteno 66r1.

ferlice ‖ færlice 55r20.

1. eo *doubtful.*
2. feo *doubtful.*

fetels: UASCULUM ‖ *pl. nom. + acc.* fetelsco [*alt. f.* fætelsco] 46v12.

fif: QUINQUE ‖ fif 83va9. fifo 47r19.

fiftig: (*a* QUINQUAGENARIUS) *b* QUINQUAGINTA ‖ fiftig 86vb13[(a)]. *dat.* fiftigum 86vb13[b].

fiond: *a* HOSTIS *b* INIMICUS ‖ fiond 50v2[a]; 54v13[b]. *sg. gen.* fiondes 18v1[b]; 48r8[b]. fiond’ 45v6[a]; 47r4[a]. *pl. nom. + acc.* fiondas 11v10[b]; 21v12[b]. *pl. gen.* fionda’ 37v19[b]. *pl. dat.* fiondum 8r13[a]; 39r4[b].

fiondlic: HOSTILIS ‖ *pl. nom. + acc.* fiondlico 59v4.

firreð: PELLERE ‖ *infl. inf.* firran’ 59r10.

afirreð: *a* AUFERRE *b* DEPELLERE *c* EXPELLERE *d* PELLERE *e* exorcizare ‖ *pres. subj. + inf.* afirra 18r14[b]. *imp. sg.* afirr 4r4[a]; 20v8[c]. *pret. sg. ind. 2* afirdest 11v10[c]. *pret. part.* afirred 54v12[e]. *pl. nom. + acc.* afirredo 60r6[d].

eft-afirreð: RETRAHERE ‖ *pret. part.* eft...afirred 8v2.

from-afirreð: ABICERE ‖ *pret. part.* from...afirr’ 59v10.

mið-afirreð: ABICERE ‖ *pret. part. sg. dat.* miðafirredum 18v11.

first: SPATIUM ‖ *pl. nom. + acc.* firsto 46v13.

fisc: PISCIS ‖ *sg. gen.* fisces 67r6; 67r19.

flæsc: CARO ‖ flæsc 8r5; 25r11. *sg. gen.* flæsces 7r17; 37v18. *sg. dat.* flæsce 37v23.

fleað: *a* FUGERE *b* effugare ‖ fleeð 61r14[a]. fleas 51r13[a]. *infl. inf.* fleanne 48r7[b]. *pres. part.* fleende 85rb8[a].

gifleað: *a* EFFUGERE *b* FUGERE ‖ *pres. subj. + inf.* giflee 58v7[a]. giflii 59r18[a]. *gifliie 52v16[b].

afleað: effugare ‖ *infl. inf.* afleanne 59r1.

of-fleað: effugare ‖ *infl. inf.* offleanne 67r9.

flegeð: *a* UOLATILE *b* UOLUCRIS ‖ *pres. part. pl. nom. + acc.* flegendo 57v9[b]; 67r18[a]. *pl. dat.* flegendum 57v6[a]; 66v2[a].

giflegeð: fugere ‖ *pres. subj. + inf.* giflega 57v8. *pret. sg. ind. 1, 3* gefleg 67r18.

aflegeð: fugere ‖ *pret. part. pl. nom. + acc.* aflegedo 67r7; 67r20.

fleme: FUGITIUUS ‖ fleme [*alt. f.* gefleme] 67r19.

flemeð: FUGARE ‖ *pret. part. pl. nom. + acc.* geflemedo 66r7.

aflemeð: FUGITIUUS ‖ *pret. part.* aflemed 67r5.

giflit(t: QUAESTIO ‖ geflit 86ra8.

fli(t)teð: DISPUTARE ‖ *pres. part.* flittende 21r19.

gifli(t)teð: CONTENDERE ‖ giflitað 3r11.

flod: DILUUIUM ‖ *sg. gen.* floedes 52v6.

from-giflloueð: AFFLUERE ‖ *pret. sg. ind. 1, 3* fromgiflæue 39r7.

foegeð: IUNGERE ‖ *pret. part.* gifoegid 52v3. gifoeged 52v7. *sg. fem.* gifoegedo 52v15.

gifoegeð: *a* CONCILIARE *b* INHAERERE *c* IUNGERE *d* SOCIARE ‖ *pres. subj. + inf.* gifoega 35v15[a]; 43v1[b]; 50r2[d]; 52r23[c].

afoegeð: *a* IUNGERE *b* SOCIARE ‖ *pret. part.* afoegid 52r17[a]. *pl. nom. + acc.* afoegedo 38r16[b].

gifoegni(s)s(e: *a* SOCIETAS *b* socius ‖ gifoegnisse 52v4[a]. gifoegnise 50v18[b].

foeleð: SENTIRE ‖ *pres. subj. + inf.* foele 57r7.

gifoeleð: SENTIRE ‖ gifoelað 10v3. *pres. subj. + inf.* gifoele 16v16; 20r21. gifoelæ 30r20. gifoela 11v21; 26r18.

foelni(s)s(e: SENSUS ‖ foelnise 81rb15.

under-on(d)-foend(e: SUSCEPTOR ‖ *pl. nom. + acc.* underondfoendo 86vb9.

foereð: *a* ABIRE *b* EGREDI *c* MIGRARE ‖ *pret. sg.* foerde 32r18[c]; 85rb6[b]. *pret. pl.* foerdon 51v4[a]; 51v13[b].

i(n)n-foereð: INTROIRE ‖ *pret. sg.* innfoerde 10v1.

ofer-foereð: TRANSIRE ‖ *pret. pl.* of’foerdon 21v9.

gifoerscipað: COMITARI ‖ gifoerscipeð 44v14. *pres. subj. + inf.* gifoerscipia 53r2.

gifoerscip(e: *a* SOCIETAS *b* socius ‖ gifoerscipe 36r18[a]. gifoerscip’ 50v17[b]. *sg. gen.* gifoerscipes’ 45r21[a].

foeð: CAPERE ‖ *infl. inf.* foanne 57r1.

gifoeð: CAPERE ‖ gefoað 85va8.

bi-foeð: CONTINGERE ‖ *pres. subj. + inf.* bifoe 34r22.

eft-on(d)-foeð: RECIPERE ‖ *pres. subj. + inf.* eftonfoe 5v17.

on(d)-foeð: *a* ACCIPERE *b* ASSUMERE *c* CAPERE *d* EXCIPERE *e* PERCIPERE *f* SUMERE *g* SUSCIPERE ‖ onfoað 3r9[a]; *57r15[f]. onfoeð 41r3[a]; 44r19[f]. *pres. subj. + inf.* onfoe 3r13[a]; 4r20[g]; 15r10[c]; 27v10[d]; 38r14[e]; 47v10[f] [*alt. f.* onfoeð]; 56r20[b]; 59r11[f]. onfoa 8v21[e]; 11r11[f]; 14v1[a]; 14v18[g]; 48r20[b]. *infl. inf.* onfoanne 57r6[d]. *pres. part.* onfoende 10v6[a]. ondfoende 19v14[e]. *sg. dat.* onfoendum 83vb9[a]. *pl. nom. + acc.* onfoendo 7v22[c]; 9r8[g]. *pl. dat.* onfoendum 58v6[f]. ondfoendum 58v16[f]. *imp. sg.* onfoh 19v16[g]; 59v7[a]; 82rb2[b]; 83rb21[e]. *pret. sg. ind. 1, 3* onfeng 41v7[a]; 50r9[g]. ondfeng 50r14[b]. *pret. sg. subj. + ind. 2* onfenge 25r11[g]; 27v19[a] [*alt. f.* onfoenge]; 49v21[b]. *pret. pl.* onfengon 15r2[e]; 29r5[a].

ðerh-foeð: *a* PERCIPERE *b* PERFICERE ‖ *pres. subj.* + *inf.* ðerhfoe 16r4[a]; 43v2[b].
ðerh-on(d)-foeð: PERCIPERE ‖ *pres. part. sg. dat.* ðerhondfoendum 20v2.
under-foeð: *a* ASSUMERE *b* SUSCIPERE ‖ underfoeð 22r16[b]. underfoað 6r1[b]. *pres. subj.* + *inf.* underfoe 1r2[b]; 4r3[b]. *pret. sg. subj.* + *ind. 2 / pret. pl.* underfenge[an] 55r10. *pret. part.* underfoen 42v6[a].
folc: *a* PLEBS *b* POPULUS ‖ folc 1r9[b]; 16v2[a]. *sg. gen.* folces 3v11[b]; *20v21[a]. *sg. dat.* folce 2v20[b]; 19r20[a]. *pl. nom.* + *acc.* folco 27r3[b]; 29v18[b]. *pl. gen.* folca 86va20[b]. *pl. dat.* folcum 1r20[b]; 7v10[a].
folgað: SEQUI ‖ *pres. subj.* + *inf.* folgiga 12v15.
for(e, -a: *a* ANTE *b* CORAM *c* OB (*d* PRAE) *e* PRO *f* PROPTER; *A—insertion* ‖ f'a 17r6[e]; 33r6[b]; 34r10[a]; 85vb14[(d)]. fore 12v12[e]; 80vb21[e]. for 55r9; 55r10. f'e 3v12[e]; 6v1[f]; 23r19[a]; 50v17[c]; 61r4[A]. f' 10v21[e]; 11r1[e]. fer 55r11; 55r12.
fore- (fora(n-) ongægn: CONTRA ‖ f'anongægn 85ra16.
for(e- (fora-) ðon: *a* ENIM *b* EO QUOD *c* ERGO *d* IDCIRCO *e* IDEO *f* IGITUR *g* NAM *h* PROPTER *i* PROPTEREA *j* QUIA *k* QUONIAM *l* praecipue, *m* quod ‖ f'eðon 4r23[j]; 9v5[e]; 9v21[i]; 43v3[d]; 66v17[k]; 81rb12[a]; 85vb12[h]. forðon 6r11[a]; 24r18[j]; 29r11[g]. f'ðon 2r8[a]; 2r11[j]; 3v9[c]; 5r24[k]; 9v6[e]; 14r5[f]; 32r2[d]; 37v1[g]; 42v20[l]; 43v5[b]; 86va9[m].
for-huon: *a* CUR *b* QUARE ‖ f'huon 85vb22[b]; 86va5[a].
forma: PRIMUS ‖ forma 60r7. f'ma 88rb23; 88va1.
forð: *a* AMPLIUS *b* PLUS *c* ULTRA ‖ *comp.* f'ðor 13r1[c]; 19v7[b]; 34r3[a].
fot: PES ‖ *pl. nom.* + *acc.* fota 78rb20. *pl. dat.* fotum 34r10; 51v20.
gifrægneð, -fraigneð: INTERROGARE ‖ gifraignað 17v17.
frætuað, freatuað: ORNARE ‖ *pret. part.* gifreatuad 1r7.
freht: AUSPICIUM ‖ *pl. dat.* frehtum 46v1.
fre(m)með: *a* AFFICERE *b* EFFICERE ‖ *pret. part.* gifremmed 51r11[b]; 54v19[b]. gifremmad 3r18[b]. *pl. nom.* + *acc.* gifremmedo 51v6[a]. gifremm' 58v5[b].
gifre(m)með: EFFICERE ‖ *pres. subj.* + *inf.* gifremme 46v22. gifremmo [*alt. f.* gifremme] 11v1. gifr...ma 38r19.
ginog-fre(m)með: SUFFICERE ‖ genogfremmað 86ra15.
u(o)el-fre(m)ming: BENEFICIUM ‖ uelfremming 85ra12.
fremni(s)s(e: EFFECTUS ‖ fremnise 32v19. fremnis' 30v11.
gifremni(s)s(e: *a* AFFECTUS *b* EFFECTUS ‖ gifremnisse 8r17[b]. gifremmnise 20r10[a]. gifremn' 9r8[a]. gifrem' 59r11[b]. *pl. dat.* gifremnissum 4v18[b]; 9r2[a].
u(o)el-fremni(s)s(e: BENEFICIUM ‖ uelfremnisse 56v18. *pl. nom.* + *acc.* uelfremnisso 40r10. uelfremniso 34v11. *pl. dat.* uelfremnisum *20r23; 28v1.
gifre(t)teð: COMEDERE ‖ gefrettað 67r14.
friað: LIBERARE ‖ *pres. ind. sg. 1* fria 5r6. *pret. part.* friad 7v16; 25v7. gifriad 24v15. gifriod 20v17. *pl. nom.* + *acc.* friado 3v13; 11r16. gifriado 8v10.
gifriað: LIBERARE ‖ *pres. subj.* + *inf.* gifrie 48r10. *imp. sg.* gifria 78va8. *pret. sg.* gifriade 30r1; 80vb24. gefriade 81va3. gifriode 29r19. *pret. sg. ind. 2* gifriadest 16v21.
afriað: LIBERARE ‖ *pret. part.* afriad 25v16. *pl. nom.* + *acc.* afriodo 26v5; 44r2.
frio, freo: LIBER ‖ frio 4r13. freo 87va21.
frio- (freo-) dom: LIBERTAS ‖ friodom 15r17. friodom' 50r16. *sg. gen.* friodomes 14r17.
gifriolic -freolic: LIBER ‖ *pl. nom.* + *acc.* gifriolico 15v18.
friond: AMICUS ‖ friond 51v17.
froecelni(s)s(e: PERICULUM ‖ froecelnis' 56r15. *pl. dat.* froecelnissum 33v12. froecelnisum 4r6; 33r22. froecilnissum 8v4.
fore- (fora-) froefrend: proconsul ‖ f'efroefrend 85vb19.
gifroefreð: CONSOLARI ‖ gifroefrað 5v24; 14r13. *pres. subj.* + *inf.* gifroefre 30v21; 35v19 [*alt. f.* gifroefreð]. *pres. part. pl. nom.* + *acc.* gifroefrendo 19v22.
frofor: *a* CONSOLATIO *b* SOLATIUM ‖ froffer 50r19[b]. *sg. gen.* frofres 19r1[b]; 20r21[a]. frof' 43r21[a]. *sg. dat.* frofre 20v17[a]. *pl. nom.* + *acc.* frofro 19r22[b].
gifrofor: CONSOLATIO ‖ *sg. gen.* gifrofres 20r17. gifrofor' 9r12. *pl. dat.* gifrofrum 19r16.
from: *a* A(B *b* DE *c* E(X; *A—insertion* ‖ from 2r7[a]; 2r23[A]; 12r7[c]; 13v9[b].
frum(m: PRIMUS ‖ *sg. gen.* frummes 17r15. *pl. dat.* frummum 46v1.
fru(m)ma: *a* EXORDIUM *b* INITIUM *c* PRINCIPIUM ‖ fruma 55v10[b]; 79va7[c]. frumma 13v22[b]; 18v11[c]; 88rb13. *pl. nom.* + *acc.* frumo 16v3[a]. frummo 50v10[b]. *pl. dat.* frummum 52r19[a].
fryht-: *see* **fyrht-**.
frymðelic: ORIGINALIS ‖ *sg. dat.* *frymðelicum 48v1.
frymðo: *a* INITIUM *b* ORIGO ‖ frymðe 33r5[a]; 46v14[b].
fugul: AUIS ‖ *pl. nom.* + *acc.* fuglas 67v3. *pl. dat.* fuglum 66r1; 66r12.
full: PLENUS ‖ full 21r15; 21r22. ful 56v4. *pl. dat.* fullum 4v17.
fullice: PLENE ‖ *comp.* fullicor 17r2.
fu(l)lni(s)s(e PLENITUDO ‖ fullnis' 53r23.
fu(l)ltum(m -tem(m: *a* ADIUTORIUM *b* AUXILIUM *c* PRAESIDIUM *d* SUBSIDIUM *e* SUFFRAGIUM ‖ fultum 41r9[b]; 81vb17[b]. *sg. gen.* fultumes 32v19[b]. *sg. dat.* fultume 16v10[b]; 78rb15[a]. fulltumme 7v11[b]; 32r6[c]; 52r20[a]. fulltume 30v21[e]; 78va19[a]. *pl. nom.* + *acc.* fultumo 4r16[c]; 16r19[d]. fultummo 35v19[e]; 44r5[e]. fultemmo 34v8[e]. *pl. dat.* fultumum 30v5[c]; 31r17[b]; 32v6[e]; 33v19[d]. fultummum 4r14[b]; 26r17[e]; 29v8[c]; 36r4[d]. fultemum 4r18[b]. fultum' 45r11[c].
fu(l)ltu(m)mað, -te(m)mað: *a* ADIUUARE *b* AUXILIARI *c* SUFFRAGARI ‖ *imp. sg.* fultuma 20v4[b]. *pres. part.* fultummende 52r17[b]. fultemmende 4r9[a]. *pl. nom.* + *acc.* fultumendo 44v17[c].
gifu(l)ltu(m)mað, -te(m)mað: AUXILIARI ‖ *imp. sg.* gifultuma 19r5.
fullunga: PERAMPLIUS ‖ fullunga 10r20.
fulni(s)s(e: SQUALOR ‖ *pl. nom.* + *acc.* fulnisso 50v3.
fuluað: BAPTIZARE ‖ *pret. part.* fulwad 55v3. *pl. nom.* + *acc.* gifwluado 12v18. gifulwwado [*alt. f.* gifulgwado, ? *read* gifwulwado] 12v17.
fuluiht: BAPTISMA ‖ fulwiht 12v19. *sg. gen.* fwlwihtes 15v15. *sg. dat.* fwlwihte 16r16.
fylgeð: *a* CONSEQUI *b* EXSEQUI *c* SECTARI *d* SEQUI ‖ fylgeð 6r3[c]. fylgað 54v2[d]; 61r7[d]. fylges 79va6[d]. *pres. subj.* + *inf.* fylga 18v14[d]; 30r2[a]. *infl. inf.* fylgenne 15r7[b]. *pres. part. pl. nom.* + *acc.* fylgendo 12v9[d].
gifylgeð: *a* ASSEQUI *b* CONSEQUI *c* EXSEQUI *d* PERSEQUI *e* PROSEQUI *f* SECTARI *g* SEQUI *h* SUBSEQUI ‖ gifylgað 23v1[g]. *pres. subj.* + *inf.* gifylga 3v23[c]; 4v15[a]; 7v21[d]; 8v12[e]; 11v12[b]; 19r11[f]; 24v19[g]; 35r15[h]. gifylge 2r23[a]; 16r20[f]. *pret. sg.* gifylgede 28r14[g]. *pret. pl.* gifylgedon 12v10[b].
fore- (fora-) fylgeð: PROSEQUI ‖ *imp. sg.* f'efylg 4v5.
soð-fylgeð: PROSEQUI ‖ *pres. subj.* + *inf.* soðfylga 14v12.
to-gifylgeð: ASSEQUI ‖ *pres. subj.* + *inf.* togifylga 44r7.
ðerh-fylgeð: SEQUI ‖ *pres. subj.* + *inf.* ðerhfylga 36r3.

under-fylgeð: SUBSEQUI ‖ *pres. subj.* + *inf.* underfylga 24v11.
fylging: SECTARI ‖ fylging 8r5. fylgincgo 27r13.
fylleð: IMPLERE ‖ *imp. sg.* fyll 1v7. *pret. part.* gifylled 29r18; 51r7. *pl. nom.* + *acc.* gifylledo 2r8. gifyldo 51v14.
gifylleð: *a* IMPLERE *b* PERIMPLERE *c* REPLERE ‖ gifylleð 3v5[a]; 78vb10[c]. *pres. subj.* + *inf.* gifylle 4v7[a]; 8r9[a]; 43r14[a]. *imp. sg.* gifyll 16r14[a]; 19r16[c]. *pret. sg.* gifylde 22r17[a]. *pret. sg. ind. 2* gifylldest [*alt. f.* gifyllest] 3r3[c]. gifyldest 2v8[a].
afylleð: REPLERE ‖ *pret. part.* afylled 45r21.
eft-gifylleð: REPLERE ‖ *eftgifylled 40v18.
eft-afylleð: REPLERE ‖ *pret. part.* eft... afylled 78ra10; 82vb4. *pl. nom.* + *acc.* eft...afylledo 45v5.
fy(l)lni(s)s(e: PLENITUDO ‖ fyllnisse 47v20. fylnisse 3v9. fylnise 31v11; 50v10.
gify(l)lni(s)s(e: PLENITUDO ‖ *sg. gen.* gifylnis' 40r7.
fyr: IGNIS ‖ fyr 18v18; 48v16. *sg. gen.* fyres 48v9; 49r8. *sg. dat.* fyre 48v4; 86va9. *pl. gen.* fyra' 48r2. *pl. dat.* fyrum 31r12; *77r21.
fyrhteð, fryhteð: TREMERE ‖ *pres. part. pl. nom.* + *acc.* fryhtendo 59v5.
gifyrhteð, -fryhteð: CONTREMESCERE ‖ *pres. subj.* + *inf.* gifyrhtia 48r14.
afyrhteð, afryhteð: TREMERE ‖ *pres. subj.* + *inf.* afyrhta 49r2.
fyrhto, fryhto: TERROR ‖ fyrhto 59v10. fryhte 28v16.
g(a)að: *a* ABIRE *b* AMBULARE *c* IRE ‖ gaað 6r12[b]; 51v11[c]. gað 6r7[b]. gæð 23v2[c]. geæð [? *read* gaæð] 44r21[c]. *pres. ind. sg. 2* gæst 26v15[c]. *pret. sg.* ead 9v1[a].
gig(a)að: *a* AMBULARE *b* EXIRE ‖ gigæð 5r11[a]. *pret. sg.* gieade 9v9[a]; 28r1[a]. *pret. sg. ind. 2* gieadest 26v12[b].
bi-g(a)að: *a* COLERE *b* EXERCERE ‖ bigaað 14v14[a]; 15r4[a]. bigað 25v21[a]; 27r15[a]. bigaas 25v14[a]. bigas 24v7[a]; 25r3[a]. *pret. sg.* bieade 11v21[b].
eft-big(a)að: RECOLERE ‖ eftbigaað 24v10.
fore- (fora-) g(a)að: ANTECEDERE ‖ *pres. subj.* + *inf.* f'egæ 41r6; 58r5.
i(n)n-g(a)að: *a* INCEDERE *b* INGREDI *c* INTRARE *d* INTROIRE ‖ *pres. ind.* + *subj. sg. 1* ingæ 82va13[d]. *pres. subj.* + *inf.* ingae 27r12[a]. in'gæ 57r9[c]. inngæ 9r16[b]. *pret. sg.* in'eade 28r1[c]; 51v15[c]. *pret. sg. ind. 2* inneadest 51v18[c].
uið-g(a)að: EUADERE ‖ *pret. pl.* wiðeadon 16v15–16.
under-g(a)að: SUBIRE ‖ *pres. subj.* + *inf.* undergaa 11v9. ungaa [? *read* und'gaa] 11r11; ungaa [? *read* und'gaa] 11v19. *pret. sg.* undereade 32r9.
galla: FEL ‖ galla 67r19. galle 67r6.
gast: SPIRITUS ‖ gast 2r8; 6r17. *sg. gen.* gastes 14v14; 18v7. gast' 14v20; 49r21. *sg. dat.* gaste 10v12; 12v13. gast' 46r20. *pl. nom.* + *acc.* *gastas 86va12.
gastlic: SPIRITALIS ‖ gastlic 8v17. *sg. gen.* gastlices 47v2; 53r20. *sg. dat.* gastlicum 22v1; 28v7. *pl. nom.* + *acc.* gastlico 4r17. gast' 56r20.
gat: CAPRA ‖ *pl. nom.* + *acc.* gæt 57v20.
gæt(t: PORTA ‖ *pl. nom.* + *acc.* gætto 60v2. gæto 9r17. *pl. gen.* gættana 28v16.
gigeadrað: *a* ADUNARE *b* SOCIARE ‖ *pres. subj.* + *inf.* gigeadriga 28v5[b]. *pret. sg. ind. 2* *gigeadridest 15v14[a].
geadrung: *a* COPULA *b* SOCIETAS ‖ geadrung 52v1[a]. *sg. acc.* + *dat.* geadrung' 53r2[b].
ge(a)fa, -o: *a* DATUM *b* DONUM *c* DOS *d* GRATIA *e* LARGITAS *f* hostia *g* oblatio *h* offerre ‖ geafa 2r5[d]; 6r9[g]; 6r16[d]. geafo 13v18[b]. gefe 2v7[d]; 13v18[a]; 43v12[h]; *56v18[e]. geafæ 2v1[d]. *sg. gen.* gefes 8r21[d]; 25r21[d]. gefe' 8r12[d]. *pl. nom.* + *acc.* geafa 42v8[b]. geafo 4r12[b]; 18r9[d]; 43v11[(f)]; 85ra22[c]. *pl. gen.* geafana 56v18[(d)]. geafona 9r12[d] [*alt. f.* geafana]; 22r4[(d)]; 45v18[b]. *pl. dat.* geafum 3v21[b]; 50v12[f].
ge(a)fað: GLORIFICARE ‖ *pret. sg.* geafade 37v20.
gig(e)afað: praestolari ‖ *pres. subj.* + *inf.* gigeafiga 10r1.
ag(e)afað: LARGIRI ‖ *pres. subj.* + *inf.* agefaiga 60v18.
eft-g(e)afung: REMUNERATIO ‖ *sg. acc.* + *dat.* eftgeafunge 28v7.
middan-geard: MUNDUS ‖ middangeard 1v7; 55r13[–]. middang' 9r4; 11r4. middan' 13v15; 49r4. *sg. gen.* middang'des 1v10. middang'es 19r12; 24v2. middangeard' 83ra10. middangear' 77r9. middang' 1v17; 55v10. middang 17r4. midg' 46r2. *mid' 78va22. *sg. dat.* middang'de 11r4; 15r15. middang' 88va20. middan' 81rb19.
uin-geard: uitis ‖ *sg. gen.* wingeard [*alt. f.* wingeardes] 2r2.
ungigearuad: NON UESTITUS ‖ ungigearuad 51v16.
gearuað: *a* INDUERE *b* PARARE *c* PRAESTARE ‖ *imp. sg.* gearua 22r8[c]; 25v18[c]. gearwa 11v6[c]. gearuig 24v8[c]; 25v5[c]. gearwig 9r5[c]; 28v8[c]. *pret. sg.* gearuade 51v2[b]. *pret. part.* gigearuad 88va 12[a]. gegearuad 80vb19[a]. gigearwad 14r7[a]. *pl. nom.* + *acc.* gigearuado 51v10[b].
gigearuað: PRAEPARARE ‖ *pret. sg.* gigearuade 36v12.
fore- (fora-) gearuað: PRAEPARARE ‖ *pres. ind. sg. 2* f'egearwast 3v21. *pret. sg.* f'egearuade 27v6. *pret. part. pl. nom.* + *acc.* f'egearuado 59r8.
gearu(u: *a* PARATUS *b* PROMPTUS (*c* existimare) ‖ gearu 77r14[b]. *sg. weak* gearua 22r9[b]. *adv.* gere 86rb8[(c)]. *pl. nom.* + *acc.* gearua 51v3[a]. *pl. dat.* gearuum 41v16[b].
agea(t)teð: EFFUNDERE ‖ *pres. ind. sg. 2* ageatas 3r2.
ald-geddung: antiquus ‖ aldgeddung 1r5.
gee, gie: *a* ETIAM *b* IAM ‖ gée 10v23[a]. gie 1r18[b].
gefend: LARGITOR ‖ gefend 47v2; 52r1.
for-gefend: praestabilis ‖ f'gefend 2v18.
gefeð: *a* DONARE *b* IMPENDERE *c* IMPERTIRE *d* LARGIRI ‖ *pres. subj.* + *inf.* gefe 18r7[a]. *imp. sg.* gef 11r21[d]; 32v9[b]; 33v1[c]; 80rb12[a]. *pres. part.* gefende 7v18[d]; 50v6[a]. *pl. nom.* + *acc.* gefendo 6r21[a].
agefeð: *a* EXHIBERE *b* IMMOLARE *c* IMPENDERE *d* INDULGERE *e* LARGIRI *f* OFFERRE *g* REDDERE ‖ *pres. subj.* + *inf.* agefe 4v6[a]; 41r12[g]. *imp. sg.* agef 8v18[c]; 19v14[g] 35v2[e]. *pret. sg. subj.* + *ind. 2* agefe 10v11[f]. *pret. part.* agefen 9v17[f]; 12r21[b]. *pl. nom.* + *acc.* agefeno 19v8[d]; 20r23[d].
for-gefeð: *a* CONCEDERE *b* DEMITTERE *c* IGNOSCERE *d* REMITTERE ‖ *pres. subj.* + *inf.* f'gefe 32r23[a]; 79ra2[b]. *imp. sg.* f'gef 1r17[a]; 32r14[c]. *infl. inf.* f'geafanne 5r21[c]. *pret. part. pl. nom.* + *acc.* f'gefeno 5v13[d]; 83rb14[d].
gefni(s)s(e: UENIA ‖ gefnise 20v4; 39v3.
eft-for-gefni(s)s(e: REMISSIO ‖ eftf'gefnise 46r17–18. eftf'gefnis' 57r18; 58r11.
for-gefni(s)s(e: *a* INDULGENTIA *b* REMISSIO *c* UENIA ‖ f'gefnisse 8v21[a]; 20r23[c]; 22v13[c]. f'gefnise 8v20[c]; 35r12[a]; 45v18[b]. forgefnis' 11v4[a].
gigegnað: OBUIARE ‖ gigegnað 22r14.
geldeð: REDDERE ‖ *pres. subj.* + *inf.* gelde 78va15. gelda 77v11.
ageldeð: REDDERE ‖ ageldes 29r15. *pres. subj.* + *inf.* agelde 26r5. agelda 6r2. *imp. sg.* ageld 33v21.
gemeleasni(s)s(e: NEGLIGENTIA ‖ *pl. dat.* gemeleasnisum 81va19.
gemeð: CURARE ‖ *pres. part. pl. dat.* gemendum 4v20.

agemeð: CURARE ‖ *pret. pl.* agemdon 21v7.
gemni(s)s(e: correptio ‖ gemnisse 21r11.
eft-bi-genga: recolere ‖ *pl. nom.* + *acc.* eftbigengo 11r18.
geond ‖ gind 55r13.
geong: *a* AMBULARE *b* GRESSUS *c* ITER ‖ geong 41v1[c]; 81rb1[c]. *sg. dat.* gionge 56r13[a]. *pl. nom.* + *acc.* geongo 78ra12[b].
gægn-geong: OBUIATIO ‖ gægngeong 87vb14.
i(n)n-geong: *a* ADITUS *b* INTROITUS ‖ inngeong 16r22[b]. in'geong 57r9[a].
ym(b)-geong: CIRCUITUS ‖ *sg. dat.* ymbgeonge 81vb11.
geongeð: AMBULARE ‖ geongað 17v18. *pres. subj.* + *inf.* geonga 12v21. gionga 18r12. *imp. sg.* geong 27v22. *pres. part.* geongende 28r2; 29v20. *pret. part.* gangen 55r17⁻.
bi-geongeð: *a* COLERE *b* EXERCERE *c* PERCOLERE *d* recensere ‖ bigeongað 14v17[a]; 24r15[a]. bigeongas 21v11[a]; 27v16[c]. *pres. subj.* + *inf.* bigeonga 36r17[a]; 83vb22[b]. *pres. part.* bigiongende 15r5[d].
eft-bi-geongeð: RECOLERE ‖ *pres. subj.* + *inf.* eftbigeonga 4v12.
i(n)n-geongeð: *a* INTRARE *b* INTROIRE ‖ *pres. subj.* + *inf.* inngeonga 4r5[b]; 50v15[a]. in'geonga 16r1[b].
bi-geonglo: CULTUS ‖ bigeongle 18v12. bigeon 12r2.
bi-geongni(s)s(e: kalendae ‖ begeongnise 85va9.
ofer-geotol, -geatul: OBLIUIOSUS ‖ of'geatul 14r18.
ofer-geotol- (geatul-) ni(s)s(e: *a* OBLIUIO *b* ignorantia ‖ of'geottolnisse 29v11[a]. *pl. nom.* + *acc.* of'giottulnisso 78rb8[b].
ger: ANNUS ‖ *sg. dat.* gere 47r20. *pl. dat.* gerum 88va13.
gere: *see* **gearu(u**.
gigerela: *a* INDUMENTUM *b* STOLA ‖ *pl. nom.* + *acc.* gigerela 23v2[b]. gigerila 49v5[a]; 49v7[a].
gerlic: ANNUUS ‖ *sg. dat.* gerlicum 7r4; 24v10. *sg. fem. acc.* + *dat.* gerlice 15r22. *pl. nom.* + *acc.* gerlico 2r22; 24r15. gerlica 26r7. gerlic' 4v16 [*alt. f.* gerlice]; 31r22.
gigerueð: INDUERE ‖ gigeruað 44r20. *pret. sg.* gigeride 22r19.
gest: HOSPES ‖ *pl. nom.* + *acc.* gestas 39v13.
get: ADHUC ‖ geet 61r16.
ond-get(t: *a* INTELLECTUS *b* INTELLIGENTIA *c* SENSUS ‖ ondget 40v7[c]; 77r15[c]. *sg. gen.* ondgetes 22v6[a]; 23r4[b]. ondgettes 22r18[a]; 40v9[a].
bi-ge(t)teð: *a* IMPETRARE *b* penetrare *c* quaerere ‖ *pres. subj.* + *inf.* bigette 8v8[a]. *pret. sg. ind. 1, 3* begætt 43v13[b]. *pret. part. pl. nom.* + *acc.* bigetno 7r9[c].
for-ge(t)teð: OBLIUISCI ‖ *pres. subj.* + *inf.* f'gette 81va18. f'geotta 78vb4.
on-ge(t)teð: *a* AGNOSCERE *b* COGNOSCERE *c* INTELLEGERE *d* NOSSE *e* ignoscere ‖ ongeattað 20v17[a]; 24v14[b]. *pres. ind. sg. 2* ongettest 19v23[e]. ongetest 83va19[c]. *pres. subj.* + *inf.* ongette 1v21[a]; 55r4[b]; 61r22[c]. ongett 19r10[b]. ongeatta 23v20[d]. *infl. inf.* ongeattanne 7v8[a]. *pret. sg. ind. 1, 3* ongæt 42r18[b]. *pret. pl.* ongeton 1r18[b]; 1v3[a].
ond-ge(t)tni(s)s(e: *a* AGNITIO *b* INTELLIGENTIA ‖ ondgetnisse 17v1[b]. ondgettnise 40r15[a]. *sg. gen.* ondgetnis' 40r5[a].
gif(e: SI ‖ gif 3v6; 4r23. gife 5r10.
gigoð: IUUENTUS ‖ gigoð 78vb15.
gigoðhad: IUUENTUS ‖ *sg. gen.* gigoðhades 78rb7. *sg. dat.* gigoðhade 79ra7.
gigoðlic: IUUENILIS ‖ gigoð' 46r22.
gimungað: NUBERE ‖ *pres. subj.* + *inf.* gimungia 52v10.
gimungo: NUPTIAE ‖ gimungo 51r22; 51v9. *gen.* gimungana 52r2; 52r11. gimunga' 34r9. *dat.* gimungum 51r23; 51v3.
gimungolic: NUPTIALIS ‖ gimungelic 51v18. *sg. dat.* gimungalicum 51v17.
gind: *see* **geond**.
aginneð: INCHOARE ‖ *pret. part. pl. nom.* + *acc.* agunneno 4v13; 4v14.
on-ginneð: *a* INCIPERE *b* INITIARE *c* INCHOARE ‖ onginnað *61v1[a]; 78r1[a]. *pres. subj.* + *inf.* onginne 7v22[a]. onginna 4r17[c]. *pres. part.* onginnenda 33v6[c]. *pl. nom.* + *acc.* onginnendo 4v5[c]; 50v9[c]. *pret. sg. ind. 1, 3* ongann 22r10[b].
yfel-giorni(s)s(e: *a* MALITIA *b* NEQUITIA ‖ yfelgiornisse 2v18[a]; 48v19[a]. *yfelgiornisse 6r20[a]. yfelgiornis' 12v3[a]. *sg. gen.* yfelgiornis' 41r21[a]. yfelgiorn' 47r6[b].
giuað: *a* APPETERE *b* EXPETERE *c* PETERE *d* POSCERE *e* POSTULARE ‖ giuað 52v8[b]. giuiað 44v5[e]; 59v6[c]. giugað 25r20[d]. *pres. ind. sg. 1* giwiga 56v7[c]. *pres. subj.* + *inf.* giuiga 50v1[a]; 82ra23[c]. *pres. part. pl. nom.* + *acc.* giuendo 82rb5[c]. *pret. part. pl. dat.* gigiuadum 59r19[b].
gigiuað: *a* APPETERE *b* COMPETERE *c* EXPOSCERE *d* POSTULARE ‖ gigiuað 49v16[c]. *pres. subj.* + *inf.* gigiuia 37r7[a]; gigiuiga 24r1[d]; 50r18[a]. *pres. part. sg. gen.* gigiuendes 23r4[b].
giung: (ADULESCENTULUS) ‖ *pl. nom.* + *acc.* giungo 53r15.
giuung: POSTULARE ‖ *sg. gen.* giwunges 19r21.
gla(d)dað: *a* LAETARI *b* LAETIFICARE ‖ *pres. ind. sg. 2* gladias 37v7[b]. *pres. subj.* + *inf.* gladia 35v4[a]; 38r16[a]. *imp. sg.* glada 32v22[b]. *pres. part. pl. nom.* + *acc.* gladiendo 4v16[a]. *pret. part.* gigladad 32v5[b]. *pl. nom.* + *acc.* gigladado 17r22[b].
gigla(d)dað: *a* GAUDERE *b* LAETARI *c* LAETIFICARE ‖ *pres. ind. sg. 2* gigladas 15v1[c]; 25v10[c]; 25v10[c]. gigladias 24v 17[c]; 25r19[c]. *pres. subj.* + *inf.* gigladia 4v18[a]; 15v23[b]; 30v19[c]; 34v18[b] [*alt. f.* gilgladia]. gigladiga 9r1[c]; 18v23[a]; 24r12[b]. *imp. sg.* giglada 27r21[c]. *pret. sg.* gigladade 85rb17[a].
glæd(d: *a* LAETARI *b* LAETUS ‖ glæd 85va11[b]. *sg. fem.* glædo 19r14[(a)]. *pl. nom.* + *acc.* glado 80vb20[(a)].
glædni(s)s(e: *a* GAUDIUM *b* LAETITIA ‖ glædnise 20r7[a]; 32v14[b]. glædnisse 14v18[b]; 35r20[b]. glæd' 23r7[b]. *sg. gen.* glædnis' 15r14[b]. *pl. nom.* + *acc.* glædniso 27v10[b].
giglædni(s)s(e: GAUDIUM ‖ *pl. nom.* + *acc.* giglædnisso 15v2.
gloed: SCINTILLA ‖ *pl. nom.* + *acc.* gloedo 41v9.
god: *a* BONUS (*b* balsamum) ‖ god 6r3[a]; 6r15[a]; 6v8[a] [*alt. f.* godum]; 17v7[a] [*alt. f.* gode]; gód 6v5[a]. *sg. gen.* godes 7v1[a]. *sg. dat.* godum 56v11[a]; 79ra11[a]. gode 13v11[a]. *pl. nom.* + *acc.* godo 17v20[a]; 22r13[a]. *pl. gen.* godra 45v8[a]; 49v13[a]. *pl. dat.* godum 7r7[a]; 81rb4[a]. *comp.* betra 24r7[a]. betre 39r8[a]. *pl. nom.* + *acc.* betro 2r11[a]. *sup.* beteste 33r11[(b)].
godcund: DIUINUS ‖ godcund 37r13; *88va22. *sg. gen.* godcundes 59r11. *sg. dat.* godcunde 46r12. *pl. dat.* godcundum 83vb23.
godcundni(s)s(e: DIUINITAS ‖ godcund' 58r3.
god(d: *a* DEUS (*b* Asmodeus) (*c* caritas) ‖ god 1r4[a]; 67r5[(b)]. go 12r5[a]. g' 58v3[a]. *sg. gen.* godes 1r10[a]; 3v1[(c)]. goddes 52r20[a]. god' 48r10[a]; 58r8[a]. *sg. dat.* gode 5r24[a]; 5v7[a]. *pl. gen.* *godana 48r17[a].
godlic: BENIGNUS ‖ *sg. dat.* godlicum 4v5.
godscip(e: BONITAS ‖ godscipe 6r13; 47v20.
godspell: *a* EUANGELIUM (*b* EUANGELIZARE) ‖ godspell 21v9[(b)]; 29r4[a]. *sg. dat.* *godspelle 56r2[a].
godspellere: EUANGELISTA ‖ godspellere 25v2; 88ra4. godspelle' 22v 18; 35r4. godsp' 88ra7; 88ra11. *sg. gen.* godspelleres 22v10. godspelle' 22v15. godspell' 22v12. *pl. nom.* +

acc. godspelleras 40r2; 55r11. godspeller' 23r7. godspelle' 54v7.
gold: AURUM ‖ gold 27v20; 41v6. *sg. gen.* goldes 39r9. *sg. dat.* golde 12r10.
gigri(p)peð: *a* APPREHENDERE *b* COMPREHENDERE ‖ *pres. subj.* + *inf.* gigrippe 22r14[a]. gigrippa 19r23[b]; 30v11[b]. gigripa 3r10[b]. *imp. sg.* gegríp 78rb14[a].
to-gigri(p)peð: APPREHENDERE ‖ *pres. subj.* + *inf.* togigripe 1v22.
grund: *a* FUNDAMENTUM *b* PROFUNDUM ‖ grund 39v15[a]. *sg. dat.* grunde 29v22[b]. *pl. dat.* grundum 83rb19[b].
bryd-guma: SPONSUS ‖ brydegume 50v20.
gylden: AUREUS ‖ gylden' 34r5. *sg. dat.* gylden' 34r7. *pl. nom.* + *acc.* gyldenno 2r15.
gyltend: LAPSUS ‖ gyltend 85va13.
agylteð: DELINQUERE ‖ *pres. part. pl. gen.* agyltendra 19v8.
gylting: *a* COMMISSIO *b* DELICTUM *c* PRAEUARICATO ‖ *sg. gen.* gyltincges [*alt. f.* giltincges] 52v13[c]. *sg. acc.* + *dat.* gyltinge 55r1[a]. *pl. nom.* + *acc.* gyltinga 78rb7[b]. *pl. dat.* gyltingum 32r14[b]; 60v21[b].
agylting: *a* CULPA *b* REATUS ‖ *sg. gen.* agyltinges 8v21[b]. *pl. gen.* agyltingo 11r21[a].
fore- (fora-) gyrdeð: PRAECINGERE ‖ *imp. sg.* f'egyrd 28r13.
ym(b)-gyrdeð: CIRCUMCINGERE ‖ *pret. sg.* ymbgyrde 38r2.
gyrdils: ZONA ‖ *sg. dat.* gyrdilse 38r3.
had: GRADUS ‖ had 87va10. *sg. dat.* hade 80vb16. *pl. dat.* hadum 87ra11.
hal: *a* SALUUS *b* SANUS ‖ hal 9v19[a]; 9v20[a]. *sg. acc. masc.* halne 80ra23[a]. *pl. nom.* + *acc.* halo 10v21[a]; 56r14[b].
hæg-hal: INCOLUMIS ‖ *pl. nom.* + *acc.* hæghalo 47r14; 80va20. hæghael 60v6.
haldend: *a* CONSERUATOR *b* CUSTOS ‖ haldend 30v4[b]; 47v1[a].
bi-hald(e)n(n)i(s)s(e: *a* CONTINENTIA *b* OBSERUANTIA *c* OBSERUATIO ‖ bihaldennisse 4v6[b]. bihaldnisse 7r5[c]. bihaldnise 3v20[b]. *sg. gen.* bihaldennisses 8r7[b]. bihaldennises 49v19[a].
haldeð: *a* CONSERUARE *b* CONTINERE *c* CUSTODIRE *d* DETINERE *e* OBTINERE *f* SERUARE *g* TENERE ‖ haldað 86va19[g]. haldes 22v16[e]. *pres. subj.* + *inf.* halde 20v23[e]. halda 15v10[c]; 43v15[g]. *pres. part.* haldende 11r7[f]; 28r7[(f)]. *pret. sg. ind. 1, 3* heald 10r14[f]. *pret. part.* halden 52r5[f]. gihalden 11r8[c]; 12r9[a]; 40v11[b]; 48v1[d]. *pl. nom.* + *acc.* gihaldeno 60v4[c].
gihaldeð: *a* ABSTINERE *b* CONSERUARE *c* CONTINERE *d* CUSTODIRE *e* OBTINERE *f* SERUARE *g* TENERE ‖ gehaldað 86vb7[g]. gihaldeð 5r12[d]. gihaldað 8r5[a]. *gihaldes 41v22[e]. *pres. subj.* + *inf.* gehalda 81va4[d]; 82vb19[d]. gihalde 14r22[d]; 15r2[g]. gihalda 2v10[e]; 49v12[d]; 58r2[g]; 61v8[b]; 77r3[f]. *infl. inf.* gihaldenne 49v15[b]. *imp. sg.* gihald 3v19[d]; 14v6[b]; 20r5[c]. gehald 82ra11[b]. *pres. part. pl. nom.* + *acc.* gihaldendo 60v5[d]. *pret. sg. ind. 1, 3* giheald 8r20[d]; 29r14[f]; 42r18[b]. geheald 88vb12[g]. *pret. sg. subj.* + *ind. 2* gihealde 42r14[b]. *pret. pl.* gihealdon 51v6[g].
ahaldeð: SERUARE ‖ *pret. part.* ahalden 52r17.
bi-haldeð: *a* ABSTINERE *b* ASPICERE *c* INTENDERE *d* INTUERI ‖ bihaldað 17v13[b]. *pres. subj.* + *inf.* bihalde 3r12[a]. bihalda 8v1[a]; 28v18[d]. *imp. sg.* bihald 7r22[c]; 7v14[b]. *pres. part. pl. nom.* + *acc.* bihaldendo 8v7[a]; 13v4[b].
eft-bi-haldeð: RESPICERE ‖ *imp. sg.* eftbihald 20r3; 20v15.
to-bi-haldeð: ATTENDERE ‖ tobihaldað 27r2.
half: (*a* ALTERUTER) (*b* UTERQUE) ‖ *pl. nom.* + *acc.* halfe 52r6[(b)]. halfa 14r13[(a)].
halgað, hælgað: *a* CONSECRARE *b* SACER *c* SANCTIFICARE ‖ *pres. subj.* + *inf.* hælgia 58v15[c]. *imp. sg.* halga 55r21. *pret. part.* gihalgad 37v1[a]. *sg. gen.* *hælgades 19r5[b]. *sg. dat.* gihalgadum 31v8[c]. *pl. nom.* + *acc.* gihalgado 33r8[c]. gehalgode 55r15. gihælgado 47r17[c]; 56r19[c].
gihalgað, -hælgað: *a* CONSECRARE *b* DEDICARE *c* SANCTIFICARE ‖ *pres. subj.* + *inf.* gihalgia 47r13[c]; 55v16[c]. gihalgiga 45r7[c]; 49v17[c]. gihælgia 55v12[c]; 56v8[c]. *imp. sg.* gihalga 11r20[c]; 36v18[c]. *pret. sg.* gihalgade 26v12[c]. *pret. sg. ind. 2* gihælgadest 28v4[a]; 55v10[c]. gihaelgadest 21v16[b]. gihælgedest 1v7[a].
halgere, hælgere: SANCTIFICATOR ‖ hælgare 30v4. *hælge' 40v3.
halgung, hælgung: creatura ‖ hælgung 66r1.
salt-halgung, -hælgung ‖ *sg. acc.* + *dat.* salthalguncge 57r10.
uæter-halgung, -hælgung ‖ waeterhalgunc 57v1. *sg. acc.* + *dat.* waeterhalguncge 56v15.
halig, hælig: (*a* MYSTERIUM) *b* SACER *c* SACRAMENTUM *d* SACRATUS (*e* SACRIFICIUM) *f* SANCTUS ‖ halig 9r1[f]; 12v6[f]. *sg. fem.* halga 10v1[f]; 32r9[f]. halgae 33v5[f]. hælgo 41r13[f]; 53r9[f]. *sg. gen.* halges 3v20[(c)]; 8r7[f]; 77v5[b]. halgæs 50r8[f]. halg' 37r14[f]; 41r8[f]. hal' 41r18[f]; 43r21[f]. hælges 2r5[f]; 22r2[(a)]. hælg' 38v9[f]. hæl' 77r13[f]. hael' 36r4[f]. *sg. dat.* halgum 34v5[f]; 79rb19[f] [*alt. f.* halge]. hælgum 55v13[f]. *sg. acc. masc.* haligne 6r17[f]; 16r21[f]. halig' 27r9[f]; 47v3[f]. *sg. weak* halga 14v5[d]; 38v10[b]; 49v22[f]. hælga 45r8[f]. hælge/[a] 66r20[f]. haelga 18r5[f]. halgan 55r9; 55r16. haligan 55r10. *pl. nom.* + *acc.* halgo 4r4[f]; 8r16[f]. halga 11v4[(c)]; 30r12[f] [*alt. f.* halgawaras]; 42v8[e]. hælgo 3v22[f]; 59r6[(c)]. halgan 55r12–13. *pl. gen.* haligra 26r16[f]; 39v14[f]. haligra' 44v12[f]. haliga' 44v8[f]. halig' 40r18[f]. halga 30v15[f]. hælgana 4r5[f]. *pl. dat.* halgum 4r16[f]; 9r4[(c)]; 36r17[c]; 41r17[b]. halig' 42r10[f]; *42v19[f]. *sup.* halgast 39v19[f].
halig- (hælig-)dom: *a* SACRAMENTUM *b* SANCTIMONIUM ‖ hæligdom 15r1[a]. *pl. nom.* + *acc.* haligdom' 47v19[b].
halig- (hælig-) ni(s)s(e: SANCTITAS ‖ halignis' 53r23.
hall: AULA ‖ hall 31v21. *sg. acc.* + *dat.* halle 45v13.
halni(s)s(e: (INCOLUMITAS) ‖ haln' 59r16.
halsað: *a* ADIURARE *b* EXORCIZARE ‖ *pres. ind. sg. 1* halsigo 48r5[b]; 67r1[a]. halsiga 57r11[b]. *pres. subj.* + *inf.* halsige 55r7[–]. *pret. part.* gihalsad 48r7[b]; 54v12[a]. gihal' 58v5[b].
gihalsað: *a* ADIURARE *b* EXORCIZARE ‖ *pres. ind. sg. 1* gihalsigo 54v6[a]; *66r4–5[a]. gihalsige 54v10[a]. *pres. subj.* + *inf.* gihalsia 57v16[b].
halsere: EXORCISTA ‖ hælsere 87ra22.
halsung ‖ *pl. nom.* + *acc.* halsuncge 55r6.
halt: CLAUDUS ‖ halt 27v18. *sg. weak* halta 28r1.
halu(o)ende: *a* SALUATOR *b* SALUTARIS *c* salubritas *d* sanctus ‖ halwoende 8r17[b]; 11v21[b]. haluoende 46v21[c]; 47v8[b]. haluoende' 78va5[d]. halwende 1v9[b]; 1v20[b]. haluende 80vb14[b]. halwoend 10r1[b]. haluoend' 41r9[b]; 59r18[c]. haluoen' 79ra15[b]. halwoend' 7r13[b]. *sg. gen.* halwoendes 22r2[b]; 22v7[b]. haluoendes 40v8[b]; 60v11[b]. halwendes 1v12[a]. *sg. dat.* haluoendum 80rb5[b]. *pl. dat.* halwoendum 8v6[b].
halu(o)endlice: SALUBRITER ‖ halwoendlice 4v20.
gihappia: *see* **giheapað**.
hat: PROMISSIO ‖ *sg. gen.* hates' 7r8.
gihat: *a* PROMISSIO *b* PROMISSUM ‖ *pl. nom.* + *acc.* gihato 44r22[a]. *pl. dat.* gihatum 16v1[b].
hat: CALIDUS ‖ hat 86rb17; 86va8.
hata: *see* **ata**.
hateð: *a* APPELLARE *b* IUBERE *c* PRAECIPERE ‖ *pres. ind. sg. 2* hates 15v20[c]. *imp. sg.* hat 57r1[b]. *pret. sg. ind. 1, 3* heht 58v4[b]. *pret. part.* haten 45v10[a].
gihateð: *a* IUBERE *b* PRAECIPERE *c* PROMITTERE ‖ *pres. ind. sg. 2* gihates 43r13[b]. *pres. subj.* + *inf.* gehate 67r2[a].

pret. sg. ind. 1, 3 giheht 31v3[b]; 57r13[a]. pret. sg. ind. 2 gihetest 49v6[c].
eft-gihateð: REPROMITTERE ‖ pret. sg. ind. 1, 3 eftgiheht 41r3.
lond-hæbbend(e: tribunus ‖ lond-hæbbende 86vb11.
hæfeð, næfeð: HABERE ‖ hæfeð 43v5; 61r20. habbað 6v10; 43v14. pres. ind. sg. 1 hafo 27v20. pres. ind. sg. 2 hæfeð 5v7. pres. subj. + inf. hæbbe 60r14; 60v7. næbbe 57v18[+]. habba 11r12; 37r3. abba [alt. f. habba] 42v11[+]. pres. part. hæbbend [alt. f. hæbbende] 34r4. næbbende 51v18[+]. pl. nom. + acc. hæbbendo 6v8; 23r12. pl. gen. hæbbendra 34r12. pret. sg. næfde 43v9[+]. pret. pl. hæfdon 37r2.
for-hæfeð: ABSTINERE ‖ pres. subj. + inf. f'habba 8r11.
hæfteð: damnare ‖ pret. part. gehæftad 88va10.
for-hæf(t)ni(s)s(e: a ABSTINENTIA b ABSTINERE ‖ f'hæf[t]nise 7r6[b]. f'hæfnise 7r23[a]. f'hæfnisse 77r9[a].
gihæld, -hald: CUSTODIA ‖ gehæld 82va9; 83ra14. gehald 81vb22. gihæld 60r14. giheaeld 82rb16.
hælend(e: a IESUS b SALUATOR ‖ hælend 10v3[a]; 11r10[b]. haelende 55r8[−]. hælen' 13v4[a]. hæl' 11v18[a]; 12v17[a]. h' 13v13[a]; 58r17[a]. sg. gen. hælendes 1v12[b]; 6v1[a]. hælend' 11r4[a]. hael' 57r21[a]. hæ' 58r8[a].
hæleð: a SALUARE b SANARE ‖ hæleð 78vb7[b]. pres. ind. sg. 2 hæles 22r6[a]. pres. subj. + inf. hæle 3r5[a]. imp. sg. hæl 79va9[a]; 79vb23[b]. pret. part. hæled 9v19[b]; 58v4[b]. gihæled 32r16[a]; 57r13[b]. pl. nom. + acc. hæledo 20v6[a]. gihæledo 8v5[a]; 57r16[b]. gihældo 13v2[a].
gihæleð: a SALUARE b SANARE ‖ pres. subj. + inf. gihæle 61v7[a]. imp. sg. gihæl 9v19[b]; *18r22[a]; 55v21[b]. pret. sg. gehælde 88vb11[a]. pret. sg. ind. 2 gihældest 17r20[a]; 49r4[a]. gihæledest 55v22[b].
hæl(i)g(-: see **hal(i)g(-**.
hælo: a SALUATIO b SALUS c SANITAS ‖ hælo 1v10[b]; 33v8[c]. haelo 58v6[c]; 81ra15[c]. hæle 47v6[b]; 57r18[c]. hæl' 14r10[b]. sg. gen. hæles 5v18[b]; 5v20[b]. hæle' 47v2[b]. hælo' 16v3[a].
hæs: a IMPERIUM b IUSSIO c IUSSUS ‖ hæs 49r6[c]; 54v18[a]; 86va18[a]. sg. dat. hæse 47r4[a]; 47r11[b].
hæsere: IMPERATOR ‖ hæsere 86va18; 86va21–2.
hæto: CALOR ‖ haeto 77r22.
hæðen: a GENTILIS b gens ‖ pl. nom. + acc. *hæðno 88vb16[a]. hædno 66v17[b]. pl. gen. hæðna 29r22[b]. hæðenra 46v6[a]. hæðinra 3v16[b]. pl. dat. hæðnum 28v5[b].
he: a ILLE b IPSE c IS d SE e SEMET f SUUS A—making a Latin Third Person B—other insertional usages ‖ sg. masc. nom. he 2v8[a]; 9v18[(b)]; 19v16[B]; 21r16[A]; 34r14[b]. sg. masc. acc. hine 1r2[c]; 3r11[d]; 6r9[e]; 9v23[a]; 37r12[B]. sg. gen. his 1v20[c]; 2r19[f]; 86vb11[B]. sg. dat. him 4r23[c]; 13r6[a]; 13r8[d]; 55r21[−]. sg. fem. acc. hia 8r4[d]; 17r2[c]; 22r14[a]. sg. fem. gen. + dat. hir 25r13[c]; 33v17[d]. hire 33v6[c]; 49v19[f]. pl. nom. + acc. hia 3r13[A]; 5r3[c]; 16r17[B]; 50r4[d]. hie 28v7[A]; 36v15[A]. pl. gen. hiora 5r4[f]; 14r22[c]; 35v8[a]. hio' 41v11[a]. hiara 2v20[c]; 2v21[c]. pl. dat. him 2r23[B]; 21v5[a]; 58r13[c].
heafod: CAPUT ‖ heafud 37v16. heafut 42r17. sg. gen. heafdes 45v22; 46r12.
hea(n)ni(s)s(e: a ALTITUDO b ALTUM c CELSITUDO d SUBLIMITAS ‖ heannisse 1r9[a]. heannise 16r2[c]. heanisse 39v22[b]. sg. gen. heannis' 1r19[c]; 46v6[d].
giheapað: ACCUMULARE ‖ pres. subj. + inf. gihappia [? read giheappia] 41r7.
h(e)ard: DURUS ‖ heard 9v6.
h(e)arpa: CITHARA ‖ pl. dat. hearpum 23r18.
h(e)arpað: CITHARIZARE ‖ pres. part. pl. gen. hearpandra 23r17.
h(e)arpere: CITHAROEDUS ‖ pl. gen. hearpara 23r17.
heart: CERUUS ‖ pl. nom. + acc. heartas 57r6.
mild-(milt-)heart: a MISERICORS b PROPITIUS ‖ mildheart 2v16[a]; 16r3[a]. miltheart 8r10[b]; 16v14[a]. miltheort 7v10[b]; 78vb5[b]. sg. weak milthearta 11v20[a]; 11v22[a]. pl. nom. + acc. miltheorto 6r21[a].
hearta: COR ‖ hearta 40v14; 61r7. hearte 1v20; 2v14. heorte 49r13. sg. gen. heart' 49v8. heart 77r6. pl. nom. + acc. hearta 2v15; 3v21. hearto 81rb16; 83ra7. heorta 79rb12. pl. dat. heartum 1r22; 1v11. heortum 8r23; 27v1.
mild-(milt-)heartlice: MISERICORDITER ‖ miltheartlice 3v13. milthe..tlice 35r1.
efne-heartni(s)s(e: CONCORDIA ‖ efneheorta' 77r24. sg. gen. efnehearta' 52r3.
mild-(milt-)heartni(s)s(e: a MISERATIO b MISERICORDIA ‖ miltheartnisse 8v3[b]; 80vb13[b]. miltheartnise 12v10[b]; 61r2[b]. miltheartnis' 7r11[b]; 12r2[b]. *miltheortnise 20v22[b]. miltheortnis' 7v15[b]. miltheart' 12v10[b]; 17r1[b]. sg. gen. miltheartniss'es 6v17[b]. miltheartnis' 29v11[b]. miltheart' 2v17[b]. pl. gen. miltheartnisa 78rb5[b]. pl. dat. miltheartnisum 22r4[a].
ofer-hebbendlic: superexaltatus ‖ of'hebbendlic 82vb9; 82vb14.
gihefeð: EXALTARE ‖ gihebbað 9r16.
ahefeð: a ERIGERE b EXALTARE c EXTOLLERE d LEUARE e ORIRI f TOLLERE ‖ ahefeð 40v11[b]. ahefað 9r15[d]; 9r16[d]. pres. subj. + inf. ahebbe 10r6[d]. imp. sg. ahef 17r10[a]; *80rb1[c]. pres. part. ahebbende 51r9[f]. pret. sg. ind. 1, 3 ahof 28r4[a]; 83ra23[d]. pret. part. ahefen 31v14[b]; 31v17[b]. sg. dat. ahefene 77r2[e].
eft-ahefeð: RELEUARE ‖ pret. part. pl. nom. + acc. eftahefeno 19r17.
ofer-ahefeð: SUPEREXALTARE ‖ pres. subj. + inf. of'ahebba 82vb17.
under-hefeð: SUBLEUARE ‖ pret. part. underhefen 38r21; 38v14.
u(p)p)-ahefeð: a ELEUARE b EXALTARE ‖ imp. sg. upahef 2v19[b]. pret. part. upahefen 1r13[a].
hefig: GRAUIS ‖ hefig 50r15; 52v17.
hef(i)gað: a AGGRAUARE b GRAUARE ‖ hefigað 24r19[b]. pret. part. gihefigad 3r6[a].
gihef(i)gað: ingrassari ‖ pres. part. sg. dat. gihefgindum 49r13.
hefigni(s)s(e: a PONDUS b molestia ‖ hefignisse 7v15[a]; 18v2[b]. hefignise 25r8[a].
heg: silua ‖ pl. dat. hegum 57v10.
heh: a ALTUS b EXCELSUS c SUMMUS d SUPERNUS e aeternus ‖ heh 1r6[b]; 17r6[c]. sg. dat. heum 48v3[c]. comp. herra 43v9[b]. sup. heista 40v15[a]; 50v14[c]. heiste 39v17[c]. hesta 17r6[c]. heste 40v12[e]; 44r16[a]. sup. sg. gen. heistes 33r9[a]; 38r22[d]. heista' 42r15[b]; 58r8[c].
hehangla: see **heh-engel**.
hehfara: a altilis b hircus ‖ pl. nom. + acc. hehfaro 51v3[a]. pl. gen. heffera 10r22[b].
heh-(heg-)stald: a UIRGO b uirginitas ‖ sg. gen. hehstaldes 25r10[a]; 50r9[b]. hehstald' 32r21[a]; 33r21[a]. sg. dat. hehstalde 33v13[a]; 61v4[a]. heghstalde 61v2[a]. pl. nom. + acc. hehstaldo 23v1[a]; 50r3[a]. pl. gen. hehstaldra 50v6[a]; 54v6[a]. hehstalda 36r6[a].
heh-(heg-)staldhad: UIRGINITAS ‖ sg. gen. hehstaldhad' 50v4. hehstald' 50v8; 50v13.
heh-(heg-)stal(d)lic: UIRGINALIS ‖ sg. acc. + dat. fem. hehstallic' 31v21.
heh-(heg-)staldni(s)s(e: UIRGINITAS ‖ hehstaldnise 22r15.
hell: INFERNUS ‖ sg. acc. + dat. helle 88va11.
helm: a GALEA b lorica ‖ sg. dat. helme 14r7[b] [deleted]; 44r20[a].
help: a ADIUTORIUM b ADIUUARE c AUXILIUM d FOUERE e SUBSIDIUM f fauor ‖ sg. acc. + dat. helpe 7v20[b];

8r7[e]; 8r12[c]; 8v12[f]; 77r5[d]; 79vb20[a]. *pl. dat.* helpum 29v9[c].
helpend: *a* ADIUTOR *b* AUXILIATOR *c* AUXILIATUS ‖ helpend 9r21[c]; 9v5[b]; 22r11[a].
helpeð: *a* ADIUUARE *b* CONFOUERE *c* FOUERE ‖ *pres. subj.* + *inf.* helpa 59v16[c]. *infl. inf.* helpanne 78va20[a]. *imp. sg.* help 81vb2[a]. *pres. part.* helpende 15v9[a]. *pret. part.* holpen 31r17[a]; 42v16[c]. giholpen 24r12[a]. *pl. nom.* + *acc.* holpeno 37v14[a]; 39v5[a]. giholpeno 27r18[a]; 40r14[b].
gihelpeð: *a* ADIUUARE *b* CONFOUERE *c* FOUERE *d* REFOUERE ‖ *pres. ind. sg. 2* gihelpes 82rb6[a]. *pres. subj.* + *inf.* gihelpe 33v5[a]; 43v19[c]. gihelpa 26r4[c]; 38v10[b]. *imp. sg.* gihelp 4v14[a]; 7v11[d]. *pret. sg. ind. 1, 3* gihalp 5v18[a].
ahelpeð: *a* ADIUUARE *b* FOUERE *c* suffragari ‖ *pret. part.* aholpen 22v16[a]; 29v9[b]. *pl. nom.* + *acc.* aholpeno 15r6[b]; 33v17[c].
gihene: caducus ‖ *pl. nom.* + *acc.* *geheno 35va8.
heneð: *a* CONTEMNERE *b* DESPICERE ‖ *imp. sg.* hen 21r4[b]. *pret. part. pl. nom.* + *acc.* gihenedo 13v7[a].
heofon: *a* CAELUM *b* caelestis ‖ heofon 56v6[a]; 79vb21[a]. *sg. gen.* heofnes 28v11[b]; 48v3[a]. heof' 78ra7[a]. *sg. dat.* heofne 21v1[a]; 23v6[a]. *pl. nom.* + *acc.* heofnas 10r7[a]; 21v2[a]. *pl. gen.* heofna 51r21[a]; 52v20[b]. heafna 1v9[a]; 31r13[a]. *pl. dat.* heofnum 12r9[a]; 59v16[a]. heofnu [? *read* heofnum] 43v9[a]. heof' 79vb 18[a]; 80vb3[a].
heofonlic: CAELESTIS ‖ heofonlic 7v8; 20v18. *sg. gen.* heofonlices 8r21; 16v6. heofonlic' 47v4. *sg. dat.* heofonlicum 8r21. heofonlic' 15r16; 17v3. heofunlicum 18v20; 32r19. *pl. nom.* + *acc.* heofonlico 9r2; 16v19. heofonlic' 45v18. heof' 46r18. hoeofonl' 45r20. *pl. dat.* heofonlicum 7r15; 16v13.
heolstrung: CALIGO ‖ heolstrung 83rb7.
heona: HINC ‖ heona 47r4.
heona-ong(e)ægn: contra ‖ heonongægn 85ra20.
heonu, -o: ECCE ‖ heono 1r2; 1r13. heone 5v19; 51v2.
her: HIC ‖ her 48r8; 55r15.
hera: MINISTER ‖ *pl. nom.* + *acc.* hero 5v23.
here: *a* AGMEN *b* EXERCITUS (*c* consul) (*d* sabaoth) ‖ here 57v19[b]; 86vb1[b]. *sg. gen.* herges 1r6[(d)]; 86va23[(c)]. hergies 17v20[(b)]. hergas 86va20[(c)]. *pl. nom.* + *acc.* hergia 54v2[a]. *pl. dat.* hergum 51v8[b].
hereni(s)s(e: LAUS ‖ herenisse 9v20; 29v18. herenise 1r1; 15r4. heren' 82vb4. herer' [? *read* heren'] 78ra10. *sg. gen.* herenis' 80va14. *pl. nom.* + *acc.* herenisso 77v11. *pl. dat.* herenissum 18v20; 60r9. herenis' 83vb23.
hereð: *a* AUDIRE *b* AUDITOR *c* SERUIRE ‖ *pres. part.* herende 9v8[a]; 59r10[c]. *pl. nom.* + *acc.* herendo 14r15[b]. *pl. dat.* herendum 6r16[a]. *pret. part.* gihered 23r1[a]; 25v4[a].
gihereð: *a* AUDIRE *b* DESERUIRE *c* EXAUDIRE *d* FAMULARI *e* SERUIRE ‖ giherað 23v5[e]; 27r2[a]; 43r10[d]. giheres 61r12[b]. *pres. subj.* + *inf.* gihere 3r7[c]; 13r2[e]; 19v15[b]; 21r12[a]. gihera 8v11[e]; 61r21–2[a]. *infl. inf.* giherann 14r2[a]. *imp. sg.* giher 3v11[c]; 3v17[c]. geher 81ra3[c]; 81rb5[c]. *pret. sg.* giherde 5v17[c]; 23r15[a]. *pret. sg. ind. 2* giherdest 78ra14[c].
hereð: LAUDARE ‖ heriað 54v1. *pres. subj.* + *inf.* herga 82vb17. *pres. part.* hergiende 28r2.
gihereð: *a* COLLAUDARE *b* LAUDARE ‖ gihergað 40v21[a]; 77v17[b]. gheriað 37r13[b]; 77v18[b]. *pres. subj.* + *inf.* gihergia 78ra5[b]. *pret. pl.* giheredon 33r16[b].
ahereð: LAUDARE ‖ *pret. part. sg. fem.* aheredo 50r17.
herg(i)endlic: *a* LAUDABILIS *b* LAUDABILITER ‖ hergendlic 82vb12[a]. hergiendlic 82vb7[a]. *adv.* hergiendlice 50r17[b].
herg(i)ere: LAUDATOR ‖ *pl. nom.* + *acc.* hergeras 60v7.
herni(s)s(e: *a* AUDITUS *b* MINISTERIUM *c* OBSEQUIUM *d* OFFICIUM *e* SERUITIUM *f* SERUITUS *g* mysterium ‖ hernisse 15r5[g]; 17v1[d]; 33v17[c]; 42v17[c] [*alt. f.* hernissum]; 56r12[a]. hernise 4v21[e]; 5v21[b]; 14v8[f]; 17v4[g]; 26r5[c]; 81va8[a]; 85vb11[d]. hernis' 16r11[g]. *sg. gen.* hernisses 40r4[b]. hernisse' 59r9[g]. hernis' 47r1[d]. *pl. nom.* + *acc.* hernisso 34r16[b]. *pl. dat.* hernisum 46v5[d].
giherni(s)s(e: AUDITUS ‖ gihernis 9v12.
ned-herni(s)s(e: SERUITUS ‖ nedhernise 3r16.
hersum(m: OBOEDIENS ‖ hersum 10v8.
gihersumað: *a* FAMULARI *b* MINISTRARI ‖ gihersumaiað 51r6[b]. *pres. subj.* + *inf.* gihersumiga 7v16[a].
hersumni(s)s(e: OBOEDIENTIA ‖ hersumnisse 47v21.
hi(d)dir: HUC ‖ hidir 51v18.
higo: *a* FAMILIA *b* FAMULUS ‖ higo 7r5[a]; 7r16[a]. *dat.* higum 15r1[b].
i(n)n-higo: DOMESTICI ‖ inhigo 39v14.
to-higung: *a* AFFECTUS *b* EFFECTUS ‖ tohigung 4r2[a]; 9r8[a]; 30v11[b]. *sg. acc.* + *dat.* tohigunge 17v6[b].
hiorde: PASTOR ‖ hiorde 5r3; 13v9. *sg. gen.* hiordes 16r2. *pl. nom.* + *acc.* hiordo 40r3; 58r5. hiord' 58r7.
hiorod: FAMILIA ‖ hiorad 8r20. *sg. gen.* hiorodes 14v6; 20r22.
hlaf: PANIS ‖ hlaf 47r18. *sg. gen.* hlafes 67r16. *sg. dat.* hlafe 22v6; 40v9. *pl. nom.* + *acc.* lafo 47r19.
hlaferd, -ard: DOMINUS ‖ hlaferd 66v19.
hlaferd- (hlafard-) scip(e: DOMINATIO ‖ *sg. gen.* [h]lafardscipes 83ra17–18.
hlæhtor: RISUS ‖ *sg. dat.* læht' 56r12.
hlear: GENA ‖ leur 2r14. *pl. nom.* + *acc.* hleawro 9v2.
i(n)n-hleaðriað: INSONARE ‖ *inleaðr... 77r4.
ðerh-hleaðriað: PERSONARE ‖ *pres. subj.* + *inf.* *ðerhleaðria[1] 77r15.
hleo: REFUGIUM ‖ hleo 19v19.
hlinað: DISCUMBERE ‖ *pres. part. pl. nom.* + *acc.* lingendo 51v16. *pl. gen.* lingendra 51v15.
gihlinað: EXCUBARE ‖ geliniað 87ra 15.
ahloefeð: EUELLERE ‖ *pres. subj.* + *inf.* ahloefa 26v20.
hlysnere: AUDITOR ‖ lysnere 14r18.
gihlytto: *a* CONSORTIUM *b* SORS ‖ gihlytto 19r8[a]; 45v19[a]. gilytto 11r13[a]. gehlytte 86ra16[b]. *dat.* gihlyttum 38r 16[a].
mið-gihlytto: CONSORTIUM ‖ *dat.* miðgihlyttum 44v21.
to-gihlytto: CONSORTIUM ‖ togihlytto 52v8.
of-dune-ahnigeð: exinanire ‖ *pret. sg. ind. 1, 3* ofduneahnag 10v5.
ahoeð: crucifigere ‖ *pret. part.* ahoen 13r1.
hoga: PRUDENS ‖ hoga 50r15.
hogascip(e: PRUDENTIA ‖ hogascip 39r8. hogascipe 39r12.
for-hogdni(s)s(e: CONTEMPTUS ‖ f'-hogdnise 49v8.
hond: MANUS ‖ hond 3r5; 9r16. *sg. acc.* + *dat.* honde 28r19 [*alt. f.* hondum]; 44r18. *pl. nom.* + *acc.* honda 55v10. *pl. gen.* honda 79rb5. *pl. dat.* hondum 10r6; 11v18.
hors: EQUUS ‖ *pl. nom.* + *acc.* hors *57v20; 58r6.
hræd: UELOX ‖ hræd 14r1.
hrædlic: *a* CELER *b* UELOCITER ‖ hrædlic 60v16[a]. *adv* hræðlice [*alt. f.* hræððe] 28r11[b].
hrægl: pallium ‖ *sg. dat.* hrægle 87va2.
hræðe: CITO ‖ hræðe 41v9.
hream: *a* GEMITUS *b* PLANCTUS ‖ hream 19v1[a]; 19v7[a]. *sg. dat.* hreame 2v14[b].

1. i *doubtful.*

hremeð: *a* IMPLORARE *b* PLANGERE ‖ hremað 58v13^a. hremið 85vb16^b.
gihremeð: IMPLORARE ‖ *pres. subj.* + *inf.* gihreme 18r11. gihrema 35r13.
hreo(u)ni(s)s(e: PAENITENTIA ‖ hreounisse 4v1.
gihreo(u)ni(s)s(e: PAENITENTIA ‖ gihreonisse 49r16.
hreo(u)sað: PAENITERE ‖ *pres. part. pl. dat.* hreosendum 81rb17.
hrif: UTERUS ‖ hrif 25r10. *sg. dat.* hrife 27r3; 27r5. ^{h}rife 26v11.
gihrin: aedificatio ‖ *sg. dat.* giríne [*alt. f.* gihríne] 6r15.
hrineð: *a* exornare *b* fabricare ‖ *pret. part.* gihrinad 50v5^a. *pl. nom.* + *acc.* girinado [*alt. f.* gihrinado] 46v6^b.
gihrineð: *a* TANGERE *b* adhaerere *c* ornare ‖ gihrineð 41r20^a; 51r11^b. *pres. subj.* + *inf.* gihrina 52r7^c. *pret. sg. ind. 1,3* gihran 26v18^a.
ðerh-gihrineð: PERTINGERE ‖ *pres. subj.* + *inf.* ðerhgihrina 26r6–7.
hring: ANULUS ‖ hring 53r21.
hroeðni(s)s(e: SAEUITIA ‖ hroeðnise 59v4.
hrof: arx ‖ *sg. dat.* hrofe 48v3.
hua: *a* ALIQUIS *b* QUIS ‖ hua 10v23^b. *sg. neut. nom.* + *acc.* huæd 19v2^b; 44v4^b. huætd 82ra20^a.
ym(b)-hu(e)arfað: CIRCUMIRE ‖ ymbhwarfað 17v12.
huil: *a* ALIQUANDO *b* INTERIM *c* quatenus ‖ *sg. acc.* + *dat.* huile 24r8^c; 85va7^b. *pl. dat.* huilum 6r11^a; 12v9^a.
gihuitað: DEALBARE ‖ *pret. pl.* gihuidadon 23v4.
hund: CENTUM ‖ *pl. nom.* + *acc.* hund' 50r3.
hundrað: *a* CENTUM (*b* CENTURIO) ‖ hundrað 23r21^a; 86vb9$^{(b)}$.
hundseofontig: SEPTUAGINTA ‖ hundseofontig 54v8.
hun(d)teantig: *a* CENTUM *b* centesimus ‖ *gen.* hunteantiges 50v3^b. *dat.* hunteantigum 86vb10^a.
hungrig: ESURIENS ‖ *sg. weak* hungrige 3r2.
hunig: MEL ‖ hunig 2r9. *sg. gen.* huniges 2r9.
to-huntað: aduenire ‖ *pres. subj.* + *inf.* tohunte' 56v17.
huntoð: UENATIO ‖ hunte 56v17. *sg. dat.* huntade 56v15$^-$.
huntung: UENATIO ‖ *pl. dat.* huntung' 57v12.
hu(o)elc, huælc: *a* ALIQUIS *b* QUI *c* QUIS ‖ huoelc 6r15^c; 17v18^b; 49r17^a.
hu(o)elc-(huælc-)huoegu: ALIQUIS ‖ huoelchuoegu 13v22; 66v13.
hu(o)er: UBI ‖ huer 12r15.
hu(o)erflung: UICISSITUDO ‖ *sg. gen.* huoerflunges 13v21.
ym(b)-hu(o)erfni(s)s(e: UICISSITUDO ‖ ymbhuoerfnise 18v3.
hu(o)eðer: *a* AUTEM *b* NUM *c* UERO ‖ huoeðer 85vb7^b. *adv.* huoeðre 12v10^a; 40r2^c.
huon: PAUCI ‖ huon 51v22.
huona: UNDE ‖ huona 86va13.
hus: *a* DOMUS *b* tabernaculum. ‖ hus 34r13^b; 47v12^a. hús 10r20^b. *sg. gen.* huses 82va13^a. *sg. dat.* huse 2v20^a; 60r5^a. use 31v5^b. *pl. dat.* husum 57r11$^-$; 59r12^a.
husincel: tabernaculum ‖ husincil 82va13; 82va21.
husul: SACRIFICIUM ‖ husul 17r4. *sg. dat.* husle 55r17$^-$.
h(u)u: *a* QUEMADMODUM *b* QUOMODO ‖ huu 43v10^a; 51v17^b. hu 86ra3$^{(a)}$.
ofer-hygd: SUPERBIA ‖ of' hygd 77r7.
hygdig: CASTUS ‖ hygdig 33r2. *sg. fem.* hygdego 52v10.
hygdigni(s)s(e: *a* CASTITAS *b* PUDOR ‖ hygdignisse 52v17^b. *sg. gen.* hygdignises 49v15^a. hygdignis' 37r21^a.
hygeð, hogað: SAPIRE ‖ hogað 6v10; 12r16. *pret. sg.* hogade 3r21.
bi-hygeð, -hogað: SOBRIUS ‖ *pret. part. pl. nom.* + *acc.* bihogodo 14r6; 14r7.
for-hygeð, -hogað: NEGLIGERE ‖ *pret. pl.* f'hogdon 51v4.
hyht: SPES ‖ hyht 2r6; 3v1. *sg. gen.* hyhtes 1r7. hygtes 2r5.
hyhteð: SPERARE ‖ hyhtað 37r7. *pres. part.* hyhtende 80rb17; 81ra7. *pl. nom.* + *acc.* hyhtendo 80ra11; 81vb15. *pl. dat.* hyhtendum 9r10.
gihyhteð: SPERARE ‖ *pres. subj.* + *inf.* gehyhte 82va11. gihyhte 9v10. *pret. pl.* gihyhton 80rb8.
ic: *a* EGO *b* EGOMET *c* MEUS *d* NOSTER *A—making a Latin First Person B—making a Latin verb-form other than a First Person C—reflexive usage* ‖ *sg. nom.* ic 1r2^A; 2r2^a; 11r3^B. ig 9v3^A. *sg. acc.* mec 2r5^a; 2r7^a. me' 2r6^a. mehc 2v21^a. *sg. poss.* min 1r2^c; 79vb23^a. mín 79ra17^c. *sg. poss. fem.* mino 2r10^c; 9v6^c. min' 2r9^c. *sg. poss. sg. gen.* mines 10r11^c; 10r12^c. min' 78rb11^a. *sg. poss. sg. gen. fem.* minræ 27r4^c. *sg. poss. sg. dat.* minum 2v20^c; 31v5^c. *sg. poss. pl. nom.* + *acc.* mino 2r21^c; 3r1^c. míno 78ra12^c; 78ra13^c. *sg. poss. pl. dat.* minum 60v21^c; 80va2^c. *sg. dat.* me 2r7^a; 2r20^a. *pl. nom.* we 1r18^A; 1v3^B; 9v15^a. ue 1r19^A; 2v10^a; 4v9^B; 39v5^d. uoe 46r12^A. uue 25v13^A. *pl. acc.* usig 2v7^a; 5v22$^{(b)}$; 8v1^C. us' 2v10^a. *pl. poss.* user 1v1^d; 17r7^a. userne 5r24^d; 7v14^d. usern' 7r13^d. user' 3v14^d; 5v1^a. usa' 4r10^d; 5v21^d. usa 20r20^d; 24r18^d. usra 3v17^d; 8v1^d [*alt. f.* usig]; 12r21^a. usræ 20v13^d. usr' 60r18^d. us' 11v18^d; 46r21^d. u' 58v21^d. ure 55r8. *pl. poss. sg. gen.* uses 12r5^d; 16r4^d. us' 11r3^d; 22r23^d. *pl. poss. sg. dat.* usum 9v12^d; 14r14^d. *pl. poss. pl. dat.* usum 1r22^d; 1v11^d. *pl. dat.* us 1v3^a; 1v13^a. ús 8v17^a.
idil: *a* UACUUS *b* UANITAS *c* UANUS ‖ idil 29r9^a. *sg. dat.* idlum 12r11^c. *pl. nom.* + *acc.* idlo 77r5^b.
idilni(s)s(e: UACUUM ‖ idilnis' 5v16.
giidlað: *a* EUACUARE *b* UACARE *c* uanescere ‖ *pres. subj.* + *inf.* giidlage 49r20^a. giidlege 47r6^c. *imp. sg.* *giidla 61r20^a. *pret. sg.* giidlade 3r22^a. *pret. sg. ind. 2* giidladest 16r12^b.
earð-ifign: TEREBINTHUS ‖ earðhifi^{g}n 33r11.
ilca: *a* IDEM *b* ILLE *c* IPSE *d* IS *e* qui ‖ ilca 5r18^c; 6v9^a; 24v18^e; 27v1^b. ilce 50r14^a; 57v1. ilcan 79vb14^a. *pl. nom.* + *acc.* ilco 81ra12^d. *pl. dat.* illcum 86va11^b.
in(n: *a* IN (*b* nusquam) *A—used insertionally with place-names* ‖ in 1r11 (2)^a, ^{a}; 57r11; 77v5$^{(b)}$; 88ra9^A. in' 87rb6^a. i' 78va1^a.
innabordes: INTUS ‖ innabord' 1v3.
innað: *a* INTERIOR *b* UISCUS ‖ *pl. nom.* + *acc.* innaðo 6v17^b. innaða 78vb2^a. *pl. dat.* i'naðum 78va2^b.
i(n)nu(e)ard: INTIMUS ‖ *pl. nom.* + *acc.* innuardo 77r6.
i(n)nu(e)ardlic: *a* INTERIUS (*b* inuocare) ‖ *sg. dat.* *innueardlicum 57r2^a. *adv.* innueardlic' 2r23^a. i'nueardlice 5r20$^{(b)}$.
intinga: CAUSA ‖ intinga 10r11; 15r 14. *pl. nom.* + *acc.* intingo 4v11. *pl. gen.* intinga 86vb8.
ioc(c: IUGUM ‖ iwocc 52v9. *sg. dat.* iwocce 52r3.
fore-(fora-)iornere: PRAECURSOR ‖ f'eiornere 27r12; 27r20.
iorneð: CURRERE ‖ iornað 3r9; 3r10. *pres. subj.* + *inf.* iorna 13v5.
giiorneð: *a* DISCURRERE *b* OCCURRERE *c* ambire ‖ giiornað 41v10^a. *pres. subj.* + *inf.* giiorne 40r5^b; 50v21^b. *pres. part.* giornende 41v17^c.
on-iorneð: INCURRERE ‖ *pres. subj.* + *inf.* oniorne 48v20.
ðerh-iorneð: PERCURRERE ‖ *pres. subj.* + *inf.* ðerhiorne 4r21.
under-iorneð: SUCCURRERE ‖ *imp. sg.* underiorn 21r6.
iorre: IRA ‖ iorre 14r3; 19v24. iorra 14r3; 14r9. irra 6r19.
iorre: IRATUS ‖ iorra 82rb2.
iorsað: IRASCI ‖ *pres. subj.* + *inf.* iorsiga 9r11. iorsia 15v19.
giiorsað: IRASCI ‖ *pres. ind. sg. 2* giiorsas 19v23.
(n)is: (*a* ABESSE) *b* ADESSE (*c* DEESSE) *d* ESSE *e* FIERI (*f* PRODESSE) (*g* imitari)

(*h* licet) *i* non + ; *A—inserted as an auxiliary; B—other insertional usages related to the Latin* ‖ is 1r6[d]; 1v14[A]; 11v14[B]. ist 32r3[d]. nis 9v9[d+]; 85vb4[i+]. bið 1r9[A]; 1r14[d]; 10v15[(c)]; 17r12[B]; 38r5[e]. *pres. sg. ind. 1* am 3r22[d]; 9r18[d]. nam 9v5[d+]. biom 9v7[A]; 9v20[d]. *pres. sg. ind. 2* arð 2r17[d]; 9v20[d]. bist 4v1[A]; 58v8[d]. *pres. pl. ind.* aron 2r11[d]; 6r18[d]. aro 13v2[d]. naro 51r17[d+]. sindon 6v14[d]; 12r14[d]. sint 7v5[d]; 12r16[d]. biðon 3r4[d]; 3v12[A]. biðo 28v13[A]. *pres. subj.* sie 1r5[e]; 1v12[A]; 9r9[d]; 11r3[(a)]; 21v11[(g)]; 44r5[(f)]. s[i]e 86vb4[(h)]. se 1v3[A]; 1v18[A]. *inf.* uosa 24v14[d]; 37v11[d]. uossa 7v11[d]; 57r1[e]. wossa 7v17[d]; 45v19[d]. *imp. sg.* uæs 50r22[d]; 59r7[b]. wæs 5v6[d]. ues 7r10[b]; 7v10[d]. uoes 19r2[b]; 30v4[d]. woes 24v12[b]; 34v10[b]. u[o]æs 21r1[d]. *imp. pl.* wosað 6r1[d]; 6r7[d]. wossað 6v9[d]. *pret. sg. ind. 1, 3* uæs 3r20[d]; 21r21[A]; 28r8[e]. uaes 88va8[d]. wæs 9v17[d]; 12r1[d]. næs 42r14[d+]. *pret. sg. subj. + ind. 2* uere 2r19[d]; 18v18[A]. were 10v4[d]; 13r1[A]. uære 28r15[d]. uoere 58v4[A]; 85rb4[d]. woere 10v4[d]; 11v18[A]. *pret. pl.* ueron 5r7[d]; 6r11[d]. weron 13v1[d]. uere 27v13[d]; 37v1[A]. were 17v5[d]. uoere 42r3[d]; 55r2[d]. woeron 10v20[d]; 88vb7[d]. uoeron 3r23[d]; 81rb25[A].

bi-tuih (-tui(e)n-) is: INTERESSE ‖ *inf.* bitwihuossa 44v20. bituienuosa 32r1.

fore- (fora-) is: PRAEESSE ‖ foreis 86vb11. f'eis 86vb14. f'ebið 86vb12.

from-is: ABESSE ‖ *pres. part. pl. dat.* fromuoesenum [?*read* fromuoesendum] 81vb13.

to-is: ADESSE ‖ *inf.* touosa 59v12.

la: *a* O *A—making a Latin vocative* ‖ la 33r2[a]; 77r17[A].

lac: HOSTIA ‖ *pl. nom. + acc.* laco 41v7.

scini-lac: *a* PHANTASIA *b* PHANTASMA *c* phantasmaticus ‖ scinilac 58v8[a]. scinelac 48r8[b]. *pl. nom. + acc.* scinelico [? *read* scinelaco] 82rb19[b]. *pl. dat.* scinelacum 47r7[c].

ofer-lad: TRANSLATIO ‖ of'lad 30r13.

laf: RELIQUUM ‖ *sg. acc. + dat.* lafe 29r14.

lam: LIMUS ‖ *sg. gen.* lames 86rb14.

lar: *a* DOCTRINA *b* ERUDITIO *c* consilium *d* documentum *e* magisterium (*f* rudimentum) ‖ lár 50r20[c]. *sg. gen.* lares 58r14[c]. *sg. acc. + dat.* lare 15r10[e]; 16v23[d]; 23r5[b]. *pl. nom. + acc.* laro 11r12[d]. lar' 38r22[(f)]. *pl. dat.* larum 22v10[a]; 29r2[a]. laru[u]m 40v2[a]. laru[u]m 60v13[a].

gilar: magisterium ‖ gilar' 15r6.

lardom: magistratus ‖ lardom 87ra1.

laruu, larua: *a* DOCTOR (*b* HAERETICUS) (*c* consul) ‖ laru 36v12[a]; 37r2[a]. larwu 86va20[(c)]; 86va23[(c)]. *sg. gen.* larwes 3v16[a]. *pl. nom. + acc.* laruas 40r3[a]; 54v10[a]. *pl. dat.* larwum 88vb8[(b)].

la(t)tað: TARDARE ‖ lattað 5v8.

gila(t)tað: TORPESCERE ‖ *pres. subj. + inf.* gilattia 61r15.

gila(t)to: IMPEDIMENTUM ‖ gilatto' 46r2.

latuu, latua: (*a* CENTURIO) (*b* DECANUS) *c* DUX (*d* QUINQUAGENARIUS) (*e* TRIBUNUS) ‖ latua 1r17[c]; 1v16[c]. latwu 86vb9[(a)]; 86vb13[(d)]; 86vb14[(b)]. latw[u]a 86vb12[(e)].

fore-(fora-)latuu, -latua: proconsul ‖ f'elatwa 86va22.

laðað: INUITARE ‖ *pret. part. pl. nom. + acc.* gilaðado 51r23; 51v10 [*alt. f.* gilaðade].

gilaðað: INUITARE ‖ *pres. part. pl. dat.* gilaðendum 51v2.

læ(d)din, lætin, latin: LATINUS ‖ lædin 87va6[()]; 87vb4[()]. latin' 87rb21. læd' 87vb2; 87vb9[−]; 87vb10[()]. *sg. gen.* lætines 87ra8.

lædeð: *a* CONFERRE *b* DUCERE *c* PRODUCERE ‖ *pres. part.* lædende 19r7[b]. *pret. part.* gilæded 60r11[b]. *pl. nom. + acc.* gilædedo 55v9[c]. *pl. dat.* gilædedum [*alt. f.* gilædde] 28v11[a].

gilædeð: *a* DEDUCERE *b* DUCERE *c* EDUCERE *d* FERRE *e* INDUCERE *f* PERDUCERE ‖ *pres. subj. + inf.* gilæde 44r22[a]; 49r12[c]; 52r8[f]; 78ra3[e]. *pret. sg.* gilædde 39r2[a]; 39v22[b]. gelædde 88va18[d]. *pret. sg. ind. 2* gilædest 49r9[c]. gilæddest 18v11[b]; 48v9[c].

eft-gilædeð: REDUCERE ‖ *imp. sg.* eftgilæd 77r8.

i(n)n-gilædeð: INDUCERE ‖ *pres. subj. + inf.* ingelæde 80vb4.

of-lædeð: EDUCERE ‖ *pret. sg.* oflædde 13v9.

ofer-lædeð: TRANSFERRE ‖ *pret. sg.* of'lædde 87ra10. *pret. sg. ind. 2* of'lædest 32r4.

soð-lædeð: PRODUCERE ‖ *pres. subj. + inf.* soðlæde 52r10.

ðerh-lædeð: PERDUCERE ‖ *pres. subj. + inf.* ðerhlæde 18r7; 79ra11. ðerhlæda 11v2; 50v11. *pret. part.* ðerhlæded 1r19.

lærend: DOCENS ‖ lærend 52r22.

læreð: *a* DOCERE *b* ERUDIRE *c* INSTIGARE *d* INSTRUERE ‖ *imp. sg.* lær 15v18[a]. *pres. part.* lærende 55r2[c]. *pret. part.* gilæred 52v18[b]. *pl. nom. + acc.* gilæredo 8v6[b]; 25v11[d].

gilæreð: *a* DOCERE *b* EDOCERE *c* ERUDIRE *d* INSTRUERE ‖ *pres. ind. sg. 2* gilæres 77r21[d]. *imp. sg.* gilær 2r22[c]; 7r15[d]; 78ra23[b]; 78rb3[a]. *pret. sg.* gilærde 23r9[a]; 27v3[b]. gelærde 87rb3[a]. *pret. sg. ind. 2* gilærdest 29v1[a].

læt(t: TARDUS ‖ lætt 14r2. hlætt 14r2.

lea: LEO ‖ *sg. gen.* leas 29r19.

leaf: *a* CARISSIMUS *b* DILECTUS ‖ leof 2r20[b]. *pl. nom. + acc.* leafa 6r7[a]; 12v11[a]. leofa 14r1[b]. *sup.* leofuste 85ra20[a]. *sup. pl. nom. + acc.* lefosta 14r1[b].

gileaf: DILECTUS ‖ *pl. nom. + acc.* gileafo 6v16.

gileafful(l: *a* FIDELIS *b* catholicus ‖ gileaffull 16v2[a]; 52v12[a]. *sg. acc. + dat. fem.* gileafful' 54v10[b]. *pl. gen.* gileaffullra 1v5[a]; 19r16–17[a]. gileaffulra 46v17[a]. gileafful' 43r3[a]. *pl. dat.* gileaffullum 4r19[a]; 35v3[a]. geleaffullum 81va6[a].

gileaffullice: FIDELITER ‖ gileaffullice 15v10; 30r15.

ungileaffu(l)lni(s)s(e: INFIDELITAS ‖ ungeleaffulnisse 88vb17.

gileafo, -a *a* FIDES *b* LICENTIA ‖ gileafa 3v1[a]; 13v15[a]. geleafa 85rb14[a]. geleafo 87va9[b]. *sg. gen.* gileafes 13v6[a]; 14r8[a].

eft-leanað: REMUNERATOR ‖ *pres. part.* eftleanend' 43r3.

leas: FALSUS ‖ *sg. dat.* leasum 48v10; 49r9.

for-leaseð: (deesse) ‖ *pret. part.* f'loren 10v15.

leasung: FALSITAS ‖ leasung 18v1.

lecedom: *a* MEDICINA *b* REMEDIUM ‖ lecedom 47v7[b]; 56r7[a]. *sg. dat.* lecedome 50r22[a]; 55v19[b]. *pl. nom. + acc.* lecedomas 15r15[b]; 22v13–14[b]. *pl. dat.* lecedomum 11v2[b]; 16r9[b].

gilefedlic: LEGITIMUS ‖ *sg. dat.* gilefedlicum [*alt. f.* gilefedra] 53r2. *adv.* gileofa' 29r12.

reht-lefend: catholicus ‖ rehtlefend 56v14.

lefeð: *a* CREDERE *b* INDULGERE ‖ *pret. part.* gilefed 38r4[a]. *pl. nom. + acc.* gilefeno 19v8[b].

gilefeð: *a* CONCEDERE *b* CREDERE ‖ gilefeð 9v12[b]; 37v13[a]. gelefeð 38r6[b]. gilefað 13r4[b]. gilefes 13v17[b]. *pres. ind. sg. 1* gelefo 78ra7[b]; 82va22[b]. *pres. ind. sg. 2* gilefes 27r17[a]; 28r22[a]. gilefest 31r17[a]. *imp. sg.* gilef 1v9[a]; 2v1[a]. *pres. part. pl. gen.* gilefendra 12r3[b]; 18r16[b]. gilefend' 58v6[b]. *pl. dat.* gilefendum 45r13[b]. *pret. sg.* gilefde 32v15[b]; 37r7[b]. *pret. pl.* gilefdon 25r13[b]; 28r6[b].

leg: FLAMMA ‖ leg 44v8; 48r3. *pl. nom. + acc.* lego 31r4; 31r8.

leger: LECTUS ‖ leger 53r22. legir 82va15.

derne-gilegere: FORNICATOR ‖ dernegileig' 51r14.

derne-gilegerscip(e: FORNICATIO ‖ dernegilegerscip' 51r13.

legeð: FULMEN ‖ *pl. dat.* legeðum 66v3.

leht: *a* LUMEN *b* LUX *c* SPLENDOR ‖

leht 1r21[a]; 3r3[b]; 77r21[c]. *sg. gen.* lehtes 1v8[a]; 6r12[b]. *sg. dat.* lehte 1v9[b]; 12v8[a]. *pl. gen.* lehta 13v20[a]. *pl. dat.* lehtum 7v3[a].

gilehtað: *a* ACCENDERE *b* LUCERE *c* recensere ‖ *pres. subj.* + *inf.* gilehta 18r23[b]; 77r16[a]. gilehta' 4r3[c].

lemb: *see* **lomb**.

lengo: LONGITUDO ‖ leng 39r10. lenge 53r12; 53r18.

lesend: REDEMPTOR ‖ lesend 10r11; 15r8.

eft-lesend: REDEMPTOR ‖ eftlesend 61v8.

on-lesend: nemar ‖ onlesend 88vb3.

leseð: REDIMERE ‖ *pret. part. pl. nom.* + *acc.* gileseno 12r11.

gileseð: *a* REDIMERE *b* parcere ‖ *pres. subj.* + *inf.* gilese 5r8[b]. *pret. sg. ind. 2* gilesdes 14v2[a].

aleseð: *a* LIBERARE *b* REDIMERE ‖ *pres. subj.* + *inf.* alese 79ra8[a]. *imp. sg.* ales 78ra4[a]; 78va11[a]. *pret. sg.* alesde 78vb8[b]; 81rb26[a]. *pret. sg. ind. 2* alesdest 48v2[a]; 48v10[a]. *pret. part.* alesed 36v15[a]. 59r13[a]. alesad 8r13[a]; 29r18[a]. alesen 45r14[a]. *pl. nom.* + *acc.* alesedo 45r5[a]; 47r7[a]. alesado 30v17[a]. *pl. dat.* alesadum 20v2[a].

eft-gileseð: REDIMERE ‖ *pret. sg. ind. 2* eftgilesdest 17v9; 22r1. eftgelesdest 48r21.

eft-aleseð: REDIMERE ‖ *pres. subj.* + *inf.* eftalesa 45r3. *pret. part. pl. nom.* + *acc.* eftalesedo 17r21.

lesing: REDEMPTIO ‖ *sg. gen.* lesinges 19r7. *sg. acc.* + *dat.* lesinge 10v1.

eft-lesing: REDEMPTIO ‖ eftlesing 60r15.

gilesni(s)s(e: REDEMPTIO ‖ *sg. gen.* gilesnisses 6r18.

gilete: EXITUS ‖ *pl. dat.* giletum 51v11.

for-letni(s)s(e: UENIA ‖ f'letnise 59v4.

bi-tuih- (-tui(e)n-) for-letni(s)s(e: INTERMISSIO ‖ bituinf'letnise 28r8.

le(t)teð: (nihilo minus) ‖ *pres. ind. sg. 1* leto 85vb3.

gile(t)teð: *a* CONCEDERE *b* PERMITTERE ‖ *pres. ind. sg. 2* giletas 28v8[b]. *pret. sg. ind. 2* gileortest 37r1[a].

for-le(t)teð: *a* CONCEDERE (*b* DEESSE) *c* DERELINQUERE *d* RELINQUERE *e* SINERE *f* committere, *g* disponere *h* relaxare ‖ *pres. subj.* + *inf.* f'leta 5r22[c]. *imp. sg.* f'let 5v10[d]; 17v9[e]; 49v2[h]; 60v3[a]. *pres. part.* f'letende 12v14[d]. *pret. part.* f'leten 10v15[(b)]; 83va19[c]. *pl. dat.* f'letum 52r19[g]; 61r6[f].

leur: *see* **hlear**.

gilic: *a* AEQUALIS *b* SIMILIS *c* SIMILITER (*d* imitari) *e* simul *f* una ‖ gilic 1v2[b]; 14r12[e]; 17r8[a]; 21v11[(d)]; 47r9[f]. gilíc 12v22[e]; 31v8[c]; 77v12[f].

ungilic: DISSIMILIS ‖ úngilic 86vb4.

efne-gilic: AEQUALIS ‖ efnegilic 10v4.

licað: IMITARI ‖ *pret. part.* gilíced 52v10.

gilicað: IMITARI ‖ *infl. inf.* gilícanne 11r9.

under-li(c)geð: SUCCUMBERE ‖ *pres. subj.* + *inf.* underlicga 39v11.

lichoma: *a* CARO *b* CORPORALIS *c* CORPUS ‖ lichoma 6v1[a]; 6v14[c]. lic-[h]oma 3r16[b]. lichome 6v21[c]; 10v12[a]. licome 52r21[c]. *sg. gen.* lichomes 1v2[a]; 4r8[c]; 4v10[b]. lichom' 56v1[c]; 78ra8[a]. *pl. nom.* + *acc.* lichoma 51r8[c]; 79rb 13[c]. lichomo 29v16[c]; 82rb22[c]. *pl. gen.* lichoma 50r11[c]; 56r11[c]. *pl. dat.* lichomum 4v20[c].

lichomlic: *a* CORPORALIS *b* CORPORALITER ‖ *adv.* lichomlice 4v6[b]. lichomlic' 55v2[b]. *pl. dat.* lichomlicum 8v1[a]; 57r16[a].

i(n)n-lichomung: *a* INCARNATIO *b* incarnare ‖ inlichomung 21v19[a]; 32r 12[b].

gilicni(s)s(e: *a* IMAGO *b* SIMILITUDO ‖ gilicnesse 52r20[a]. gilicnis' 43v17[b].

on-licni(s)s(e: *a* HABITUS *b* SIMILITUDO ‖ onlicnisse 10v6[b]; 10v7[a]. onlicnise 46r1[a].

alieð: ACCOMODARE ‖ *imp. sg.* alih 20r14.

lif: *a* UITA (*b* UIUERE) ‖ lif 2v10[a]; 6v1[a]. *sg. gen.* lifes 2r5[a]; 2r6[a]. *sg. dat.* life 5r12[a]; 15r2[(b)]. lífe 16r13[a].

lifbrycgung: *see* **lif-bru(c)cung**.

long-lif(e: LONGAEUUS ‖ *sg. fem.* longlif' 52v12.

lifeð, liofað: *a* UIUERE *b* UIUUS ‖ liofað 13r9[a]; 17r13[a]. liof' 48r14[a]; *49r21[a]. lifað 13r8[a]; 13r9[a]. lifeð 29v17[a]. lifigað 6r23[a]. *pres. ind. sg. 2* liofas 48v6[a]. liofað 17r22[a]; 58r18[a]. *pres. subj.* + *inf.* lifia 13r10[a]; 14r12[a]. lifiga 13r5[a]; 16r7[a]. *pres. part.* lifiende 28r5[b]. lifigende 82ra7[a]. lifigiend' 58v2[b]. *sg. gen.* lifigiend' 56r6[b]. *pl. gen.* lifigiendra 13r12[b].

gilifeð, -liofað: UIUERE ‖ gilifeð 5r12.

liffæst: UIUIFICUS ‖ *sg. acc.* + *dat. fem.* liffæste 45r4.

liffæsteð: UIUIFICARE ‖ *pret. part.* giliffæsted 10v12; 12v13. *pl. nom.* + *acc.* giliffæstedo 13r18.

giliffæsteð: *a* CONUIUIFICARE *b* UIUIFICARE ‖ giliffæstað [*alt. f.* giliffæstaðe] 5r19[b]. *pret. sg.* giliffæstade 13v1[a].

unlifi(g)ende: DEFUNCTUS ‖ *pl. dat.* unlifigendum 80rb11. unlifiendum 81va6.

liflic: UITALIS ‖ *sg. gen.* liflices 45r17.

i(n)n-lihtend: ILLUMINATOR ‖ inlihtend 1r20.

gilihteð: LUCERE ‖ *pres. subj.* + *inf.* gelihta 81va12.

i(n)n-lihteð: ILLUMINARE ‖ *imp. sg.* inlihta 18r16. *pret. part. sg. fem.* giinlihtado 22v10.

gi-i(n)n-lihteð: *a* ACCENDERE *b* ILLUMINARE *c* ILLUSTRARE ‖ giinlihteð 78ra 16[b]. *pres. subj.* + *inf.* giinlihta 18r20[b]; 59v7[c]. giinlihte 46v19[c]. *imp. sg.* giinlihta 18r18[b]; 59v20[c]. giinlichta 47v 13[c]. giinlihte 22v9[c]. geinlihte 1v19[b]. giinliht 1v20[a].

under-lihteð: SUBLEUARE ‖ *pret. part.* underlihtad 25r9. *pl. nom.* + *acc.* underlihtado 34v12.

lim: MEMBRUM ‖ *pl. nom.* + *acc.* lioma 51v8; 51r9. *pl. gen.* liomana 15v22; 56r22. *pl. dat.* liomum 56r10.

gilimplic: successus ‖ *pl. dat.* gilimplicum 77v3.

liode ‖ *gen.* lioda 88ra6.

giliorendlic: TRANSIRE ‖ *sg. gen.* giliorendlices 8v16–17.

bi-liorendlic: PRAETERIRE ‖ *pl. nom.* + *acc.* biliorendlica 79ra3–4. *pl. dat.* bileorendlicum 60r12.

ofer-lioreð: TRANSIRE ‖ *pres. subj.* + *inf.* of'liora 8r18.

liorneð: legere ‖ liorniað 87ra5.

giliorneð: DISCERE ‖ *pres. subj.* + *inf.* giliornia 21v11; 23v17. giliorniga 16v19.

giliorni(s)s(e: *a* EXITUS *b* OBITUS *c* depositio ‖ giliornise 41r22[a]; 42v16[c]; 60v2[b].

lixað: *a* CORUSCARE *b* MICARE ‖ *pres. part. pl. gen.* lixendra 37v2[b]. *pl. dat.* licxændum 1v14[a].

eft-gilixað: RESPLENDERE ‖ *pres. subj.* + *inf.* eft...gilixia 26r20.

lixung: SPLENDOR ‖ *sg. acc.* + *dat.* lixunge 1v19. licsunge 18v22.

eft-locung: RESPECTUS ‖ eftlocung 41v8.

lo(e)sað: PERIRE ‖ *pres. subj.* + *inf.* loesia 20r5. *pret. sg.* losade 78ra6.

lof: LAUS ‖ lof 1r1; 1e4. *sg. dat.* lofe 15r4.

lomb, lemb: AGNUS ‖ lomb 54v2; 78va22. lemb 23r11; 23v1. *sg. gen.* lombes 12r12; 23v4. le/[o]mbes 34r9.

gilomlic: *a* CONTINUARE *b* CONTINUUS (*c* FREQUENTARE) ‖ *sg. fem.* gilomlica 35v17[b]; 42r10[a]. gilomlico 35v22[b]; 36r13[b]. *sg. dat.* gilomlicum [*alt. f.* gilomlico] 36v14[a]. *sg. dat.* + *adv.* gilomlic' 43v21[b]. gilomlice 38v11[(c)]. *pl. nom.* + *acc.* gilomlica 31r15[a]; 32r20[c]. *pl. dat.* gilomlicum 36r17[b]; 37r11[b].

lond: *a* REGIO *b* TERRA *c* uilla ‖ lond

87va13[a]. *sg. dat.* londe 8v15[a]; 51v4[c]; 88ra6[b]. *pl. dat.* londum 87va7[c].

for-longe: DUDUM ‖ f'longe 87ra18.

longsum(m: *a* DIUTURNUS *b* hodiernus ‖ *sg. acc. masc.* longsumne 1r16[b]. *pl. dat.* longsummum 20r18[a].

losuist: INTERITUS ‖ losuist 78vb8.

bi-lu(c)ceð: *a* CONCLUDERE *b* EXCLUDERE ‖ *infl. inf.* bilucanne 57r19[b]. *imp. sg.* biluc 78rb16[a].

eft-bi-lu(c)ceð: RESERARE ‖ *pres. subj.* + *inf.* eftbiluce 14v10–11.

eft-on-lu(c)ceð: RESERARE ‖ *pret. sg. subj.* + *ind. 2* eft...onlece [*alt. f.* ? eft...onluce] 23r3.

lufað: *a* AMARE *b* CREDERE *c* DILIGERE ‖ lufað 3v4[c]. *pres. subj.* + *inf.* lufia 21v12[c]; 23r8[a]. lufiga 7v8[c]; 15v19[a]. lufige 3v4[c]. *imp. sg.* lufa 3v7[c]. *pres. part. pl. dat.* lufendum 41r4[c]; 44v6[c]. *pret. sg.* lufade 23r9[b].

gilufað: DILIGERE ‖ *pres. subj.* + *inf.* gilufia 50r17; 50v1. *pret. sg.* gilufade 6r8.

luf(i)end: AMATOR ‖ lufend 48v22; 50r12.

lufsum(m: AMABILIS ‖ lufsum 52v11.

lufsumni(s)s(e: *a* DILECTIO *b* IOCUNDITAS ‖ lufsumnise 22r20[b]. *sg. gen.* lufsumnis' 2r4[a]; 6v10[a].

lufu, -o, -a: *a* AMOR *b* CARITAS *c* DILECTIO *d* FIDES ‖ lufu 3v1 (2)[d],[(b)]; 3v8[c]; 14v20[a]. lufa 1r18[d]. lufe 24v1[a]; 28v3[d] *sg. gen.* lufes 18v17[d]; 52v9[c]. lufe' 24r16[d]. *pl. dat.* lufum 44v9[c]; 44v10[d].

broðer-lufu, -o, -a: CARITAS ‖ broðerlufu 3v2.

lust: *a* ARDOR *b* DESIDERIUM *c* SPONTE *d* UOLUNTARIE ‖ lust 77r16[a]; 78vb11[b]. *sg. dat.* luste 46r3[b]. *pl. nom.* + *acc.* lusto 16v18[b]. *adv.* lustume 13v21[d]; 45r13[c].

lustlice: LIBENTER ‖ lustlice 3r19.

lyft: AER ‖ lyft 3r15.

lytel: *a* MODICUS (*b* NIHILO MINUS) *c* PARUULUS *d* PARUUS *e* PAUCUS *f* ne (*g* necnon) *h* ne forte (*i* nequire) *j* quominus ‖ lytel 3r20[c]; 10v17[a]. *sg. gen.* lytles 3r23[c]. *pl. dat.* lytlum 23v14[d]. lytlum' 41v3[e]. *comp.* læassa 87va10[d]. læsse 54v8[(g)]. *comp. adv.* læs 3r6[(i)]; 3r16[h]; 5v12[f]; 54v21[(g)]; 85vb3[(b)]; 86ra1[j]. *sup.* læsest 29r6[d].

mac(c)ca: unicus ‖ maca 77v7.

gima(c)ca: *a* COMPAR *b* imitator ‖ gimacca 77r17[a]; *77r24[a]. gimaca 77v 7[a]. *pl. nom.* + *acc.* gimaco 6r7[b].

gimana: (MARITALIS) ‖ gimane 52v7.

mæg(e: (*a* NEQUIRE) *b* POSSE *c* UALERE *d* possibilitas ‖ mæge [*alt. f.* mæhge] 85vb6[b]. maege 38r15[c]; 55r21. mægi 3r6[(a)]; 4v7[c]; 5r20[b]; 85vb16[b]. maegi 22r2[c]; 79vb10[c]. *pres. sg. ind. 1, 3* mæg 58r1[b]. *pres. pl.* mægon 47r15[c]. magon 30v1[c]; 32r15[c]. mægo 44r6[b]. *pret. sg.* mæhte 23r21[b]; 23v20[b]. *pret. pl.* mæhton 34r2[c]. maehton 21r20[b]. mæhto 39v4[d].

mæg(e)n: *a* ROBUR *b* UIGOR *c* UIRTUS *d* UIS ‖ mægen 37v8[c]; 77r15[b]. mægn 3r18[c]; 18v17[c]. mægin 59r8[c]. mæg' 59r3[c]. *sg. gen.* mægnes 46r5[c]; 52r18[c]. mæg' 59v1[c]. *sg. dat.* mægne 15r19[c]; 52v16[a]. *pl. nom.* + *acc.* mægno 12v7[c]; 25r17[c]. mægna 54v4[c]; 59v3[d]. *pl. gen.* mægna 18r12[c]; 18r15[c]. *pl. dat.* *mægnum 41r19[c].

ned-mæg(e)n: UIS ‖ nédmægn 57r6.

mæht: *a* POTENTIA *b* POTESTAS *c* UIRTUS *d* possibilitas ‖ mæht 11v10[b]; 46v7[a]; 49r15[c]. *sg. gen.* mæhtes 2r6[c]; 24v21[a]. mæht' 59v1[c]. *sg. acc.* + *dat.* mæhte 7v23[c]; 52r18[b]. *pl. nom.* + *acc.* mæhto 22v16[d]; 55r4[c]. *pl. gen.* mæht' 54v4[b].

mæhtig: *a* POTENS *b* POTIS *c* potentia ‖ mæhtig 6v6[a]; 59v5[a]. *pl. nom.* + *acc.* mæhtigo 34v11[b]. *sup.* mæhtigust 39r6[c].

all-mæhtig: OMNIPOTENS ‖ allmæhtig 85vb9. allmaeht' 80va18. allm' 1v5; 1v9. allm 11r14. alm' 8r15; 11v6. *sg. gen.* allmæhtiges 57r20–1. allmæht' 48r6. allm' 48r10; 48r12. *sg. acc. masc.* allmæhtigne 66r2; 66v19.

gimænsumni(s)s(e: *a* COMMUNIO *b* communis ‖ gimænsum' 54v11[a]. gimænsumn' 12r2[b].

gimære: *a* FINIS *b* TERMINUS ‖ gemære 82rb13[b]. *pl. gen.* gimæro 78va 17[a] [*alt. f.* gimære]; 81rb6[a].

gimæreð: DETERMINARE ‖ *pres. part.* gimaerende 77v4.

meard: *a* MERCES *b* PRAEMIUM (*c* PRETIUM) ‖ meard 5v15[a]; 44r15[a]; 77v5[b]. *sg. acc.* + *dat.* mearde 18v20[a]; 51r 18[(c)]. *pl. nom.* + *acc.* mearda 8v19[b]. meardo 25r7[b]; 32r23[b]. *pl. dat.* meardum 41v17[b]; 41v20[b].

mea(s)sa: FESTA ‖ *pl. nom.* + *acc.* measso 27v16.

mega: AMICA ‖ mego 2r14; 2r17.

megð: PROUINCIA ‖ megð 88rb2; 88rb12. meghð 88ra13; 88ra17. mægð 85vb21. *sg. acc.* + *dat.* megðe 88ra23; 88rb6. meghðe 88ra9.

menig: *see* **monig**.

mennisc: HUMANUS ‖ mennisc 45r3. menisc 17r14. *sg. gen.* mennisces 45r15; 47v1. mennisc' 16r18; 21r1. mennis' 61r18. menn' 59r5. *sg. dat.* menniscum 11r9; 56v22. mennisc' 15r19; 23v22. menn' 46r5. *pl. nom.* + *acc.* mennisco 19r22. *pl. dat.* menniscum 46v14.

menniscni(s)s(e: HUMANITAS ‖ mennisscniss 1v16.

gimeodni(s)s(e: DIGNITAS ‖ *pl. dat.* gemeodnissum 86va16–17.

meodomað: DIGNARE, -ARI ‖ *pret. part.* gimeodumad 17r18; 18r7. gimeadomad 11r18. gimoedumad 52r 10. gimeodum' 45r3. gimeodu' 48r13; 48r20.

gimeodomað: DIGNARE, -ARI ‖ *pres. ind. sg. 2* gimeodumes 46v7. gimeodomest 46v19. *pres. subj.* + *inf.* gimeodumia 59v12; 59v15. gimeodomia 18r14; 45v3. gimeodomiga 52r13. gmeodumia 50r2. gimeodum' 47r13; 48v2. gimeodu' 49v17; 57v17. gimeodo' 48v18. gmeodu' 48v15. gimeod' 61v7. *imp. sg.* gemeoduma 67v1; 83ra1. gemeadoma 56v8. gimeoduma 53r17; 55v12. *pret. sg.* gimeodumade 55v2.

meodomlice: DIGNE ‖ meodomlice 1v13.

gimeodomlice: *a* DIGNANTER *b* DIGNE ‖ gimeodomlice 9r11[b]. gimeodumlice 16v17[a].

mercað: *a* SIGNARE *b* SIGNIFICARE ‖ *pret. part. pl. nom.* + *acc.* gimercado 6r17[a]; 56v21[b].

gimercað ‖ *pret. sg.* gimercade 32r12.

to-gimercað: ASSIGNARE ‖ *pret. sg.* togimercade 28r5.

mersað: *a* CELEBRARE *b* CONCELEBRARE *c* praedicare ‖ mersað 34v3[c]. mersiað 30v11[a] [*alt. f.* gimersiað]; 41v19[a]. mersias 21v13[a]. mersigað 17r 23[a]. *pres. ind. sg. 1* mersigo 3r17[c]. *pres. subj.* + *inf.* mersia 33v6[a]; 36r8[a]. *pres. part.* mersande 44r12[b]. *pl. dat.* mersandum 30r13[a].

gimersað: *a* CELEBRARE *b* praedicare ‖ gimersas 32r7[a]. *pres. subj.* + *inf.* gimersia 4v21[a]; 15r11[b]. gimersiga 1v13[a]; 39r17[a]. *infl. inf.* gimersanne 15v17[a]. *pres. part. pl. nom.* + *acc.* gimersando 44v13[a].

mersere: praeco ‖ *sg. gen.* merseres 27v7.

mersung: *a* CELEBRARE *b* CELEBRITAS *c* fauor ‖ *sg. acc.* + *dat.* mersunge 4v5[c]; 4v16[b]; 40r17[a]. mersunga 35r22[b].

gimersung: CELEBRITAS ‖ *sg. acc.* + *dat.* gimersunge 23v15. *pl. dat.* gimersungum 37r11.

gimetfæstni(s)s(e: MODESTIA ‖ gimetfæstnis' 6v18.

metgað: *a* MITIGARE *b* TEMPERARE ‖ *pret. part. pl. nom.* + *acc.* gimetgado 55v6[b]. *pl. dat.* gimetgadum 9r2[a].

gimetgað: *a* FRENARE *b* MITIGARE *c* TEMPERARE ‖ gimetgað 77r20[c]. *pres. subj.* + *inf.* gimetga 77r4[c]. *pres. part.* *gimetgende 77r3–4[a]. *pret. sg. ind. 2* gimetgadest 48r2[b].

met(t: CIBUS ‖ met 50r22. *sg. gen.* metes 77r7. *sg. dat.* mætte 6v12.
gimet(t: MENSURA ‖ gimett 39v21; 40r6. *sg. gen.* gimetes 52r11.
micil: (*a* INGENS) *b* MAGIS (*c* MAGNALIA) *d* MAGNUS *e* MULTUS *f* qualitas *g* tantus ‖ micil 13v10^{d}; 85va6$^{(a)}$. *micel 88vb12^{d}. *sg. fem.* micla 12r6^{d}; 19v2^{f}. *sg. gen.* micles 23r16^{d}; 24r16^{g}. *sg. dat.* miclum 13r13^{d}; 21v4^{d}. *adv.* micle 10v21^{e}. *sg. acc. + dat. fem.* micle 23v3^{d}; 78rb10^{d}. *pl. nom. + acc.* micla 21r16^{d}; 37r15$^{(c)}$. micilo 48v1^{d}. *pl. dat.* miclum 4r6^{g}. *comp.* mara 3v2^{d}; 10v 21^{b}. *sup.* maast 85va21^{d}. *sup. pl. nom. + acc.* maasta 59r5^{d}.
med-micil: pusillanimis ‖ *pl. nom. + acc.* metmiclo 5v23.
gi-med-micil: infirmus ‖ *pl. nom. + acc.* gimetomicla 24v4.
micilni(s)s(e: MAGNITUDO ‖ micilnise 61r22. *sg. gen.* micelnis' 2r4.
miclað: MAGNIFICARE ‖ *pres. part.* miclande 44v18. *pret. part.* gimiclad 57v6. gemiclad 66v15.
gimiclað: MAGNIFICARE ‖ *imp. sg.* gimicla 41v15. *pret. sg.* gimiclade 37v19.
midd: MEDIUS ‖ *sg. dat.* middum 5r4; 22r17. *pl. dat.* middum 1r11.
milc: LAC ‖ milc 12v5.
mildelice: *a* PROPITIUS *b* propitiatus ‖ mildelice 4r10^{a}; 20v1^{b}. mildeldelice [? *read* mildelice] 45r4^{a}.
mil(d)sa: *a* MISERATIO *b* MISERICORDIA *c* PROPITIATIO ‖ milsa 19v18^{a}; 78rb10^{b}. milsæ 20v6^{a}. milse 78vb12^{a}. *sg. gen.* milsa' 20v10^{a}; 32v11^{c}. milse' 35v1^{c}. *pl. gen.* milsa 5v2^{a}; *78rb4^{a}. *pl. dat.* milsum 22r4^{a}.
mil(d)sað: *a* MISERARI *b* MISERERI *c* PROPITIUS *d* misericordia ‖ *imp. sg.* milsa 56r3^{b}; 79rb21^{b}. *pres. part.* milsend 5r23^{b}; 17v15^{c}; 33r20^{a}. milsend' 7v11^{a}. *pl. dat.* milsendum 20v4^{d}. *pret. part. pl. nom. + acc.* gimilsado 9r10^{b}.
gimil(d)sað: *a* MISERERI *b* PROPITIARI ‖ gimilsageð 10r3^{a}. *pres. subj. + inf.* gimilsia 79ra21^{a}. gimils^{i}a 61v9^{a}. gimilsage 19v16^{a}. *imp. sg.* gimilsa 5v1^{a}; 52r14^{b}. gimildsa 43r9^{b}; 43r17^{b}. gemilsa 82ra5^{a}. *pret. sg.* gimilsade 56r3^{a}.
mil(d)sung: MISERATIO ‖ *sg. gen.* milsunga' 34v7.
min: *see* **ic.**
mind: DIADEMA ‖ mind 44r17.
missenlic: DIUERSUS ‖ *pl. gen.* missenlicra 45v11. *pl. dat.* missenlic' 83va9.
missenlicni(s)s(e: DIUERSITAS ‖ missenlic'e 15v13.
mist: CALIGO ‖ *sg. gen.* mistes 5r7. *sg. dat.* miste 18r3; 18v10. mist' 16v21. *pl. nom. + acc.* misto 79va18.
mistig: CALIGOSUS ‖ mistig 9r15.
mitteð: INUENIRE ‖ *pres. ind. sg. 1* mitto 82va20.
gimitteð: INUENIRE ‖ *pres. subj. + inf.* gimitta 5r20; 7r9.
mið: *a* APUD *b* CUM *A—making a Latin ablative* ‖ mið 1v4^{b}; 4v1^{A}; 7r16^{a}. m' 1v22^{b}; 17r8^{b}.
mið-symlinga, -unga: CONTINUUS ‖ miðsymlinga 8r20.
mið-ðy: *a* CUM *b* DUM *A—insertion* ‖ miððy 2r19^{b}; 3r2^{a}; 10v13^{A}.
eð-mod: HUMILIS ‖ *pl. nom. + acc.* eðmodo 7v18. *pl. gen.* eðmoda 19v19.
ru(m)-mod: *a* BENIGNUS *b* CLEMENS *c* paracletus ‖ rummod 7r22^{a}; 35v11^{b}; 53r21^{c}. rummód 2v16^{a}. *sg. dat.* rummodum 77r11^{c}; 77r18^{c}. rummode 7v11^{a}; 77v7^{c}. *sg. weak* rummode 77v10^{b}.
u(o)el-ru(m)-mod: BENIGNUS ‖ *pl. nom. + acc.* uelrummodo 6r21.
gi-eð-modað: HUMILIARE ‖ *pret. sg.* gieðmodade 10v8.
moder: MATER ‖ moder 2r4; 22r15. *sg. gen.* moder' 27r4. *sg. dat.* moeder 61v6; mo^{e}der 33r14.
eð-modlic: *a* HUMILITER *b* SUPPLEX *c* SUPPLICITER ‖ *adv.* eðmodlice 19r3^{c}; 58v13^{a}. *pl. nom. + acc.* eðmodlic' 48v7^{b}.
ru(m)-modlic: *a* BENIGNUS *b* CLEMENTER *c* PROPITIUS ‖ *sg. dat.* rummodlicum 8v12^{a}. *adv.* rummodlice 3v11^{b}. rumodlice 7v13^{b}. *sg. weak* rummodlice 1r17^{c}; 19v5^{a}.
eð-modni(s)s(e: HUMILITAS ‖ eðmodnise 6v17. eðmodnis' 11r10; 16r1.
ru(m)modni(s)s(e: *a* BENIGNITAS *b* CLEMENTIA *c* PROPITIATIO ‖ rummodnise 20r7^{b}; 50r15^{a}. rummodnis' 8v7^{c}; 61r4^{b}. rummod' 6v17^{a}.
gimoede: PROSPERUS ‖ *pl. nom. + acc.* gimoedo' 24v1.
uiðir-moede: *a* CONTRARIUS *b* aduersitas ‖ *pl. nom. + acc.* uiðirmoedo 60r5^{a}. *pl. dat.* wiðirmoedum 25v6^{b}.
ungimoedni(s)s(e: ADUERSITAS ‖ *pl. dat.* ungimoednisum 30v17.
uiðir-moedni(s)s(e: *a* ADUERSITAS *b* ADUERSUM *c* PRAUITAS ‖ wiðirmoednise 16v13^{c}. uiðermoednise 42v21^{a}. *pl. dat.* uiðermoednisum [*alt. f.* uiðermoednusum] 39v12^{b}. uiðirmoednisum 36r9^{b}; 44r2^{a}. wiðirmoednisum 51r3^{a}.
moeteð: INUENIRE ‖ *pret. part.* gimoeted 10v2; 10v7. gim^{o}oeted [? *read* gimoeted] 50r5. *pl. nom. + acc.* gimoetedo 42r1.
gimoeteð: *a* INUENIRE *b* REPERIRE *c* uenire ‖ gimoetað 17v19^{a}. gimoetas 51v12^{a}. *pres. subj. + inf.* gimoeta 35r20^{b}. gimoetta 60r13^{a}. gimoete 50v6^{c}. *pret. sg.* gimoete 37v17^{a}; 39r7^{a}. gimoette 41v5^{a}; 42r19^{a}. *pret. pl.* gimoeton 17v14^{a}; 51v14^{a}.
gimoeting: CONUENTIO ‖ *sg. acc. + dat.* gimoetinge 53r8.
mona: LUNA ‖ mona 33r18.
gimong: (aroma) ‖ *pl. nom. + acc.* gimongo 2r13. gimonge 2r13.
monig, menig: *a* MULTUS *b* PLURES *c* TOT ‖ monig 5r24^{a}. *pl. nom. + acc.* monigo 28r6^{a}. menigo 34r5^{a}; 43v3^{b}. mengo 40v21^{a}. *pl. gen.* monigra 23r15^{a}. menigra 86va19^{a}. *pl. dat.* monigum 20r2^{c}; 78vb20^{a}. menigum 41v4^{a}.
monigfald: *a* LARGUS *b* MULTIPLEX *c* MULTIPLICARE *d* MULTUS *e* copiosus ‖ monigfald 48r17^{d}; 60r1^{a}. *sg. gen.* monigfald' 2v17^{d}. *sg. dat.* monigfald' 35v18–19^{b}. *pl. nom. + acc.* monigfald' 46v20^{a}; 56v16^{e}. *pl. dat.* monigfaldum 22r4^{c}; 35v6^{b}.
monigfaldað: *a* ABUNDARE *b* MULTIPLICARE ‖ *pres. subj. + inf.* monigfaldiga 6v8^{a}. *pret. part. pl. nom. + acc.* gimonigfaldado 53r11^{b}. *pl. dat.* gimonigfaldadum 60v17^{b}.
gimonigfaldað: *a* ABUNDARE *b* MULTIPLICARE ‖ *pres. ind. sg. 2* gimonigfaldes 14v22^{b}. *pres. subj. + inf.* gimonigfaldia 53r18^{b}. gimonigfaldiga 6v6^{a}. *imp. sg.* gimonigfalda 4r12–13^{b} [*alt. f.* gimonigfaldia]; 34v4^{b}.
monigfal(d)lic: *a* ABUNDANTER *b* MULTIMODUS *c* MULTIPLEX *d* MULTIPLICARE *e* copiosus ‖ monigfallic' [*alt. f.* monigfallice] 30v14^{e}. *sg. dat.* monigfallicum 35r17^{c}. monigfallic' 30r6^{c}. monigfalli' 30v20^{c}. *adv.* monigfaldlice 6v22^{a}. *pl. dat.* monigfaldlicum 52r4^{d}. *comp. adv.* monigfald'cor 23r1^{e}. monigfald' 25v4^{e}. *sup.* monigfald'cost 59r 7–8^{b}.
monigfaldni(s)s(e: *a* MULTIPLICATIO *b* MULTITUDO ‖ monigfaldnisse 8v15^{b}. monigfaldnise 10r3^{b}; 29r22^{b}. monigfaldnis' 40r11^{a}; 61r10^{b}.
mon(n: (*a* ADOLESCENTULUS) (*b* CENTURIO) (*c* DECANUS) *d* HOMO (*e* NEMO) (*f* QUINQUAGENARIUS) (*g* QUIS) ‖ monn 14r1^{d}; 58r21^{d}. mon 56r4. ᛗ 6r2$^{(g)}$; 6v12$^{(e)}$; 10v7^{d}. man 55r19. *sg. acc.* monno 13r16 (2)^{d,d}. *sg. gen.* monnes 21v2^{d}; 54v13^{d}. *sg. dat.* menn 3v3$^{(e)}$; 51r22^{d}. *pl. nom. + acc.* menn 48r18^{d}; 53r15$^{(a)}$. men 55r21. *pl. gen.* monna 10v6^{d}; 86vb13$^{(f)}$. mon' 86vb9$^{(b)}$; 86vb14$^{(c)}$. *pl. dat.* monnum 33r4^{d}; 34r13^{d}.
aldor-mon(n: *a* DUX *b* PRAESUL *c*

PRINCEPS *d* principatus ‖ aldormonn 18v15[c]. aldormon' 86vb16[c]. aldormon 82rb16[b]; 87rb22[c]. aldorm' 54 v4[d]; 87vb4[c]. *pl. nom.* + *acc.* aldormenn 27r8[c]. aldormen' 9r17[a]; 87ra3[c]. *pl. dat.* aldormonnum 28v20[c]; 29r2[b]. aldorm' [*alt. f.* alldorm'] 29v5[c].

embeht- (embiht-) mon(n: EPIDIACONUS ‖ *pl. nom.* + *acc.* *embihtmen[1] 87rb4.

heh-aldor-mon(n: PATRICIUS ‖ *sg. dat.* hehaldorm' 86vb4. *pl. nom.* + *acc.* hehaldormenn 86vb1.

heh-scire-mon(n: PROCURATOR ‖ *pl. nom.* + *acc.* hehsciremenn 86vb7.

scire-mon(n: UICARIUS ‖ *sg. gen.* scir' 87va6.

ðegnung-mon(n: NATHINNAEUS ‖ *pl. nom.* + *acc.* ðegnungmen' 87rb6.

uif-mon(n: *a* FEMINA *b* MULIER ‖ *wifmon[2] 88va12[b]. *pl. gen.* uifmonna 52v11[a]. wifmonna 85vb2[b].

mor: MONS ‖ mor 9r15. *sg. dat.* more 5v5; 23r11. *pl. dat.* morum 1r11; 83ra24.

morgen: (AURORA) ‖ morgen 33r17.

morgenlic: MATUTINUS ‖ *sg. dat.* morgenlicum 82va9. *pl. dat.* morgenlicum 18r6; 18r11.

ar-morgenlic: *a* AURORA *b* MATUTINUS ‖ armorgenlic 83rb9[a]. *pl. dat.* armorgenlicum 60v6[b].

gimot: negotium ‖ *pl. dat.* gimotum 29r10.

mus: MUS ‖ *pl. nom.* + *acc.* mys 66r8.

muð: OS ‖ muð 9v18; 22r17. *sg. gen.* muðes 2r11. *sg. dat.* muðe 6r14; 12v16. *pl. dat.* muðum 29r19.

gimynd: *a* COMMEMORATIO *b* MEMORIA ‖ gimynd 2r10[b]; 30r14[a]. gemynd 81va7[b]. *sg. acc.* + *dat.* gimynde 35v8[a]; 42v10[a].

efne-gimynd: COMMEMORATIO ‖ *sg. gen.* efnegimyndes 27v16.

gimyndgað: MEMINISSE ‖ *pres. subj.* + *inf.* gemyndge 81va20.

eft-gimyndgað: *a* RECORDARI *b* REMINISCI ‖ *pres. ind. sg. 1* eft...gimyndga 9r19[a]. *imp. sg.* eftgimyndga 78rb4[b].

gimyndig: MEMOR ‖ gimyndig 5v6; 21r1.

eft-gimyndig: RECORDATUS ‖ eftgimyndig 27r4.

gimyne: COMMEMORATIO ‖ *gimyne[3] 41r13.

gimyneð, -monað: MEMINISSE ‖ *imp. sg.* gimyne 78rb9; 78rb11.

eft-myneð, -monað: RECOLERE ‖ eftmonað 16v2.

1. em *doubtful.*
2. on *doubtful.*
3. n *doubtful.*

næbbe: *see* **hæfeð.**

næfra, -e: *a* NUMQUAM (*b* NUSQUAM) ‖ næfra 52r23[a]. næfre 77va5[(b)].

næht: *a* NOX *b* noxius ‖ næht 14v5[a]; 23v5[a]. *sg. gen.* næhtes 14r5[a]; 18r6[a]. *sg. acc.* + *dat.* næhte 18r2[a]; 83ra1[a]. *pl. nom.* + *acc.* næhta 82rb19[b].

næhtlic: NOCTURNUS ‖ *pl. nom.* + *acc.* næhtlica 79va17–18.

nænig: *see* **ænig.**

ne: (*a* ABESSE) *b* NE *c* NEC (*d* NECDUM) (*e* NEMO) (*f* NEQUE) (*g* NESCIRE) *h* NON ‖ ne 2v9[h]; 2v19[b]; 3r6[(f)]; 3v3[(e)]; 12v15[c]; 23v22[(d)]; 51r10[(a)]; 51r15[(g)]; 55r17.

gineað: INHAERERE ‖ *pres. subj.* + *inf.* ginea 16v22.

nebb: nardus ‖ nebb 2r19.

ned: *a* NECESSITAS *b* debere ‖ ned 51r1[b]. *pl. dat.* ned' 81rb25[a].

nedra: *a* SERPENS *b* scorpius ‖ nedre 61r15[b]. *sg. gen.* nedres 59v11[a].

nedunga: (RAPERE) ‖ nedunga 88 va17.

neh: (*a* DEMUM) *b* IUXTA *c* PROPE *d* PROXIMUS *e* SECUNDUS ‖ neh 5r21[c]; 31v17[b]. *sup.* nest 86va21[e]. nesta 85ra23[(a)]. neste 3v4[d]; 3v7[d]. *sup. sg. gen.* nestes 3v8[d]. *sup. pl. nom.* + *acc.* nesta 77r16[d]. *sup. pl. dat.* nestum *61r4[d4]; 81ra22[d].

gineh: PROXIMUS ‖ *sup. pl. dat.* ginestum 40v12.

gineoleceð: APPROPINQUARE ‖ *pres. part.* gineolecende' 45v1.

to-gineoleceð: APPROPINQUARE ‖ *pret. sg. ind. 2* to...gineolecdest 10r9.

ginereni(s)s(e: ereptio ‖ *sg. gen.* ginerenise' 14v17.

nereð: ERUERE ‖ *pret. part.* genered 33r23.

ginereð: *a* ERUERE *b* eripere ‖ *pres. ind. sg. 2* gineres 28v15[a]. *pres. subj.* + *inf.* genere 26v17[a]; 81vb12[b]. *imp. sg.* ginere 78va7[b]; 78va9[b]. *pret. sg.* ginerede 13r21[b]; 28r19[b].

neten: *a* ANIMAL *b* PECUS ‖ *pl. nom.* + *acc.* netena 57v19. netna 61r17[a]. netno 23r20[a]; 58r1[a]. *pl. dat.* netnum 56r9[b].

nett: RETE ‖ *pl. nom.* + *acc.* netto 56v16; 56v22.

dæl-ni(m)mend(e: PARTICEPS ‖ dælnimmende 17v4.

ni(m)með: *a* ABSTRAHERE *b* ATTOLLERE *c* AUFERRE (*d* IMITARI) (*e* TOLLERE) ‖ niomað 30r16[(d)]. *pres. ind. sg. 2* nimmes 78va22[e]. *pret. part.* ginumen 46v14[a]. ginummen 6r20[e]. *sg. fem.* ginumene 52v6[c]. *pl. nom.* + *acc.* numeno 36r5[b].

4. stum *doubtful.*

gini(m)með: *a* AUFERRE *b* CAPERE (*c* IMITARI) (*d* RAPERE) ‖ *pres. subj.* + *inf.* ginime 24r9[(c)]; 27v17[(c)]. ginimme 23r5[b]. giniomma 9r3[b]. ginioma 22r2[b]. *imp. sg.* ginim 78va4[a]. *pret. sg. ind. 1, 3* genom 88va17[(d)].

to-gini(m)með: ATTOLLERE ‖ *imp. sg.* toginim 29v8.

niolni(s)s(e: ABYSSUS ‖ *pl. nom.* + *acc.* niolniso 39r14.

ned-ni(o)m(m)o: RAPINA ‖ ednioma 10v4.

giniosað: UISITARE ‖ giniosað 5r3. *pres. subj.* + *inf.* giniosiga 14r21. giniosige 5r6. giniosia 59v17. *imp. sg.* giniosa 80rb5.

oft-giniosað: FREQUENTARE ‖ oftginiosað 7v9. *pres. part. pl. dat.* *oftginiosendum[5] 44v19.

nið: (Zabulus) ‖ nið 86rb8.

niðrung: CONDEMNATIO ‖ *sg. acc.* + *dat.* niðrunge 12r1.

giniuað: *a* INNOUARE *b* frequentare ‖ *pres. subj.* + *inf.* giniwia 4v12[b]. giniwge 17r18[a].

eft-niuað: *a* REFORMARE *b* RENOUARE *c* REPARARE *d* RESTITUERE *e* recensere ‖ *pres. ind. sg. 2* eftniwas 9r4[b]; 16r14[c]. eftniuas 17r10[c]. eftniues 46r8[d]. *pres. part. pl. nom.* + *acc.* eftniuando 4v15[e]. *pret. part.* eftginiuad 78vb14[b]. *pl. nom.* + *acc.* eftniuado 1v3[a]. eftginiwado 14v8.

i(n)n-niuað: INNOUARE ‖ *imp. sg.* inniua 78va2. *pret. part. pl. nom.* + *acc.* ginniwado 16v5.

niue: *a* NOUUS (*b* rudimentum) ‖ niue 23t19[a]; 47r16[a]. *sg. fem.* niwa 14v6[a]; 15v22[a]. niua 46r16[a]. *sg. gen.* niues 47r18[a]; 54v9[a]. *sg. dat.* niwum 14v22[a]. *pl. nom.* + *acc.* niua 38r22[(b)].

niuung: *a* NOUARE *b* NOUITAS *c* nouus ‖ *sg. acc.* + *dat.* niwunge 12r20[c]; 12v 20[b]. *pl. dat.* niwungum 1v11[a].

eft-niuung: REPARATIO ‖ *sg. gen.* eftniuaw[u]nges [? *read* eftniuuw[u]nges] 4r2. eftniwawnges [? *read* eftniwuwnges] 15r13.

i(n)n-niuung: INNOUATIO ‖ *sg. acc.* + *dat.* inniwang' [? *read* inniwung'] 14v14.

no: *a* NON (*b* NECNON) (*c* NIHILOMINUS) ‖ no 2v15[a]; 54v8[(b)]; 85vb3[(c)].

ginoh: (SUFFICERE) ‖ genog 86ra15.

noht: NIHIL, -UM ‖ noht 18r1; 50r16. *sg. dat.* nohte 52r18.

noma: NOMEN ‖ noma 42v4; 66r10. nome 1r4; 3v13. nom' 58r8. naman 55r7⁻; 55r7–8⁻. *sg. gen.* nomes 81vb4. nome' 15v14; 27r4. nom' 40r14; 59v9. *pl. dat.* nomum 66r4; 67r1.

5. t *doubtful.*

nomað: *a* NOMINARE *b* nomen ‖ *pret. part.* *genomad 88va4[a1]; 87va24[a2]. ginomad 88ra20[b]. *pl. nom.* + *acc.* genomado 87rb19[a]; 87vb1[a].
ginomað: NOMINARE ‖ *pret. sg.* genomade 66v21. *pret. sg. ind. 2* genomadest 66r4; 67r16.
nu: *a* MODO *b* NUNC ‖ nu 5v19[b]; 12v4[a].
ginyhtsum(m: LARGUS ‖ ginyhtsu' 49v14.
ginyhtsumni(s)s(e: *a* ABUNDANTIA *b* LARGITAS *c* UBERTAS *d* abundans ‖ ginyhtsumnisse 60v17[a]; 81ra18[a]. ginyhtsumnise 19v21[a]; 35v1[a]. ginyhtsum' 45r21[c]; 47r20[d]. ginyht' 46v15[b].
oefistað: FESTINARE ‖ *pres. subj.* + *inf.* oefistia 46r1. *imp. sg.* oefistig 80va25.
oehtere: PERSECUTOR ‖ *pl. dat.* oehterum 21v13.
fore-(fora-)oehtere: PERSECUTOR ‖ *pl. dat.* f'eoehte'um 21v17.
oehteð: *a* ADUERSARI *b* PERSECUTOR ‖ *pres. part.* oehtende 31r8[b]. *pl. dat.* oehtendum 81rb8[a].
gioehteð: PERSEQUI ‖ gioehtas 78rb17. *pres. part.* gioehtende 29r7.
oele: OLEUM ‖ oele 88vb15.
oest: *a* DEUOTIO *b* deuotus *c* uotiuus *d* uotum ‖ oest 7r22[a]; 50r14[d]. *sg. gen.* oestes 9r7[a]; 15v12[a]. *sg. acc.* + *dat.* oeste 2r23[a]; 3v22[a]. oest' 36v9[a]. *pl. nom.* + *acc.* oesto 9r1[a]; 14v11[d]; 33v3[c]; 38v10[c] [*alt. f.* oestiga]. *pl. dat.* oestum 4v11[b]; 30v10[d].
oestig: *a* DEUOTUS *b* UOTIUUS ‖ oestig 7v11[a]; 33v16[a] [*alt. f.* oestigo]. *sg. fem.* oestigo 34v20[a]. *sg. dat.* oestigum [*alt. f.* oestigo] 19v15[a]. *pl. nom.* + *acc.* oestigo 15r4[a]; 41r10[b]. *pl. dat.* oestigum 32v7[a].
oestlic: *a* DEUOTUS *b* UOTIUUS ‖ *sg. dat.* oestlic' 4v21[a]. *adv.* oestlice 15v9[a]. *pl. nom.* + *acc.* oestlico 8v23[b]. oestlica 26r20[b]. *pl. dat.* oestlicum 4v15[a].
oeðel: PATRIA ‖ *sg. gen.* oedles 87va15.
of: *a* A(B *b* DE *c* EX *A—making a Latin ablative* ‖ of 1r18[c]; 2v21[b]; 17r2[A]; 49v20[a].
ofer: *a* SUPER *b* SUPRA *c* ULTRA ‖ ofer 9r15[a]; 56r5. of' 2r8[a]; 17r15[b]; 57v17[c].
ofon: *a* CAMINUS *b* FORNAX ‖ ofen 41v6[b]. *sg. dat.* ofone 48v9[a]; 49r7[a]. ofne 49r8[b].
oft: (*a* QUOTIES) *b* SAEPE ‖ oft 86ra8[(a)]. *comp.* oftor 30r7[b].
of-ðon: *a* DEINDE *b* EXINDE *c* INDE ‖ ofðon 48v2[b]; 85ra21[a]; 86rb14[c].
on: (*a* ALTERUTER) (*b* IBIDEM) *c* IN (*d* RETRORSUM) (*e* UTERQUE) *A—making a Latin ablative* ‖ on 1r1[a]; 9v1[(d)]; 14r13[(a)]; 48v1[(b)]; 52r6[(e)]; 55r7; 87 va6[A].
onda: TIMOR ‖ onde 37v19.
ondeslic: *a* TERRIBILIS *b* horror ‖ ondeslic 33r18[a]; 77r4[b].
ondesni(s)s(e: TIMOR ‖ *sg. gen.* ondesnis' 2r4. ondes' 58r15.
ondetere: CONFESSOR ‖ ondetere 34v 15; 36v10. ondet'e 43r8. *sg. gen.* ondeteres 24r4; 31r22. ondeter' 36v7; 37r10. ondete' 37r14. ondet' 43r4. *pl. gen.* ondetera 43v19 [*alt. f.* ondetere]; 43v21. ondetra 35v22; 44r6. ondet' 36r6; 36r16. ond' 54v6. *pl. dat.* ondeterum 44r1.
ondetni(s)s(e: *a* CONFESSIO *b* PROFESSIO ‖ ondetnisse 8v21[a]; 35r16[b]. ondetnise 30r19[a]; 36r22[a]. *pl. dat.* ondetnissum 44r8[a].
giondetni(s)s(e: CONFESSIO ‖ *sg. gen.* giondetnisses 28v9.
onde(t)teð: *a* CONFITERI *b* FATERI *c* PROFITERI *d* confessio ‖ *pres. ind. sg. 1* ondeto 78vb16[a]. *pres. part.* ondettende 60r21[a]. ondetende *23v22[c]; 49v1[a]. *sg. fem.* ondetenda 50v1[c]. *pl. nom.* + *acc.* ondettendo 60v1[a]; 81va16[a]. ondetendo 23v10[a]. *pl. gen.* ondettendra 19v4[a]. *pl. dat.* ondetendum 20v3[a]; 30r9[d]. *pret. part.* giondeted 23v12[b].
gionde(t)teð: *a* CONFITERI *b* PROFITERI ‖ giondetað 7v7[b]; *40v20[a3].
ondu(e)ard: *a* PRAESENS *b* absens ‖ ondueard 48v16[a]. *sg. gen.* ondueardes 46v4[a]. ondueard' 32r22[a]; 50v12[a]. *sg. dat.* ondueardum 13r21[a]; 32r4[a]. *sg. acc. masc.* ondueardne 23v20[a]. *sg. acc.* + *dat. fem.* ondueard' 43r18[a]. *pl. dat.* ondueardum 80rb15[b].
ondu(e)ardað: PRAESENTARE ‖ *pret. part.* gionducardad 2v4–5. *pl. nom.* + *acc.* gionduardedo [*alt. f.* giondeuardedo] 2v6.
eft-giondu(e)ardað: REPRAESENTARE ‖ *imp. sg.* eftgiondueard a 60v5.
ondu(e)ardlic: PRAESENS ‖ *sg. acc.* + *dat. fem.* ondueardlic' 33v13. *pl. nom.* + *acc.* ondueardlica 79ra4.
ondu(e)ardni(s)s(e: PRAESENTIA ‖ onduærdnis' 59v11.
on-gægn: CONTRA ‖ ongægn 4r17; 7r19.
ongol: HAMUS ‖ *ongel[4] 88va19.
onn: *a* INDULGERE *b* praestabilis ‖ *pres. part.* unnende 19v8[a]. unnend 2v17[b].
gionn: *a* PRAEBERE *b* PRAESTARE ‖ *pres. ind. sg. 2* + *subj.* + *inf.* giunna [*alt. f.* giunne] 8v20[a]. giw[u]nne 20r10[b]. giwunne 55v20[b]. giwnne 32v19[b]; 82rb5[b]. giuunne 55v15[b]. giw[u]nna 48v18[b]. giunne [*alt. f.* gionne] 25v13[b]. giwnna 35v18[b]. *imp. sg.* gionn 1v2[b]; 1v17[b]. geonn 30v7[b]. gion' 11v6[b]; 36r20[b]. *pret. sg.* giuðe 54v17[a]. geuðe [*alt. f.* gewuðe] 88va6[b]. *pret. sg. ind. 2* giuðes 34v8[b]. giwðes 15v18[b].
onseade: *see* **on-sendeð.**
ordal ‖ *sg. dat.* ordale 55r18.
oroð: ANHELA ‖ oroð 86va3. *pl. nom.* + *acc.* oroðo 86va7.
oð: USQUE ‖ oð 10v9.
oðer: *a* ALIUS *b* CETERUS *c* RELIQUUS ‖ oðer 51v4[a]; 51v5[a]. oðor 86va7[a]; 86va8[a]. *pl. nom.* + *acc.* oðro 24v21[b]; 40r2[a]; 51v5[c]. oðero 51v1[a]. *pl. gen.* oðerra 45v4[b]. oðer'a 86vb8[a]. *pl. dat.* oðrum 3r17[a]. oðerum 22r9[a].
oð-to: USQUE AD ‖ oðto 27r6.
oðða: *a* AUT *b* SIUE *c* UEL *d* an ‖ oðða 85ra2[a]. oððe 6v5[b]; 51r10[d]; 55r19; 86rb5[c].
oð-ðæt: *a* DONEC *b* QUATENUS *c* QUOUSQUE *d* USQUE ‖ oðþ 1r18[a]; 18r8[b]; 52v21[d]; 80va19[c].
oð-uið: USQUE AD ‖ oðuið 27r6.
oxa: BOS ‖ *pl. nom.* + *acc.* exen 58r6.
pælma, palma: PALMA ‖ pælm' 31v14; 37v3. paelm' 45v7. *pl. gen.* palma' [*alt. f.* paelma'] 45v3.
unapinadlic: IMPUNE ‖ unapinedlic 54v17.
pinung: *a* POENA *b* TORMENTUM ‖ pinung 11v19[b]; 60r10[a]. *sg. acc.* + *dat.* pinunge 49v3[a]. *pl. nom.* + *acc.* pinungo 41v2[b]. *pl. gen.* pinunga 31r6[b].
plæca: PLATEA ‖ *pl. dat.* plæcum 17v14.
giplontað: PLANTARE ‖ *pres. subj.* + *inf.* giplontia 27r1.
of-plontað: EXPLANTARE ‖ *pres. subj.* + *inf.* ofplontia 59r3.
plontung: PLANTATIO ‖ plontung 31v15.
mea(s)s(a)-preost: PRESBYTER ‖ *measp'eost 87rb11. *pl. nom.* + *acc.* *measap'stas 87rb13. *pl. gen.* measap'sta' 87va11. meas' 87va23; 87va25.
prim: PRIMA ‖ prim 78r1; 79va6.
pund: PONDUS ‖ pund 86rb13; 86rb15. *pl. nom.* + *acc.* pundo 86rb12.
ra: capra ‖ *pl. nom.* + *acc.* ra 57v20. [h]rao 57r6.
on-rad: inequitare ‖ onrad 58r2.
rap: rete ‖ *pl. nom.* + *acc.* rapas 56v16; 56v22. *pl. dat.* rapum 57v10.
ræceð: *a* PORRIGERE *b* TRIBUERE ‖ *imp. sg.* ræc 19r20[a]; *20r10[b]. rǽc 11r19[b]; 15v11[b] [*alt. f.* girǽc].
giræceð: *a* EXTENDERE *b* PORRIGERE *c* TRIBUERE ‖ *pres. subj.* + *inf.* giræce 15v6[c]; 19v5[c]. *imp. sg.* giræc 7r21[a]; 22v13[c]. girǽc 32v11[a]; 42v15[c]. giræcg

1. genom *doubtful.*
2. mad *doubtful.*
3. gi *doubtful.*
4. on *doubtful.*

60r18[c]. *pret. sg.* girahte 33r12[a]. *pret. sg. ind. 2* girahtest 48v12[b].
ræcing: DETENTIO ‖ hræcing 31v12.
rædend: DISPOSITOR ‖ rædend 52r1.
rædeð: DISPONERE ‖ *pret. part.* giræded 41v4.
girædeð: *a* DISPENSARE *b* PROPONERE ‖ *pres. ind. sg. 2* giraedes 34r17[a]. *pres. subj. + inf.* girǽde 52r7[a]. *infl. inf.* girædenne 44v7[b].
fore-(fora-)rædni(s)s(e: PROPOSITUM ‖ f'aræden' 13v5.
fer-ræsend: REPENS ‖ *pl. nom. + acc.* feeræsenda 61r17.
ræst, rest: REQUIES ‖ ræst 31v2; 80rb12. rest 32r7.
giræst, -rest: ACCUBITUS ‖ *sg. acc. + dat.* giræste 2r19.
giræsteð, -resteð: *a* ACCUBARE *b* REQUIESCERE ‖ geresteð 88ra8[b]; 88ra 19[b]. giresteð 43r18[b]. gerestað 88rb8[b]; 88rb13[b]. gerestes 88ra22[b]. *gerest'[1] 88rb18[b]. geræst' 88rb24[b]. *pres. subj. + inf.* giresta 5r8[a]. gihresta 60v9[b]. gehræste 81va13[b]. *pret. sg.* gereste 88ra 12[b]; 88ra16[b]. gireste 31v9[b] [*alt. f.* giræste]; 88rb13[b].
eft-giræsteð, -resteð: REQUIESCERE ‖ *pret. sg.* eftgireste 31v5.
read: RUBEUS ‖ read 86rb16.
bi-reafað: EXUERE ‖ *pret. part.* bireafad 27v7; 38r12.
re(c)cone: CITO ‖ recone 81va22.
recels: *a* INCENSUM *b* balsamum *c* myrrha *d* turibulum ‖ recels 42v4[a]. recilc 31v18[b]; 31v19[c]; 33r11[(b)]. ræcelc 34r5[d]. *sg. gen.* recelces 2r20[c].
red: *a* LECTIO *b* STUDIUM ‖ *sg. dat.* rede 61v1[a]. *pl. nom. + acc.* rædo 17v21[b].
redere: LECTOR ‖ redere 87ra17. *pl. nom. + acc.* rederas 87ra17.
redeð: RECITARE ‖ *pres. subj. + inf.* reda *56r4[-]; 56v4[-]. *infl. inf.* redanne 87vb8.
regn: (IMBER) ‖ regn 40v19.
regol: CANON ‖ *pl. nom. + acc.* reglas 88vb23. regulas 88v26. *regul' 88v26[-].
reht: IUS ‖ reht 85va3; 85va4. *sg. gen.* rehtes 85rb12; 85va3.
reht: RECTUS ‖ reht 48v4; 78va2. *sg. acc. masc.* reht' 49r1. *pl. nom. + acc.* rehto 7v5.
unreht: *a* INIQUITAS *b* in iure ‖ unreht 85va5[b]. *pl. gen.* unrehtra 81va 21[a].
ned-reht: DEBITUM ‖ nedreht 42v22.
rehtlice: *a* AEQUUS *b* IUSTE *c* POTIUS *d* RECTE ‖ rehtlice 21r2[b]; 45r13[d]; 52r2[a]. rehtelice 86ra11[d]. *comp.* rehtlicor 9r 10[c].
unrehtuis: *a* INIQUUS *b* iniquitas *c* nequitia ‖ unrehtwis 5r22[a]. *sg. dat.* unrehtuisum 78va8[a]. *pl. nom. + acc.* unrehtuisso 4r4[b]. unrehtuiso 4r17[c].
rehtuislice: rationabile ‖ rehtuislice 12v4.
unrehtuisni(s)s(e: INIQUITAS ‖ unrehtuisnisse 5r15. unrehtuisnise 5v3. unrehtuissnise 5r16. unrehtuisnis' 37v 10. unrehtwisn' 9v17. unrehtuis'se 24v13. unreht' 78va12. unrehtuisnis' 81vb20. *pl. nom. + acc.* unrehtwisn' 9r18. unrehtuis'a 61r1. unreht' 78rb 24. *pl. dat.* unrehtuisnisum 32r8. unrehtuisnissum 78vb6.
cneo-reso: *a* GENERATIO *b* PROGENIES ‖ cneoreso 33r2[a]; 41r1[a]. cneorese 41r1[a]. cneorise 52v21[b].
gi-cneo-reso: GENERATIO ‖ gecneoreso 2r10.
æfter-cneo-reso: nepos ‖ *pl. nom. + acc.* æft'cneoreso 29v13.
eft-cneo-reso: REGENERATIO ‖ eftcneoreso 52r7–8.
-)rest(-: *see* -)**ræst(-**.
ric: REGNUM ‖ ric 29r20; 51r21. ríc 16v9; 39r2. *sg. gen.* rices 16r22; 28v11. *pl. nom. + acc.* rico 26v20; 52v20.
heofon-ric: CAELESTE REGNUM ‖ heofneric 16v9. heofnæric 87va4. *sg. gen.* heofonrices 16r21–2.
ricsað: *a* DOMINARI *b* GUBERNARE *c* REGERE *d* REGNARE ‖ ricsað 47r9[d]; 57v14[d]. ric' 49r22[d]. *pres. ind. sg. 2* ricsas 58r18[d]; 66v5[d]. ricsað 66r11[d]; 79ra23[d]. *pres. part.* ricsande 61v6[d]; 66v19[a]. *ricsende[2] 66r2[a]. *pl. gen.* *ricsandra[3] 48r18[a]. *pret. part.* giricsad 11r7[c]; 19r7[b].
giricsað: *a* DOMINARI *b* GUBERNARE *c* REGERE *d* REGNARE ‖ giricsað 13r12[a]; 41v11[d] [*alt. f.* giricsas]. *imp. sg.* giricsa 4r12; 38r9[b]. gericsa 81ra12[c].
ricsere: dominatio ‖ *pl. nom. + acc.* ricsares 54v3. ricsa's 86vb20[-].
rics(i)end: *a* DOMINARE *b* RECTOR ‖ *ricsand[4] 48v21[b]. ricsend 13r7[a].
ricsung: DOMINATIO ‖ ricsung 79va1. *sg. gen.* ricsunges 80va3; 81vb25.
ridend: ASCENSOR ‖ *pl. nom. + acc.* ridenda 87ra7.
rif: FEROX ‖ *sup. pl. nom. + acc.* rifista 61r17.
rihteð: DIRIGERE ‖ *pret. part.* girihtad 19r13. *pl. nom. + acc.* girihto 44r21.
girihteð: DIRIGERE ‖ *pres. subj. + inf.* gerihta 80va17; 83ra4. girihte 79rb9. *infl. inf.* girihtanne 78rb20. *imp. sg.* giriht *79rb2; 79rb6. girihte 78rb2.
riht- (reht-)ni(s)s(e: *a* AEQUITAS *b* RATIO ‖ rihtnisse 54v15[b]. rehtnise 48v22[a]. *pl. dat.* rihtnissum 16r6[b].
giriht-(reht-)ni(s)s(e: RECTITUDO ‖ girihtnise 27v1.
unriht-(reht-)ni(s)s(e: INIQUITAS ‖ *sg. gen.* unrehtnises 80rb21.
giriord: *a* ALIMENTUM *b* CENA *c* CIBUS *d* EPULA *e* EPULATIO *f* ESCA *g* PRANDIUM *h* UICTUS ‖ giriord 8v17[h]; 34r9[b]; 47r20[a] [*alt. f.* giriorde]; 51v2[g]. giriord 56v8[d]; 56v9[e]; 57v11[a]. *pl. gen.* giriorda 56r13[c]. *pl. dat.* giriordum 8r5[a]; 8r10[f]; 8v13[a].
riordað: reficere ‖ *pret. part. pl. nom. + acc.* giriordado 7v2.
giriordað: *a* CIBARE *b* EPULARI *c* SATIARE ‖ *pres. ind. sg. 2* giriordest 8v16[c]. *pres. subj. + inf.* gihriordiga 12r22[b]. *imp. sg.* geriord 66v8[c]. *pret. sg.* giriordade 22v6[a]; 40v9[a].
eft-riordað: reficere ‖ *pret. part.* eftgihriordad 18v4.
eft-giriordað: reficere ‖ *pres. ind. sg. 2* eftgihriordest 60v1.
giriorde: *a* ELOQUIUM *b* LOCUTIO ‖ giriorde 78vb18[b]. *pl. nom. + acc.* giriodo 40v19[a].
rip: MESSIS ‖ *sg. dat.* hrippe 66r1; 67r4. *pl. dat.* hrippum 67r13.
giriseð: CONSURGERE ‖ *pret. pl.* girioson 12r14.
ariseð: *a* CONSURGERE *b* EXSURGERE *c* INSURGERE *d* ORIRI *e* RESURGERE *f* SURGERE ‖ ariseð 3r3[d]. arisað [*alt. f.* girisað] 27r8[a]. *pres. subj. + inf.* arise 14v21[e]; 83rb10[f]. *imp. sg.* aris 27v22[f]; 28r11[f]. arís 78rb15[b]. *pres. part.* arisende 33r18[a]. *pl. nom. + acc.* arisendo 18r10[b]. *pl. dat.* arisendum 78va10[c]. *pret. sg. ind. 1, 3* aras 13r5[f]. *pret. sg. subj. + ind. 2* arise 77v12[f]. *pret. pl.* arioson 21r17[f]. *pret. part.* arisen 1v12[d]; 45r16[d].
eft-ariseð: RESURGERE ‖ *pres. subj. + inf.* eftarisa 79vb9–10. eft...arisa 14v 15; 32r8. *pret. sg. ind. 1, 3* eftaras 12v 19; 13r11. *pret. sg. subj. + ind. 2* eftarise 45r16.
rod(a: CRUX ‖ rod 11r11; 45r4. rode 11r3; 45r15. hroda 88vb5. *sg. gen.* rodes 10v9; 35r4. ródes 11v9. rod' 11v19; 45r10.
heh-giroefa: COMES ‖ heghgeroefa 86vb5.
rosa: ROSA ‖ *sg. gen.* rosæs 31v15.
rotni(s)s(e: *a* maeror *b* tristatus *c* tristitia ‖ rotnisse 87ra2[b]. rotnise 33v9[c]. rótnise 20r7[a].
unrotni(s)s(e: MAEROR ‖ unrotnise 50r19.
girotsað: contristari ‖ girotsiað 27r 20.

1. st *doubtful.*
2. ende *doubtful.*
3. dr *doubtful.*
4. ricsa *doubtful.*

unrotsað: CONTRISTARI ‖ *pres. subj.* + *inf.* unrotsiga 6r17.
roueð: NAUIGARE ‖ *pres. part. pl. dat.* roendum 81rb4.
rum: SPATIUM ‖ *sg. dat.* rume 18r6. *pl. nom.* + *acc.* rumo 79va21; 82ra13.
rumlic: *a* BENIGNUS *b* CLEMENTER *c* PROPITIUS ‖ *sg. weak* rumlice' 50r11[a]. *adv.* rumlice 21r7[c]; 24r10[b]; 36r12[a]. rum' 8r23[a].
u(o)el-rumlic: BENIGNUS ‖ *sg. weak* uelrumlice 20r9; 20r15.
giryne: *a* MYSTERIUM (*b* SACRAMENTUM) ‖ giryne 1v13[(a)]; 52v2[(b)]. *sg. gen.* gihrynes 3v20[(b)]. *pl. nom.* + *acc.* giryno 11v14[a]; 15v5[(b)]. gihryno 59r5[(b)]. *pl. dat.* girynum 9r4[(b)].
sacerd: SACERDOS ‖ sacerd 42r11; 87va17. sac' 87va22. *sg. gen.* sacerdæs 30r12. *pl. nom.* + *acc.* sacerdas 43v3; 43v10. sac' 87vb1.
sacerdhad: SACERDOTIUM ‖ sacerdhad 42v1; 42v3; 43v6 [*alt. f.* sacedhad].
sacerdlic: *a* SACERDOTALIS *b* sacerdotium ‖ sacerdlic 12v6[b]. sacerlichad [? *read* sacerdlic] 87va20[a].
salm: PSALMUS ‖ salm 78va14. *pl. nom.* + *acc.* salmas 83va21; 83vb11. salm' 83va9.
salt: *a* SAL *b* SALSUS ‖ salt 57r15[a]; 58v5[a]. *sg. gen.* saltes 56v21[a]; 57r5[a]. *pl. nom.* + *acc.* salto 86rb18[b].
sar ‖ *sg. dat.* sare 55v15.
sau(e)l: ANIMA ‖ sauel 1r3; sawel 3r2; 5r14. saul 82ra1. *sg. gen.* saueles 79vb9. saules 47r22; 47v10. sawles 10r11; 14v15. *sg. acc.* + *dat.* saule 25r6. sawle 9v22. *pl. nom.* + *acc.* sauelo 57r9. saulo 20r5; *41r20. *pl. gen.* sauela 50r12. saula 1v5; 4v10. saulo 43r3. *pl. dat.* saulum 34v4. sawlum 17v19.
sæ: MARE ‖ sæ 82vb22. sae 56v6; 78va18.
uið-sæ(c)ceð: RESPUERE ‖ *pres. part.* wiðsæcg/[c]ende 16v18.
unasæcgendlic: *a* INEFFABILIS *b* INENARRABILIS ‖ unasæcgendlic 16r14[a]. *unasægcgendlic[1] 17r16[a]. *sg. dat.* unasæcgendlicum 18v9[b]. *sg. acc.* + *dat. fem.* unasæcgendlic' 3v20[a]. *pl. dat.* unasæcgendlicum 9r4[a]. unasæccendlicum 52r6[a].
asægdni(s)s(e: *a* hostia *b* oblatio (*c* sacrificium) ‖ asægdnisse 6r9[a]; 52r9[b]. asægdnise 50v16[b]. asægdnis' 60v19[b]. *pl. nom.* + *acc.* asægdnisso 42v8[(c)]. asægdniso 61r3[b].
sægeð: *a* ANNUNTIARE *b* DICERE *c* NARRARE *d* REFERRE ‖ sægeð 87ra22[d]. sæcgað 29v17[c]. *imp. sg.* sæge 86va12[b]. sægi 86va5[b]. *pres. part.* sæcgende 25r11[a]. *pret. pl.* sægdon 29v17[c].
gisægeð: *a* ANNUNTIARE *b* PRONUNTIARE ‖ *pres. subj.* + *inf.* gisæcge 12v7[a]; 29v18[b]. *imp. sg.* gisægi 2v19–20[a].
asægeð: offerre ‖ *pret. sg.* asægde 12v12.
ascæ(c)ceð: *a* CONCUTERE *b* DISCUTERE ‖ *pret. part.* asceæccen 28v9[a]. *pl. dat.* ascæccenum 18r11[b].
scæft: CREATURA ‖ scæft 33r9.
giscæft: *a* CREATURA *b* RES *c* elementum ‖ giscæft 46r20[a]; 47r18[a]; 57v3[a] [*alt. f.* giscæfto]. gescæft 66r1[a]; 66r5[a]. gesceæft 66v13[a]. *sg. gen.* giscæftes 13v2[a]2. *sg. dat.* giscæfte 54v21[a]; 59r7[c]. *pl. nom.* + *acc.* giscæfto 43r10[c]. *pl. gen.* giscæfta *77r20[b][2]; 77v2[b].
giscæp(p: *a* HABITUS *b* SEXUS ‖ giscæp 24v22[b]. giscæp' 49v11[a].
scæ(p)pend: *see* **sce(p)pend.**
gisceadeð: *a* DISCERNERE *b* DISTINGUERE *c* SEPARARE *d* destituere ‖ *pres. ind. sg. 2* gisceadas 18r2[a]. *imp. sg.* giscead 18r3[b] *pret. sg. ind. 2* gisceadest 7v23[d]; 15r20[d]. gesceadest 83rb3[c].
asceadeð: *a* SEGREGARE *b* destituere ‖ *pret. part.* asceaden 9r6[b]; 43v8[a].
to-sceadeð: deferre ‖ *pret. pl.* tosceadon 42v10.
sceal ‖ *scall 56r4.
bryd-sceamol: TORUS ‖ *sg. dat.* brydsceam' 52v15.
gisceapað: CREARE ‖ *imp. sg.* gisceap' 78va1.
scearo: TONDERE ‖ *sg. gen.* sceares 46r16.
sceaða: LATRO ‖ sceaðe 60r21.
gisceauað: *a* CERNERE *b* CONSIDERARE *c* CONSPICERE *d* INTUERII ‖ gisceawað 17v13[b]. *pres. ind. sg. 2* gisceauas 82vb10[d]. gisceawast 3v14[c]. *pres. subj.* + *inf.* gisceauia 31r16[d]; 38v11[c]. gisceawiga 17v5[a].
heh-sceauere: pontifex ‖ hehsceaware 10r19.
i(n)n-sceauere: INSPECTOR ‖ insceawre 87rb17. *pl. nom.* + *acc.* insceawras 87rb18–19. *pl. gen.* insceaura 87rb23.
sceauung: ASPECTUS ‖ *sg. acc.* + *dat.* sceaunge 35v9.
fore-(fora-)sceauung: PROUIDENTIA ‖ *sg. gen.* f'esceaunges 53r1. *sg. acc.* + *dat.* f'esceaunge 27v5; 47r11. f'esceauunge 52r6.
ym(b)-sceauung: *a* CIRCUMSPECTIO *b* CONTEMPLARI ‖ ymbsceawung 22v5[a]. *sg. acc.* + *dat.* ymbsceaunge 40v8[a]. ymbsceaw'ge 1r18[b].
sceld: SCUTUM ‖ sceld 44r21; 78rb14.
unscended: *a* ILLAESUS *b* INCORRUPTUS ‖ unscended 12r8[b]. unscende'd [? *read* unscended] 49r11[a]. *pl. gen.* unscendenda' [? *read* unscendeda'] 50r11[b].
ungiscended: ILLAESUS ‖ ungiscended 66v14.
unascended: ILLAESUS ‖ *pl. nom.* + *acc.* unascendedo 55r3–4. unascendado 48v9; 79vb2.
scendeð: *a* CONFUNDERE *b* CORRUMPERE ‖ *pres. ind. sg. 1* scendo 1r12[a]. *pres. part.* scendende 59r14[b]. *pret. part.* giscended 40v11[a].
scendung: afflictio ‖ *scendung 41r22.
sceoma: *a* CALUMNIA *b* CONFUSIO *c* CONTUMELIA *d* OPPROBRIUM ‖ scoma 85vb10[d]. sceoma 48v20[a]. sceome 13v7[b]. *pl. nom.* + *acc.* sceomo 51v6[c].
sceomað: *a* CONFUNDERE *b* rubeta ‖ *pres. part.* sceomiende 38r6[a]; 61r14[b]. sceomigende 9v5[a]; 9v7[a].
gisceomað: CONFUNDERE ‖ *pres. subj.* + *inf.* gisceomiga 61r8.
sceomfull: PUDICUS ‖ sceomfull 52r5.
sceomful(l)ni(s)s(e: UERECUNDIA ‖ sceomfull [? *read* sceomfull'] 52v17.
sceomlic: corruptibilis ‖ sceomlic 3r12.
unsceomlic: incorruptus ‖ *sg. acc.* + *dat. fem.* unsceomlic' 3r13.
sceondlic: corruptibilis ‖ *pl. dat.* sceondlicum 12r10.
gisceoð: CALCIARE ‖ *imp. sg.* gisceo 28r13.
sce(p)pend, scæ(p)pend: *a* AUCTOR *b* CONDITOR *c* CREATOR ‖ scæppend 53r19[c]; 66r13[c]. scæpend 82rb14[c]. sceppend 31v4[c]; 47v1[c]. scepend 16r18[b]. *sg. gen.* scependes 16v7[a].
frum-sce(p)pend, -scæ(p)pend: AUCTOR ‖ frumsceppend 59v1. frumscepend 8r8.
sce(p)peð, scæ(p)peð: FORMARE ‖ *pret. sg. ind. 1, 3* sceop 27r5.
gisce(p)peð, -scæ(p)peð: *a* CONDERE *b* CREARE *c* FORMARE ‖ *pret. sg. ind. 1, 3* gisceop 31v4[b]. *pret. sg. subj.* + *ind. 2* gisceope 26v11[c]; 52r21[a]; 61r21[b].
asce(p)peð, -scæ(p)peð: CREARE ‖ *pret. part.* ascæpen 33r5.
scereð: TONDERE ‖ *infl. inf.* scearanne 46v1.
gisce(ð)ðendlic: NOCIUUS ‖ *pl. nom.* + *acc.* gisceððendlica 57v9.
sce(ð)ðeð: *a* NOCERE *b* NOXIUS *c* aduersarius ‖ *pres. part.* sceððende 78rb12[a]. *pl. nom.* + *acc.* sceðend' 61r17[b]. *pl. gen.* sceððendra 77r23[b].

1. *1st* g *inchoate, perhaps deliberately left to be read as* c.

2. a *doubtful.*

pl. dat. sceððendum 8r11[b]; 54v21[c]; 77r3[a].

gisce(ð)ðeð: *a* NOCERE *b* aduersari ‖ gisceðeð 4r23[a]. gesceððað 67r13[b]. *pres. subj. + inf.* gesceððe 81vb21[a]. gisceððe 49v2[a]; 56r11[a].

scildend: PROTECTOR ‖ scildend 7v 14; 46v17. *sg. gen.* scildendes 36v20.

scildeð: *a* DEFENDERE *b* PROTEGERE *c* TUERI ‖ *pres. ind. sg. 2* scildes 36v4[b]. *imp. sg.* scild 32v23[a]; 38r7[c]. *pres. part.* scildende 49v11[b]. *pret. part.* scildad 36r7[a]. giscilded 16v13[a]; 19v11[b]. giscildad 18r17[b]. *sg. fem.* giscildado 59r20[a]. *pl. nom. + acc.* giscildado 37r6[b].

giscildeð: *a* CONTEGERE *b* DEFENDERE *c* PROTEGERE *d* TEGERE *e* TUERI *f* TUTARE ‖ giscildað 33v23[c]. *pres. ind. sg. 2* giscildes 30r10[c]. giscildis 44r9[c]. *pres. subj. + inf.* gescilde 66v1[b]. gescilda 83rb8[c]. giscilde 24r21[e]; 43v20[e]; 44r 18[d]; 44r19[b]. giscilda 18r21[b]; 59v16[e]; 60v12[e]; 77r5[a]. *imp. sg.* gescild 81vb 18[e]. giscild 4r22[e]; 28v19[b]; 30r3[c]. *pret. sg.* giscilde 39r4[f].

ascildeð: PROTEGERE ‖ *pres. subj. + inf.* ascilda 36r14. *pret. part.* ascildad 36r9; 38v8.

scilding: TUTUM ‖ scilding 47v16.

scildni(s)s(e: *a* DEFENSIO *b* PROTECTIO *c* PROTEGERE *d* TUITIO *e* TUTELA ‖ scildnisse 15r21[b]; 39v10[a]; 47v11[e]. scildnise 3v16[b]; 42r7[a]; 45r17[d]; 57r8[e]. scildnis'e 4r11[c]. scildnis' 36r6[b]. *sg. gen.* scildnisses 31r10[b]. scildnises 8v9[b]. scildnis'e 26r17[b]. scildnis' 46v2[b].

giscildni(s)s(e: *a* DEFENSIO *b* PROTECTIO *c* TUITIO *d* TUTELA ‖ giscildnisse 19r4[a]. giscildnise 8r21[b]; 30r4[a]; 56v1[d]. *sg. gen.* giscildnisses 30r7[c]; 57r8[a]. giscildnises 47v5[a].

scineð: SPLENDIDUS ‖ *pres. part.* scinende 1r21.

giscineð: *a* FULGERE *b* INNITERE ‖ giscineð 41v9[a]. *pres. subj. + inf.* giscina 7r17[a]; 32v4[a]. *pret. sg. ind. 1, 3* giscean 22r10[b].

eft-scineð: REFULGERE ‖ *pret. sg. ind. 1, 3* eftscean 28r10.

eft-giscineð: REFULGERE ‖ *pres. subj. + inf.* eftgiscine 41r19.

scip: OUIS ‖ scip 78ra6. *pl. nom. + acc.* scíp 5r2. scip 5r6; 5r8; 17v8 [*alt. f.* scipo]. scipo 9v15. scip' 58r6. *pl. gen.* scípa 13v10. scipa 5r4.

scir: UICUS ‖ *pl. dat.* scirum 87va7.

giscir: actio ‖ gescír 85ra4.

meg-scir: decurio ‖ *sg. acc. + dat.* megscire 86vb15.

scort: BREUIS ‖ scort 85ra8. *sg. acc. masc.* scortne 85ra9.

giscrinceð: ARESCERE ‖ *pres. subj. + inf.* giscrinca 61r18.

giscroepe: APTUS ‖ *pl. nom. + acc.* giscroepo 56v22.

unascry(u)ncen: IMMARCESCIBILIS ‖ *sg. acc. + dat. fem.* unascryuncan' 12r8.

scyld: UITIUM ‖ scyld 55r18⁻. *pl. gen.* scylda' 50v3.

giscyld: REATUS ‖ *pl. dat.* giscyldum 38r11.

scyldig: *a* DEBITOR *b* NOCENS *c* REUS ‖ scyldig 61r6[a]. *pl. nom. + acc.* scyldigo 24v14[c]. *pl. gen.* scyldigra 11v19[b].

unscyldig: INNOCENS ‖ unscyldig 43v7; 48r9. *sg. fem.* unscyldig' 52v19. *pl. nom. + acc.* unscyldigo 23v9.

deað-scyldig: REUS ‖ *pl. nom. + acc.* deadscyldigo 37v11.

scyldigni(s)s(e: REATUS ‖ scyldignis' 49v3.

unscyldigni(s)s(e: INNOCENTIA ‖ unscyldignisse 24r2.

deað-scyldigni(s)s(e: REATUS ‖ ðeað...scyldignis' 20v16.

giscynað: METUERE ‖ *pres. subj. + inf.* giscynia 15v19.

on-scynað: *a* FORMIDARE *b* METUERE ‖ onscynað 61r13[b]. *pres. subj. + inf.* onscynia 24v2[a].

scyrteð: ABBREUIARE ‖ *pret. part. sg. fem.* giscyrtedo 3r5.

scytil: MOMENTUM ‖ *pl. nom. + acc.* sgytila 79va21.

scy(u)a: UMBRA ‖ scya 78rb19.

fore-(fora-)scy(u)a: UMBRA ‖ f'ascya 6v14.

ascy(u)feð: DEPONERE ‖ ascyfað 12v3.

of-scy(u)feð: DEPONERE ‖ *pres. part.* ofscyfende 16r7. *pret. pl.* ofscyufon 46r12.

fore-(fora-)scy(u)uung: OBUMBRATIO ‖ f'ascywung 13v21.

ym(b)-sean: INTUITUS ‖ *sg. acc. + dat.* ymbseane 17v5.

sed: *a* SEMEN *b* semita ‖ sed 29v12[a]; 29v14[a]. *pl. nom. + acc.* sedo 66v11[a]. *pl. dat.* sedum 17v16[b].

sedlic: SEMINALIS ‖ *sg. acc. + dat. fem.* sedlic' 66v9.

gisegnað: CONSIGNARE ‖ *imp. sg.* gisægna 58r15.

fore-(fora-)segnað: PRAESIGNARE ‖ *pret. sg. ind. 2* f'esegnadest 52v2.

se(i)sta: SEXTUS ‖ seista 60r15.

giseleni(s)s(e: *a* DONATIO *b* TRADITIO ‖ giselenise 25r21[a]. *sg. gen.* giselenisses [*alt. f.* giselenissese] 12r12[b].

eft-seleni(s)s(e: RETRIBUTIO ‖ *pl. nom. + acc.* eftseleniso 78vb4.

giselig: FELIX ‖ giselig 33v6.

seliglice: FELICITER ‖ *seliglice[1] 38r 15.

se(l)lend: DATOR ‖ sellend 47v1; 49v13.

se(l)leð: *a* DARE *b* DONARE *c* PRAEBERE *d* TRADERE *e* TRIBUERE ‖ sellað 85ra23[a]. *pres. ind. sg. 1* sello 1r4[e]; 82va16[a]. sila 27v21[a]. *pres. ind. sg. 2* seles 26r7[e]. *pres. subj. + inf.* selle 81va15[d]. *imp. sg.* sel 1r20[a]; 24v1[e]. *pres. part. pl. nom. + acc.* sellendo 5v20[a]. *pret. sg.* salde 2r19[a]; 6r22[b]. *pret. sg. ind. 2* saldest 15r10[e]; 52r21[a]. *pret. pl.* saldon [*alt. f.* gisaldon] 23v16[c]. *pret. part.* sald 6r23[d]; 22v17[b]; 39v20[a]. gisald 34r5[a].

gise(l)leð: *a* DARE *b* DONARE *c* PRAEBERE *d* TRADERE *e* TRIBUERE *f* praestare ‖ giselið 40v14[d]. gisilið 23v19[f]. gisileð 5v14[a]. *pres. ind. sg. 2* giseleð 2r23[e]; *44v20[e2]. *pres. subj. + inf.* giselle 6r16[a]; 30v20[c]; 33v3[e]. geseallа 85rb2[a]; 86ra12[a]. *imp. sg.* gisel 35r15[e]; 35r19[e]. *pret. sg.* gisalde 2r18[a]; 6r8[d]. gesalde 81rb20[a]. *pret. sg. ind. 2* gisaldes 23r8[e]; *38r22[b]. gisaldest 14v7[a]; 28v 12[d]; 31r5[e]; 36v12[b].

eft-se(l)leð: *a* REDDERE *b* RETRIBUERE ‖ *imp. sg.* eftsel 81vb8[b]. *pret. sg. ind. 2* eftsaldest 46v15[a].

ym(b)-se(l)leð: CIRCUMDARE ‖ *pres. ind. sg. 2* ymbseles 30r10; 36v4. ymbselið 44r9. *pres. subj. + inf.* ymbselle 16v11–10.

sendeð: MITTERE ‖ sendeð 85va15. sendas 51v20. *pres. subj. + inf.* sende 26v15; 56r6. senda 57r13; 59v15. *imp. sg.* send 31v7; 47v3. sende 58r11. *pres. part.* sendend 48r9. *pret. sg.* sende 26v18; 28r19. *pret. part.* gesended 85va17. *pl. nom. + acc.* gisendedo 49r8.

gisendeð: *a* EMITTERE *b* MITTERE ‖ gisendeð 40v19[b]. gisendes 49r11[b]. *pres. ind. sg. 1* gisendo 61r4[a]. *pres. subj. + inf.* gisende 48r11[b]; 48v2[b]. *pret. sg.* gisende 48v17[b]; 51v1[b].

of-sendeð: effundere ‖ *imp. sg.* ofsend 78rb16.

on-sendeð: IMMITTERE ‖ *pret. sg.* onseade [? *read* onsende] 81vb10.

ðerh-sendeð: PERMITTERE ‖ *imp. sg.* ðerhsend 53r20; 66r15.

gisene: UIDERE ‖ gisene 1r9; 41r21.

gisenelice: UISIBILITER ‖ gisenelice 49v9.

seofa(n)fald: SEPTIFORMIS ‖ seofafald 58r12.

seofa(n)fal(d)lice: septies ‖ seofanfallice 86ra17.

seolf: IPSE ‖ seolf 5r2; 9v18[0]. seolfa 3r17. seolfe 6r9. *sg. acc. masc.* seolfne

1. igli *doubtful.*

2. le *doubtful.*

3v7; 10v5. *pl. nom.* + *acc.* seolfa 5v22; 14r16. *pl. dat.* seolfum 6v19.
seolfor, sulfor: ARGENTUM ‖ sulfer 27v20. *sg. gen.* seolferes 39r9. *sg. dat.* seolfre 12r10. sulfere [*alt. f.* sulferne] 2r16.
se(t)teð: *a* CONSTITUERE *b* FUNDARE *c* INSTITUERE *d* PONERE ‖ *imp. sg.* sett 80rb25[d]; 81vb22[d]. *pret. part.* gisetted 4v21[c]. gesetted 85rb13[b]; 86vb2[a]. *pl. nom.* + *acc.* gisetedo 4r6[a]. gesettedo 87va7–8[a]. *pl. dat.* gisettedum 21v4[d].
gise(t)teð: *a* CONSTITUERE *b* FUNDARE *c* PONERE *d* STATUERE ‖ *pres. subj.* + *inf.* gisette 81rb10[d]. gesetta 87va9[a]. *imp. sg.* gesett 83ra14[c]. *pres. part.* gisettende 29v5[a]. *pret. sg.* gisette 9v16[d]; 26v19[a]; 38r2[d]; 39r13[b]. [gi]sette 9v6[c]. *pret. sg. ind. 2* gisettest 45r15[a].
ase(t)teð: *a* CONSTITUERE *b* FUNDARE *c* INSTITUERE *d* PONERE *e* REPONERE ‖ *pret. part.* asetted 29r14[e]; 42v7[a]; 52r22[c]; 58r1[d]. astetted [? *read* asetted] 28v15[b].
fore-(fora-)se(t)teð: PROPONERE ‖ *pret. part.* f'aset' 13v6.
i(n)n-se(t)teð: INSTITUERE ‖ *pret. part.* ingesetted 85va2.
of-se(t)teð: DEPONERE ‖ *infl. inf.* ofsettenne 45v22.
to-se(t)teð: APPONERE ‖ *pres. subj.* + *inf.* tosette 80rb22; 81vb21.
set(t)ni(s)s(e: INSTITUTUM ‖ *pl. dat.* settnissum 52r15.
gise(t)tni(s)s(e: PROPOSITUM ‖ gisetnise 49v10 [*alt. f.* gisetnisum]; 50r9. gisetnis' 49v19.
frum-se(t)tni(s)s(e: auctoritas ‖ frumsettnesse 60r6.
i(n)n-se(t)tni(s)s(e: INSTITUTUM ‖ *pl. nom.* + *acc.* *insetniso[1] 53r1. *pl. dat.* insetnissum 16v15. insetnis'um 9r5.
on-se(t)tni(s)s(e: INSIDIAE ‖ *pl. nom.* + *acc.* onsetnis' 59r15.
on-se(t)tnung: INSIDIAE ‖ *pl. nom.* + *acc.* onsettnungo 67r17.
gise(t)to: INSIDIAE ‖ giseto 18r18.
seðel: SEDES ‖ seðel 57r9. *sg. gen.* sedles 13v8. *sg. dat.* sedle 23r19.
heh-seðel: *a* THRONUS *b* TRIBUNAL ‖ *sg. dat.* hehseðle [*alt. f.* hehseðile] 6v3[b]. hehsedle 23v5[a]; 34r7[a]. *pl. nom.* + *acc.* hehsedlo 54v3[a].
sex: SEX ‖ sex 56v10.
sgytila: *see* **scytil**.
sibb: *a* PAX *b* foedus ‖ sibb 6v10[a]; 6v20[a]. sib 19v6[a]; 43r22[a]. *sg. gen.* sibbes 6v10[a]; 13v9[a]. *sg. acc.* + *dat.* sibbe 1r21[a]; 10r14[b]. sibe 81rb17[a]. *pl. nom.* + *acc.* sibba 52r2[b].
sibsum(m: PACIFICUS ‖ *sg. fem.* sibsum' 19r12. *pl. nom.* + *acc.* sibsumo 39r12.
sida: LATUS ‖ side 28r11. sido 55v8.
sig: *a* TRIUMPHUS *b* UICTORIA *c* brabeum ‖ sig 3r9[c]; 13v15[b] [*alt. f.* gisig]; 24v22[b]; 31r11[a]. *pl. nom.* + *acc.* *sig' 41v19[b].
sigfæst: TRIUMPHATOR ‖ sigfæst 59v2.
sigfæstað: coronare ‖ *pret. part.* gisigfæstad 29r12. *pl. nom.* + *acc.* gisigfæstado 23v23.
gisigfæstað: coronare ‖ *pret. sg.* gisigfæstade 78vb12.
sigfæstni(s)s(e: *a* TRIUMPHUS *b* UICTORIA ‖ *sg. gen.* sigfæst' 45v7[b]. *pl. dat.* sigfæstnissum 44v11[a]. sigfæstnisum 36r14[a].
i(n)n-sigle: SIGNACULUM ‖ insiglae [*alt. f.* insigloe] 14v1.
gisihð: UISUS ‖ *sg. acc.* + *dat.* gisihðe 28r16; 56r12. gisihde *77r4⁻.
siið: UIDERE ‖ *pres. ind. sg. 1* sium 21v2.
gisiið: *a* CONSPICERE *b* UIDERE ‖ giseað 6r2[b]; 27r8[a]. *pres. ind. sg. 2* gisiist 20r2[a]; 34v22[a]. *pres. subj.* + *inf.* gisii 52v20[b]; 61r21[b]. gisea 2v10[b]; 7v4[b]. *imp. sg.* gisih 34r11[b]. *pret. sg. ind. 1, 3* gisæh 21v1[b]; 23r11[b]. *pret. sg. subj.* + *ind. 2* gisege 2v9[b]; 27v18[b]. gisegi 51v15[b]. *pret. pl.* gisegon 33r14[b].
bi-siið: *a* ASPICERE *b* CONSPICERE *c* RESPICERE ‖ *pres. ind. sg. 2* bisiist 7v23[b]; 15r19[b]. *imp. sg.* besih 49v18[c]; 82rb1[a]. biseh 4r10[c]; 4v2[c]. bisih 11v17[c]. bisigh 7v12[c].
eft-bi-siið: RESPICERE ‖ *pres. subj.* + *inf.* *eft...besii[2] 61r1. eft...bisii 48v13. *imp. sg.* eftbesih 46r15; 50r8. eftbesigh 45v16. eftbisih 11r6; 19v24. eftbiseh 8r10.
ðerh-bi-siið: PERSPICERE ‖ ðerhbisið 14r17.
sin: SUUS ‖ sin 2r18; 9v11. *sg. gen.* sines 2r11; 9v9. *sg. dat.* sinum 1v21; 2r19. *pl. gen.* sinra 10r4. *pl. dat.* sinum 23r18; 37v19.
singal: diurnus ‖ *pl. nom.* + *acc.* singal 77v3.
singeð: CANTARE ‖ *pres. subj.* + *inf.* singa 78ra11; 82vb5. *imp. sg.* sinc 55v15⁻.
gisingeð: *a* CANERE *b* CANTARE *c* DECANTARE ‖ *pres. subj.* + *inf.* gisinga 77r9[a]. *imp. sg.* gesing 83va12[c]; 83va 21[c]. *pret. pl.* gisungan 23r19[b].
gisinigscip(e: CONNUBIUM ‖ gisinigscip' 52r5. *sg. gen.* gisinig' 51v21.
on-sion(e: *a* CONSPECTUS *b* FACIES *c* UULTUS ‖ onsione 26v16[b]; 34v6[a]; 46r4[c]. onsion 9v2[b]; 53r5[c].
sitteð: SEDERE ‖ sitteð 13v8. sittes 78rb19. *pres. part.* sittende 12r15.
gisitteð: *a* CONSEDERE *b* SEDERE *c* constituere ‖ gesittes 82vb11[b]. *pres. subj.* + *inf.* gisitte 13v3[a]. *pres. part.* gisittende 28v20[c].
efne-sitteð: CONSEDERE ‖ *pres. part.* efnesittende [*alt. f.* efnesittendum] 17r10.
eft-asitteð: RESIDERE ‖ *pres. subj.* + *inf.* eftasitta 59r14.
i(n)n-sitteð: INSTITUERE ‖ *pret. part. pl. dat.* insetenum 4r14.
siðða: DEINDE ‖ siðða 43v11.
slaeð: *a* OCCIDERE *b* PERCUTERE ‖ *pres. part. pl. dat.* slændum 9v2[b]. *pret. part. pl. nom.* + *acc.* gislægno 51v3[a].
of-slaeð: OCCIDERE ‖ *pret. pl.* ofslogon 51v7. *pret. part.* ofslægen 14v2.
ðerh-slaeð: PERCUTERE ‖ *pret. part.* ðerhslægen 20v10.
mon(n)-slaga: HOMICIDA ‖ *pl. nom.* + *acc.* monslago 51v8.
slep: *a* DORMITATIO *b* SOMNUS ‖ slep 82va17[b]; 82va18[a].
slepeð: DORMIRE ‖ *pres. subj.* + *inf.* slepa 14r5; 14r11. *pres. part. pl. gen.* slependra 13r15.
fore-(fora-)slepeð: OBDORMIRE ‖ *pret. sg.* f'eslepde 21v6.
sli(t)teð: DISCORDARE ‖ *pres. part. pl. dat.* slitendum 81rb13.
gisli(t)teð: RUMPERE ‖ *pres. subj.* + *inf.* geslita 86ra14.
to-sli(t)teð: *a* DISRUMPERE *b* LACERARE ‖ *pres. ind. sg. 1* toslito 1r10[a]. *pret. part. pl. nom.* + *acc.* tosliteno 17v10[b].
smeað: *a* MEDITARI *b* TRACTARE ‖ *infl. inf.* smeanne 3v22[b]. *pres. part.* smeande 22v4[a]; 40v7[a].
gismeað: *a* EXCOGITARI *b* SCRUTARI ‖ gismeað 10r5[b]; 44v4[b]. *pres. subj.* + *inf.* gismeaiga 78vb22[a].
smeauung: COGITATIO ‖ smeaung' [*alt. f.* smeaungo] 44r16. *sg. acc.* + *dat.* smeaunge 78vb18. smeawnge 10v14. *pl. nom.* + *acc.* smeawngo 5r25.
smirini(s)s(e: UNGUENTUM ‖ *sg. gen.* smirenisse 56r8. smirinise 56r16. *pl. gen.* smirenis' 2r12.
smirueð: UNGERE ‖ *pret. part.* *gesmiruad[3] 88vb14.
smolt: (IMBER) ‖ smolt 40v19.
smylte: sincerus ‖ smylte 23v18. *pl. dat.* smyltum 3v22; 8r15.
smyltlic: *a* SERENUS *b* TRANQUILLUS *c* sincerus ‖ *sg. dat.* smyltlicum 19r13[b]. *pl. dat.* smyltlicum 47v13[a]. smyltlic' 4v7[c].
smyltni(s)s(e: *a* QUIES *b* TRANQUILLITAS ‖ smyltnisse 15v6[b]; 83vb9–10[a].

1. inset *doubtful.*
2. ii *doubtful.*
3. mir *doubtful.*

smyltnise 19v14[b]. *sg. gen.* smylt' 59r17[a].

sno(t)tor: SAPIENS ‖ snotor 50r15. snottor 52v12.

unsno(t)tor: INSIPIENS ‖ *pl. gen.* unsnotterra 41r21.

sny(t)tro: SAPIENTIA ‖ snytro *21r20[1]; 22v3. *snyttro 40v21. snytre 29v17; 39r7. snyttre 39r12. *sg. gen.* snytres 22r18; 22v7. snyttres 40v8; 58r13.

to-socni(s)s(e: ACQUISITIO ‖ tosocnis' 14r9.

to-socnung: ACQUISITIO ‖ tosocnung 39r8.

soeceð: (*a* FREQUENTARE) *b* QUAERERE *c* UISITARE ‖ soecað 2v21[b]; 5r20[b]. soecas 61r8[b]. *pres. ind. sg. 1* soeco 5r3[c]. *pres. subj.* + *inf.* soeca 7r9[b]; 38v11[(a)]. *pres. part.* soecende 9v23[b]; 17v15[b]. *pl. dat.* soecendum 20v4[b]. *pret. sg.* sohte 81ra25[b].

gisoeceð: *a* QUAERERE *b* REQUIRERE ‖ *pres. subj.* + *inf.* gisoece 10r5[a]. *imp. sg.* gisoec 80va10[b]. *pret. sg.* gisohte 31v2[a].

eft-soeceð: REQUIRERE ‖ *pres. ind. sg. 1* eftsoeca 5r2.

to-gisoeceð: assequi ‖ *pres. subj.* + *inf.* togisoeca 37r16.

unsofte ‖ unsofte 55r21.

somnað: CONFERRE ‖ *pret. part. pl. nom.* + *acc.* gisomnado 16r19.

gisomnað: *a* COLLIGARE *b* COLLOCARE *c* CONGREGARE *d* COPULARE *e* amplificare ‖ gisomniað 33r21[c]. *pres. subj.* + *inf.* gisomniga 20v19[e]; 79vb7[c]. gisomnia 52r13[d]. *pret. sg. ind. 2* gisomnadest 48r22[a]; 49v19[b]. *pret. pl.* gisomnadon 51v13[c].

somnung: *a* CONGREGATIO *b* synagoga ‖ *sg. gen.* somnunges 80ra12–13[a]. *sg. acc.* + *dat.* somnunge 21r17[b].

lof-song: *a* CANTICUM *b* CARMEN ‖ lofsong 23r19[a]; 23r21[a]. *pl. nom.* + *acc.* lofsongas 77v17[b].

or-sorg: SECURUS ‖ orsorg 40v5. *sg. dat.* orsorgum [*alt. f.* orsorgo] 36v15. *pl. nom.* + *acc.* orsorgo 7v19; 33v21.

sorgleas: SECURUS ‖ sorgleas 27r13; 30v6. *sg. dat.* sorgleasum 4r20; 8v10. *sg. acc. masc.* sorgleasne 19v14.

soð: UERUS ‖ soð 1r5; 18r13. *sg. acc. masc.* soðne *58v3.

soðfæst: *a* IUSTUS *b* UERAX ‖ soðfæst 5r10[a]; 77r20[b]. soð' 49r1[a]. *sg. fem.* soðfæsta 40v14[a]. *sg. gen.* soðfæstes 2v7[a]; 37v16[a]. *sg. weak* soðfæsta 39r2[a]. *pl. nom.* + *acc.* soðfæsto 41v9[a]; 42r1[a]. soðfæsta 41r20[a]. *pl. gen.* soðfæstra 36r17[a]; *81va2[a2]. *sup.* soðfæst' 49r19[a]. *sup. sg. fem.* soðfæstisto 49r14[a].

1. ro *doubtful.*
2. soðfæ *doubtful.*

unsoðfæst: INIUSTUS ‖ *pl. dat.* unsoðfæstum 10v11; 12v12.

soðfæstað: IUSTIFICARE ‖ *pret. part.* gisoðfæsted 13r2.

soðfæstni(s)s(e: *a* IUSTITIA *b* UERITAS ‖ soðfæstnise 8r5[a]; 49r14[b]. soðfaestnis' 79va12–13[a]. soðfæstnis' 5r10[a]; 19v21[a]. soðfæstn' 5r12[b]; 5r18[a]. soðfæst' 5v3–4[a]; 18r23[b]. soðf' 18r20[b]. soð' 49r19[b]. *sg. gen.* soðfæstnises 12v2[b]; 38r3[a]. soðfæstnis' 2r5[b]; 16v22[b]. soðfæst' 19r9[b]; 29v11[a].

soðlice: *a* AMEN *b* IAM *c* IUSTE *d* QUIDEM *e* TAMEN *f* UERACITER *g* UERE ‖ soðlice 1v21[f]; 10v19[a]; 12v12[d]; 13r6[b]; 19v23[c]; 25r12[g]; 86rb4[e].

soðni(s)s(e: UERITAS ‖ soðnise 6r13.

spærað: PARCERE ‖ *pres. subj.* + *inf.* spæria 19v16. *imp. sg.* spær 19v4; 20v5.

gispærað: PARCERE ‖ *pret. sg.* gispærede 11r1.

spærni(s)s(e: PARCITAS ‖ spærnisse 77r7.

spilleð: DISSIPARE ‖ *pres. subj.* + *inf.* spilla 27r1. *pret. part. pl. nom.* + *acc.* gispilledo 10r15.

gispilleð: *a* PERDERE *b* usurpare ‖ *pres. subj.* + *inf.* gispilla 52v14[b]. *pret. sg.* gispilde 51v8[a].

hago-spind: GENA ‖ hagospind 2r14.

gispitteð: CONSPUERE ‖ *pres. part. pl. dat.* gispittendum 9v3.

sprædung: PROPAGATIO ‖ sprædung 52r15.

sprec: *a* LOCUTIO *b* LOQUI ‖ spréc 78vb18*a*. *sg. acc.* + *dat.* spréce 23v9[b].

soð-sprec: ELOQUIUM ‖ *pl. nom.* + *acc.* soðspreco 79va14.

tui-sprec: detractio ‖ *pl. nom.* + *acc.* tuispreco 12v2.

spre(c)ceð: LOQUI ‖ *inf.* sprecan 55r21⁻. *infl. inf.* spreccanne 14r2. *pres. part.* spreccende 23v16. sprecend 51r20; 81ra23. *pret. sg. ind.* spræc 3r20. *pret. part.* *spreccen[3] 21r21.

gispre(c)ceð: LOQUI ‖ gispreceð 23v11. *pres. ind. sg. 2* gispreces 26v16.

aspringeð: deficere ‖ aspringað 11r15. *pres. subj.* + *inf.* aspringa 8v18; 35r1.

sprot(t: (ARUNDO) ‖ sprott 41v9.

e-spryng: FONS ‖ *sg. dat.* esprynge 15v14. *pl. nom.* + *acc.* espryngo 1r10.

ond-spurneð, -spyrneð: OFFENDERE ‖ ondspurnað 35v15. *pres. ind. sg. 2* ondspyrnas 4v1.

spyrd: STADIUM ‖ *sg. dat.* spyrde 3r8.

ond-spyrni(s)s(e: *a* OFFENDICULUM *b* OFFENSIO *c* OFFENSUM ‖ ondspyrnisse 19v8[b]. ondspyrnis' 5v11[a]; 5v20[b]. *pl. nom.* + *acc.* ondspyrniso 20r20[c]. *pl. dat.* ondspyrnissum 20v12[c]. ondspyrnisum 4r13[c].

3. *Probably one or more letters (illegible) after* n.

stalo: FURTUM ‖ stale 54v14.

stan: LAPIS ‖ stan 85v12.

huo(m)m-stan: ANGULARIS LAPIS ‖ *sg. dat.* huomm'stane 39v17.

gistaðolað: STABILIRE ‖ *pret. sg.* gistaðelade 39r13.

gistaðolfæstnað: SOLIDARE ‖ *pres. subj.* + *inf.* gistaðolfæstniga 10v18.

staðolfæstni(s)s(e: status ‖ staðolfæstnisse 52r11.

unstaðolfæstni(s)s(e: INSTABILITAS ‖ *unstaðolfæstnis'[4] 86va2.

stæf: LITTERA ‖ *sg. dat.* *stæfe 88va2. *pl. dat.* stafum 88va3.

stænen: (hydria) ‖ stænen 56v10.

stearra: STELLA ‖ stearre 1r16; 1v17. *pl. gen.* stearra' 44v3.

stef(e)n: UOX ‖ stefn 23r16; 23v22. stefen 23v6. *sg. acc.* + *dat.* stefne 2v19; 9r16.

stenc: ODOR ‖ stenc 31v19; 33r11. stencg 42v5. *sg. gen.* stences 31v20; 57r7.

gistenc: ODOR ‖ gistenc 6r10. *sg. gen.* gistences 2r2.

suot-stencende: (AROMATIZARE) ‖ suotstencende 31v18.

stencni(s)s(e: ODOR ‖ stencgnis' 2r18. stengcnis' 2r12.

gistencni(s)s(e: ODOR ‖ *sg. gen.* gistencnis' 2r3.

ste(p)peð: GRADI ‖ *pres. part.* steppende 18v14.

giste(p)peð: GRADI ‖ *pres. subj.* + *inf.* gistepe 25r1. gistepa 31v1.

gistigeð: DESCENDERE ‖ *pres. subj.* + *inf.* gistige 46v19.

gistigeð: DESCENDERE ‖ *pres. subj.* + *inf.* gistige 46v19.

astigeð: *a* ASCENDERE *b* DESCENDERE ‖ astigeð [*alt. f.* gistigeð] 9v13[a]. *pres. ind. sg. 1* astigo 82va15[a]. *pres. subj.* + *inf.* astige 47v13[b]. *pres. part.* astigende 39v21[a]. *pret. sg. subj.* + *ind. 2* astige 60r16[a].

ofdune-stigeð: DESCENDERE ‖ *ofdunestig' 45r23. *pres. subj.* + *inf.* ofdunestige 57v19. ofdunestiga 59v20. *pres. part.* ofdunestigende 13v19. *pret. sg. subj.* + *ind. 2* ofdunestige 48r19; 48r21.

u(p)p-stigeð: ASCENSOR ‖ *pres. part. pl. nom.* + *acc.* upstigendo 87ra6.

stioreð: GUBERNARE ‖ *pret. part.* gistiored 28v19; 29r2.

gistioreð: GUBERNARE ‖ *pres. subj.* + *inf.* gestiora 80va18. *pres. part.* gistiorende 50r10.

4. unsta *doubtful.*

gistiðað: INDURARE ‖ *pres. subj. + inf.* gistiðia 49r13.
stol: STOLA ‖ stól 22r18.
stondenni(s)s(e: SUBSTANTIA ‖ stonden' 16r8.
under-stondenni(s)s(e: SUBSTANTIA ‖ understondennis' 15v12. underst' 59r6.
ym(b)-stondenni(s)s(e: CIRCUMSTANTIA ‖ *sg. gen.* ymbstondennisses' 83ra16. ymbstondennisse 81vb24.
stondeð: *a* STARE *b* STATOR ‖ stondað 17v17[a]. stondas 29r5[a]. *pres. part.* stondende 21v1[a]; 21v3[a]. *pl. nom. + acc.* stondendo 87ra9[b].
gistondeð: *a* ASSISTERE *b* CONSISTERE *c* EXSISTERE *d* STARE ‖ gistondes 34r18[a]. *pres. subj. + inf.* gistonde 32v7[b]; 34v21[b]. *pret. sg. ind. 1, 3* gistod 28r1[d]; 33v2[c].
astondeð: EXSISTERE ‖ *pres. subj. + inf.* astonde 21v17.
æt-gistondeð: ASSISTERE ‖ *pret. sg. ind. 1, 3* ætgistod 28r10; 29r17.
i(n)n-stondeð: INSTARE ‖ instondað 77v6. *pres. part. pl. dat.* instondum [? *read* instondendum] 33r22.
to-stondeð: ASSISTERE ‖ *imp. sg.* tostond 52r16. *pres. part.* tostondende 10r19.
ðerh-stondeð: PERSISTERE ‖ *pres. part.* ðerhstondende 28v17.
uið-stondeð: *a* ABSISTERE *b* RESISTERE ‖ *pres. subj. + inf.* uiðstonde 47r5[a]; *21r20[b].
under-stondeð: SUBSISTERE ‖ *pres. subj. + inf.* understonda 20r2.
stou(a: LOCUS ‖ stoue 17v22; 34r2. stou 81vb25; 82va20. *pl. dat.* stoum 5r6; 59r12.
stream: FLUMEN ‖ *pl. nom. + acc.* streamas 1r11.
astregdeð: ASPERGERE ‖ *pret. part.* astrogden 57r17; 57v18.
eft-astregdeð: RESPERGERE ‖ *pret. sg.* eftastrægde 59r12. eftastrogden 58v 18.
to-stregdeð: *a* DESTRUERE *b* DISPERGERE *c* DISSIPARE ‖ *pres. subj. + inf.* tostregda 26v20[a]. *pret. sg. ind. 1, 3* tostrægd 81rb20[b]. *pret. part.* tostrogden 13r1[a]. *pl. nom. + acc.* tostrogdeno 5r7[b]; 21v8[b]. *pl. gen.* tostrogdenra 5r5[c].
strengo: *a* FORTITUDO *b* UALETUDO *c* UIRTUS ‖ strengo 88vb12[a]. strenge 21r15[a]. *sg. gen.* strencges 58r14[a]. *pl. nom. + acc.* strengo 55r4[c]; 56r21[b].
gistrioneð: *a* GIGNERE *b* THESAURIZARE ‖ *pret. sg.* gestrionde 85rb18[a]. gistrionde 22r20[b].
strogdni(s)s(e: ASPERSIO ‖ strogd' 59r17.
gistrogdni(s)s(e: CONSPERSIO ‖ gistrogdnisse 12r21.
astrogdni(s)s(e: ASPERSIO ‖ *astrogdnise[1] 56v20.
strong: *a* FORTIS *b* TENAX ‖ strong 39r5[a]; 77v2[b]. *adv.* strongi 85rb13[a]. *pl. nom. + acc.* strongo 30r19[a]; 36r22[a]. stronga 24v5[a].
stronglic: UALIDUS ‖ *comp. pl. dat.* stronglcrum [*alt. f.* stronglicum, ? *read* stronglicrum] 29v9.
strynd: TRIBUS ‖ strynd 37v17. *sg. acc. + dat.* strynde 86vb12.
soð-gistrynd: PROGENIES ‖ soðgistrynd 14v7.
sturtað: EXSILIRE ‖ *pres. part.* sturtende 28r1.
styð: (*a* IBIDEM) (*b* NUSQUAM) ‖ *sg. dat.* styde 48v1[(a)]; 77va5[(b)].
stydfæstni(s)s(e: CONSTANTIA ‖ stydfæstnise 24v11.
unstydful(l: apostaticus ‖ *pl. dat.* unstydfu'llum [? *read* unstydfullum] 59r3.
unstydfu(l)lni(s)s(e: *a* INFESTATIO *b* INSTABILITAS ‖ unstydfullnisse 86 va1[b]. unstydfulnis' 59v9[a].
u(o)elig-styd(i)ende: LOCUPLETANS ‖ uoeligstydende [*alt. f.* uoegligstydende] 47r2.
styreni(s)s(e: PERTURBATIO ‖ *pl. dat.* styrenissum 28v8.
gistyreni(s)s(e: tribulatio ‖ *pl. dat.* gistyrenisum 20r2.
ðerh-styreð: PERTURBARE ‖ ðerhstyriað 25v17–18.
suat: SUDOR ‖ suat 86rb20.
suæ, sua: *a* ITA *b* PROUT (*c* QUANTUS) *d* QUASI *e* QUEMADMODUM *f* QUOMODO (*g* QUOTIENS) *h* SIC *i* SICUT (*j* TAMQUAM) (*k* TANTUS) (*l* TOT) *m* UT (*n* abesse) ‖ suæ 2r14[i]; 2v10[a]; 3r10[h]; 3r20[m]; 6v4[b]; 12v19[f]; 29v8 (2)[(c),(k)]; 31v19[d]; 47r21[(j)]; 51r10[(n)]; 80rb7[(e)]; 86ra8[(g)]. suae 8v13[i]; 12v19[m]; 86ra3[e]. sua 2v5[a]; 3r14[h]; 20r2[(l)]; 33r18[m]; 80vb2[i].
suæ-(sua-)hua: *a* QUICUMQUE *b* QUISQUIS ‖ *sg. neut. nom. + acc.* suahuæd 58v17[b]. suæhuæd 43r13[a]; 59r11[b]. suæhuædd 6v23[a]. suaehuæd 51r14[a].
suæ-(sua-)hui(d)dir: *a* QUICUMQUE *b* qui ‖ suahuidir 23v1[a]. suæhuidder 26v15[b].
suæ-(sua-)hu(o)elc, -huælc: *a* QUICUMQUE *b* QUISQUE ‖ suahuoelc 47v9[(a)]. suæhuoelc 47r14[(a)]. suæhuælc 56r22[(a)]. *pl. nom. + acc.* suahuoelc 24v5[b]. suæhuoelc 12v17[a]; 59r5[b].
suæ- (sua-) hu(o)er: UBICUMQUE ‖ suahuoer 59v8. suæhuoer 57v18[0]. suaehuoer 57r17[0].

1. o *doubtful.*

suæ-(sua-)hu(o)eðer: SIUE ‖ suahuoeðer 14r11.
ond-suæra: sententia ‖ ondsuære 52v6.
suæð: *a* SEMITA *b* UESTIGIUM ‖ *sg. dat.* swæðe[2] 12v15[b]. *pl. nom. + acc.* suæðo 39r11[a]; 78ra13[b]. *pl. dat.* suæðum 78ra19[a]. suo[a]eðum 78ra12[a].
suæ-(sua-)ðæh: *a* QUAMUIS *b* TAMEN ‖ suaðæh 23v13[b]. suæðeah 32r11[b]. suæðeh 86ra9[a].
suereð: IURARE ‖ *pret. part. sg. gen.* gesuorenes 85va4.
e-suic(c: simulatio ‖ *pl. nom. + acc.* ésuico 12v3.
e-sui(c)ca: SEDUCTOR ‖ *pl. dat.* esuicum 39r4.
gisuiceð: SEDUCERE ‖ *pres. subj. + inf.* gisuica 6v15.
bi-suiceð: *a* FALLERE *b* LUDERE *c* SEDUCERE ‖ *pres. ind. sg. 1* besuico 85va13[b]. *pres. part. pl. nom. + acc.* bisuicendo 14r16[a]. *pret. part.* bisuicen 54v14[c]. besuicen 88va9[c].
suigeð: SILERE ‖ suigað 61r14.
gisuigeð: OBMUTESCERE ‖ *pret. sg.* gisuigade 51v19.
suigunga: SILENTIUM ‖ suigunga 10r1.
suin: PORCA ‖ *pl. nom. + acc.* *suin[3] 57v21.
suinga: UERBER ‖ *pl. gen.* suinca' 19v21.
asuingeð: FLAGELLARE ‖ *pret. part. pl. nom. + acc.* asungeno [*alt. f.* asunguno] 20v5.
sui(p)pa: FLAGELLUM ‖ *pl. nom. + acc.* su[y]oppa 4v2. syuipa 20r20. syppo 7v13. *pl. dat.* suippum 20v10.
suira: COLLUM ‖ suire 2r15.
suið: *a* DEXTER (*b* INGENS) *c* NIMIS (*d* TANTUS) *e* UALDE (*f* gemere) *g* quam ‖ *sg. dat. + adv.* suiðe 1r14[e]; 29v8[(d)]; 33r2[g]; 78vb17[c]; 85va6[(b)]; *88va16[(f)]. *comp.* suiðra 4r11[a]; 33v11[a]. suiðræ 46r4[a]. suiðre 7r20[a]; 12r15[a]. *comp. pl. dat.* suiðrum 21v1[a]; 21v3[a].
for(e)-(fora-)suiðeð: *a* UINCERE *b* confundere *c* praecedere ‖ f'suiðeð 13v14[a]; 13v15[a]. *pres. ind. sg. 2* f'suiðes 24v5[b]. *pres. subj. + inf.* f'esuiðe 4r9[a]. *pret. sg.* f'suiðde 16r2[c].
ofer-suiðeð: *a* EXSUPERARE *b* SUPERARE *c* UINCERE ‖ of'suiðas 81rb14[a]. *pres. ind. sg. 2* of'suiðest 59v4[b]. *pres. subj. + inf.* of'suiðe 31r6[b]; 45v6[b]. of'suið' 13v16[c].
sulfor: *see* **seolfor**.
sum(m: QUIDAM ‖ sum [*alt. f.* sum oðer] 27v18. *pl. nom. + acc.* sumo 40r1 (2). summo 21r17.

2. e *incomplete.*
3. n *doubtful.*

unasundradlic: INSEPARABILIS ‖ unasundradlic 59v1. *sg. dat.* unasundradlic' 52r20.

gisundrað: destinare ‖ *pret. sg. ind. 2* gisundradest 27v5.

asundrað: destituere ‖ *pret. part.* asundrad 4r14.

sunna: SOL ‖ sunna 33r18; 77v16. sunne 77r8.

sunu: FILIUS ‖ sunu 2v3; 5v7. sun' 58r17. *sg. gen.* sunu 11r16; 55r22. sun' 56r17. suna 55r7[-]. *pl. nom. + acc.* sunu 6r7.

su(o)ef(e)n: *a* SOMNIUM *b* SOMNUS ‖ suoefen 82va17[b]. *pl. nom. + acc.* suoefno 82rb18[a].

su(o)elc, suælc: *a* QUASI *b* SICUT *c* TAM *d* TAMQUAM *e* UELUT *f* UT ‖ *adv.* suoelce 2r2[a]; 3r4[b]; 23r15[d]; 52r23[c]; 86rb5[e]. soelce 9v6[f]; 33r17[a]. suælce 2r15[b]; 2v19[a].

su(o)enc: *a* TENTATIO *b* TRIBULATIO ‖ *pl. dat.* suencum 83va10[a]. suoencum 83va18[b].

gisu(o)enc: AFFLICTIO ‖ gisuoenc 20r22; 21r4.

su(o)enceð: *a* AFFLIGERE *b* fatigare ‖ *pret. part. sg. gen.* gisuoenctes 19v23[a]. *pl. nom. + acc.* gisuoencdo 20v12[b].

gisu(o)enceð: AFFLICTOR ‖ *pres. part. pl. gen.* gisuoencendra 20r3.

asu(o)enceð: AFFLIGERE ‖ *pret. part.* asuoenc' 3r3. *sg. gen.* asuoenctes 20v15. *pl. nom. + acc.* asuoencte 21r11. asuoencde 3v12. *pl. dat.* asuoenctum 21r3.

su(o)estren: SORORES ‖ *dat.* soest'num 81ra20.

suoete: DULCIS ‖ suoet' 2r9.

suo(e)tni(s)s(e: *a* DULCEDO *b* SUAUITAS ‖ suoetnisse 55v5[a]; 56v13[b]. suotnise 31v19[b]. suoetnis' 2r2[b]. *sg. gen.* suotnisses 42v5[b]. suoetnises 6r10[b].

suore(t)tung: SINGULTUS ‖ *sg. acc. + dat.* suoretunge 10r8.

asuungenni(s)s(e: fragilitas ‖ *sg. gen.* asuuncgennisse[1] 21r1.

symbe(l)lice: SOLLEMNITER ‖ symbellice 4v9; 24r2.

symbelni(s)s(e: *a* FESTIUITAS *b* SOLLEMNITAS ‖ symbelnise 24r15[b]. symbelnis' 1v10[a]; 15r15[b]. *sg. gen.* symbeln' 27v10[a].

symlað: FREQUENTARE ‖ symligað 7v9.

symle: SEMPER ‖ symle 1v11; 1v18; 40r21 [*alt. f.* symse]. sym' 15r12.

symlinga, -unga: *a* CONTINUATUS *b* CONTINUUS *c* IUGITER ‖ symlinga 16r20[c]; 22r1[a]. symlu/[i]nga 32v21[c]. symlung [*alt. f.* symlunge] 29r1[b].

1. u *and* c *intercalated.*

syndirlic: *a* excellens *b* excellenter ‖ *sg. dat.* syndirlicum 52r23[a]. *adv.* syndirlice 23r4[b].

syndrig: PROPRIUS ‖ syndrig 19v16. *sg. gen.* syndriges 16v2. *sg. dat.* syndrigum 11r1; 44v16. *sg. acc. masc.* syndrigne 85vb18–19. *pl. nom. + acc.* syndrigo 6v4[0].

syndurae: *see* **syndir-æ.**

synn: *a* CRIMEN *b* CULPA *c* DELICTUM *d* PECCATUM (*e* SCELUS) *f* UITIUM *g* peccator *h* pectus ‖ synn 12v15[d]; 48v20[b]. *sg. acc. + dat.* synne 8r6[b]; 13r2[d]; 48v10[a]; 80rb24[d] [*alt. f.* synnum]; *sg. gen.* synnes 16r10[d]; 52v5[d]. syn' 13r1[d]. *pl. nom. + acc.* synno 2v21[d]; 4v1[b]. synna 60r12[d]; 79ra6[(e)]. synne 79ra3[d]. syn' 78va22[d]. *pl. gen.* synna 3v18[d]; 18r12[f]; 46v17[h]. synna' 19v17[c]. sy'na 11r21[b]. *pl. dat.* synnum 3v12[d]; 8v13[f]; 8v19[g]; 40v16[c]; 45r4[d] [*alt. f.* synna]. syn' 8v7[f]; 78rb23[d].

heh-synn: *a* CRIMEN *b* FACINUS *c* SCELUS ‖ hehsynn 85ra18[a]. *pl. nom. + acc.* hehsynno 20v7[b]; 79ra5[a]. hehsynna 2v20[c]. *pl. dat.* hehsynnum 78vb20[a].

sy(n)nful(l: PECCATOR ‖ *sg. acc. masc.* synnfullne 78vb24. synfulne 60v20. *pl. nom. + acc.* synnfullo 10v20; 21r2. *pl. dat.* synnfullum 43r9; 43v8.

sy(n)ngað: PECCARE ‖ *pres. part. pl. gen.* syngendra 20r5. *pret. sg.* syngade 78vb17; 79vb23. syn'de 79rb23. *pret. pl.* syngadon 5v3.

gisy(n)ngað: PECCARE ‖ gisynngað 5r14. gisynngiað 51r15. *pret. sg. ind. 2* gisyngades 5v12.

synnig: CULPABILIS ‖ synnig 48v17; 49r12. synn' 48r10.

deað-synnigni(s)s(e: REATUS ‖ ðeaðsynnignise 20v16.

gitacnað: SIGNIFICARE ‖ getacnað 86va11.

tacon: *a* SIGNUM *b* uexillum ‖ tacon 45r7[b]. *sg. dat.* tacne 49v16[a]; 58r16[a].

soð-tacon: PRODIGIUM ‖ *pl. nom. + acc.* soðtaceno 21r16.

tal: NUMERUS ‖ tal 53r14.

unataladlic: INNUMERABILIS ‖ *pl. dat.* unataladlicum 60v21.

to-talo: reputatio ‖ *sg. gen.* totales' 48v15.

tan: FRONS ‖ *pl. nom. + acc.* tanas [*alt. f.* danas] 45v11.

tea: (*a* DECANUS) *b* DECEM ‖ tea 86vb14[(a)]. teno 86vb15[b]; 86vb16[b].

team: SUBOLES ‖ *sg. dat.* teame 52v19.

tear, te(h)her: LACRIMA ‖ *pl. nom. + acc.* tearo 20v15. tehhero 19v24. tehero 86rb18.

teað ‖ tihð 55r19.

giteað: contendere ‖ giteð 3r11.

tederlic: FRAGILIS ‖ *sg. dat.* tederlicum 24v22. *comp. pl. nom. + acc.* tederlico' 29v8.

tederni(s)s(e: FRAGILITAS ‖ tedernise 4r7; 32r6. tederniss' 4r1. tedern' 22v18. *sg. gen.* tedernises 25v3. tedernis'e 51r2.

ra(c)cen-teg: CATENA ‖ racenteg 19v17. *pl. gen.* racentego 28r12.

teleð: *a* CONTEMNERE *b* DESPICERE ‖ *pret. part. sg. dat.* giteledum [*alt. f.* giteledo] 31r8[a]. *pl. dat.* giteldum 31r12[b].

giteleð: DESPICERE ‖ *pres. subj. + inf.* gitela 21r4; 24v2.

ateleð: UITUPERARE ‖ *pret. part.* ateled 5v21.

telga: RAMUS ‖ *pl. nom. + acc.* telgo 33r12.

te(l)leð: *a* EXISTIMARE *b* statuere ‖ *pres. subj. + inf.* tele 21v5[b]. *pret. part.* giteled 41r22[a].

gite(l)leð: AESTIMARE ‖ *pret. sg.* gitelede 28r16.

ate(l)leð: REPUTARE ‖ *pret. part.* ateled 48r9.

ðerh-te(l)leð: PERPENDERE ‖ *pres. ind. sg. 2* ðerhteles 42r3.

tempel: TEMPLUM ‖ tempel 51r16. *sg. dat.* temple 2v4; 23v5.

hus-tempel: tabernaculum ‖ *sg. dat.* hustemple 87ra15–16.

tid: *a* HORA *b* TEMPUS *c* iam ‖ tid 5v15[b]; 79ra8[a]. tíd 83va11[a]. tiid 5v14[b]; 45v1[a]. *sg. gen.* tides 79va22[b]. *sg. acc. + dat.* tide 5v17[b]; 60r7[a]; 77r2[c]. tiide 83vb16[b]. *pl. nom. + acc.* tido 18v3[b]; 79va20[a]. *pl. gen.* tidana 46v13[b]. *pl. dat.* tidum 18r7[a] [*alt. f.* tido]; 60v6[a].

heh-tid: SOLLEMNE ‖ *pl. nom. + acc.* hehtido 4r20.

non-tid: HORA NONA ‖ tid non 83va22–3. tiid non 60r20.

symbel-tid: *a* FESTIUITAS *b* FESTUM *c* NATALICIA *d* SOLLEMNE *e* SOLLEMNITAS ‖ symbeltid 16v12[e]; 31r22[e]. symbbeltid 1v6[e]. symbelt' 33v3[e]; 37r19[e]. *sg. gen.* symbeltid' 15v4[a]. *sg. acc. + dat.* symbeltide 15v1[e]; 23r8[a]. symbeltid' 15r20[a]; 17r23[d]; 26r13[e]. *pl. nom. + acc.* symbeltido 14v14[d]; 15r3[b]; 24r5[e]; 24r15[e]. sym'tido 40r18[b]. *pl. dat.* symbeltidum 38v13[e]; 39v7[e].

tidlic: *a* TEMPORALIS *b* TEMPORALITER ‖ tidlic 15v5[a]; 32r11[a]. *sg. gen.* tidlices 35r18[a]. *sg. dat.* tidlicum 11v13[a]; 30v9[a]. *adv.* tidlice 38v11[b]. *pl. nom. + acc.* tidlico 15v2[a]. *pl. dat.* tidlicum 4r13[a]; 9r6[a].

heh-tidlic: SOLLEMNIS ‖ *sg. acc. + dat.* hehtid' 4v19.

gitimbirni(s)s(e: AEDIFICATIO ‖ gitimbernisse 40r4. gitimbernise 39v 17–16.

timbreð: CONSTRUERE ‖ *pret. part.* gitimbred 39v16.

gitimbreð: AEDIFICARE ‖ gitimbrað 14r13. *pres. subj. + inf.* gitimbra 27r1.

æc-gitimbreð: COAEDIFICARE ‖ æc-gitimbrað 39v18–19.

ofer-timbreð: SUPERAEDIFICARE ‖ of'timbras 39v14–15.

tinterga: gehenna ‖ *sg. gen.* *tint'ges 31r2.

ungetiono ‖ ungetionu 57v19–20.

titt: UBER ‖ *pl. nom. + acc.* titto 2r21. tido 2r12.

to: *a* AD *b* TENUS *c* de *d* in (*e* quoque) *A—making a Latin dative B—with an inflected infinitive* ‖ to 1r7[A]; 1r18[a]; 3v22[B]; 34v2[b]; 37v8[(e)]; 45r21[c]; 50r6[d]; 56v15. tó 55r17.

here-toga: *a* COMES *b* DUX ‖ heretoga 86vb3[b]; 86vb5[a].

tosca: RANA ‖ tosca 61r15.

toð: DENS ‖ *pl. gen.* toðana 51v21.

tou(e)ard: *a* AD FUTURUM *b* FUTURUS *c* UENTURUS ‖ *sg. dat.* toweardum 33r5[a]. *sg. acc. masc.* toueardne 39r15[c]. *sg. acc. + dat. fem.* toueard' 36v6[c]. *pl. nom. + acc.* toueardo 33v14[b]. *pl. gen.* toweardra 6v14[b]. towardra 10r19[b]. *pl. dat.* toweardum 60r13[b].

tou(e)ardlic: FUTURUS ‖ *pl. nom. + acc.* toueardlica 79ra4.

trahtað: INTERPRETARI ‖ *pret. part. pl. nom. + acc.* getrahtado 87ra3–4.

tre(o): *a* ARBOR *b* LIGNUM ‖ tree 47r11[a]; 60r16[b]. *sg. gen.* trees 45r15[b]. *pl. gen.* treona 45v11[a].

galga-tre(o): PATIBULUM ‖ galgatré 11v9. galgatree 60r20.

gitriue: *a* FIDELIS *b* confisus *c* idoneus ‖ gitriua 32v6[b]; 34v19[b]. gitriwa 52v9[a]; 87vb9[a]. *pl. nom. + acc.* gitriua 40v2[a]. getriuo 42r3[c]. gitriuao [? *read* gitriuuo] 60v12[a]. *pl. dat.* gitriwum 4v8[a].

gitriuelice: FIDELITER ‖ gitriwalice 11v21; 15r2.

gitriueð: *a* CONFIDERE *b* FIDERE ‖ gitriuað 29v4[a]; 51r4[a]. *pres. subj. + inf.* gitriwa 11v15[a]. *pres. part.* gitriunde 30r4[a]. *pl. nom. + acc.* gitriundo 33v20[a]. gitriwendo 7r11[a]. *pl. dat.* gitriwendum 19r2[b]. *pret. pl.* gitriuadon 3v15[a].

mis-triueð: DIFFIDERE ‖ mistriuað 19v2.

triuleas: PERFIDUS ‖ *pl. gen.* triwleasra 12r2. trioleasra 28v17.

trumlice: FIRME ‖ *comp.* trumlicor 16v22.

trymmeð: *a* FIRMARE *b* MUNIRE *c* OFFIRMARE *d* commendare *e* testari ‖ *pret. part.* trymmed 31r10[b]. gitrymmed 8r2[b]; 31v7[a]; 54v12–13[c]. gitrymed 27r16[b]; 39v11[b]. *sg. fem.* gitry'meðo 52v9[b]. *pl. nom. + acc.* trymmedo 40r22[b]. gitrymmedo 3v16[b]; 11v15[e]. gitrymedo 42r9[b]; *42v18[d]. *pl. dat.* gitrymmedum [*alt. f.* gitrymmedo] 40v4[b].

gitrymmeð: *a* CONFIRMARE *b* CONFORTARE *c* EXHORTARI *d* HORTARI *e* ROBORARE *f* SOLIDARE *g* UALERE ‖ gitrymmeð 5v16[d]. gitrymmað 6v9[c]. *pres. subj. + inf.* gitrymma 8v21[g]; 10v18[a]. *imp. sg.* gitrymme 78va6[a]. *pret. sg.* gitrymmede 29r17[b]; 42r17[a]. *pret. sg. ind. 2* gitrymedest 28v10[f]. gitrymmedest 24r23[e].

untry(m)mig: INFIRMUS ‖ *pl. dat.* untrymigum 81rb23. untrymmigum 6r1.

trymni(s)s(e: *a* FIRMITAS *b* testamentum ‖ trymnisse 86rb2–3[b]. trymnise 15v21[a].

gitrymni(s)s(e: *a* HORTAMENTUM *b* SOLIDITAS ‖ gitrymnise 28v15[b]. *pl. nom. + acc.* gitrymniso 27r12[a].

untrymni(s)s(e: INFIRMITAS ‖ untrymnisse 50r22; 52v16. untrymnise 18v4; 24r18. untry[u]mnise 4r10. untrymn' 11r15. *pl. nom. + acc.* untrymnisso 56r21. *pl. dat.* untrymnissum 3r19; 43v17.

tu(i)a: (uidelicet) ‖ tua 86rb6.

gitu(i)a: AMBIGUITAS ‖ gituia 50r19.

gituiað: DUBITARE ‖ *pret. sg.* gitui[e]da 11v18.

tuifal(d)lic: GEMINATUS ‖ *pl. nom. + acc.* tuifallico 27v10.

tuigga: RAMUS ‖ *pl. nom. + acc.* tuiggo 33r12; 45v4.

tunga: LINGUA ‖ tunga 23v11; 77r15.

tungul: SIDUS ‖ *sg. dat.* tungle 77r2.

tuoege: DUO ‖ tuoegi 54v8. twoego 86va6. tuu 51r12. *gen.* tuoegra 56r2.

tu(o)elf: DUODECIM ‖ tuoelf 66r4; 66v21. *gen.* tuoelfa' 37v17.

tur: TURRIS ‖ *pl. dat.* turum 81ra18.

turtur: TURTUR ‖ *sg. gen.* turtures 2r14.

untyneð: *a* APERIRE *b* INHIARE ‖ untyneð 22r17[a]; 40v16[a]. *pres. ind. sg. 1* untyno 1r11[a]. *pres. ind. sg. 2* untynest 50v9[a]. *pres. subj. + inf.* untyne 14v1[a]; 46r6[a]. untyna 16v19[b]. *pret. sg.* untynde 9r22[a]; 9v18[a]. *pret. sg. ind. 2* untyndest 48v11[a]; 56r1[a]. *pret. part. pl. nom. + acc.* untyndo 21v2[a]; 56r4[a]. *pl. dat.* untynedum 50v14[a].

bi-tyneð: laudari ‖ *pret. part.* bityned 45v3.

on-tyneð: absoluere ‖ *pres. subj. + inf.* ontyne 17r8.

ða: *a* QUANDO *b* TUM *c* TUNC ‖ ða 3r22[a]; 9r8[c]; 86rb1[b].

ða-geana: ADHUC ‖ ðageane 10v20.

ða-get: (NECDUM) ‖ ðaget 23v22.

giðafað: competere ‖ *pres. part.* giðafende 4r2.

giðafung: CONSENSUS ‖ giðafung 54v 16.

ðæccilla: *a* LAMPAS *b* LUCERNA ‖ ðæccelle 78ra16[b]; 78ra18[b]. ðæccille 50v 20[a]. *pl. dat.* ðæccillum 50v5[a].

ðæh: (*a* ETSI) *b* licet ‖ ðæh 23v13[b]; 32r18[(a)]; 86vb4[(b)].

giðæhtung: CONSILIUM ‖ giðæht' 1r5.

ðe: *a* HIC *b* IDEM *c* ILLE *d* IPSE *e* IS *f* QUAM *g* QUI *h* QUIA (*i* QUICUMQUE) *j* QUOD *k* QUONIAM *l* UT (*m* ne) (*n* necnon) (*o* nequire) *A—making an Anglo-Saxon group "definite article + nomen" vis-à-vis a Latin nomen (or, occasionally, another Latin part of speech); B—other miscellaneous insertional usages related to the Latin; C—instrumental usages of type* the more the merrier ‖ ðe 1r3[(g)]; 5r18[(d)]; 47r14[(i)]; 85va2[(b)]. ð 1v5[(g)]; 11v19[g]. te 1r17[(l)]; 1r22[(g)]; 6v1[(l)]; 13r4[(h)]; 13r16[(k)]; 17r6[A]; 17v 10[B]; 51r8[(j)]. *sg. masc. nom.* se 1v4[(g)]; 5r15[A]; 11r16[g]; 47r14[(i)]. *sg. masc. acc.* ðone 1v2[g]; 3r9[A]; 7r2[d]; 39r2[A] [*alt. f.* ðe]; 58v10[e]. *sg. neut. nom. + acc.* ꝥ 1r17[(l)]; 1r21[c]; 1r22[(g)]; 1v3[B]; 1v8[A]; 1v13[g]; 2v3[l]; 3r8[j]; 7v10[f]; 10r21[e]; 13r4[(h)]; 13r16[(k)]; 23r21[A]; 85va2[(b)]. ðæt 18v18[g]; 48v19[(b)]; 77v11[l]. ðaet 55r8. *sg. gen.* ðæs 1v1[g]; 10v22[d]; 11r12[(d)]; 16r7[c]; 36v19[(b)] [*alt. f.* his]. ðaes 55r9. *sg. dat.* ðæm 3r2[A]; 4r12[e]; 6v20[g]; 10v19[d]; 12v18[c]. ðaem 81ra3[g]. *sg. instr.* ðon 6r17[g]; 16r1[e]; 54v8[(n)]. ðy 3r6[(o)]; 5v12[(m)]; 8v8[C]. *sg. fem. nom. + acc.* ðiu 1r7[g]; 83rb8[A]. ðio 4v3[(g)]; 5r14[d]; 13v15[g]; 29v19[A]. sio 61r14[A]. ða 8r20[g]; 15r21[e]; 27v1[(c)]; 54v10[A]; 55r10; 60r17[c]. þa 52r10[g]. *sg. fem. dat.* ðær 17v18[e]; 21r17[A]; 54v17[c]; 57v11[d]. *sg. fem. gen. + dat.* ðære 24v23[g]; 45r8[(b)]. ðaere 24v10[g]; 55r16. *pl. nom. + acc.* ða 1r17[(g)]; 3r8[a]; 3r12[c]; 4r8[e]; 4v5[A]; 6v14[g]; 21r19[(g)] [*alt. f.* ðar]; 24r1[d]; 28r12[A] [*alt. f.* ðara]; 57r15[(g)] [*alt. f.* se]. *pl. gen.* ðara 6v14[A]; 15r6[g]; 21r18[e]; 44r16[c]. *pl. dat.* ðæm 5r7[g]; 6r1[A]; 10r16[a]; 21r15[c]; 29v14[e]; 47v16[d].

ðea: *a* FAMULUS *b* SERUUS ‖ ðea 46r16[a]; 49v1[a]. *sg. gen.* ðeas 25r6[a]. *pl. nom. + acc.* ðea 48r3[a]; 79ra20[a]. *pl. gen.* ðeana 3v19[a]; 33r20[b]. *pl. dat.* ðeaum 30v15[a].

ðeadom: SERUITUS ‖ *sg. gen.* ðeadomes 4v12. *sg. dat.* ðeadome 3r16.

ðeadscip(e: disciplina ‖ *sg. gen.* ðeadscipes 37v23. ðeatscipes 52v16. *pl. dat.* ðeadscipum 7r15.

ðeaf: LATRO ‖ *pl. dat.* *ðeafum 57v21.

ned-ð(e)arf: NECESSITAS ‖ nedðarf 43v10.
ned-ð(e)arfa: NECESSARIUS ‖ *pl. nom.* + *acc.* nedðærfo [*alt. f.* nedðærfa] 18v3.
ðearfo: AZYMA ‖ *dat.* ðearfum 12v1.
ðeau: MOS ‖ *sg. dat.* ðeaue 59v8. *pl. dat.* ðeau^{u}m 23v12.
ðeauað: CAPTIUUS ‖ *pret. part. pl. dat.* geðeadum 81rb23.
ðeg(e)n: *a* DISCIPULUS *b* FAMULUS *c* MINISTER *d* angelus ‖ ðegin 37r1^{c}. *pl. nom.* + *acc.* ðegnas 16r22^{b}; 34r1^{d}. *pl. gen.* ðegna 32r14^{b}. *pl. dat.* ðegnum 33v1^{b}; 51r20^{a}.
giðegnað: MINISTRARE ‖ *pret. sg.* giðegnade 33r7.
ðenceð: MEDITARI ‖ *pres. part. pl. nom.* + *acc.* ðencendo 18r4.
giðenceð: *a* COGITARE *b* EXCOGITARE ‖ giðenceð 22v4^{a}. *pres. part.* giðengende 40v7^{a}. *pret. sg.* giðohte 3r21^{a}; 22v4^{a}. *geðohte 87rb1^{b}.
aðenneð: TENDERE ‖ *pres. subj.* + *inf.* aðenne 15v11.
ðer: *a* IBI (*b* IBIDEM) *c* ILLIC *d* QUO (*e* UBICUMQUE) ‖ ðer 48v1$^{(b)}$; 51v16^{a}; 57r17$^{(e)}$; 58v8^{d}; 59r13^{c}.
ðerh: PER ‖ ðerh 1r19; 1v2. ð 4v4; 4v7. *ð' 52r1. ðe'h 20v3.
ðersceð: UERBERARE ‖ *pres. ind. sg. 2* ðersces 21r2. *pres. part.* ðerscende 3r15.
ðerscing: UERBER ‖ *pl. gen.* ðerscingra[1] 19v21.
ðes, ðis: *a* HIC *b* hinc *c* is *d* iste *e* qui ‖ ðes 5r12^{a}; 12r2^{d}. ðis 4v19^{a}; 53r22^{d}; 55r21. ðiss 56v13^{d}. ꝥys [*alt. f.* ꝥus, ? *read* þys] 55r17. *sg. acc. masc.* ðiosne 18r8^{a}; 38v5^{a}. ðios' 47v18^{d}. *sg. fem. nom.* + *acc.* ðios 13v15^{a}; 33r17^{d}. ðas 1v5^{a}; 47v7^{d}. ðass 60r7^{a}. ðas' 49r11^{a}; 56v9^{d}. *sg. gen.* ðisses 4v16^{a}; 55v21^{d}. ðissæs 85va1^{a}. ðisis 56r16^{a}. ðis' 79va7^{a}. *sg. dat.* ðissum 45v6^{a}; 80rb23^{d}; 85rb22^{b}. ðisum 45v21^{a}. ðissu 53r21^{a}. ðis' 48v14^{a}; 48v16^{a}. ðassum 47r11^{a}; 48v 15^{a}. ðassum 30v13^{a}; 79va10^{a}. ðas' 48v13^{a}; 48v14^{a}. *sg. dat. fem.* ðisser 83ra6^{d}. *pl. nom.* + *acc.* ðas 1r11^{a}; 3v2^{a} [*alt. f.* ðasum]; 45v12^{c}; 53r15^{d}; 86ra6^{e}. þas 45v3^{a}. *pl. gen.* ðisra 3v2^{a}. *pl. dat.* ðissum 29r2^{a}; 47v15^{a}. ðisum 7r6^{a}. ðasum 3v2^{a}.
ði(d)dir: ILLUC ‖ ðiðer 15v11.
ðiið: PROFICERE ‖ *pres. part.* ðiiende 19r6.
giðiið: *a* PRODESSE *b* PRODIRE *c* PROFICERE *d* excipere ‖ *pres. subj.* + *inf.* giðia 30r11^{c}; 34v2^{c}. giðii 7r14^{c}; 9r5^{c} [*alt. f.* giðiie]; 33v15^{a}; 41r11^{d}. *pret. pl.* giðungon 9r8^{b}.

1. s *intercalated.*

ðing: *a* RES *b* munus (*c* patrocinium) ‖ ðing 7v8^{b}; 86ra10^{a}. *sg. gen.* ðinges 37v4^{b}. ðincges 38r22^{b}. *sg. dat.* ðinge 19r6^{b}. *pl. nom.* + *acc.* ðing 24v7$^{(c)}$. ðingo 30^{c}v2$^{(c)}$; 35r18$^{(c)}$. *pl. gen.* ðinga 77v2^{a}; 82rb14^{a}. ðingana 86ra12^{a}. ðing' 86ra13^{a}. *pl. dat.* ðingum 33v 20$^{(c)}$; 86ra13^{a}. ðing' 41r6$^{(c)}$.
giðingað: *a* INTERCEDERE *b* INTERUENIRE ‖ *pres. subj.* + *inf.* giðingage 29v3^{b}; 32r5^{a}. giðingiga 35r3^{b}. *pres. part.* giðingende 15r20^{b}; 25v5^{a}. giðingande 11r15^{a}. *pl. dat.* giðingendum 30v16^{a}; 44r1^{a}.
eft-ðingað: RECONCILIARE ‖ *pret. part. pl. nom.* + *acc.* eftgiðingado 10v21.
eft-giðingað: RECONCILIARE ‖ *pres. subj.* + *inf.* eftgiðingiga 17r7.
fore-(fora-)giðingað: *a* INTERPELLARE *b* INTERUENIRE ‖ *pres. part.* f'egiðingende 17r6^{a}. *sg. dat.* f'egiðingendum 16v12^{b}.
ðingere: *a* INTERCESSOR *b* INTERUENTOR ‖ ðingere 37r2^{a}; 38r18^{b}.
giðingere: INTERCESSOR ‖ giðingere [*alt. f.* giðingehere] 21v17.
ðingleas: immunis ‖ *pl. nom.* + *acc.* ðingleaso 55r3.
ðingung: *a* INTERCESSIO *b* intercessor ‖ ðingung 33v23^{a}. *sg. gen.* ðingunges 32r8^{a}. ðingunge' 28v12^{a}. *sg. acc.* + *dat.* ðingunge 26v5^{a}; 30r22^{a}; 37v12^{a} [*alt. f.* ðingenge]. ðincgunge 22v17^{a}. *pl. gen.* *ðingunga 38r21^{a}. *pl. dat.* ðingungum 25r13^{a}; 35v2^{b}.
giðingung: *a* INTERCESSIO *b* intercessor ‖ *sg. acc.* + *dat.* giðingunge 30r20^{a}; 34r20^{a}. *pl. dat.* giðingungum 60v17^{b}.
eft-ðingung: RECONCILIATIO ‖ eftðingung 42r13.
fore-(fora-)ðingung: INTERCESSIO ‖ *sg. acc.* + *dat.* f'eðingunge 24r20.
on-ðiodeð: inhaerere ‖ *pres. part. pl. nom.* + *acc.* onðiodendo 4v17.
under-ðiodeð: *a* SUBDERE *b* SUBICERE ‖ *pres. part.* underðiodende 46v17^{a}. *pret. part.* underðioded 19v10^{b}; 20v18^{b}. underðiodded 61r12^{b}. underðiode' 20v21^{b}. *pl. nom.* + *acc.* underðiodo [*alt. f.* wunderðiodo] 1v7^{a}.
ðiofend: FURTUM ‖ *sg. dat.* ðiof'te 49r10. *pl. nom.* + *acc.* ðiofento 49r19.
ðiofo ‖ *pl. dat.* ðiofum 57v20.
ðiostro: TENEBRAE ‖ ðiostro 3r4; 18r14. *gen.* ðiostres 6r11. ðiostra 14r5; 18r2. *dat.* ðiostrum 3r3; 9v9.
aðiostrað: TENEBRARE ‖ *pret. part. pl. nom.* + *acc.* aðiostrado 61r17.
ðir(d)da: TERTIUS ‖ ðirdda 60r10. ðirde [*alt. f.* ðirdung] 29v22. ðirðan 52v21.

ðiua: FAMULA ‖ ðiua 49v9. *pl. dat.* ðiwum 11v11.
ðiuena: *a* FAMULA *b* familia ‖ ðiuen' 50v7^{a}; 51r1^{a}. ðioen' 49v21^{a}; 50r12^{a}. ðioenne 49v18^{a}. *sg. gen.* ðioen' 50v12^{a}; 50v16^{a}. *pl. dat.* ðiuonum 7r5^{b}.
ðo(e)lað: PATI ‖ *pres. part.* ðolende 55v20.
giðo(e)lað: PATI ‖ giðoligað 4r8. *pres. subj.* + *inf.* giðole 54v17. giðoeliga 18r1. *imp. sg.* giðola 55r4.
ðoht: *a* COGITATIO *b* MENS *c* SENSUS *d* anima ‖ ðoht 7r17^{b}; 8v1^{c}. *sg. gen.* ðohtes 4r7^{b}; 47r22^{d}. *sg. dat.* ðohte 7v2^{b}; 22v4^{c}. *pl. nom.* + *acc.* ðohto 7r14^{b}; 7v3^{b}. *pl. gen.* ðohta 24r1^{b}. ðohta' 86va2^{b}. ðohto 15v15^{b}. *pl. dat.* ðohtum 1v18;^{b} 4r5^{c}; 44r3^{a}; 57r16^{d}.
giðoht: *a* COGITATIO *b* animus ‖ *pl. nom.* + *acc.* giðohtas 15v18^{b}. *pl. dat.* giðohtum 8r2^{a}.
ðona: *a* INDE *b* QUA *c* QUO ‖ ðona 15v12^{c}; 45r16^{a}; 80ra22^{b}.
giðoncað: GRATULARI ‖ *pres. subj.* + *inf.* giðoncia 35v8. giðoncage 15r13.
eft-ðoncað: remunerari ‖ *pres. ind. sg. 2* eftðonces 18v21.
giðoncol: *a* GRATUS *b* SUPPLEX *c* intentus ‖ *pl. nom.* + *acc.* giðoncolo 6v 21^{a}; 8r13^{c}. giðoncle 2v2^{b}. *pl. dat.* giðoncum [? *read* giðonclum] 8v20^{b}.
ðoncung: GRATIA ‖ *pl. nom.* + *acc.* ðoncungo 80va20. ðoncunco 6r5; 60v4(). ðoncunga 7r1; 56v18(). ðoncunca 22r4(). ðoncuncgo 18v9(). ðoncgunco 18r5().
ðonne: *a* QUANDO *b* TUNC ‖ ðon' 5r4^{a}; 12r18^{b}.
ðorfend: *a* PAUPER *b* puer ‖ ðorfend 80vb23^{a}. *sg. gen.* ðorfendes 45v10^{b}. *pl. nom.* + *acc.* ðorfendo 81va24^{a}. *pl. gen.* ðorfendra 19v19^{a}; 81va17^{a}. *pl. dat.* ðorfendum 81rb20–1^{a}.
ðorfendni(s)s(e: PAUPERTAS ‖ ðorfendnisse 50r21.
ðor(f)fæst: (*a* prodesse) *b* utilis ‖ ðorfæst 86rb7^{b}. *pl. nom.* + *acc.* ðorfæsta 44r5$^{(a)}$.
unðor(f)fæst: ineptus ‖ unðorfæst 82ra21.
u(o)epen-giðræc(c: framea ‖ uoepengiðræcc[2] 78rb16.
ðræl: SERUUS ‖ *sg. gen.* ðræles 10v5.
ðreat: TURBA ‖ *pl. dat.* ðreattum 45v2.
giðreað: *a* CORRIPERE *b* INCREPARE ‖ giðreað 5v24^{a}. *pres. part. pl. dat.* giðreandum 9v3^{b}.
ðrifald: TERNI TRINI ‖ ðrifald 53r14. *pl. nom.* + *acc.* ðriffaldo 87ra9.
ðriga: TER ‖ ðriga 86ra23.

2. gi *intercalated.*

ðrini(s)s(e: TRINITAS ‖ ðrinisse 77v 15. ðrinesse 55r10.
ðrio, ðreo: (*a* TRECENTI) *b* TRES (*c* TRIGINTA) ‖ ðrio 48vb8[b]; *88vb23[(a)]; *88vb25[(c)]. ðreo 88vb23[b]. ðria 49r6[b]. ðriga 86rb1[b]. *gen.* ðrea 1r22[b]; 83vb 18[b]. *dat.* ðrim [*alt. f.* ðrio] 3v2[b]. ðriim 48r2[b].
ðri(t)tig: TRIGINTA ‖ ðrittig 86vb6. *dat.* ðrit'gum 88va11,13.
ðrouað: *a* PATI *b* crucifigi ‖ *pres. part.* ðrowende 10v14[a]. *pret. part.* giðrowad 11r4[b]; 12v14[a].
giðrouað: *a* COMPATI *b* PATI ‖ *pres. subj.* + *inf.* giðrouia 43v16[a]. *pret. sg.* giðrowade 10v13[b]; 10v17[b]. *pret. pl.* giðrouadon 41v2[b].
ðrouere: MARTYR ‖ ðrouere 25v2; 88rb23. ðrouræ 37r17; 38v10. ðroure 24r22; 25v6. ðrow' 87vb10. *sg. gen.* ðroueres 24r11; 24r14. ðroures 22r6; 24r19. ðrou' 31r12; 36r5. *pl. nom.* + *acc.* ðroueras [*alt. f.* ðroueres] 23v9. ðrouras 30r18; 36r20. ðroueres 58r4. ðrou' 42r5. *pl. gen.* ðrouera 25v20; 26r3. ðroura 26r13; 34v18. ðrouara 30v19. ðrouerana 21v15. ðrouara' 30v8; 41v19. ðrou' 41v21.
ðrouung: *a* MARTYRIUM *b* PASSIO ‖ ðroung 27v12[b]. *sg. gen.* ðrounges 11v4[b]; 24v22[a]. ðrownges [*alt. f.* ðrowenges] 11r16[b]. ðrou[u]nges 37v3[a]; 37v9[b]. ðrowunges 38v6[a]. *sg. acc.* + *dat.* ðrounge 11v7[b]; 17r21[b]; 24r23[b] [*alt. f.* ðrouenge]. *ðrownge 11v20[b]. ðrou' 41r14[a].
giðry(c)ceð: COMPRIMERE ‖ *imp. sg.* geðrycg 82rb21.
aðry(c)ceð: *a* OPPRIMERE *b* PREMERE ‖ *pret. part.* aðryht 7v15[b]; 39v12[a]. *pl. nom.* + *acc.* aðryhto 25r8[b].
eft-for-ðry(c)ceð: REPRIMERE ‖ *pres. ind. sg. 2* eftf'ðryces 59v3.
of-ðry(c)ceð: DEPRIMERE ‖ *pret. part.* ofðryht 32r11.
mæg(e)n-ðrym(m: MAIESTAS ‖ mægenðrym 2v2; 42r8. mægenðrymm 7r21; 40r10. *sg. gen.* mægenðrymmes 4r11. *sg. dat.* mægenðryme 16r15. mægenðrymme 32v20; 35v14. mæginðrymme 42r4. *pl. nom.* + *acc.* mægenðrymmo 35r9.
ðu: *a* TU *b* TUUS *c* UESTER *d* UOSMET *e* qui; *A—with a Latin verb in the Second Person*; *B—with a Latin verb not in the Second Person*; *C—other insertional usages* ‖ ðu 1r3[(e)]; 1r23[A]; 2r17[a]; 31r16[B]; 78ra2[e]. *sg. acc.* ðec 1r3[a]; 15v10[C]; 50v4[B]. *sg. poss.* ðin 1r5[b]; 1r6[b]. ðín [*alt. f.* ðínum] 11v17[b]. *sg. poss. sg. gen.* ðines 1r19[b]; 1v8[a]. ðin' 41r14[a]; 46v 12[b]. *sg. poss. sg. dat.* ðinum 3v16[b]; 5v6[b] [*alt. f.* ðine]; 7v10[b] [*alt. f.* ðine]; 47v22[C]. *sg. poss. sg. acc. masc.* ðinne 14v9[b]; 27r9[b]. *sg. poss. sg. acc.* + *dat. fem.* ðine 7r5[b]. *sg. poss. sg. gen.* + *dat. fem.* ðinræ 18r10[b]; 18v6[b]. ðinre 23r8[b]; 45v14[b]. *sg. poss. sg. dat. fem.* ðinra 58v15[b]; 82ra13–14[b]. *sg. poss. pl. nom.* + *acc.* ðino 2r12[b]; 2r18[b]. ðinno 80ra18[b]. *sg. poss. pl. gen.* ðinra 2r12[b]; 40r18[c]. ðin' 40v1[b]. *sg. poss. pl. dat.* ðinum 1r20[b]; 19r2[b]. *sg. dat.* ðe 1v7[a]; 2r16[a]; 55r18. ð' 52r9[a]. *pl. nom.* gie 2r8[A]; 10v13[a]; 39v15[B]. ge 55r10; 55r17. *pl. acc.* iuih 5v16[a]; 10v14[A]; 14r16[d]. eow 55r7. *pl. poss.* iuero 2v15[c]; 12r 18[c]. iwero 12r17[c]. iuere 12r11[c]. iuer' 2v16[c]; 5v14[c]. iur' 17v21[c]. *pl. poss. sg. gen.* iueres 51r17[c]. *pl. poss. sg. dat.* iuerum 6r14[c]; 13r14[c] [*alt. f.* iuerw, *alt. f.* iuero]. *pl. poss. pl. dat.* iurum 17v23[c]. iwrum 17v19[c]. iur' 6v20[c]. *pl. dat.* iuh 5v15[a]; 6v19[d].
aðuað: LAUARE ‖ *pret. pl.* aðuogon 23v3.
ungiðuerni(s)s(e: UECORDIA ‖ ungeðuærnise 77r6.
heh-ðungen: sublimis ‖ hehðungen 1r13.
ðunur: TONITRUUM ‖ *sg. gen.* ðunures 23r16.
sceoh-ð(u)ong: CALIGA ‖ *pl. dat.* sceohðongum 28r14.
ðusend: MILLE ‖ ðusendo 23r12; 23r22. ðusenda 50r3; 54v5 [*alt. f.* ðusende]. *dat.* ðusendu [? *read* ðusendum] 66v12.
ðuslic: TALIS ‖ ðuslic' 43v7. *pl. dat.* ðuslicum 31r16.
giðyld: PATIENTIA ‖ giðyld 6v18; 13v5. *sg. gen.* giðyldes 11r12.
ðyldig: PATIENS ‖ ðyldig 48r16.
giðyldig: PATIENS ‖ giðyldig 2v17; 48v21. *pl. nom.* + *acc.* giðyldigo 6r1.
giðyll: AURA ‖ giðyll 59r14.
ðyngo: PROFICERE ‖ ðynge 40r17.
giðyngo: *a* PROUECTUS *b* expiare ‖ giðynge 11v1[b]; 24v9[a].
ðyrsteð: SITIRE ‖ *pres. part.* ðyrstende 1r12. *sg. dat.* ðyrstendum 9v14.
ua(c)can: *a* UIGILARE *b* incitamentum ‖ *sg. dat.* uacene 40v14[a]. *pl. nom.* + *acc.* wacana 30v20[b].
on-ua(c)can: incitamentum ‖ *pl. nom.* + *acc.* onwaccano 35v18.
in-uadað: illustrare ‖ *pret. sg. subj.* + *ind. 2* inwode 14v6.
uala, uæla: *a* DIUITIAE *b* PROSPERA *c* PROSPERITAS ‖ wala 7v18[b]; 39r10[a]. uale 33v13[c].
Rom-walas: QUIRITES ‖ *gen.* romwala 85va4.
ualer, uæler: LABIUM ‖ *pl. dat.* uælerum 80va2. uæler' 83ra16. ualerum 81vb24.
uall: MOENIA ‖ *pl. nom.* + *acc.* uallas 60r21.
ualleð: FERUERE ‖ *pres. part.* uallende 48v16; 49r5.
giualleð: *a* FERUERE *b* FERUESCERE ‖ *pres. subj.* + *inf.* giualla 48v4[b]; 50r16[a] [*alt. f.* giuallia].
uallung: FERUOR ‖ *sg. acc.* + *dat.* wallunge 31r14.
uaras: UIRI ‖ waras 21v7; 29v11. *gen.* warana 86vb6.
burg-waras: CIUES ‖ burgwaro 39v 14.
halg(a)-uaras: SANCTI ‖ halgauaras 44r17. halgawaras 23r19. halgaua' 44r20; 44v7. halgawar' 28r3. halga' 80ra18; 80vb20. *gen.* halgauara 29v 16; 31v12[1]. halgawara 23v21; 24r7. halgauara' 26v3. halgawara' 39r3. halgaua' 26v6; 36r6. halgawa' 29v19; 30r9. halguara 22r1; 34r6.
hell-waras: *a* INFERI *b* INFERNI ‖ *gen.* helluarana 5v8[a]. elluar' 28v15[b]. *dat.* helluarum 48r21[a].
uat, nat: *a* NESCIRE *b* NOUISSE *c* SCIRE (*d* existimare) ‖ uat 21v13[b]; 44v4[c]; 86rb8[(d)]. wat 9v7[c]. *pres. ind. sg. 2* uast 4r6[c]. *pres. subj.* witto 66v17[c]. witen 55r18. *inf.* w[u]tta 23v20[b]. *pres. pl.* wuton 32v4[b]; 44v6[c]; 51r10[(a)]. nuton 3r8[c+]; 81rb12[a+]. *imp. pl.* [w]utað 14r1[c]. wutas 12r10[c]. *pres. part.* witende 13r5[c]. *pl. nom.* + *acc.* witendo 12v22[c]. *pret. sg.* uiste 39r5[c]. wiste 26v11[b]. nyste 28r15[a+].
giuat: SCIRE ‖ *inf.* [gi]uta 3r1.
uæ(c)ceð: UIGILARE ‖ *pres. subj.* + *inf.* woæca 14r11. *pres. part. pl. nom.* + *acc.* wæccendo 18v20.
giuæ(c)ceð: UIGILARE ‖ *pres. subj.* + *inf.* giwoeca 14r6. giuæcge 60v10.
giuæld: coma ‖ giuæld 45v22; 46r12.
on-uæld: *a* DOMINATIO *b* IMPERIUM *c* POTESTAS ‖ onwæld 10v19[b]; 61r13[c]. *sg. gen.* onuældes 59v3[a].
on-uældeð: DOMINARI ‖ onuældað 6v19.
gi-on-uældeð: DOMINARI ‖ gionuældeð 4r24. gionwældiað 13r7. gionuældas 41v10.
uælm: *a* FERUOR *b* FUROR ‖ *sg. dat.* uælme 83rb13[b]. wælme 45v13[a].
auælteð: uexare ‖ *pret. part. pl. nom.* + *acc.* auæltedo 41v3.
giuærleð: DECLINARE ‖ *pret. sg.* giwærlde 9v16.
auærleð: DECLINARE ‖ *pres. subj.* + *inf.* awærle 19r21.
bi-uærleð: carere ‖ *pres. subj.* + *inf.* beuærle 58v18; 59r13.
uæst(e)m: FRUCTUS ‖ uæstim 45v7;

1. *Third* a *intercalated.*

47r16. uæstm 44r13. wæstem 7v1. wæstm 2r3. *sg. gen.* wæstmes' 50v4. *sg. dat.* uæstme 4v10. *pl. nom. + acc.* uæstmo 57v5. wæstmo 66v10. *pl. dat.* wæstmum 26v2.

on-uæst(e)m: INCREMENTUM ‖ on-uæstem 33v4. *pl. dat.* onwæstum [? *read* onwæstmum] 19r6.

uæst(e)mlic: FRUCTUOSUS ‖ wæstimlic 9r7.

uæstmað: FRUCTIFICARE ‖ *pret. sg.* wæstmede 2r2.

uæ(t)ter: *a* AQUA (*b* HYDRIA) ‖ wæter 55r21. uæt' 55v12[a]; 57v16[a]. wæt' 49r5[a]. wætter 55v1[a]. *sg. gen.* uætres 48v3[a]; 56v20[a]. wætres 40v9[a]; 56v11[a]. uættres 66r5[a]. uæt's 56v10[(b)]. *sg. dat.* uætre 1r12[a]; 31v17[a]. wætre 16r21[a]; 22v6[a]. uæt' 58r10[a]; 58v20[a]. wæt' 57v8[a]. *pl. nom. + acc.* uætro 55v3[a]; 55v5[a]. wætro 55v1[a]. uætro 55v17[a]; 59r6[a].

uæx: (CERARIUS) ‖ uæx 87vb7.

uæxeð: *a* CRESCERE *b* progenitus ‖ uæxeð 39v18[a]. *pres. part.* uæxende 47r12[b].

giuæxeð: *a* ACCRESCERE *b* CONCRESCERE *c* CRESCERE *d* proficere ‖ *pres. subj. + inf.* geuæxe 81vb18[d]. giuæxe 4v10[d]; 26v2[a]. gewæxe 1v18[c]. giwæxe 12v5[c]. *pret. pl.* giuoxon 39r14[b].

dor-u(e)ard: *a* IANITOR *b* OSTIARIUS ‖ dorweard 87ra12[b]. *pl. nom. + acc.* dorweardas 87ra14[a].

erf(e)-u(e)ard: HERES ‖ erfeueard 85rb21.

for-u(e)ard: *a* EXORDIUM *b* initium *c* principium ‖ f'ueard 18v11[c]; 33v3[a]. foruard 80va13[b].

gi-erf(e)-u(e)ardað: HEREDITARE ‖ gierfeuardeð 40v13. *pres. subj. + inf.* gierfeueard' 31v6. *pret. sg.* gierfeueardade 22r21.

erf(e)-u(e)ardni(s)s(e: HEREDITAS ‖ erfeueardnisse 12r7–8. erfeueardnisse 80ra25. erfeueardnise 31v3. erfeuardnise 31v11; 37v16. erfeweardnis' 2r9. *pl. nom. + acc.* erfeuardnisso 29v13. erfwardniso 10r15.

ufa: SURSUM ‖ ufa 13v19.

uidilni(s)s(e: POLLUTIO ‖ uidðil' 47r6.

unwidlad: IMPOLLUTUS ‖ unwidlad 43v8.

unawidlad: INCONTAMINATUS ‖ unawidlad 12r8. *sg. gen.* unawidlades 12r13.

uidlað: *a* COINQUINARE *b* POLLUERE ‖ *pret. part. pl. nom. + acc.* giuidlado 23r23[a]. gewidlado 82rb21[b].

giuidlað: INQUINARE ‖ *pret. pl.* giwidladon 50r4.

uidua: UIDUA ‖ *pl. nom. + acc.* widua/o 28r5. widuas 14r21.

uif: *a* MULIER *A—glossing a name* ‖ uif 48v10[A]; 52v3[a]. wif 22r15[a]. *sg. gen.* uifes 52r20[a]. *sg. dat.* uife 28r4[A]. *pl. dat.* uifum 23r23[a]; 50r4[a].

uiflic: FEMINEUS ‖ *sg. dat.* uiflicum 52r21.

uigbed: ALTAR ‖ *sg. dat.* uigbede 34r4; 34r6. wigbede 55v11.

uiht: animal ‖ *pl. nom. + acc.* wihto 66r9.

uil: *a* NOLLE + *b* UELLE ‖ uil 50r1[b]. wil 66v9[b]. *pres. sg. ind. 2* nylt 20r5[a+]. *pres. pl.* uallað 3r1[b]. nællað 6r17[a+]. *pres. subj.* uælle 40v18[b]; 49r19[b]. *imp. sg.* nælle 26v14[a+]; 78vb4[a+]. *pret. sg.* ualde 45v3[b]; 55r2. walde 9v18[b]. *pret. sg. ind. 2* ualdest 25r11[b]; 45r7[b]. waldest 11v10[b]; 17v5[b]. *pret. pl.* naldon 51r23[a+].

uillo: *a* DESIDERIUM *b* UOLUNTAS ‖ uillo 6r5[b]; 7r17[a]. willo 13r22[b]. willa 13v12[b]. *pl. nom. + acc.* willo 3v21[b].

uilnað: *a* CONCUPISCERE *b* DESIDERARE ‖ uilniað 44v4[b]. wilnig' 12v5[a]. *pres. part.* *uilnende 35r22[b].

giuilnað: CONCUPISCERE ‖ giwilnigað 2r7.

uin: UINUM ‖ win 48v8. *sg. dat.* wine 2r12; 55v4.

uind: UENTUS ‖ wind 86va14. *sg. gen.* windes 86va2. *sg. dat.* winde 86va10. *pl. gen.* windana 86va16.

uindung, uyndung: (zizania) ‖ *wyndnung [? *read* wynndung] 88vb 19.

uinneð: LABORARE ‖ *pres. part.* winnende 20r18. *pret. sg. ind. 1, 3* wann 33r10.

uinstra: SINISTER ‖ winstræ 39r10. ui/ynst 58r4.

uisdom: SCIENTIA ‖ wisdom 18v12; 39r3. *sg. gen.* wisdomes 58r14.

unuisdom: IGNORANTIA ‖ *sg. gen.* unwisdomes 18v11.

uisfæst: perfectus ‖ uisfæst 27v5; 36v12. wisfæst 13v18[1]; 14r17. *sg. fem.* uisfæsto 33r13. *sg. dat.* wisfæstum 40r6. *sg. acc. + dat. fem.* uisfæste 50v10. wisfæst' 15r17. *pl. nom. + acc.* wisfæsto 6v9.

uisfæstlice: perfectius ‖ wistfæstlice [? *read* wisfæstlice] 10r20.

unuisnis(s)(e: nequitia ‖ *sg. gen.* unwisnise 12v1.

uitga: PROPHETA ‖ uitga 58v3. uitge 58r4. witge 26v12. *pl. nom. + acc.* witgo 40r2. *pl. gen.* uitgana 39v15. *pl. dat.* witgum 87ra20.

1. *First* s *intercalated.*

giuitgað: PROPHETARE ‖ *pret. sg.* giuitgade 27v8.

uitni(s)s(e: SCIENTIA ‖ witn' 87va12.

giuitni(s)s(e: TESTIS ‖ gewitnesse 55r20⁻. giwitnis' 87vb10.

bil-uitni(s)s(e: *a* LENITAS *b* MANSUETUDO *c* MODESTIA *d* SIMPLICITAS *e* SINCERITAS ‖ biluitnisse 37v22[a]; 47v20[b]. biluitnise 50r15[c]; 87ra8[d]. bilwitnis' 53r23[a]. *sg. gen.* biluitnises 12v1[e].

uið: *a* ADUERSUS *b* CONTRA *c* USQUE *d* cum ‖ uið 27r6[c]; 34r1[d] [*written above* mið]; 54v13[a]; 54v19[b]. wið 3v15[b]; 55v15. w' 17v23[c].

uiðir: ADUERSUS ‖ uiððir 78rb17.

uiðiru(e)ard, -uord: *a* ADUERSUS (*b* Asmodeus) (*c* hereticus) ‖ *sg. gen.* *wiðirwordes 59v3[a]. *sg. weak* wiðirwearda 67r5[(b)]. wiðirworda 67r18[(b)]. *pl. nom. + acc.* uiðiruorda 60r5[a]. wiðirweardo 24v2[a]; 61r18[a]. *pl. dat.* wiðirwordum 88vb8[(c)].

uiðiru(e)ardað, -uordað: ADUERSARI ‖ *pret. part.* giwiðirworded 54v21.

uiðiru(e)ard- (-uord-)ni(s)s(e: *a* ADUERSITAS *b* ADUERSUM *c* aduersor *d* prauitas *e* prauus ‖ *uiðirweardnisse 18r20[d]. uiðerwordnise 4r23[a]. wiðirwordnise 7r11[a]. *pl. nom. + acc.* wiðirwordnisso 7v19[b]. *wiðirwordniso 3v 15[b]. wiðerwordnis' 7r20[c]. *pl. dat.* wiðirweardnissum 8r1[a]. wiðirweardnisum 11r14[b]. uiðirwearðnisum 45r 18[b]. wiðirwordnissum 3v18[a]. uiðirwordnisum 44r3[e]. wiðirwordnisum 19v14[a].

uið-ðæt: USQUE QUO ‖ uiðþ *80ra7; 81rb17.

aulencað: DITARE ‖ *pret. part. pl. nom. + acc.* awlencedo 28v7.

ond-uliota: *a* FACIES *b* FRONS ‖ ondwliote 5v11[a]. ondwlioto 9v6[a]. *pl. dat.* ondliotum [*alt. f.* ondwliotum] 23r 11[b].

giulitgað: DECORARE ‖ *pres. subj. + inf.* giwlitga 50v8. giwlitgega 50v4.

ulit(t: decus ‖ *sg. gen.* ulittes 44r17. *sg. dat.* wlite 46v1.

fore-(fora-)ulit(t: fasciculus ‖ f'awlit 2r20.

meg-ulit(t: *a* SPECIES *b* maiestas ‖ megwlite 1r19[a]. megewlit 1r9[b]. *sg. gen.* m'gwlit' 44r17[a].

under: SUB ‖ under *35r21; 60v15.

au(o)e(c)ceð: SUSCITARE ‖ *pres. subj. + inf.* awoece 10r15. *pret. sg.* awoehte 28r11. *pret. sg. ind. 2* awoehtest 10r15; 48v12.

eft-giu(o)e(c)ceð: RESUSCITARE ‖ *pret. sg.* eftgiwoehte [*alt. f.* eftawoehte] 13v3.

u(o)ede: *a* UESTIMENTUM *b* UESTIS ‖

woede 49v5a; 49v14b. *pl. nom.* + *acc.* uoedo 2v15a.
giu(o)ede: UESTIS ‖ *pl. nom.* + *acc.* giwoedo 51v18.
giu(o)edeð: INDUERE ‖ gioedes [*alt. f.* giwoedes] 6v16.
u(o)eg(e: UIA ‖ uoeg 44v2. woeg 17v18; 27r11. weg 5r22; 9v16. uoegi 79rb13. uægi 78rb20. *pl. nom.* + *acc.* uoegas 39r11 (2). woegas 17v12; 17v17. uegas 3r1. wegas 10r5. *pl. gen.* woegena 51v11. *pl. dat.* uoegum 51v13.
u(o)el: BENE ‖ uel 41v4; 81rb3. wel 5v7.
u(o)elgað: DITARE ‖ *pret. part. pl. nom.* + *acc.* giwoelgado 28v7.
unu(o)emmed: IMMACULATUS ‖ *sg. fem.* unuoemmedo 50r6. *sg. weak* unwoemmedo 50r6.*
unau(o)emmed: IMMACULATUS ‖ *sg. fem.* unawoemmedo 14r20. *sg. gen.* unawoemmed' 12r13. *sg. acc. masc.* unawoemmed' 14r22.
unau(o)emmedlic: immortalitas ‖ *sg. dat.* unawoemmedlicum 16r17.
un-ym(b)-u(o)endedlic: IMMOTUS ‖ unymbuoendedlic 77v2.
u(o)endeð: CONUERTERE ‖ *pret. part.* giuoendad 60r17.
giu(o)endeð: CONUERTERE ‖ *pres. subj.* + *inf.* giuoende 80ra7. giwoende 56v12. *imp. sg.* geuoend 82rb3. giuoend 80ra4. gewoend 81rb17.
eft-giu(o)endeð: REUERTI ‖ *pres. subj.* + *inf.* eftgiwoende 5r23.
eft-ym(b)-u(o)endeð: REUERTI ‖ *pret. sg.* eftymwoende 28r18.
from-u(o)endeð: AUERTERE ‖ *imp. sg.* fromwoend 20v7.
ym(b)-u(o)endeð: *a* AUERTERE *b* CONUERTERE *c* IMMUTARE *d* MOUERE *e* UERTERE *f* uellere ‖ ymwoendes 5r17a. *pres. subj.* + *inf.* ymbwoende 10r8a. *imp. sg.* ymbuoend 21r9a. ymbwoend 4v4a; 7v13a. *pres. part. pl. dat.* ymbwoendendum[1] 9v2f. *pret. sg. ind. 2* ymbuoendest 55v4b; 55v6e. *pret. part.* ymbuoended 5v4a; 46r4c. *pl. nom.* + *acc.* ymbuoendedo 56v11b; 78ra13d.
ym(b)-u(o)ending: *a* CONUERSATIO *b* uegetatio ‖ ymbwoending 8r18b; 30v5a.
ofer-ym(b)-u(o)endni(s)s(e: TRANSMUTATIO ‖ of'ymbwoendnise 13v20.
ðun-u(o)enge: TEMPORA ‖ *pl. dat.* ðunwoengum 82va19.
u(o)epen: ARMA ‖ *pl. nom.* + *acc.* uoepeno 78rb14.

1. b *intercalated.*

uoepeð: FLERE ‖ *pres. subj.* + *inf.* woepa 9r11.
u(o)epnað: ARMARE ‖ *pret. part. sg. dat.* uoepnedum 47v4. gewoepnadum 66r17.
giu(o)epnað: ARMARE ‖ giwoepnigað 10v14.
u(o)er: *a* UIR (*b* maritalis) ‖ uoer 3r22a. woer 17v14a; 40r6a. uer 5r10a; 22v3a. wer 5r22a. *sg. gen.* woeres 52r21a. ueres 52v7(b). weres 14r3a. *sg. dat.* uoere 52r13a; 78va8a. woere 52v3a. uere 52v12a. *pl. dat.* uærum 78va13a.
port-u(o)er: CIUIS ‖ portuer 85ra17.
u(o)erc: *a* ACTIO *b* DOLOR *c* LABOR *d* OPERATIO *e* OPUS ‖ uoerc 55v20b. woerc 5v14e; 6v8e [*alt. f.* woerce]. *sg. gen.* uoerces 52r1e; *87rb15e. woerces 7v1e; 14r19e. *sg. dat.* uoerce 79ra9e; 79ra11e. woerce 6v23e. *pl. nom.* + *acc.* uoerco 79rb2e; 79rb5e. *pl. gen.* uoerca 44v1c; 45v8e. *pl. dat.* woercum 4v17a; 7r7e; 44r6d.
hond-giu(o)erc: MANU FACTUS ‖ hondgiwoerc 10r20. *pl. dat.* hondgiuoercum 47v15; 60r2.
yfel-u(o)erc: MALEFICIUM ‖ yfeluoerc 49r17.
unau(o)erded: ILLAESUS ‖ *pl. nom.* + *acc.* unawoerdedo 49r8.
u(o)erdeð: uitium ‖ *pres. part. pl. gen.* woerdendra 18r14.
au(o)erdeð: AFFLIGERE ‖ *pret. part. sg. fem.* awoerdedo 3r3. *pl. nom.* + *acc.* awoerdedo 11v7; 20v13. awoerdeno 19v21.
u(o)erding: LAESIO ‖ woerding 48v18.
u(o)erdni(s)s(e: *a* AFFLIGERE *b* NOXIUS *c* UITIUM ‖ woerdnise' 8r4a. *pl. dat.* woerdnisum 8r11c; 8v2b.
giu(o)ereð: DETEGERE ‖ *pres. subj.* + *inf.* giwoeria 49r19.
uoeste(r)n: *a* DESERTUM *b* exterminium ‖ woesten 1r8a. *sg. gen.* woest'es 41v1b. *sg. dat.* woesterne 27v3a. uoest'ne 47r19a.
uoestig: DESERTUS ‖ *sg. dat.* woestigum 8v15.
uoeðni(s)s(e: LENITAS ‖ uoeðnisse 47v20.
giuoeðni(s)s(e: LENITAS ‖ giwoeðnise 50r15.
uoh: PRAUUS ‖ *pl. dat.* woeum 25v7. woewum 8r2.
uoh: PRAUITAS ‖ *sg. gen.* woe 18r20. w^u^oe 16v12.
uohful(l: *a* NEQUAM *b* nequitia ‖ wogfull 13r21a. *pl. nom.* + *acc.* woghfulla 56r20b.
uohfulni(s)s(e: NEQUITIA ‖ woghful' 58v8; 58v19. *pl. nom.* + *acc.* *woghfulniso 59v5.

uolcen: NUBIS ‖ *sg. gen.* uolcenes 5r7. uolcnes 86rb23. *pl. nom.* + *acc.* wolceno (*alt. f.* wolgceno) 39r14.
uomb: *a* UENTER *b* UULUA ‖ *sg. acc.* + *dat.* uombe 26v12b; 27r3a.
uomm: MACULA ‖ *sg. dat.* uomme 46r13.
uona: (DEESSE) ‖ uona 42r9.
uonað: MINUERE ‖ *imp. sg.* wona 5v11.
giuonað: DEESSE ‖ *pres. subj.* + *inf.* giwonia 34v9.
auonað: MACERARE ‖ *pret. part.* awonad 7r23.
nerxna-uong: PARADISUS ‖ *sg. gen.* nerxnawong' 60r21. neirxnawongas 60v2.
uonung: MACERATIO ‖ *sg. acc.* + *dat.* wonunge 7r18.
uop: *a* FLETUS *b* PLANCTUS ‖ wop 51v 21a. wop' 21v8b. *sg. dat.* uope 2v14a. *pl. dat.* wopum 19v9a.
uord: *a* SERMO *b* UERBUM ‖ uord 21v9b. word 6r14a; 6v21b. *sg. gen.* uordes 23r2b. wordes 14r15b; 18v16b. *sg. dat.* worde 3v6b; 6v23b. *pl. nom.* + *acc.* worda 26v19b. *pl. dat.* wordum 37v19b.
on-uorpeð: illabi ‖ *imp. sg.* onuorp 18v13.
to-uorpeð: DISPERGERE ‖ *pres. subj.* + *inf.* toworpa 27r1.
plæce-uorð: PLATEA ‖ plægiword 17v13.
uorð: PRETIUM ‖ *sg. dat.* worðe 13r13.
uorðað: *a* ADORARE *b* HONORIFICARE *c* UENERARI ‖ uorðiað 23v18c. worðiað 24v18c. *pres. ind. sg. 1* worðigo 1r4b. *pres. subj.* + *inf.* worðiga 32v3c [*alt. f.* worðia]; 36r2c. uorðia 34v5a. worðia 31r2c; 31r10c. *infl. inf.* worðanne 45r4a. *pret. sg.* uorðade 34r10a. *pret. part.* giworðiad 2r23c.
giuorðað: *a* ADORARE *b* UENERARI ‖ giworðigað 27r8a. *pres. subj.* + *inf.* giuorðia 60v16b. giworðia 35r22b. *pret. pl.* giworðadon 60v15b.
uorðeð: FIERI ‖ *pret. part. sg. dat.* giwordnum 52r20.
giuorðeð: FIERI ‖ *pres. subj.* + *inf.* giworðe 48r7; 54v12.
auorðeð: FIERI ‖ *pret. pl.* awurdon 48r17. *pret. part.* auorden 42r13; 86rb 14. aworden 3r22; 10v6. *pl. nom.* + *acc.* auordeno 81va24–5. awordeno 43v3 [*alt. f.* awurdeno]; 85rb10. awordno 85rb7.
uorðlice: HONORABILITER ‖ worðlice 4v14.
uorðung: *a* HONOR *b* UENERATIO ‖ worðung 50r19a. *sg. gen.* uorðunges 44r13a. worðunges 33r12a; 87rb15a. *sg. acc.* + *dat.* worðunge 29r1a; 35v4b.
uor(u)ld: SAECULUM ‖ uoruld 81rb22.

woruld 33r5; 77r11. uorld 58v11. world 82va12. wor' 57r22. *sg. gen.* uoruldes 8v16. woruldes *88vb18. uorld' 81rb22. *sg. acc. + dat.* uorulde 32r4; 45v6. worulde 13r21; 17v23. weorolde 55r15[-]. worlde 14r23. uorld' 81vb9. *pl. nom. + acc.* uorulda 79rb20; 82rb11. worulda 53r7. worul'da 29r21. worulde 77v18. wuoruldo 77v13. woruld' 47r10; 66r11. uorul' 58r18; 82vb9. worul' 55r5; 57v14. worlda [*alt. f.* worlde] 10v19. world' 66v6. uorl' 82vb14; 83ra13. wor' 56v3. wo' 49r22. *pl. gen.* woruldo 2r10. uoruld' 66r11; 66v6. woruld' 53r7; 55r6. uorld' 79rb20. world' 10v19. uorl' 47r10; 58r19. wor' 56v3. wo' 49r22. *pl. dat.* woruldum [*alt. f.* woruldo] 29v17.

uor(u)ldlic: SAECULARIS ‖ *sg. dat.* woruldlicum 46r3. *pl. dat.* woruldlicum 29r10.

uo(s)sa: CONUERSATIO ‖ wosa 12r11; 40v4.

giuo(s)sa: CONUERSATIO ‖ giwosa 16r7. *sg. gen.* giuossa' 36r2. giwos'a 24v18.

up(p: SURSUM ‖ upp 12r14; 12r15.

urað: IRATUS ‖ *urað 82rb2.

uræðeð: *a* FREMERE *b* IRASCI ‖ *pret. sg.* uræðde 88va14[a]. w[u]ræðde 51v7[b].

uræ(ð)ðo, ura(ð)ðo: *a* INDIGNATIO *b* IRA *c* IRACUNDIA *d* iniuria ‖ wræððo 6r19[a]; 7v13[c]; 50r20[d]. wræðo 5v4[b]. uræððo 20r12[a]. uraððo 4v3[c]. *sg. gen.* wræððes 42r13[c].

under-ure(ð)ðeð: *a* FULCIRE *b* SUFFULCIRE *c* SUSTENTARE ‖ *pres. ind. sg. 2* underwreððes 22r7[c]. *imp. sg.* underureð 18v2[c]. *pret. part.* underwreðed 36v5[a]. *pl. nom. + acc.* underwreððedo 34r21[b].

uri(g)ils: *a* UELAMEN *b* UELAMENTUM ‖ wrigils 44v2[b]. *sg. dat.* wriilcse 50v18[a].

uriið: OPERIRE ‖ *infl. inf.* wrianne 49v16.

eft-unauriið: REUELARE ‖ eftunawriað[1] 10r17.

urit(t: SCRIPTURA ‖ urit 38r5.

giurit(t: CONSCRIPTUM ‖ giwritt' 16r10.

aurit(t: SCRIPTURA ‖ *pl. nom. + acc.* awriotto 54v9.

hond-giurit(t: CHIROGRAPHUM ‖ hond-giwrit 16r10.

auri(t)teð: SCRIBERE ‖ *imp. sg.* auritt 34r8. awritt 23v6. *pret. part.* awritten 23r13.

urixl: UICIS ‖ *pl. nom. + acc.* wrixla 77r21.

user: *see* **ic.**

uta: *a* EXTERIOR *b* EXTRINSECUS *c* FORIS ‖ uta 1v3[c]; 2r22[b]. *sup.* utmeste 27r6[a]. *sup. pl. nom. + acc.* y/[u]tmesto 48r22[a]. ytmesto 51v21[a].

utacund: alienus ‖ *pl. dat.* utacundum 78rb22; 80ra2 [*alt. f.* utatcundum].

uuldrað: *a* GLORIARI *b* GLORIFICARE ‖ wuldriað 51r18[b]. wuldriaðg 13r13[b]. *pres. ind. sg. 1* wuldrigo 3r19[a]. *pres. subj. + inf.* wuldrige 11r3[a]; 38v14[a]. *pret. part.* wuldrad 20r24[a]. *pl. nom. + acc.* wuldrado 34v6[a].

auuldrað: GLORIARI ‖ *pret. part.* awuldrad 38r15.

uuldrig: GLORIOSUS ‖ wuldrig 25v19; 33v8. wuld[u]rig 23v13. *sg. fem.* wuldrigo 24r20; 35r15 [*alt. f.* wuldriga]. *sg. gen.* wuldriges 33v22. *sg. dat.* wuldrigum 36v4. *pl. nom. + acc.* wuldrigo 28r22; 30r18; 36r20 [*alt. f.* wuldrigum]; 40r9 [*alt. f.* gwuldrigo]. *pl. dat.* wuldrigum 32v7; 34v20. wuldrium 44r8.

uuldrung: GLORIFICATIO ‖ wuldrung 27v11. *sg. gen.* wuld'es 41r11.

uuldur: GLORIA ‖ uuldur 34v2. wuldur 10v19; 12v20. wuldor 1v7; 85rb20. *sg. gen.* *uuldres 38r3. wuldres 1v19; 22r18. wuld' 48r14. *sg. dat.* wuldre 1r7; 3v13. wuldure 21r5.

uuldurlic: GLORIOSUS ‖ wuldurlic 82vb13. wuldorlic 82vb8. *sg. dat.* wuldurlicum 43r19. *pl. dat.* wuldirlicum 30r10.

uunað: *a* MANERE *b* PERMANERE *c* morari ‖ uunas 81rb21[a]. wunað 3v1[a]; 43v5[a]. wuniað 29v12[b]. wniað 29v15[a]. *pres. ind. sg. 1* uniga 31v3[c]. *pres. subj. + inf.* wunia 46r13[b]. *pres. part.* wunigende 60r3; unigende 40v6[c]. wnigende 22v3[c]. *pl. dat.* wunigendum 47v16[a].

giuunað: *a* HABITARE *b* PERMANERE *c* commorari ‖ giwuneð 2r21[c]. *pres. subj. + inf.* giuunia 43v4[b]. *pret. sg. ind. 2* giw[u]nedest 31v20[a].

ðerh-uunað: PERMANERE ‖ ðerhwunað 14r18. *pres. subj. + inf.* ðerhuuniga 82ra16. ðerhwuniga[2] 79vb1. ðerhwunige 34v20. ðerhuunia 66v15. ðerhu[u]nia 32v7. ðerhwunia 52v11; 52v15. *ðerhunia 50r5. *pres. part.* *ðerhwunigende 77v2–3. *pret. pl.* ðerhwunedon 50r3.

uundur: (*a* MAGNALIA) *b* MIRABILE *c* MIRACULUM ‖ *pl. nom. + acc.* wundra 24v21[c]. w[u]ndra 37r15[(a)]. wundro 23v13[b]. *pl. dat.* wundrum 1v14[c].

uundurlic: *a* ADMIRABILIS *b* MIRABILIS *c* MIRUS *d* immensus ‖ uundurlic 38v5[b]. wundurlic 1r5[b]; 15v5[b]. *sg. fem.* wundurlico 58v12[d]. *sg. dat.* wundurlicum 34r16[c]; 44v2[b]. wundurlic' 1v10[b]. wunderlicum 12v8[a].

giuunu: USUS ‖ giwunu 58v14; 56v22.

uun(u)lic: SOLITUS ‖ *sg. fem.* wunulico 82rb15. wnulic' 17r20.

giuun(u)lice: ASSIDUE ‖ giwunulcei 54v1.

uununi(s)s(e: *a* HABITACULUM *b* HABITATIO *c* PERSEUERANTIA ‖ w[u]nunisse 33r6[b]. wununise 28r10[a]; 33r10[b]; 50v13[c].

giuununi(s)s(e: *a* HABITACULUM *b* USUS ‖ giwununise 60r3[a]. giwunun' 59v18[a]. *pl. dat.* giwununissum 46v14[b].

uuted: CERTUS ‖ *sg. dat.* wutedum 44r22. *sg. acc. masc.* wutedne 44r19. *pl. nom. + acc.* uutedo 79va21.

unuuted: INCERTUS ‖ *pl. nom. + acc.* *unw[u]tedo 51r2.

uutedlice: *a* AUTEM *b* ETIAM *c* IAM *d* QUIDEM *e* UERO ‖ wuted' 3r9[d]; 43v4[a]. wut' 3r12[d]; 3r13[a]; 8r21[b]; 39v13[c]; 51v5[e].

giuu(t)ta: CONSCIUS ‖ giwuta' 54v16.

(u)uð-(u)u(t)ta: senior ‖ *pl. nom. + acc.* wuðwuto 54v1.

uynsum(m: *a* IOCUNDUS *b* adultus ‖ *pl. nom. + acc.* wynsumo 32r1[a]. wynsum' 46r21[b].

uynsu(m)mað: *a* EXSULTARE *b* LAETARI *c* exaltare ‖ wynsumiað 1r8[a]. *pres. part.* wynsummende 1r13[a]. wynsumiende 46v1[b]; *60r8[a]. *sg. fem.* wynsumændo 31v13[c].

giuynsu(m)mað: EXSULTARE ‖ giwynsumiað 1r8. *pres. subj. + inf.* giwyinsumia 29r2. giwynsumiga 6v20.

uynsumni(s)s(e: *a* EXSULTATIO *b* IOCUNDITAS ‖ wynsumnise 22r20[a]; 24v8[a]. wynsumnis' 4r3[a]; 49v6[b]. wynsumnise 41r11[b].

uyrcend: FACTOR ‖ wyrcend 14r18.

brycg-uyrcend(e: pontifex ‖ brycg-wyrcende 87va3.

yfel-uyrcend(e: MALEFICUS ‖ *pl. nom. + acc.* yfelwyrcendo 49r18.

uyrceð: *a* FACERE *b* OPERARI ‖ wyrceð 3v8[b]. wyrcað 5v14[b]. *pres. ind. sg. 2* wyrces 23v14[b]. *pres. part.* wyrcende 8r8[b]; 47r8[b]. wyrcend 5r18[b]; 14r19[a]. uyrc' 78va12[b]. *pret. sg.* worhte 51r22[a]; 80vb8[a]. *pret. sg. ind. 2* worhtest 45r11[a]; 48v8[a]. *pret. pl.* worhton 21v7[a].

giuyrceð: *a* OPERARI *b* gerere ‖ giwyrcað 14r3[a]. *pres. subj. + inf.* giuyrca 61r16[a]. gewyrce 67r4[a]. *pret. sg. ind. 2* giworhtest 79ra6[b].

auyrceð: FACERE ‖ *pret. part.* *aworht 88va1.

1. un *intercalated.*

2. ðerh *intercalated.*

efne-giuyrceð: COOPERARI ‖ efnegiwyrcað 44v6.

uyrcing: *a* OPERARI *b* OPERATIO ‖ wyrcing 15r13[b]; 21r10[a]. *sg. acc.* + *dat.* wyrcinge 78vb19[b]. *pl. nom.* + *acc.* wyrcengo 7v21[b].

giuyrd: CONDITIO ‖ giwyrd 32r18.

uyrdeð ‖ *pres. subj.* + *inf.* wyrde 55r20.

giuyrht ‖ *pl. dat.* gewyrhtum[1] 55r19.

uyrhta: AUCTOR ‖ wyrhte 13v6.

frum-uyrhta: AUCTOR ‖ frumwyrhta 17r11; 52v13. frumwyrhte 18r13; 52r16.

uyrm: UERMIS ‖ *pl. nom.* + *acc.* wyrmas 57v9. w^u^yrmas 66r8. *pl. dat.* wyrmum 57v5; 66v1.

uyrt: *a* HERBA (*b* aroma) ‖ *pl. nom.* + *acc.* wyrto 49r17[a]. *pl. gen.* wyrtana 2r13[(b)]. wyrteno 2r13[(b)].

uyr(t)tru(m)m(a: RADIX ‖ wyrtrum 9v14. *pl. nom.* + *acc.* wyrtrumo 31v7. wyrttrum' 61r18.

1. h *intercalated.*

giuyr(t)tru(m)mað: ERADICARE ‖ *pret. sg.* giwyrtrumade 31v10.

of-uyr(t)tru(m)mað: ERADICARE ‖ *pres. subj.* + *inf.* *ofwyrttrumia 59r2.

ar-uyrðað: UENERARI ‖ arwyrðed 33v16.

gi-ar-uyrðað: HONORIFICARE ‖ giarwyrðigeð 1r3.

uyrðe: DIGNUS ‖ wyrðe 14v1; 29r7. *sg. fem.* wyrðo 53r9. *pl. nom.* + *acc.* wyrðo 5v7; 11v1.

unuyrðe: INDIGNUS ‖ unwyrðe 47r1; 60v20.

ar-uyrðe: *a* HONORIFICATUS *b* UENERABILIS *c* UENERANDUS *d* pius ‖ arwyrðe 31r19[c]; *52v17[b]. *sg. fem.* arwyrðo [*alt. f.* arwyrðe] 22r15[a]. *sg. dat.* arwyrðum 31v10[a]. *sg. acc. masc.* arwyrðne 23r6[c]. *pl. nom.* + *acc.* arwyrðo 4r19[c]; 11v14[c]. *sup.* arwyrðesta 77r17[d]; 82rb23[d].

dior-uyrðe: *a* PRETIOSUS *b* SPECIOSUS (*c* pretium) ‖ diorwyrðe 31v16[b]; 43v 19[a]. *sg. dat.* diorwyrðum 45r6[a]; 51r 18[(c)]. *pl. nom.* + *acc.* diorwyrðo 44r12[a].

uyrð(e)lic: *a* DIGNANTER *b* DIGNUS ‖ *sg. dat.* wyrðelicum 17v6[b]; 39r17[b]. *sg. dat.* + *adv.* wyrðelice 42r6[b]; 59v7[a].

ar-uyrð(e)lic: UENERABILIS ‖ *sg. acc. masc.* arwyrðlicne 37r19.

uyrðni(s)s(e: DIGNITAS ‖ wyrðnise 17r15.

yfel: MALUS ‖ yfel 3v8; 6r2. *sg. dat.* yflum 78va7; 79ra9. yfle 6r2 [*alt. f.* yfele]; 29r20. *pl. nom.* + *acc.* yflo 20r3; 25v17. yfla 9r11; 27r20. *pl. gen.* yfelra 7v14; 23v10. *pl. dat.* yflum 8v10; 25r4.

ym(b: *a* CIRCA *b* DE ‖ ymb 22r4[a]; 86rb10[b]. ymbe 87ra11[b].

ymen: HYMNUS ‖ ymmon 83vb17.

y(p)peð: MANIFESTARE ‖ *pret. part.* giypped 6v1; 49r15. geypped 85va19. *pl. nom.* + *acc.* giyppedo 6v3. giypedo 1v16.

ay(p)peð: experiri ‖ *pret. part.* aypped 33v17.

y(p)ping: MANIFESTATIO ‖ ypping 87vb13.

yð: *a* FLUCTUS *b* UNDA ‖ yð 59r12[b]. *pl. dat.* yðum 29v20[a].

rusalem laudem in terra.
Ecce seruus meus suscipiam eum electus meus
honorificabit te anima mea. [illegible] in tuo quia fa
Dne ds nr honorificabo te et laudem tribuam nomi
cis mirabilia pro consilium tuum antiquum uerum fiat.
Dne excelsum est brachium tuum ds sabaoth. coro
na spei que ornata est gloriae.
Exultet desertum exultent solitudines iordanis
et populus meus uidebit altitudinem dni et maiesta
tem di. [illegible] dns campis fontes diffu
Haec dicit dns. aperiam in montibus flumina. in me
pam. et terram sitientem sine aqua confundam.
Ecce puer nr exaltabitur et eleuabitur et sub
limis erit ualde.

Ds qui hodierna die unigenitum tuum gentibus stel
la duce reuelasti. concede propitius. ut qui
iam te ex fide cognouimus usque ad contempla
ndam speciem tuae celsitudinis perducamur. per eundem.
Ds illuminator omnium gentium. da populis tuis per
petua pace gaudere. et illud lumen splendidum
infunde cordibus nris quod trium magorum mentibus
aspirasti. per.

1v

IIII non feb. Purificatio scē marię

Ego quasi uitis fructificaui suauitatē odoris. Et
flores mei fructū odoris & honestatis.
Ego mater pulchre dilectionis & timoris & magnitu
dinis & scē spei. In me gratia omnis uite & ueritatis. In me omnis spes uitae & uirtutis.
Transite ad me omnes qui concupiscitis me & a ge
nerationib; meis implemini. Sps enim meus sup
mel dulcis. & hereditas mea sup mel & fauum
memoria mea in generationes saeculorum
Osculetur me osculo oris sui quia meliora sunt
ubera tua uino & odor unguentorū tuorū sup
omnia aromata.
Pulchra est gena tua amica mea sicut turtur
is collum tuū sicut monilia murenulas au
reas faciemus tibi uermiculatas argento.
Ecce tu pulchra es amica mea ecce tu pulchra oc
culi tui columbarū. dit odorē suū
Dum esset rex in accubitu suo nardus mea de
fasciculus myrrhe dilectus meus mihi inter
ubera mea commorabitur.
Erudi qs dne plebē tuā. & que extrinsecus annua
tribuis deuotione uenerari interius assequi gratia

tiae tuae luce concede. p dnm nrm.
Omps sempr ds. maiestatem tuam supplices exor
amus. ut sicut unigenitus filius tuus hodierna
die cum nrae carnis substantia intemplo est pr
esentatus. ita nos facias purificatis tibi mentib;
praesentari. p eundem.
Perfice innobis qs dne gratiam tuam qui iusti
symeonis expectationem inplesti. ut sicut il
le mortem non uidit priusquam xpm dnm uid
ere mereretur. ita & nos uitam optineamus ae
ternam. p eundem

Incipiunt capitula in capud ieiunii.

Haec dicit dns. Conuertimini adme intoto
corde uro inieiunio & fletu & planctu & scin
dite corda ura & non uestimenta ura.
Conuertimini addnm dm urm quia benignus & mi
sericors est patiens & multae misericordiae & prae
stabilis sup malitia.
Clama necesses quasi tuba exalta uocem tuam. & an
nuntia populo meo scelera eorum & domui iac
ob peccata eorum me & enim de die indiem qua

stiga weges mine willad

erunt & semite uias meas uoluit.

Cum effuderis esurienti animam tuã & animã
afflictã repleueris orietur in tenebris lux
tua & tenebre tuae erunt sicut meridies.

Ecce n̄ est adbreuiata manus dñi. ut saluã
re nequeat neq; adgrauata est auris eius
ut non exaudiat. Incipit capitula de lec

Frs. Nescitis quod hi qui in stadio currunt
omñs quidẽ currunt. sed unus accepit bra
diũ. Sic currite ut conprehendatis.

Frs. Omnis q in agone contendit ab omnib; re
abstinet. & illi quidẽ ut corruptibilẽ coronã
accipiant nos autẽ incorruptam.

Frs. Ego igitur sic curro non quasi in incertũ
sic pugno. non quasi aerem uerberans. sed
castigo corpus meũ & in seruitutẽ redigo. ne
forte cum aliis predicauerim ipse reprobus ef
ficiar. In lx. Ut inhabitet in me uirt. xpi.

Frs. Libenter gloriabor in infirmitatib; meis

Frs. Cum essem paruulus loquebar ut par
uulus sapiebam ut paruulus cogitabã ut par
uulus. quando h factus sum uir euacuaui
que erant paruuli.

Frs. Nunc autem manent fides spes caritas.
tria haec. maior autē horū est caritas.
Frs. Nemini quicquā debeatis. nisi ut in
uicem diligatis. qui enim diligit pximum
legem impleuit.
Frs. Si quod est mandatū in hoc uerbo insta
uratur. diliges pximū tuū sicut te ipsū.
Frs. dilectio pximi malum non operatur
plenitudo ergo legis est dilectio.
Hae sunt collectiones in septuagesima
Preces populi tui qs dne clementer exau
di. ut qui iuste p peccatis nris affligimur.
p tui nominis gloria misericorditer liberemur.
Ds qui conspicis quia ex nulla nra actio
ne confidimus. concede ppitius ut contra adu
rsa omia doctoris gentiū ptectione muniamur. p
Preces nras qs dne clementer exaudi. atq; a pec
catorū uinculis absolutos ab omi nos aduersit
ate custodi. p dnm. mulorū tuorū
Ds qui p ineffabilē obseruantium sacramti fa
praeparas uoluntates. donis gratiae tuae corda nra
purifica. ut quae sca est deuotione tractandum. sin
ceris mentib; exequamur. p dnm.

Concede qs omps ds. fragilitate nre sufficientia com
petente. ut sue reparationis affectu. et pia conuer
satione recenseat. et cum exultatione suscipiat. p.

Aufer a nobis dne qs iniquitates nras. ut ad sca sco
rum puris mereamur sensib; introire. p.

Ds qui nos in tantis periculis constitutos scis fra
gilitate non posse subsistere da nobis salute men
tis et corporis. ut ea q; p peccatis nris patimur te
adiuuante uincamus. per.

Omps sempr ds. infirmitate nram ppitius respice.
atq; ad ptegendu nos dextera tue maiestatis extende. p

Rege qs dne populu tuu. et gratie tue in eo dona mul
tiplica. ut ab omnib; liberi offensis. et temporalib; non
destituatur auxiliis. et sempiternis gaudiat institutis. p

Feria .IIII. caput ieiunii.

Concede nobis dne presidia militie xpiane scis
inchoare ieiuniis. ut contra spiritales nequitias pu
gnaturi. continentie muniamur auxiliis. p.

Presta dne fidelib; tuis. ut ieiuniorum ueneranda so
lemnia et congrua pietate suscipiant et secura
deuotione percurrant. p dnm.

Tuere dne populu tuu. et ab omnib; peccatis clementer
emunda. quia nulla ei nocebit aduersitas si nulla
ei dominetur iniquitas. p

Ds qui culpa offenderis penitentia placaris. preces populi tui supplicantis propitius respice. et flagella tuae iracundiae quae pro peccatis nostris meremur auerte. per dominum.

Inchoata ieiunia qs dne. benigno fauore prosequere. ut obseruantiam quam corporaliter exhibemus mentibus ualeamus implere sinceris. per d.

Da qs dne. fidelibus tuis ieiuniis paschalibus conuenienter aptari. ut suscepta solempniter castigatio corporalis cunctis ad fructum proficiat animarum. p.

Fac nos qs dne salutis nrae. causas et deuotius semper frequentare et deuotius recolere principaliter inchoatas. per dnm.

Adiuua nos ds nr. ut inchoata ieiunia honorabiliter recensenter deuotis mentibus assequamur. p.

Obseruationis huius annua celebritate laetantes qs dne. ut paschalibus actionibus inhaerentes plenius eius effectibus gaudeamus. per d.

Adesto dne supplicationibus nris. ut hoc solemne ieiunium quod animis corporibusque curandis salubriter institutum est deuoto seruitio celebremus. p.

[Inc]ipit in quadragesima .I.

[H]aec dicit dominus deus. Ecce ego ipse requiram oves meas et visitabo eas sicut visitat pastor gregem suum in die quando fuerit in medio ovium suarum dissipatarum.

[V]isitabo oves meas et liberabo eas de omnibus locis
in quibus dispersae fuerant in die nubis et caliginis.
[E]go pascam oves meas. et ego eas accubare faciam
dicit dominus. & Inter virum et virum
[v]ir si fuerit iustus et fecerit iudicium et iustitiam
in praeceptis meis ambulaverit. et iudicia mea cus-
todierit ut faciat veritatem hic iustus est vita viv-
et ait dominus. & rietur filius non por-
[H]aec dicit dominus deus. anima quae peccaverit ipsa mo-
tabit iniquitatem patris. et pater non portabit
iniquitatem filii. & in impietate sua

[H]aec dicit dominus deus. Cum averterit se impius ab
iniquitate sua quam operatus est et fecerit iudicium et iustitiam ipse
animam suam vivificavit.

Quaerite dominum dum inveniri potest invocate eum
dum prope est. & ignoscendum

Derelinquat impius viam suam et vir iniquus
cogitationes suas. et revertatur ad dominum et miserebitur eius. et ad deum nostrum quoniam multus est ad &

isere re mei ds omnium. et respice nos et
ostende nobis lucē miserationum tuar[um] uos.
Peccauimus iniquitatē fecimus. dn̄e in omī ius
ti tia tua auertatur obsecro ira tua et
furor tuus a ciuitate tua hierusalē et monte
sco tuo.   Bnes offer. memor esto
ili si habes bene fac tecū et dō dignas oblatio
nem mors non tardat. et testamentū inferio
rum quia demonstratum est tibi
Fili conuertere ad dm̄. et relinque peccata tua
precare autem faciem eius et minue offendiculū.
Fili peccasti ne adicias iterū. Sed et de pristinis dep
recare ut tibi remittantur.
Frs. operamini opus ūm ante tempus et dabit
uobis dn̄s mercedē uestram in tempore suo.
Frs. ortamur uos ne in uacuū gratiam dī reci
piatis. ait enim tempore accepto exaudiuite
et in die salutis adiuuite.
Frs. ecce nunc tempus acceptabile ecce nunc
dies salutis. nemini dantes ullā offensionē ut
non uituperetur ministerium nostrū. sed in
omnib; exhibeamus nos met ipsos sicut dī mi
nistros.   Bmini pusillanimes.
Frs. rogamus uos corripite inquietos consola

suscipite infirmos. patientes estote ad omnes.
Frs. uidete ne quis malum pro malo alicui reddat.
sed semper quod bonum est sectamini inuicem et in omnes.
Frs. semper gaudete. sine intermissione orate. in
omnibus gratias agite. haec est uoluntas dei in xpo
ihu in omnibus uobis.
Frs. estote imitatores dei sicut filii karissimi et ambu
late in dilectione sicut et xps dilexit nos. et tra
didit semet ipsum pro nobis. oblationem et hosti
am deo in odorem suauitatis.
Frs. aliquando tenebrae. nunc autem lux in dno.
ut filii lucis ambulate. fructus enim lucis est
in omni bonitate et iustitia et ueritate.
Frs. omnis sermo malus ex ore uestro non procedat.
sed si quis bonus ad edificationem oportunita
tis ut det gratiam audientibus.
Frs. nolite contristari spm scm in quo signati
estis in die redemptionis.
Frs. omnis amaritudo et ira et indignatio et clamor
et blasphemia tollatur a uobis cum omni malitia.
Frs. estote inuicem benigni misericordes. donantes
inuicem sicut et ds in xpo donauit uobis.
Frs. semper nos qui uiuimus in mortem tradimur

ppter ihm ut et uita ihu manifestetur in car
ne nra mortali. nal xpi ut re

Frs. Omnes nos manifestari oportet ante tribu
ferat unusquisque ppria corporis. prout ges
sit siue bonum siue malum.

Frs. Potens est ds. omnem gratiam abundare face
re in uobis. ut in omnibus semp omnem sufficienti
am habentes abundetis in omne opus bonum.

Frs. gaudete pfecti estote exortamini idem
sapite. pacem habete. et ds dilectionis et pa
cis erit uobiscum.

Frs. Nemo uos iudicet in cibo aut in potu aut in
parte diei festi. aut neomenie aut sabbatorum
que sunt umbra futurorum corpus autem
xpi nemo uos seducat.

Frs. Induite uos sicut electi di sci et dilecti uis
cera misericordie. benignitatem humilitatem
modestiam. patientiam. supportantes inuicem
et donantes uobismet ipsis.

Frs. pax xpi exultet in cordibus uris in qua et uo
cati estis in uno corpore et grati estote uerbum
xpi habitet in uobis abundanter.

Frs. Omne quodcumque facitis in uerbo aut in opere.

omnia in nomine dñi ihū facite gratias agen
tes dō & patri per ipsum.

collectiones unde supra

Ds qui aecclesiam tuā annua quadragesimali
obseruatione purificas. presta familiae tuae.
ut quod ate optinere abstinendo nititur hoc
bonis operibus exequamur. p

Da nobis qs omp ds. & aeternae promissionis gaudia
gustare. & terrena citius inhibere. per

Adesto qs dne supplicationib; nris. & in tua
misericordia confidentes abomni nos aduersi
tate custodi. per.

Conuerte nos ds salutaris noster & ut nobis
ieiunium quadragesimale proficiat. mentes nos
tras caelestib; instrue disciplinis. per

Respice dne familiā tuā & presta. ut apud te
mens nra tuo desiderio fulgeat quae se carnis
maceratione castigat. per

Preces nras qs dne clementer exaudi. & con
tra cuncta nobis aduersantia dexterā
tuae maiestatis extende. per.

Deuotionem populi tui qs dne benignus in
tende. ut qui per abstinentiā macerantur

incorpore. per fructum boni operis per-
ficiantur in mente. per.
Mentes nr̄as qs̄ dn̄e lumine tuae claritatis
inlustra ut uidere possimus quae agen-
da sunt et quae recta sunt agere ualeamus. p dn̄m.
Da qs̄ dn̄e populis xp̄ianis et quae pfiten-
tur agnoscere. et caeleste munus diligere quod frequentant. per.
Esto dn̄e ppitius plebi tuae. et quam tibi facis
esse deuotam benigno refoue miseratus auxilio.
opulum tuu dn̄e qs̄ ppitius respice. atq; ab eo
flagella tuae iracundiae clementer auerte. p.
Protector nr̄ aspice ds̄. et qui malorum nr̄orum
pondere premimur. pcepta misericordia libera tibi mente famulemur. per.
desto qs̄ dn̄e supplicationib; nr̄is. ut esse te
largiente mereamur. et inter pspera humiles.
et inter aduersa securi. p dn̄m.
Actiones nr̄as qs̄ dn̄e et aspirando praeueni et ad-
iuuando prosequere. ut cuncta nr̄a operatio et a te semper incipiat et per te coepta finiatur. p.
s qui conspicis omni nos uirtute destitui inte-

rius exterius q; custodi· & ut ab omnib; aduersitati
bus muniamur in corpore & a prauis cogitationib;
mundamur in mente· per·
praesta qs omps ds· ut familia tua que se affligen
do carne ab alimentis abstinet· sectando iustitia
a culpa ieiunet· per dnm·
Respice qs dne benignus in nobis obseruantiae sce sub
sidium· ut que te auctore facienda cognouimus te op
ante impleamus· p & carnalib; precipis
opulum tuū dne propitius respice· & quos ab escis
abstinere iubes a noxiis quoq; uitiis cessare concede· p
Presta nobis dne qs auxiliū gratiae tuae· ut ieiuniis &
orationib; conuenienter intenti liberemur ab hostib;
mentis & corporis· per d
a qs omps ds· ut sacro nos purificante ieiunio· since
ris mentib; ad sca uentura facias peruenire· p·
Da qs dne nris effectū ieiuniis salutare ut castigatio
carnis assumpta ad nrarū uegetationem transeat
animarum· per dnm·
amilia tua qs dne continua pietate custodi· ut que in
sola spe gratiae caelestis innititur· caelesti etiā protec
tione muniatur· per dnm·
ordib; nris qs dne benignus infunde· ut sicut ab escis

16

corporalibus abstinemus. ita sensus quoq; nos
tros a noxiis retrahamus excessib; per.

Sub ueniat nobis dne misericordia tua. ut ab in
minentib; peccatorum nostrorum periculis te mere
amur protegente saluari. per dnm.

Presta nobis qs dne. ut salutarib; ieiuniis eru
diti. a noxiis quoq; uitiis abstinentes. propitiatione
tuam facilius impetremus. per.

Concede qs omps ds. ut qui protectionis tuae gratiam
quaerimus liberati ab omnib; malis secura tibi
mente seruiamus. per.

Ieiunia nra qs dne benigno fauore prosequere.
ut sicut ab alimentis in corpore ita a uitiis ie
iunemus in mente. per dnm.

Ds qui in deserta regione multitudinem populi
tua uirtute satiasti. in huius quoq; saeculi transe
untis excursu. uictum nobis spiritalem ne defici
amus impende. per.

Ds qui et iustis premia meritorum et peccatorib; per
ieiunium ueniam prebes miserere supplicib; tuis ut re
atus nostri confessio indulgentiam ualeat percipe
re delictorum. per dnm.

Presta quaes omps ds. ut qui nos ieiunia uotiua ca

tigant. Ipsa quoq; deuotio sca laetificet. ut terrenis affectib; mitigatis. facilius caelestia capiamus. per dnm.

Ds qui ineffabilib; mundu renouas sacramentis praesta qs. ut aeclesia tua et aeternis pficiat institutis. et temporalib; n destituatur auxiliis. p

Fiat dne qs. p gratia tua fructuosus nre deuotionis affectus. quia tunc nobis pderunt suscepta ieiunia. si tuae sint placita pietati. p

Ds qui sperantib; in te misereri potius eligis quam irasci. da nobis digne flere mala que fecimus ut tue consolationis gratia inuenire ualeamus. per xpm.

Super montem caligosum leuate signu exaltate uoce leuate manu et ingrediantur portas duces. [iniqui]tates tuas ppt

Haec dicit dns. Ego sum ego sum qui deleo iniquitates tuas propter me et peccatorum tuorum non recordabor.

In tempore placito exaudiui te. et in die salutis auxiliatus sum tui.

Dns ds aperuit mihi aurem ego autem non con

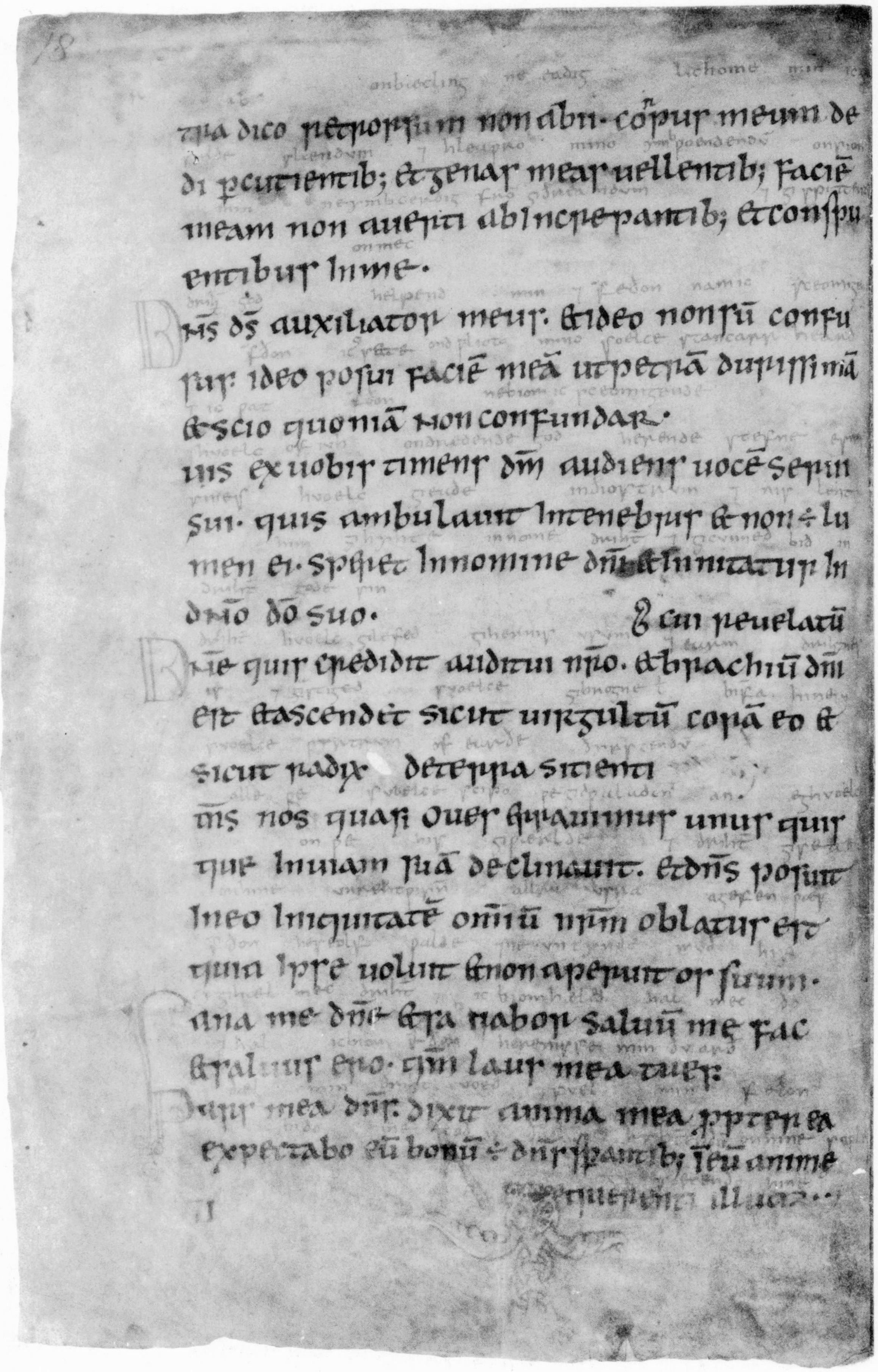

18

tra dico retrorsum non abii. corpus meum de
di percutientibus et genas meas uellentibus faciem
meam non auerti ab increpantibus et conspu
entibus in me.

Dominus deus auxiliator meus. et ideo non sum confu
sus. ideo posui faciem meam ut petram durissimam
et scio quoniam non confundar.
Quis ex uobis timens dominum audiens uocem serui
sui. quis ambulauit in tenebris et non est lu
men ei. speret in nomine domini et innitatur in
domino deo suo. et cui reuelatum

Domine quis credidit auditui nostro. et brachium domini
est. et ascendet sicut uirgultum coram eo et
sicut radix de terra sitienti
Omnes nos quasi oues errauimus unusquis
que in uiam suam declinauit. et dominus posuit
in eo iniquitatem omnium nostrum oblatus est
quia ipse uoluit et non aperuit os suum.
Sana me domine et sanabor saluum me fac
et saluus ero. quoniam laus mea tu es.
Pars mea dominus dixit anima mea propterea
expectabo eum bonus est dominus sperantibus in eum animae
quaerenti illum.

Bonum est prestolari cum silentio salu
tare dni quia non repellet in sempiternum dns
sed miserebitur secundum multitudinem mise
ricordiarum suarum.

Scrutetur vias nostras et quaeramus et reverta
mur ad dnm levemus corda nostra cum manib
us ad dnm in caelos.

Ne avertas dne aurem tuam a singultu meo et cla
mib; adpropinquasti in die quando invocavi te
dixisti ne timeas quia ego sum dns ds tuus.
iudicasti dne causam animae me redemptor vite
me dne ds meus. et auxiliatus sum

In tempore placito exaudivi te et in die salutis
tui et servavi te et dedi te in foedus populi. ut s
uscitares terram et possideres hereditates dis
sipatas. ut diceres his qui vincti sunt exite
et his qui in tenebris revelamini.

Xps. Xps adsistens pontifex futurorum bonorum
per amplius et perfectius tabernaculum non manu
factum. id est non huius creationis. neque per san
guinem hircorum et vitulorum sed per proprium san

20

gur. Introiuit semel in scā aeterna redem
ptione inuenta. & Cum in forma dī es

F rs. hoc et sentite in uobis quod et in xpo ihu. qui
set non rapinā arbitratus esse se equalem
dō. Sed semet ipsum exinaniuit formā serui
accipiens. In similitudinē hominū factus et
habitu inuentus ut homo.

F rs. xps humiliauit semet ipsum factus obedi
ens usq; ad mortē mortē autem crucis.

rs. xps semel pro peccatis nris mortuus est
iustus pro iniustis: ut nos offerret dō mortifi
catus carne uiuificatus autem spu.

F rs. xpo igitur passo in carne et uos eadem co
gitatione armamini quia qui passus est in c
arne desiit a peccatis.

rs. ds aut omnis gratiae qui uocauit nos in aeter
nam suā gloriā in xpo ihū modicū passos
ipse perficiet. et confirmabit. solidabitq; ip
si gloria et imperiū in scła scłorū amen

F rs. Cum adhuc peccatores essemus xps pro no
bis mortuus est. multo magis reconciliati sal
ui erimus in uita ipsius.

F rs. Si ds pro nobis quis contra nos. qui etiā

Filio suo proprio non pepercit sed pro nobis omnibus
tradidit illum.
Fratres. Michi autem absit gloriari nisi in cruce domini nostri
ihesu christi. per quem mundus crucifixus est et ego mundo.
Deus omnipotens deus familiam tuam propitius respice. ut te
largiente regatur in corpore. et te seruante
custodiatur in mente. per dominum
Omnipotens sempiterne deus. qui humano generi ad imitandum
humilitatis exemplum. saluatorem nostrum carnem
sumere et crucem subire fecisti. concede propiti
us. ut et patientiae ipsius habere documenta
et resurrectionis consortia mereamur. per eun
Da quaesumus omnipotens deus ut qui in tot aduersis ex
nostra infirmitate deficimus intercedente
unigeniti filii tui passione liberemur. qui te
Adiuua nos deus salutaris noster et ad benefi
cia recolenda quibus nos instaurare digna
tus es tribue uenire gaudentes. per
Sanctifica quaesumus domine nostra ieiunia et cunctarum
nobis propitius indulgentiam largire cul
parum. per dominum.
Ista tibi domine quaesumus sint accepta ieiunia.

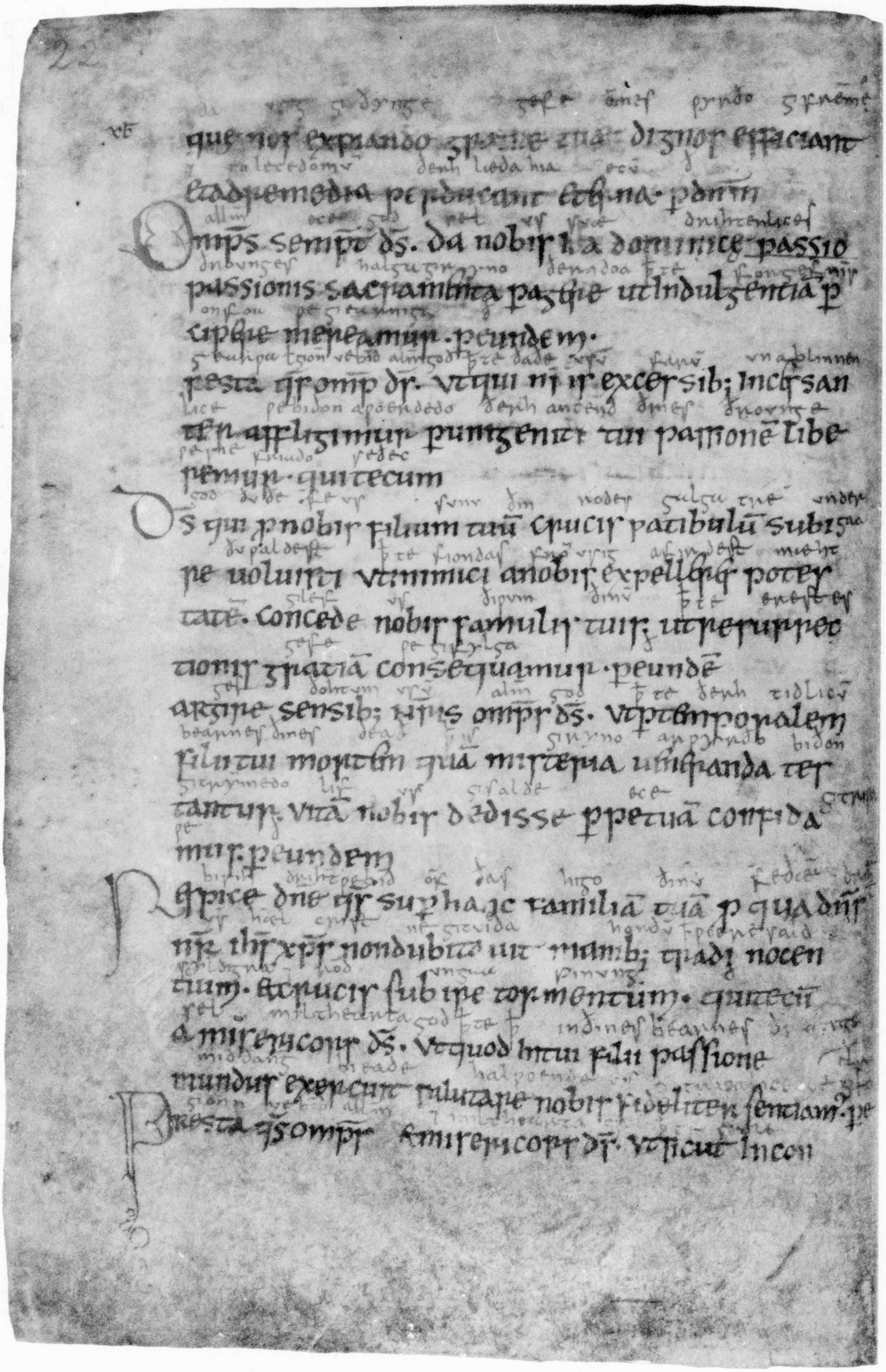
22

que nos expiando gratie tue dignos efficiant
et ad remedia perducant eterna. per dominum
Omnipotens sempiterne deus. da nobis ita dominice passionis
passionis sacramenta peragere ut indulgentiam per
cipere mereamur. per eundem.
Presta quesumus omnipotens deus. ut qui nostris excessibus incessan
ter affligimur per unigeniti tui passionem libe
remur. qui tecum
Deus qui pro nobis filium tuum crucis patibulum subi
re voluisti ut inimici a nobis expelleres potes
tatem. concede nobis famulis tuis ut resurrec
tionis gratiam consequamur. per eundem
Arripe sensibus nostris omnipotens deus. ut per temporalem
filii tui mortem quam misteria veneranda tes
tantur. vitam nobis dedisse perpetuam confida
mus. per eundem
Respice domine quesumus super hanc familiam tuam pro qua dominus
noster ihesus christus non dubitavit manibus tradi nocen
tium. et crucis subire tormentum. qui tecum
Omnipotens et misericors deus. ut quod in tui filii passione
mundus exercuit salutare nobis fideliter sentiamus. per
Presta quesumus omnipotens et misericors deus. ut sicut in con

11 v

demnatione . filii tui ualeat . domini ut sint piaculi rei

donum ita pro misericordia tua communis sit salutis ut

te credentium . per eundem .

Benedictus deus et pater domini nostri ihesu christi . qui secundum

magnam misericordiam suam regenerauit nos in spem

uiuam per resurrectionem ihesu christi ex mortuis in here-

ditatem incorruptam et incontaminatam et inmarcescibi-

lem conseruatam in caelis .

Fratres . Scientes quod non corruptibilibus argento uel au-

ro redempti estis de uana uestra conuersatione paternae

traditionis sed pretioso sanguine quasi agni incon-

taminati et inmaculati christi .

Fratres . Si consurrexistis cum christo quae sursum sunt

quaerite ubi christus est in dextera dei sedens . quae sursum

sunt sapite non quae super terram .

Fratres . Mortui estis et uita uestra abscondita est cum christo

in deo . cum autem christus apparuerit uita uestra tunc et

uos apparebitis cum ipso in gloria .

Fratres . Expurgate uetus fermentum ut sitis noua con-

spersio . etenim pascha nostrum immolatus est christus .

Fratres . Epulemur non in fermento ueteri neque in fermento

malitiae et nequitiae sed in azimis sinceritatis et
ueritatis. Omnes et inuidias et omnes de-
FRS. deponentes omnem malitiam et omnem dolum et simulati-
tractiones. sicut modo geniti infantes rationabile et sine
dolo lac concupiscite ut in eo crescatis in salutem.
FRS. Vos genus electum regale sacerdotium gens sancta populus adquisitionis ut uirtutes adnuntietis eius qui
de tenebris uos uocauit in admirabile lumen suum qui
aliquando non populus nunc autem populus dei qui non consecuti misericordiam nunc autem misericordiam consecuti.
FRS. Christus semel pro peccatis nostris mortuus est iustus
pro iniustis ut nos offerret deo mortificatus quidem
carne uiuificatus autem spiritu.
FRS. Christus passus est pro nobis uobis relinquens exemplum
ut sequamini uestigia eius. qui peccatum non fecit nec
inuentus est dolus in ore eius.
FRS. quicumque baptizati sumus in christo iesu in morte ipsius baptizati sumus. consepulti enim sumus cum illo
per baptismum in mortem. ut quomodo resurrexit christus
a mortuis per gloriam patris ita et nos in nouitate
uitae ambulemus.
FRS. hoc scientes quia uetus homo noster simul cru-

cifixus ÷ ut destruatur corpus peccati ut ultra
non seruiamus peccato qui enim mortuus est iusti
ficatus ÷ a peccato.

Rs. Si mortui sumus cum xpo credimus quia sim
ul etiam uiuemus cum xpo scientes quod xps sur
gens a mortuis iam non moritur. mors illi ultra
non dominabitur.

Rs. Nemo nostrum sibi uiuit. et nemo sibi moritur. si
ue enim uiuimus dno uiuimus siue morimur dno
morimur. siue ergo uiuimus siue morimur dni sumus.

Rs. In hoc xps mortuus est et resurrexit. ut et
mortuorum et uiuorum dominetur.

Rs. Empti estis pretio magno. glorifi cate et
portate dm in corpore uro.

Rs. Resurrexit a mortuis primitie dormientium.
quoniam enim per hominem mors et per hominem resurrectio
mortuorum. et sicut in adam omnes moriuntur ita
et in xpo omnes uiuificabuntur.

Rs. Gratia uobis et pax a do patre nro et dno
ihu xpo. qui dedit semet ipsum pro peccatis
nris ut eriperet nos de presenti seculo nequa
secundum uoluntatem di et patris nri.

Frs. Cum essemus mortui peccatis. conuiuifica-
uit nos xpo. cuius gratia estis saluati. Et con-
resuscitauit et consedere fecit in caelestibus
in xpo ihu. Fr tamen. aspicientes in a-
rs. per patientiã curramus ppositũ nobis cer-
uctore fidei et consũmatore ihm qui pposito
sibi gaudio sustinuit crucẽ confusione contem-
ta atq; in dextera sedis dĩ sedet.

Frs. Ds pacis qui eduxit de mortuis pastorẽ
magnũ ouiũ in sanguine testamenti aeterni dñm
nrm ihm xpm. aptet uos in omni bono ut facia-
tis uoluntatẽ eius faciens in uobis quod placeat
coram se. per ihm xpm.

Kmi. Omne quod natũ est ex dõ uincit mundum.
Et haec est uictoria quae uincit mundũ fides
nra. quis est autem qui uincit mundũ nisi qui
credit quoniam ihs est filius dĩ.

Kmi. Omne datũ optimum et omne donũ per-
fectũ de sursum est descendens a patre lumi-
nũ apud quẽ non est transmutatio nec uicissi-
tudinis obũbratio. uoluntarie genuit nos uerbo ueritatis. ut simus initiũ aliquod creaturae eius.

Scitis fratres mei dilectissimi. Sit autem omnis homo uelox ad audiendum. tardus autem ad loquendum et tardus ad iram. Ira enim uiri iustitiam dei non operatur.

R.S. Omnes uos filii lucis estis et filii dei. non sumus noctis neque tenebrarum. Igitur non dormiamus sicut et ceteri. sed uigilemus et sobrii simus.

F.S. Nos qui diei sumus sobrii simus. induti loricam fidei et caritatis et galeam salutis.

R.S. Non posuit nos deus in iram. sed in adquisitionem salutis per dominum nostrum iesum christum qui mortuus est pro nobis. ut siue uigilemus siue dormiamus simul cum illo uiuamus.

R.S. Consolamini inuicem et aedificate alterutrum in christo ihesu domino nostro.

R.S. Estote factores uerbi et non auditores tantum fallentes uos met ipsos.

R.S. Qui perspexerit in legem perfectam libertatis et permanserit. non auditor obliuiosus factus sed factor operis hic beatus in facto suo erit.

R.S. Religio munda et inmaculata apud deum et patrem haec est. uisitare pupillos et uiduas in tribulatione eorum. et inmaculatum se custodire ab hoc seculo.

Dignus es domine accipere librum et aperire sig
naculum eius. qui occisus es et redemisti nos deo
in sanguine tuo.
Ds qui hanc sacratissimam noctem gloria dominice resurrec
tionis inlustras. conserua innoua familiae tuae
progenie adoptionis spiritum quem dedisti. ut corpore
et mente renouati puram tibi exhibeant seruitutem. per
Ds qui hodierna die per unigenitum tuum
aeternitatis nobis aditum deuicta morte rese
rasti. uota nostra quae praeueniendo adspiras etiam ad
iuuando prosequere. per
Concede quaesumus omnipotens deus. ut qui resurrectionis domi
nice solemnia colimus innouatione tui spiritus a m
orte animae resurgamus. per eundem.
Presta quaesumus omnipotens deus. ut qui resurrectionis do
minice solemnia colimus ereptionis nostrae sus
cipere laetitiam mereamur. per eundem.
Presta quaesumus omnipotens deus. ut qui gratiam dominicae
resurrectionis agnouimus ipsi per amorem spiritus
a morte animae resurgamus. per eundem.
Ds qui ecclesiam tuam nouo semper foetu multi

plicat. Concede famulis tuis ut sacramentum
uiuendo teneant quod fide perceperunt. per
Concede quaesumus omnipotens deus. ut per haec paschalia festa
que colimus deuoti in tua semper laude uiuamus. per
Paschale misterium recensentes apostolorum domine
beatorum precibus foueamur quorum magisterium
cognouimus exequendum. per.
Deus aecclesiae tuae redemptor atque perfector fac quaesumus
ut apostolorum precibus paschalis sacramenti dona ca
piamus quorum nobis ea tribuisti magisterio
predicari. per dominum.
Concede quaesumus domine semper nos per haec mysteria paschalia
gratulari. ut continua nostrae reparationis opera
tio perpetua nobis fiat causa laetitiae. per
Deus qui solemnitate paschali mundo remedia
contulisti. populum tuum quaesumus caelesti dono prosequere;
per. ut et perfectam libertatem consequi mereatur
et ad uitam proficiat sempiternam. per
Deus qui conspicis familiam tuam omni humana uir
tute destitui paschali interueniente festiui
tate. tu eam brachii protectione custodi. per
Deus. Qui nos resurrectionis dominicae annua

sollemnitate laetificas concede propitius ut per te-
poralia festa que agimus peruenire ad gaudia
aeterna mereamur. per eundem.

Da quesumus omnipotens deus ut qui paschalis festiuitatis mirabile sacramentum et temporalem
nobis tranquillitatem tribuat et uitam conferat
sempiternam. per eundem.

Deus qui nos per paschalia festa laetificas concede propitius ut ea que deuote agimus te adiuuante fideliter teneamus. per dominum.

Tribue quesumus omnipotens deus ut illuc tendat christiane deuotionis affectus quo tecum est nostra substantia. per

Deus qui diuersitatem gentium in confessione
tui nominis adunasti. da ut renatis fonte
baptismatis una sit fides mentium et pietas
actionum. per eundem.

Deus qui nobis ad celebrandum paschale sacramentum liberiores animos praestitisti doce-
nos et metuere quod irasceris et amare quod
praecipis. per dominum.

Da quesumus omnipotens deus ut ecclesia tua et suorum firmitate membrorum et noua semper fecunditate
laetetur. per.

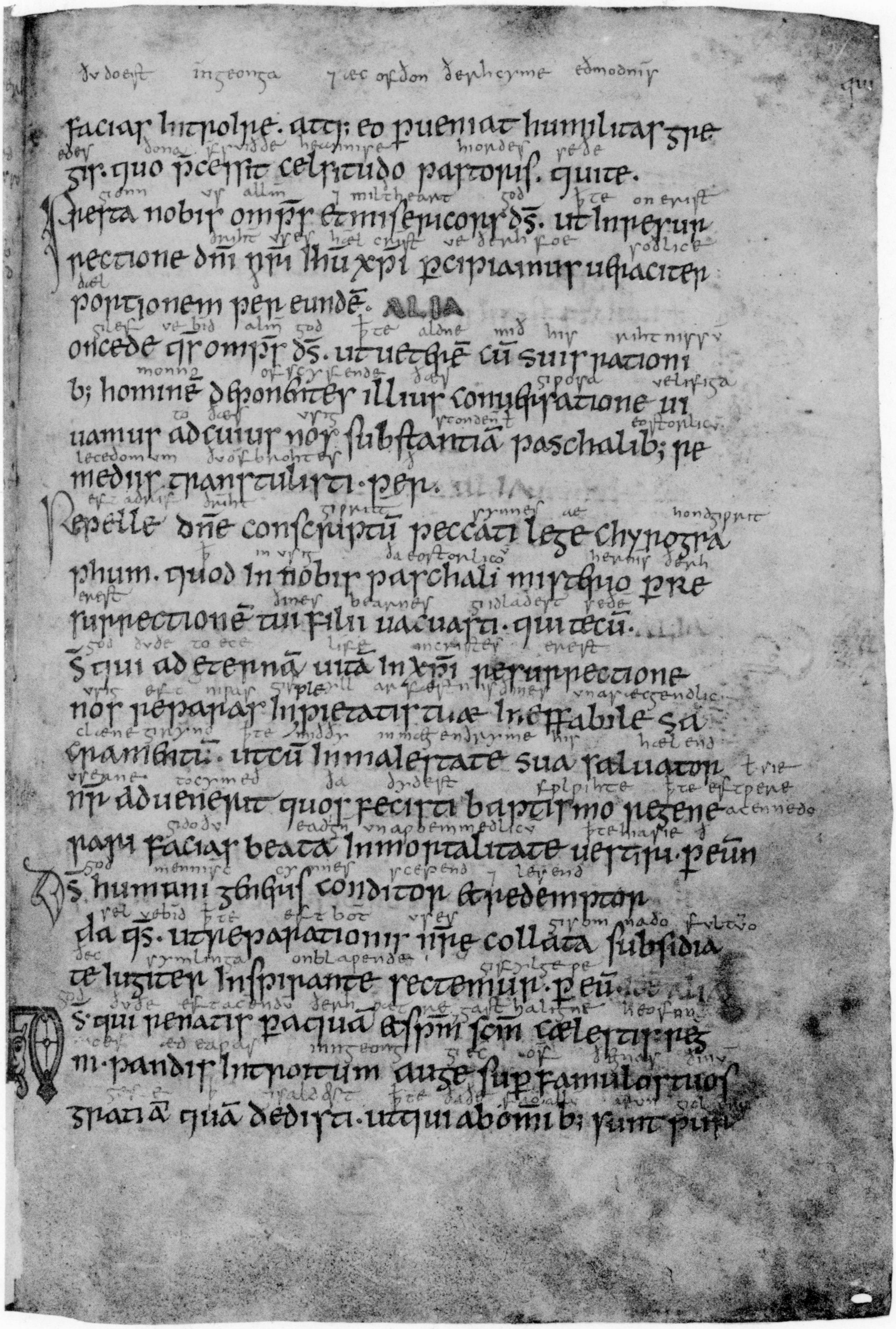

faciat in corpore. atque eo perueniat humilitas gre-
gis. quo precessit celsitudo pastoris. qui te.
Presta nobis omnipotens et misericors deus. ut in resurrectione domini nostri ihesu christi percipiamus ueraciter
portionem per eundem. ALIA
Concede quaesumus omnipotens deus. ut ueterem cum suis passioni-
bus hominem deponentes illius conuersatione ui-
uamus ad cuius nos substantiam paschalibus remediis transtulisti. per.
Repelle domine conscriptum peccati lege chyrogra-
phum. quod in nobis paschali mysterio per resurrectionem tui filii uacuasti. qui tecum.
Deus qui ad eternam uitam in christi resurrectione
nos reparas inpietatis tuae ineffabile sacramentum. ut cum in maiestate sua saluator
noster aduenerit quos fecisti baptismo regene-
rari faciat beata inmortalitate uestiri. per eun.
Deus humani generis conditor et redemptor
da quaesumus. ut reparationis nostrae collata subsidia
te largiter inspirante recolamus. per eundem.
Deus qui renatis ex aqua et spiritu sancto caelestis regni pandis introitum auge super famulos tuos
gratiam quam dedisti. ut qui ab omnibus sunt puri-

16 r

gati peccatis: a nullis preteritis premissis. per
Gaudeat domine plebs fidelis. et cum propriae recolit
saluationis exordia eius promoueatur augmentis. per
Deus omnipotens. ut qui paschalibus remediis
innouati similitudinem terreni parentis euassi
mus ad formam caelestis transferamur
auctoris. per dominum
Deus qui nos fecisti hodierna die paschalia fes
ta celebrare. fac nos quaesumus in caelesti regno gau
dere. per. det auxilio ut pas
Familiam tuam quaesumus domine dextera tua perpetua circum
chali interueniente solemnitate. ab omni pra
uitate defensa donis caelestibus prosequatur. per
Concede quaesumus omnipotens deus. ut qui paschali
bus exequimur institutis. fructiferum nobis
omni tempore sentiamus. per
Paschalibus nobis quaesumus domine remediis dignanter
inpende ut terrena desideria respuentes dis
camus inhiare caelestia. per dominum.
Conserua in nobis quaesumus domine misericordiam
tuam et quos ab erroris liberasti caligine.
ueritatis tuae firmius inherere facias
documento. per

Omips sempt ds. ppensius his dieb; tuam mise
ricordiā consequamur quib; eā plenius te
largiente cognouimus. p dnm

Ds qui psalute mundi sacrificiū paschale
fecisti. ppitiare supplicationib; nris ut
ut interpellans pnobis pontifex summus
nos p id qd nri est similis reconciliet p id
quod tibi est equalis absoluat. qui tec

Ds qui ad aeternā uitā in xpi resurrectione
nos reparas. erige nos ad consedentem in dex
tera tua nre salutis auctore. ut qui ppter
nos iudicandus aduenit. pnobis iudicaturus
ut adueniat qui tecum uiuit.

Omips sempt ds. qui humanā naturam
supra prime originis reparas dignita
tem. respice pietatis tuae ineffabile sa
cramentum. ut quos regenerationis mis
terio innouare dignatus es in his dona tua
ppetuae gratiae ptectione conserua. p

Solita qs dne quos saluasti pietate custodi
ut qui tua passione sunt redempti tua
resurrectione laetentur. qui uiuit.

Presta qs dne ds nr. ut q; solemni celebram

34

officio purificatę mentis intellegentia
consectamur. per dnm.

Caelesti lumine qs dne semper et ubique nos
preueni. ut misterium cuius nos participes
esse uoluisti et puro cernamus intuitu
et digno percipiamus effectu. per.

Gregem tuum pastor bone qs dne placatus
intende. et oues quas pretioso sanguine
tuo redemisti diabolica non sinas incur
sione lacerari. qui tecum

Haec sunt capitula in laetania maiore.

Haec dicit dns. circuite uias hierusalem
et aspicite et considerate. et querite in pla
teis eius an inueniatis uirum facientem
iudicium et querentem fidem et propitius ero
eius. [illegible] et de [illegible] Sta
te super uias et uidete. et interrogate
quis que sit uia bona et ambulate in ea
et inuenietis refrigerium animabus uestris.

Exercituum ds israel. bonas facite
uias uestras et studia uestra. et habitabo uobis
cum in loco isto in terra quam dedi patri
bus uestris a seculo et usque in seculum.

III

om

nihil patiamur h(ostis) i(n)sidiis. p(er) d(ominu)m

Ds qui diem discernis a nocte actus n(ost)ros a tenebr
arum distingue caligine. ut semp(er) que s(an)c(t)a sunt me
ditantes in tua iugiter luce uiuamus. p(er)

Gratias agimus d(omi)ne s(an)c(t)e pat(er) om(ni)p(otens) (et)e(r)ne ds.
qui nos transacto noctis spatio. ad matutinas
horas p(er)ducere dignatus es. q(uesumu)s ut dones nobis die(m)
hunc sine peccato transire quatenus ad uesperum
tibi do gratias referamus. p(er) d(ominu)m.

Exsurgentes de cubilib(us) n(ost)ris auxiliu(m) gratiae tuae ma
tutinis d(omi)ne p(re)cibus implora(m)us. ut discussis tene
bris uitioru(m) ambulare mereamur in luce uirtu
tum.

Te luce(m) ueram et lucis auctore(m) d(omi)ne dep(re)camur. ut
digneris a nobis tenebras depellere uitioru(m). et cla
rificare nos luce uirtutum. p(er)

Illumina d(omi)ne q(uesumu)s. in luce corda credentiu(m). ut tuo se
mp(er) munimine. et tuo auxilio p(ro)tegamur. p(er).

Illumina q(uesumu)s d(omi)ne tenebras n(ost)ras. et totius noctis
insidias tu repelle p(ro)pitius. p(er) d(ominu)m.

Qua nos d(omi)ne uisitas semp(er) inluminet. et a bono in pra
uitate defendat. p(er) d(ominu)m.

Salua nos om(ni)p(otens) ds. et luce(m) nobis concede p(er)petua(m)

Veritas tua q(uesumu)s d(omi)ne luceat in cordib(us) n(ost)ris et falsitas dissipatur inimici. p.

Ds dne ds nr diei molestias noctis quiete sustenta. ut necessaria temporum uicissitudine succedente nostra reficiamur infirmitas. per.

Exaudi nos misericors ds. et mentibus nostris gratiae tuae lumen ostende. per.

Auge in nobis dne quaesumus fidem tuam. et spiritus sci lucem in nobis semper accende. p.

Gratias agimus inenarrabili pietati tuae omnips ds. qui nos depulsa noctis caligine ad diei huius principium duxisti et abiecta ignorantiae caecitate ad cultum tui nominis atq; scientiam reuocasti. Inlabere sensibus nostris omnips pater. ut in praeceptorum tuorum lumine gradientes te duce sequamur et principem. per.

Ds qui tenebras ignorantiae uerbi tui luce depellis. auge in cordibus nostris uirtutem fidei quam dedisti. ut ignis quem gratia tua fecit accendi nullis temptationibus possit extingui. per.

Ds qui uigilantes in laudibus tuis caelesti mercede remuneras tenebras de cordibus nostris auferre digneris. ut splendore luminis tui semper gaudeamus. p dnm.

solationis auxilium. per.

Adesto dne populis tuis in tua protectione fidentib; et tuae dexterae suffragia implorantib; perpetua defensione conserva. p

Humiliate dne populo tuo ut sacrae devotionis proficiens incrementis et tuo semper munere subornetur et ad redemptionis aeterna perveniat te ducente consortium. p

Da populo tuo qs dne spm veritatis et pacis. ut et tota mente cognoscat et quae tibi sunt placita tota corde sectetur. per dnm

Da nob dne qs. ut et mundi cursus pacificus nob tuo ordine dirigatur et ecclesia tua tranquilla devotione laetetur. per.

Da salute dne qs populo tuo mentis et corporis et spiritus consolationib; tuorum reple corda fidelium. ut protectione tua relevati et pia devotione conplaceant. et tua semper beneficia consequantur. per.

Porrige dexteram tuam qs dne plebi tuae misericordiam tuam postulanti. per quam et presens declinet humanorum et solatia vitae mortalis accipiat et sempiterna gaudia conprehendat. p.

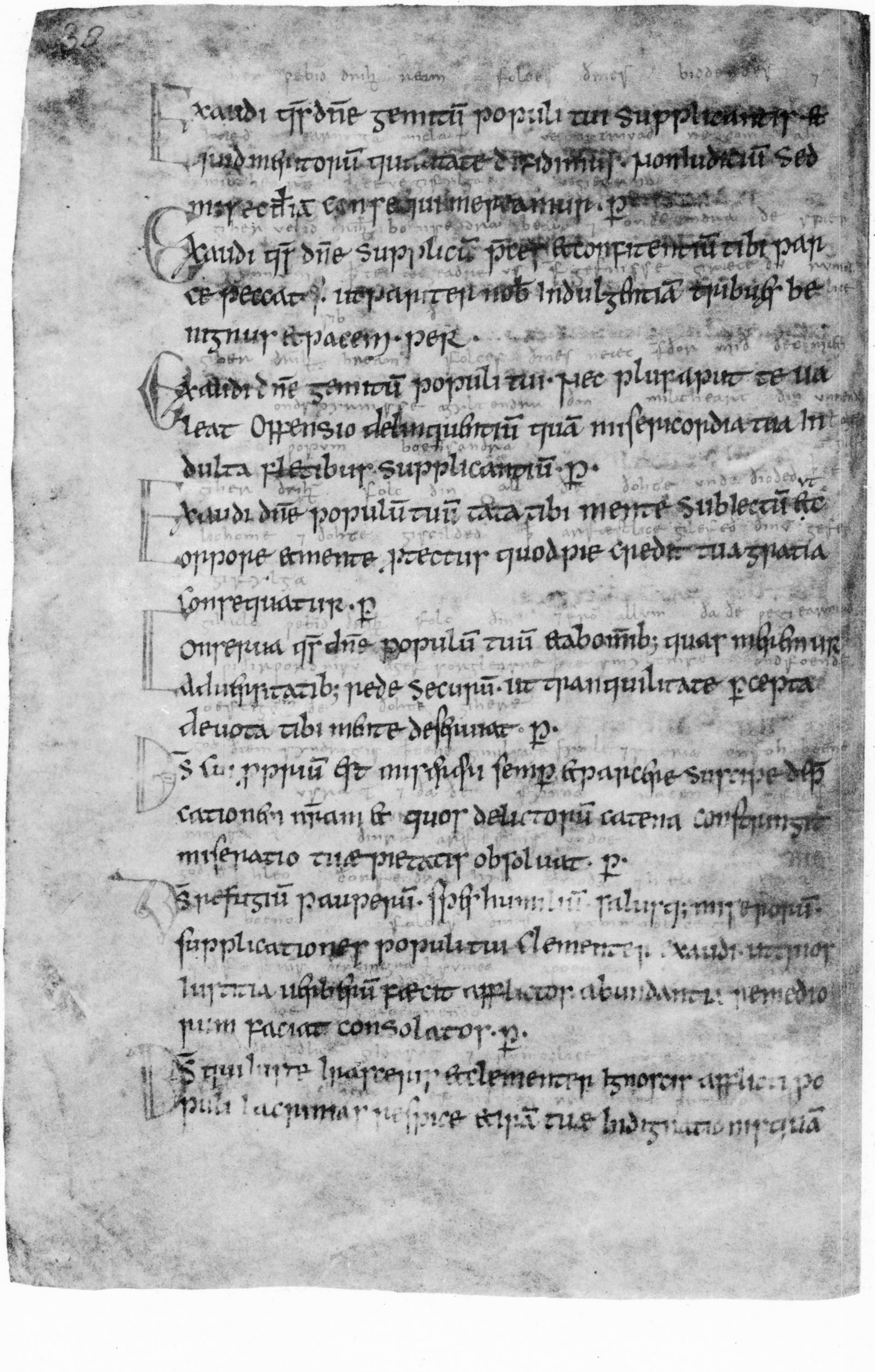

Exaudi quaesumus domine gemitum populi tui supplicantis et
qui de meritorum qualitate diffidimus. non iudicium sed
misericordiam consequi mereamur. per.

Exaudi quaesumus domine supplicum preces et confitentium tibi par
ce peccatis. ut pariter nobis indulgentiam tribuas be
nignus et pacem. per.

Exaudi domine gemitum populi tui. nec plus apud te ua
leat offensio delinquentium quam misericordia tua in
dulta fletibus supplicantium. p.

Exaudi domine populum tuum tota tibi mente subiectum et
corpore et mente protectus quod pie credit tua gratia
consequatur. p.

Conserua quaesumus domine populum tuum et ab omnibus quas meretur
aduersitatibus redde securum. ut tranquillitate percepta
deuota tibi mente deseruiat. p.

Deus cui proprium est misereri semper et parcere suscipe depre
cationem nostram et quos delictorum catena constringit
miseratio tuae pietatis absoluat. p.

Deus refugium pauperum. spes humilium. salusque miserorum.
supplicationes populi tui clementer exaudi. ut quos
iustitia uerberum fecit afflictos. abundantiae remedio
rum faciat consolatos. p.

Deus qui iuste irasceris et clementer ignoscis afflicti po
puli lacrimas respice et iram tuae indignationis quam

lustre [illegible] misericordiae propitiatus attende. p.

Ds qui nos conspicis [illegible] perturbationibus non posse subsistere afflictorum gemitum propitius respice et mala omnia quae meruimus auerte. p.

Ds qui peccantium animas non uis perire sed culpas, con-
tine quam meremur iram et quam precamur super nos effun-
de clementiam ut de merore gaudium tuae misericordiae consequi mereamur. p.

Deprecationem nostram quaesumus omnipotens deus benignus exaudi et quibus supplicandi praestas affectum tribue defension-
is auxilium. p. — Cognouimus misericor-

Parce quaesumus omnipotens deus ut qui iram tuae indignationis ag-
diae tuae indulgentiam consequamur. p.

Precibus nostris quaesumus domine aurem tuae pietatis accommoda et
orationes supplicum occultorum cognitor benignus exaudi ut te largiente adiuta perueniant sempiterna. p.

Praesta populo tuo domine quaesumus consolationis auxilium et
diuturnis calamitatibus laborantem propitius respirare concede. p. — Agnoscimus tuae con-

Praesta quaesumus omnipotens deus ut qui offensa nostra per flagella co-
solationis gratiam sentiamus. p.

Afflictionem familiae tuae quaesumus domine intende placatus ut
indulta uenia peccatorum de tuis beneficiis semper gloriemur. per dominum.

Ab omnibus nos quaesumus domine peccatis propitiatus absolue ut
percepta uenia peccatorum liberis tibi mentibus ser
uiamus. per dominum.
Quaesumus domine nostra confitentibus
Auxiliare domine querentibus misericordiam tuam et da ue
niam supplicibus ut qui nostris meritis flagellamur
tua miseratione saluemur. per dominum
Auerte quaesumus domine iram tuam propitiatus a nobis et facinora
nostra quibus indignationem tuam prouocamus expelle. per.
Pietatis tuae quaesumus domine precibus nostris inclina. ut qui
peccatorum nostrorum flagellis percutimur miseratio
nis tuae gratia liberemur. per.
Quaesumus omnipotens deus ut qui nostris fatigamur offensis et merito
nostrae iniquitatis affligimur pietatis tuae gratiam
consequi mereamur. per.
Quaesumus omnipotens deus afflicti populi lacrimas respice et iram
tuae indignationis auerte. ut qui reatum nostrae infir
mitatis agnoscimus tua consolatione liberemur. per.
Subiectum tibi populum quaesumus domine propitiatio caeles
tis amplificet. et tuis semper faciat seruire mandatis. per dominum.
Oculat pietatem tuam quaesumus domine subiectae tibi plebis af
fectus. et misericordiam tuam supplicatio fidelis obti
neat. ut quod meritis non praesumit indulgentiae
tuae largitate percipiat. per.

Memor esto qs dne fragilitatis humane & qui
iuste uerberas peccatores parce ppitiatus
afflictis. p. per dnm.
Ne despicias omps ds populu tuu in afflictione
clamante. sed ppter gloria nominis tui tribu
lantis succurre placatus. p dnm.
Tribulatione nram qs dne ppitius respice & i
ram tuae indignationis qua iuste meremur
ppitiatus auerte. p.
Intende qs dne preces nras. & qui non operando
iustitia. correptione meremur afflicti. in
tribulatione clamantes respirare mur auditi. p.

Hic incipiunt cap maior. per circulu anni
In nat sci stephani martyris
In diebus illis Stephanus plenus gratia et for
titudine faciebat prodigia et signa magna in populo.
Surrexerunt aut quida de sinagoga que apellatur liber
tinorum & cyrenensium & alexandrinorum. & eorum
qui erant a cilicia et asia disputantes cum ste
phano & non poterant resistere sapientiae
& spu quae loquebatur.
Erat aut stephanus plenus spu sco intendens

42

In celum uidit gloriā dī et ihm stantē ad dexteris
dī. et ait ecce uideo celos apertos et filiū homi
nis stantē ad dexteris dī.

Positis genib; stephanus clamauit uoce mag
na dicens: dne ne statuas illis hoc peccatū. et
cum hoc dixisset obdormiuit in dno.

Curauerunt stephanū uiri timorati. et fecerunt
planctū magnū sup eū. Igitur qui dispersi er
ant transiebant euangelizantes uerbū dī.

Item collecte unde supra

Da nobis qs dne imitari qd colimus ut disca
mus et inimicos diligere quia eius natalicia
celebram qui nouit etiā p persecutorib;
exorare. p.

Natali leuite ste

Omps sempt ds. qui primitias martyrū in be
ati leuite ste phani sanguine dedicasti. tribue qs ut pro nob
intercessor existat. qui p suis etiā persecutorib;
exorauit. per

Ds qui unigeniti tui clementer incarnatione

redemisti. da nobis patrocinia continuata scorum quib; capere ualeamus salutaris myste-
rii portionem. per dnm.

Gratias agimus dne multiplicatis circa nos mise-
rationibus tuis qui et filii tui natiuitate nos sal-
uas: et beati martyris stephani deprecatione
sustentas. per eundem.,,

Presta qs omps ds. ut beatus stephanus leuita
magnificus sicut ante alios imitator dominice
passionis et pietatis innituit. ita sit fragilitatis nr
promptus adiutor. per eundem.

VI. Kl. Ianu. Nt. Sci Iohan euang.

Qui timet dm faciet bona. et qui continens est iustitiae adprehendet illam. et obuiauit illi quasi ma-
mater honorificata et quasi mulier a uirgini-
tate suscipiet illu.,

In medio ecclesiae aperuit os ei et impleuit eu
dns spu sapientiae et intellectus et stola gloriae induit eum.,

Iocunditatem et exultationem thesaurizabit super eum. et nomine aeterno hereditabit illum dns ds noster.,

Ps. benedictus ds et pater dni nri ihu xpi qui

benedixit nos in omni benedictione spiritali in caelestib; in xpo ihu dno nro.,
Beatus uir qui in sapientia sua morabitur et qui
in iustitia meditabitur et in sensu cogitabit circum spectionem di.;
Cibauit illum pane uite et intellectus et aqua
sapientiae salutaris potabit illu dns ds nr.,

Item collectiones
Ecclesiam tuam dne benignus inlustra ut beati iohannis euangelistae inluminata doctrinis ad dona
perueniat sempiterna. per
Beati iohannis euangelistae qs dne supplicatione placatus et ueniam nobis tribue et remedia sempiterna concede.,
Beati euuangeliste iohannis qs dne precib; adiuuemur ut qd possibilitas nra non optinet eius
nobis intercessione donetur. per.
Sit dne beatus iohannes euuangelista nrae fragilitatis adiutor ut pro nob tibi supplicans copi-

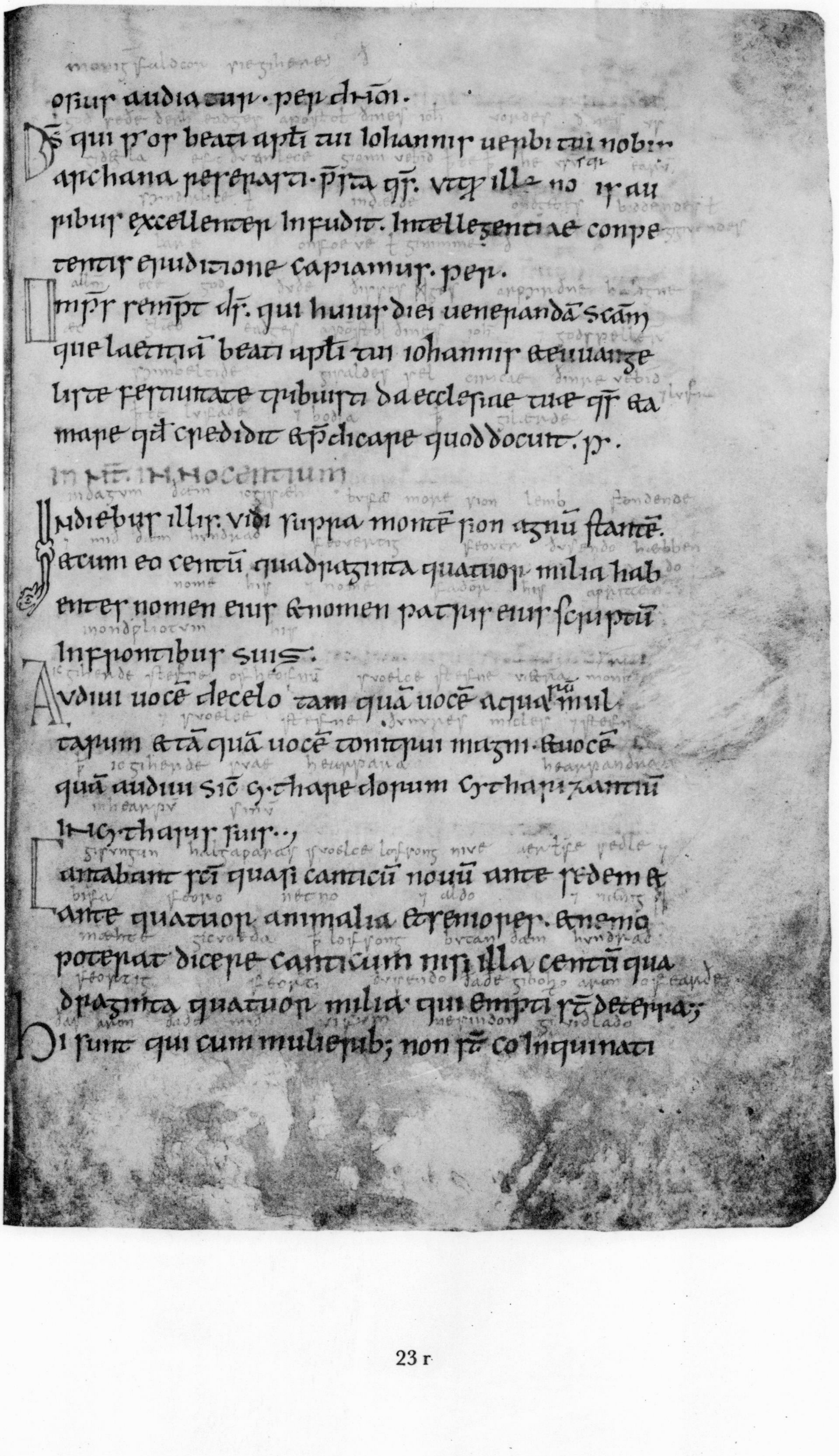
orsus audiamur. per dnm.
Ds qui per os beati apostoli tui iohannis uerbi tui nobis
archana reserasti. praesta qs. ut quod ille nostris au
ribus excellenter infudit. intellegentiae conpe
tentis eruditione capiamur. per.
Omps sempt ds. qui huius diei uenerandam scam
que laetitiam beati apostoli tui iohannis et euuange
liste festiuitate tribuisti da ecclesiae tuae qs et a
mare quod credidit et praedicare quod docuit. per.
IN NT. INNOCENTIUM
In diebus illis. Vidi supra montem sion agnum stantem.
et cum eo centum quadraginta quattuor milia hab
entes nomen eius et nomen patris eius scriptum
in frontibus suis.
Audiui uocem de caelo tamquam uocem aquarum mul
tarum et tamquam uocem tonitrui magni. et uocem
quam audiui sicut citharedorum citharizantium
in citharis suis.
Cantabant sci quasi canticum nouum ante sedem et
ante quattuor animalia et seniores. et nemo
poterat dicere canticum nisi illa centum qua
draginta quattuor milia. qui empti sunt de terra;
Hi sunt qui cum mulieribus non sunt coinquinati

23 r

uirgines enim sunt hi sunt qui secuntur agnum quocum-
que ierit. ;

Hi sunt qui uenerunt de tribulatione magna et la-
uerunt stolas suas et dealbauerunt eas in sanguine agni. Ideo sunt ante thronum dei et seruiunt ei die ac nocte in templo
eius. Audiui uocem de celo dicentem. Scribe beati mortui qui in domino moriuntur. ; Item collectiones

Deus cuius hodierna die preconium ad innocentes
innocentes martyres non loquendo sed morien-
do confessi sunt. Omnia in nobis uitiorum mala mortifi-
ca ut fidem tuam quam lingua nostra loquitur etiam
moribus uita fateatur. ;

Deus qui licet sis magnus in mirabilia tamen gloriosi-
us operaris in minimis. Da nobis quesumus in eorum
celebritate gaudere qui filio tuo domino nostro
testimonium prebuerunt etiam non loquentes. per

Discat ecclesia tua deus infantium quos hodie
ueneramur exemplo sinceritatem tenere pietatis que prius uitam prestitit sempiternam quam
posset nosse presentem. ; p.

Adiuua nos domine quesumus eorum deprecatione sanctorum.
qui filium tuum humana necdum uoce profitentes
caelesti sunt per eius natiuitate gratia coronati q

[L]argire nobis quaesumus domine semper posculent mentium puritatem
quorum innocentiam hodie solemniter celebramus. p.

.ii. kl. ian. nat. sci siluestri

[D]a quaesumus omnipotens deus. ut beati siluestri confessoris tui at
que pontificis ueneranda solemnitas. et deuotionem
nobis augeat et salutem. per. .xuiiii. kl. febru.

[C]oncede quaesumus omnipotens deus. ut ad meliorem uitam sanctorum tuorum. sce feli cis
exempla nos prouocent. quatenus quorum solemnia
agimus etiam actus imitemur. per. .xuii. kl. febru.

[P]reces populi tui quaesumus domine clementer exaudi. sce marcelle
ut beati marcelli martyris tui atque pontificis
meritis adiuuemur cuius passione letamur. p.

.xu. kl. febr. nat. sce prisce m.

[D]a quaesumus omnipotens deus. ut qui beate prisce martyris tuae
natalicia colimus. et annua solemnitate laetemur
et constantiae fidei proficiamus exemplo. p.

.xiii. kl. febr. nat. sci fabiani mar.

[I]nfirmitatem nostram respice omnipotens deus. et quia pondus
propriae actionis nos grauat beati fabiani mar
tyris tui atque pontificis intercessio gloriosa
nos protegat. per d. eodem die sci sebastiani

[D]eus qui beatum sebastianum martyrem tuum uirtute
constantiae in passione roborasti. ex eius nobis

imitatione tribue famulis tuis ... di despicere et nulla eius aduersa formidare. p.

Omnipotens sempiterne ds qui infirma mundi eligis ut fortia quaeque confundas: concede propitius ut qui beatae agnetis martyris tuae sollemnia colimus, eius apud te patrocinia sentiamus. p.

Praesta qs dne mentibus nostris cum exultatione profectum, ut beatae agnetis martyris tuae cuius diem passionis annua deuotione recolimus etiam fidei constantiam subsequamur. p.

Adesto qs dne supplicationibus nostris. ut qui ex iniquitate nostra reos nos esse cognoscimus beati uincentii martyris tui intercessione liberemur. p.

Ds qui nos annua beatae agnetis martyris tuae sollemnitate laetificas. da qs ut quam ueneramur officio etiam piae conuersationis sequamur exemplo. per dnm nrm.

Ds qui inter cetera potentiae tuae miracula etiam in sexu fragili uictoriam martyrii contulisti concede propitius ut cuius natalitia colimus colimus perueniat ad te exempla gradiamur. per

[P]resta quesumus omnipotens deus. xvi. decima kl. mai. sci ualentini
ut qui beati martyris tui natalitia colimus
a cunctis malis imminentibus eius intercessione
liberemur. per. viii id. mart. sci gregorii pap.

[D]eus qui anime famuli tui gregorii aeterne beatitu
dinis premia contulisti concede propitius ut qui
peccatorum nostrorum pondere premimur eius apud
te precibus subleuemur. per. viii kl. april. adnunt.

[D]eus qui beate uirginis utero uerbum sce marie.
tuum angelo annuntiante carnem suscipere uolui
sti presta supplicibus tuis ut qui uere eam genetri
cem dei credimus eius apud te intercessionibus ad
iuuemur. per eundem. dominum. xviii. kl. mai.

[P]resta quesumus omnipotens deus ut qui sanctorum tuorum tiburtii et uale
tiburtii et ualeriani et maximi solemnia colimus
eorum etiam uirtutes imitemur. per dominum.

[D]eus qui nos beati georgii ix kl. mai. sci georgii
martyris tui meritis et intercessione letificas
concede propitius ut qui eius beneficia pos
cimus donatione gratie consequamur. per

50

vii. kł mai. nat. sci marci euaǥ

Sit dñe beatus marcus martyr et euangelista.
nrae fragilitatis adiutor. ut p nobis tibi suppli
cans copiosius audiatur. p. IIII. kł mai sci uitalis

Presta qs omnip ds. ut intercedente beato marť.
uitale martyre tuo. et cunctis aduersitatib; libe
remur in corpore. et prauis cogitationib; munde
mur in mente. p. kł mai aptoꝝ pilipi et iacobi

Ds qui nos annua aptoꝝ tuorū philippi et
iacobi solennitate laetificas psta qs ut quoꝝ
gaudemus meritis instruamur exemplis. p.

v. nō mai scoꝝ alexandri euenti et theodoli

Presta qs omnip ds. ut qui scorū tuorū alexan
dri euenti et teodoli natalicia colimus. a cunc
tis malis inminentib; eorū intercessionibus
liberemur. p. ii. n mai. sci iohan. ante portam

Ds qui conspicis quia nos undiq; mala nra per
turbant. presta qs ut beati ioh apti tui in
tercessio gloriosa nos ptegat. p. vi. id mai. sco

Da qs omnip ds. ut qui beatorū mar
tyrū gordiani atq; epimachi solemnia colim

eorum aput te intercessionibus adiuuemur. p.

Semper nos domine martyrum tuorum nerei et achill
ei et pancratii foueat quaesumus beata sollemnitas. et
tuo dignos reddat obsequio. per.

Concede quaesumus omnipotens deus. ad eorum nos gaudia aeterna per
tingere. de quorum nos uirtute tribuis annua sol
emnitate gaudere. per. d. VIII. kl. iun. Sci urbani
Da quaesumus omnipotens deus. ut qui beati urbani martyris tui atque
pontificis solemnia colimus eius aput te interc
essionibus adiuuemur. per dominum. IIII. kl. iun. Scorum mar...
Deus qui nos annua beatorum marcellini et petri
martyrum tuorum solemnitate laetificas: praesta quaesumus
ut quorum gaudemus meritis, prouocemur exemplis. p.
Fac nos domine quaesumus. V. id. iun. Scorum primi ...
scorum tuorum primi et feliciani semper festa sec
tari. quorum suffragiis protectionis tuae dona
sentiamus. per dominum. II. id. iun. Scorum basilidis ...
Scorum basilidis cyrini naboris et na
zarii quaesumus domine natalitia nobis uotiua resplende

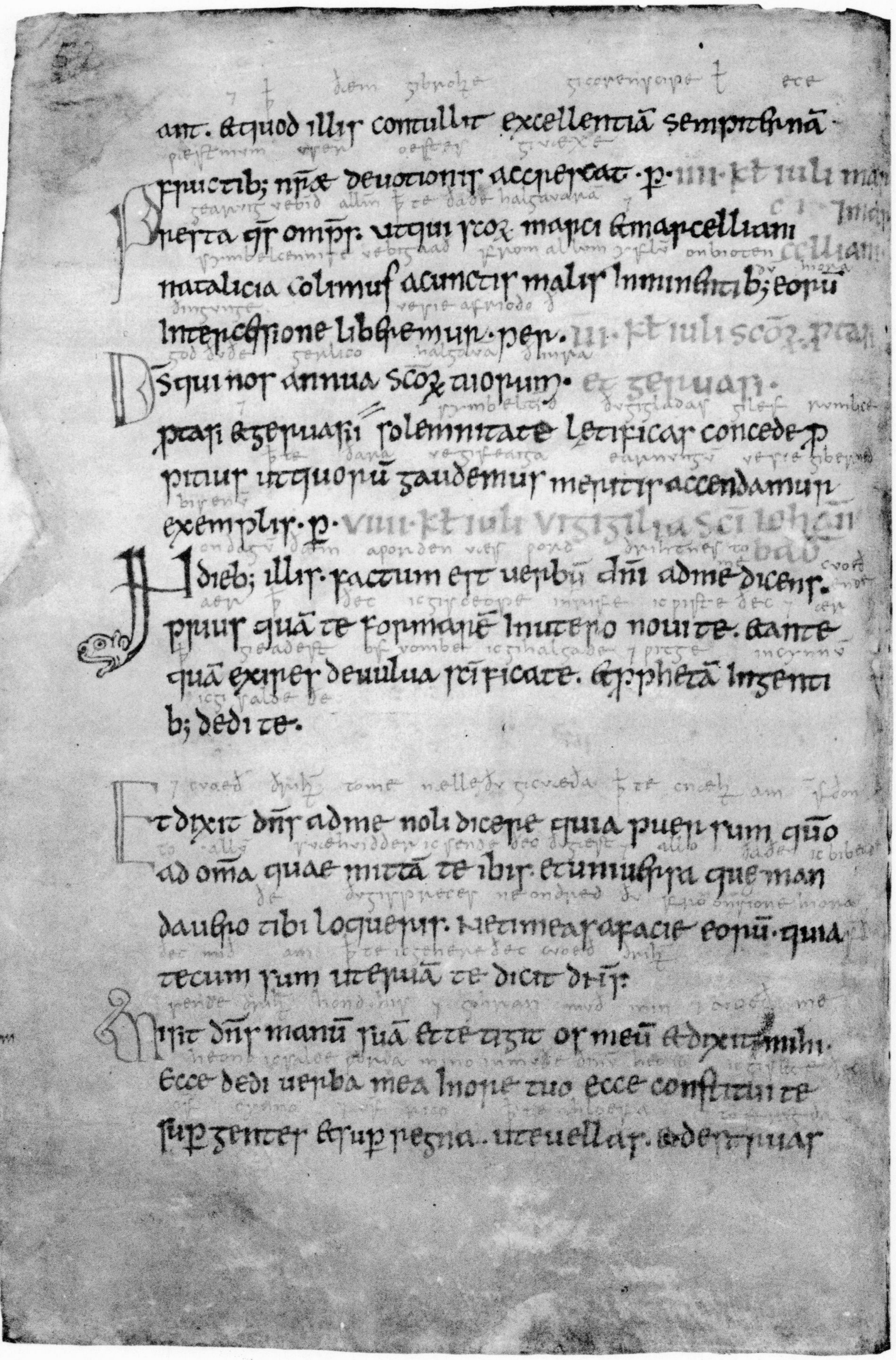

ant. et quod illis contulit excellentiā sempiternā

fructib; nr̄ae deuotionis acceperat. p. IIII. K IULI MAR

Praesta qs omps. ut qui scor. marci et marcelliani

natalicia colimus a cunctis malis inminentib; eorū

intercessione liberemur. per. III. K IULI SCOR. PROT

Ds qui nos annua scor. tuorum. et geruasi.

protasi et geruasii solemnitate letificas concede p

pitius ut quorū gaudemus meritis accendamur

exemplis. p. VIII. K IULI VIGILIA SCI IOHAN BAB

In dieb; illis. factum est uerbū dni ad me dicens.

priusquā te formarē in utero noui te. et ante

quā exires de uulua scificate. et pphetā in genti

b; dedi te.

Et dixit dns ad me noli dicere quia puer sum quō

ad omā quae mittā te ibis. et uniuersa quae man

dauero tibi loqueris. ne timeas a facie eorū. quia

tecum sum ut eruā te dicit dns.

Misit dns manū suā et tetigit os meū et dixit mihi.

Ecce dedi uerba mea in ore tuo ecce constitui te

sup gentes et sup regna. ut euellas. et destruas

et dispendas et dissipes. et aedifices et plantes. dicit dominus.

Haec dicit dominus deus. Audite insulae et adtendite
populi de longe. dominus ab utero uocauit me de uen
tre matris meae recordatus est nominis mei.

Haec dicit dominus. formans me ex utero seruum sibi dedi
te in lucem gentium ut sis salus mea usque ad extre
mum terrae. ℞ bunt propter dominum deum

Reges uidebunt et consurgent principes et adora
tuum et sanctum israhel qui elegit te.

it(em) collecta

Praesta quaesumus omnipotens deus. ut familia tua per uiam salutis
incedat et beati iohannis praecursoris ortamenta
sectando. ad eum quem praedixit secura perueniat. qui

Concede quaesumus omnipotens deus. ut qui beati iohannis baptis
te solemnia colimus eius apud te intercessione
muniamur.

Deus qui nos beati iohannis baptistae concedis nata
licia perfrui eius nos tribue misericordiae adiuuari. per

Deus qui conspicis quia nos undique it(em) ut supra
mala nostra contristant per praecursorem gaudii
corda nostra laetifica. per dominum..

Omps sempt̃ ds da cordib; nris illã tuarũ rectitudinem semitarum quã beati iohannis baptiste in deserto uox clamantis edocuit. per.

Omps sempitne ds qui beatũ iohannẽ baptistã iohannẽ tua puidentia destinasti ut pfectã plebẽ xpo dño ppararet. da qs. ut familia tua huius in tercessione pconis et a peccatis omib; exuatur et ad eum quẽ pphetauit. puenire mereamur. p.

Quessumus omps ds. ut nos geminata letitia hodiernẽ festiuitatis excipiat. que de beatorũ iohannis et pauli glorificatione pcedit quos eadẽ fides et passio uere fecit ee. germanos. per.

Ds qui beatum leonẽ pontificẽ scorũ tuorũ meritis coequasti concede ppitius ut qui com memorationis eius festa pcolimus in te quoq; imitemur exempla. p dnm

Claudus quidã cum uidisset petrũ et iohannẽ rogabat ut elimosinã acciperet. petrus ħ dix. argentũ et aurũ non ẽ. mihi qđ autẽ habeo hoc tibi do in nomine ihu xpi nazareni surge et ambula.

Exiliens claudus stetit et ambulabat. et intrauit
cum illis in templum ambulans et exiliens et lauda
ns dm̄. eam et cum uocasset scōs
In dieb; illis. dans petrus manū thabite erexit
et uiduas adsignauit eam uiuā. Notum h' factū
est per uniuersā Ioppen. et crediderunt multi in dn̄o.,
Petrus quidē seruabatur in carcere. Oratio
aut̄ fiebat sine intermissione ab aecclesia ad
dm̄ pro eo; lo carceris percusoque
Angelus dn̄i adstitit et lumē refulsit in habitacu
lo et latere petri suscitauit eū dicens. Surge uelo
citer et ceciderunt cataene de manibus eius.,
Dixit angelus ad petrū precingere et calciate
calligas tuas et fecit sic. et exiens sequeba-
tur eū et nesciebat quia uerū est quod fiebat per
angelum estimabat aut̄ se uisū uidere.
Petrus ad se reuersus dix. nunc scio uere quia
misit dn̄s angelū suū et eripuit me de manu
herodis et de omi expectatione plebis iudeorū
Ds qui nobis apostolorū beatorū petri et pau Secun
li natalicia gloriosa prebere concedis. tri collecte

bue qs eorum nos semper · et beneficiis preuenire
et orationib; adiuuari · per
Ds qui aecclesiã tuã apti tui petri fide · et nomine
consecrasti quiq; beatum illi paulum ad predicandũ
gentibus gloriã tuã sociare dignatus es. concede ut
omnes qui ad apostolorũ tuorum solemnia conuenerunt
spiritali remunerare ratione ditentur · per.
Presta qs omps ds. ut nullis nos permittas perturba
tionib; concuti quos in apostolice confessionis petra
solidasti · per   Ligandi atq; soluendi
Ds qui apto tuo petro collatis clauib; regni celestis
pontificiũ tradidisti · concede ut intercessionis eius
auxilio a peccatorũ nostrorũ nexib; liberemur · p.
Omps sempt ds. qui aecclesiã tuã in apos
tolica soliditate fundatã ab inferorũ erui
terrore portarũ · presta ut in tua ueritate persi
stens nulla consortia perfidorũ · per
Familiã tuã dne propitius intuere et apostolicis
defende presidiis ut eorũ precib; gubernetur quib;
nititur te constituente principibus · p.
Ds omps beatorũ apostolorũ tuorũ ·

petri et pauli honore continuo plebs tua semper
exultet et his praesulibus subsistetur quorum doctrinis
gaudet et meritis. Per. II. kl. Sci pauli apti.
Fratres notum uobis facio euangelium quod praedicaui uobis
quod et accepistis in quo et statis per quod et saluemini.
Ego enim sum minimus omnium apostolorum
qui non sum dignus uocari apostolus quoniam per
secutus sum ecclesiam dei. gratia dei sum id quod
sum. et gratia eius in me uacua non fuit. Ne
mo militans deo implicat se negotiis secularibus
ut ei placeat cui se probauit. Nam et qui certat in a
gone non co ronatur nisi legitime certauerit.
Bonum certamen certaui cursum consummaui
fidem seruaui. In reliquo reposita est mihi
corona iustitie quam reddet mihi dominus in illa die
iustus iudex. Ut me predicatio
Dominus michi adstitit et confortauit me ut per
impleatur. et audiant omnes gentes. Et liberatus
sum de ore leonis. liberauit me dominus ab omni opere
malo et saluum faciet regnum suum caeleste cui glo
ria in secula seculorum amen. ctione
Deus qui multitudinem gentium beati pauli apostoli predica

29 r

docuisti da nobis qs. ut cuius natalicia colimus et
apud te patrocinia sentiamus. p.

Concede qs dne apostolos tuos intervenire pro nobis quia
tunc nos saluari posse confidimus si eorum precibus tua
subiungetur aecclesia quibus te constituente princi
pibus. per.

Apostolicis nos dne qs beatorum petri et pauli ad
tolle presidiis. ut quanto fragiliores sumus tanto
ualidioribus auxiliis foueamur. per.

.iii. id. iul. octauas apostolorum

Hii sunt uiri misericordiae quorum iustitiae obliuio
nem non acceperunt. cum semine eorum permanent
bona hereditas sca nepotes eorum et in testamentis
stetit semen eorum et filii eorum propter eos usque in
aeternum manent.

Corpora scorum in pace sepulta sepulta sunt et nomina
eorum uiuet in secula sapientiam eorum narrabunt
omnis populi et laudem eorum pronuntiet omnis
ecclesia sanctorum. Sequitur coll.

Deus cuius dextera beatum petrum ambulantem in fluc
tibus ne mergeretur erexit et coapostolum eius
paulum tercio naufragantem de profundo pelagi

liberauit. exaudi nos propitius et concede ut amborum
institutis et eternitatis gloriam consequamur. per.

Protege domine populum tuum. et apostolorum tuorum
patrocinia confidentem perpetua defensione conserua. per.

Omnipotens sempiterne deus. qui nos beatorum apostolorum petri et pau
li. multiplici facis celebritate gaudere. da quesumus eo
rum semper iterata solemnitas. sit tuitio
nis augmentum. per. VI. N. IUL. SCORUM PROCESSI ET MARTI[NIANI]

Deus qui nos sanctorum tuorum processi et martiniani confes
sionibus gloriosis circumdas et protegis da nobis et eorum
imitatione proficere et intercessione gaudere. per

Sci sacerdotis. IIII. N. IUL. TRANSLATIO BEATI MARTINI

Deus qui martini hodie translationem celebrantibus
tribue nobis domine. ut sicut commemorationem
eius deuotissime colimus ita et opus fideliter im
mitemur. per.

VII. ID. IUL. SCORUM VII FRATRUM FILIORUM SCE FELICITATIS

Presta quesumus omnipotens deus. ut qui gloriosos martyres fra
tres in sua confessione cognouimus pios apud
te in nostra intercessione sentiamus. per.

V. ID. IUL. N. SCI BENEDICTI ABB.

Intercessio nos domine quesumus beati benedicti abbatis

6

commendat. ut qui nostris meritis non ualemus eius
patrocinio assequamur. per.

VIII. Kl. Augusti. Nat. sci Iacobi apostoli.

Esto domine plebi tuae sanctificator et custos. ut apostoli
tui Iacobi munita presidiis. et conuersatione tibi
placeat. et secura deseruiat. per. IIII. Kl. ... Felicis

Praesta domine quaesumus. ut sicut populus christianus
martyrum tuorum felicis simplicii. faustini
et beatricis temporali sollemnitate congau
det. ita perfruatur aeterna. et quod uotis
celebrat. comprehendat effectu. per.

III. Kl. Augustus. Scorum Abdo et Sennes.

Deus qui sanctis tuis abdo et sennen ad hanc gloriam
ueniendi copiosum munus gratiae contulisti.
da famulis tuis suorum ueniam peccatorum. ut sanctorum
tuorum intercedentibus meritis ab omnibus mereamur
aduersitatibus liberari. per. Kl. Agustus. Scorum

Fraterna nos domine Machabeorum VII fratrum cum matre
martyrum tuorum corona laetificet. quae et fidei
nostrae praebeat incitamenta uirtutum. et multiplici
nos suffragio consoletur. per.

IIII. Non. Agustus. sci Stephani epis. et martyris.

cede propitius ut omnes qui martyrii eius merita
ueneramur intercessionibus eius ab aeternis gehenne
incendiis liberemur. per

Da nobis quaesumus omnipotens deus uitiorum nostrorum flammas ex
tinguere. qui beato laurentio tribuisti tor
mentorum suorum incendia superare. per

Deus cuius caritatis ardore beatus laurentius ae
daces incendii flammas contempto persecutore
deuicit. concede ut omnes qui martyrii eius merita
ueneramur. protectionis tuae auxilio muniamur. per

Da quaesumus omnipotens deus ut triumphum beati laurentii
martyris tui. quem despectis ignibus consumma
uit in terris perpetua caelorum luce conspicuum dig
no feruore fidei ueneremur. per

Beati tiburtii nos domine foueant continuata prae
sidia quia non desinis propitius intueri quos talibus
auxiliis concesseris adiuuari. per

Da nobis omnipotens deus ut beati ypoliti martyris
tui ueneranda sollemnitas et deuotionem nobis
augeat et salutem. per

Deus qui nos beati eusebii
confessoris tui annua sollemnitate laetificas
concede propitius ut cuius natalitia colimus

per eius adte exempla gradiamur. p[er].

In omnibus requiem quesiui
et in hereditate domini morabor. tunc precepit
et dixit mihi creator omnium et qui creauit
me requieuit in tabernaculo meo.
In iacob inhabita et in israhel hereditare et
in electis meis mitte radices et sic in sion fir
mata sum et in ciuitate sanctificata similiter
requieui et in hierusalem potestas mea.
Et radicaui in populo honorificato et in partes
dei mei hereditas illius et in plenitudine sanctorum
detentio mea. Ⱶ Cipressus in
Quasi cedrus exaltata sum in libano et quasi
montem sion. et quasi palma exaltata sum in cad
es et quasi plantatio rose in hiericho et
quasi oliua speciosa in campis et quasi pla
tanus exaltata sum iuxta aquam in plateis.
Sicut cynnamomum et balsamum aromatizans
odorem dedi quasi myrrha electa dedi suauita
tem odoris. Collecta.
Ⱶ Habitaper elizepe
Deus qui virginalem aulam beate marie in qua
dignatus es. da quesumus ut tua nos defensione

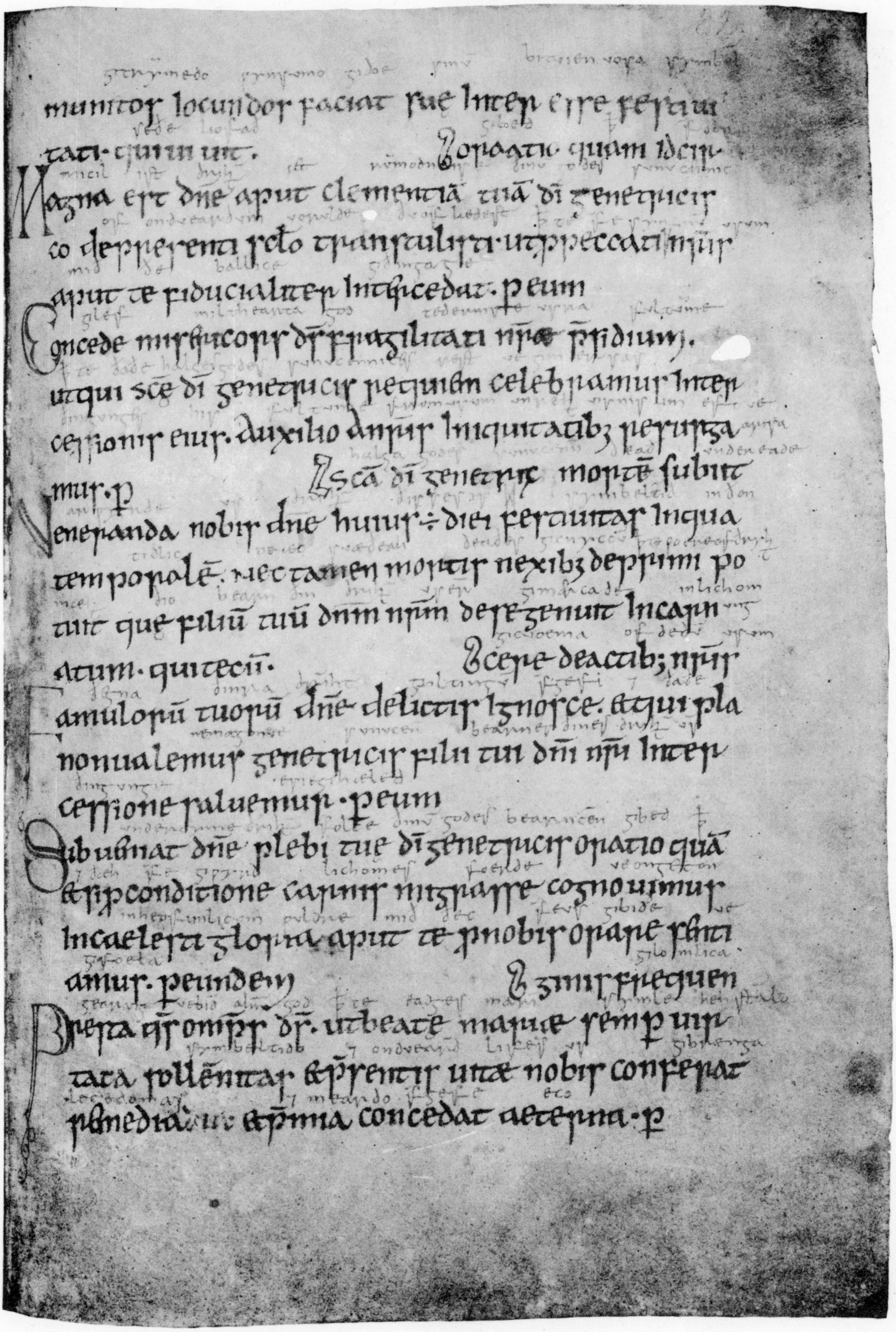

munitos iocundos faciat sue interesse festiui
tati. Qui cum uiuit. oratio quam idcir-
Magna est domine apud clementiam tuam dei genetricis
co de presenti seculo transtulisti ut pro peccatis nostris
apud te fiducialiter intercedat. Per eum
Concede misericors deus fragilitati nostre presidium;
ut qui sancte dei genetricis requiem celebramus inter
cessionis eius auxilio a nostris iniquitatibus resurga
mus. Per. sancta dei genetrix mortem subiit
Veneranda nobis domine huius ÷ diei festiuitas in qua
temporalem. nec tamen mortis nexibus deprimi po
tuit que filium tuum dominum nostrum de se genuit incarn
atum. Qui tecum. placere de actibus nostris
Famulorum tuorum domine delictis ignosce. et qui pla
non ualemus genetricis filii tui domini nostri inter
cessione saluemur. Per eum
Subueniat domine plebi tue dei genetricis oratio quam
et si pro condicione carnis migrasse cognouimus
in caelesti gloria apud te pro nobis orare senti
amus. Per eundem ginis frequen
Presta quaesumus omnipotens deus ut beatae mariae semper uir
tata sollemnitas et presentis uitae nobis conferat
remedia et praemia concedat aeterna. Per.

xvii kl sept. octauas sci laurentii

Iterata festiuitate beati laurentii natalitia
ueneramur que in caelestib; beatitudine ful
gere nouimus sempiterna. per xv kl sept sci a[gapiti]

Laetetur aecclesia tua ds: beati agapiti mar
tyris tui confisa suffragiis atq; eius precib;
gloriosis et deuota permaneat et secura consistat. p.

xi kl sept sci thimothei.

Auxilium tuum nobis dne quaesumus placatus inpende et in
tercedente beato timotheo martyre tuo. dexteram
sup nos tuae propitiationis extende. p.

viii kl sept sci bartholomei apostoli

Omnipotens sempiterne ds. qui huius diei uenerandam scam
que laetitiam beati apostoli tui bartholomei festiui
tate tribuisti da ecclesiae tuae quaesumus et amare quod cre
didit et praedicare quod docuit. p.

Sci iohannis baptiste iiii kl sept par iohannis

et martyris tui dne quaesumus ueneranda festiuitas sa
lutaris auxilii nobis praestet effectum. p.

Maiestatem tuam dne iii kl sept sci felicis
suppliciter deprecamur. ut sicut nos iugiter
scorum tuorum commemoratione laetificas ita
semper supplicatione defendas. p.

VI idus sept. Nativitas sancte marie.

O quam pulchra est casta generatio cum cla-
ritate. Inmortalitas est in memoria illius quoniam apud deum nota est et apud homines.

Ab initio ante saeculum creata sum et usque ad futurum saeculum non desinam. Et in habitatione sancta coram ipso ministravi. Et sic in sion firmata sum et in civita-
te sanctificata. Natura. Ego quasi libanus.
Ego ex ore altissimi prodivi primogenita ante omnem cre-
non incisus vaporavi habitationem meam et quasi balsamum non mixtum odor meus. Et quasi terebintus
extendi ramos meos et rami mei honoris et gratie.

Una est columba mea perfecta mea. Item capitula.
una est matri sue electa genetrici sue. Viderunt
illam filiae et beatissimam eam predicaverunt reginae et
concubinae laudaverunt eam. Item ut supra.

Que est ista que progreditur quasi aurora consur-
gens pulchra ut luna electa ut sol terribilis ut acies
ordinata. Item collectio. ut qui in nativita-

Supplicationem servorum tuorum deus miserator exaudi.
tate dei genetricis semper virginis congregamur eius intercessionibus complacatus a te de instantibus periculis eru-
amur. per eundem.

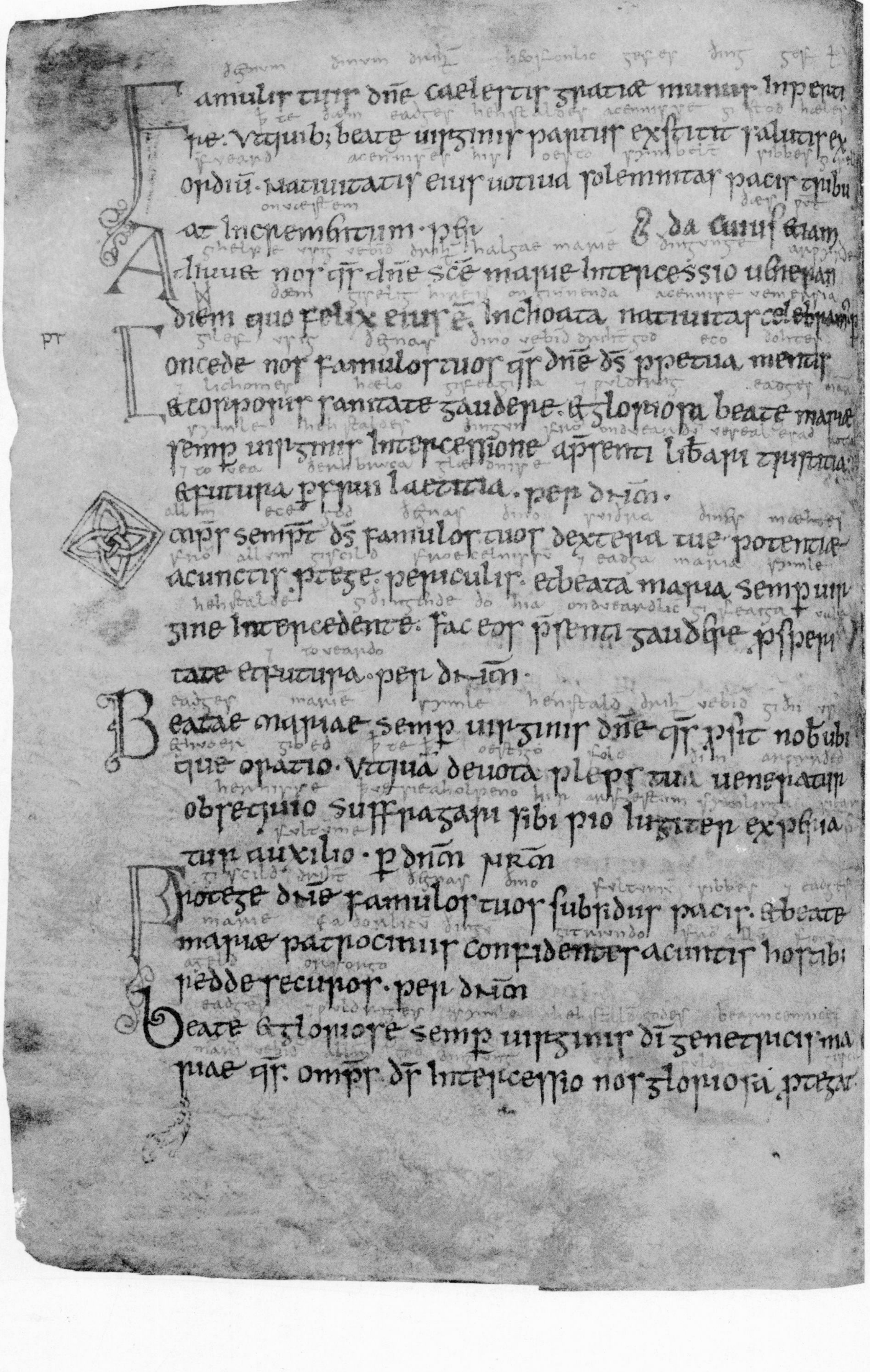

Famulis tuis dne caelestis gratiae munus inpertire. ut quibus beatae uirginis partus extitit salutis exordium. natiuitatis eius uotiua sollemnitas pacis tribuat incrementum. per. Et da eius etiam

Adiuuet nos qs dne sce mariae intercessio ueneranda diem quo felix eius est inchoata natiuitas celebrantes.

Concede nos famulos tuos qs dne ds perpetua mentis et corporis sanitate gaudere. et gloriosa beatae mariae semper uirginis intercessione a presenti liberari tristitia et futura perfrui laetitia. per dnm.

Omnips sempiterne ds famulos tuos dextera tuae potentiae a cunctis protege periculis. et beata maria semper uirgine intercedente. fac eos presenti gaudere prosperitate et futura. per dnm.

Beatae mariae semper uirginis dne qs prosit nobis ubique oratio. ut qua deuota plebs tua ueneratur obsequio suffragari sibi pio iugiter experiatur auxilio. per dnm nrm.

Protege dne famulos tuos subsidiis pacis. et beatae mariae patrociniis confidentes a cunctis hostibus redde securos. per dnm.

Beatae et gloriosae semper uirginis di genetricis mariae qs omps ds intercessio nos gloriosa protegat

et angeli eius preliabantur cum dracone. et draco pu-
gnabat et angeli eius et non ualuerunt. neque locus inuentus est eorum amplius in caelo.

Angelus uenit et stetit ante altare habens turri-
bulum aureum et data sunt illi incensa multa ut
daret de orationibus sanctorum omnium super altare aureum quod est ante thronum.

In diebus illis dixit mihi angelus scribe beati qui
ad caenam nuptiarum agni uocati sunt.

Cecidi ante pedes angeli ut adorarem eum et dixit
mihi uide ne feceris conseruus tuus sum et fratrum tuorum habentium testimonium ihesu. deum adora.

Ecce tabernaculum dei cum hominibus et habitabit cum
eis. et erit eorum deus et ipsi populus eius erunt et ipse dominus cum eis erit eorum deus.

Deus qui miro ordine angelorum ministeria
hominumque dispensas. concede propitius ut quibus
tibi ministrantibus in caelo semper adsistitur ab
his in terra nostra uita muniamur.

Beati archangeli tui michaelis intercessione
suffulti supplices te domine deprecamur. ut quos
honore prosequimur contingamus et mente. per

Da nobis omnipotens deus beati archangeli michaelis
eo tenus honore proficere ut cuius gloriam predica
mus in terris eius precibus adiuuemur in celis.

Multiplica domine uniuersitatem tuam in animabus
supplicum ut dum te in templo sancto iugiter adoramus in
conspectu tuo cum sanctis angelis gloriemur. per

Perpetuum nobis domine tue miserationis presta sub
sidium. quibus et angelica prestitisti suffragia non
deesse. per

Adesto plebi tue misericors deus et ut gratiae tue
beneficia potiora percipiat. beati michaelis
archangeli fac supplicem deprecationibus sub
leuari. per

Exaudi domine preces nostras et interueniente bea
to marco confessore tuo atque pontifice. sup
plicationes nostras placatus intende. per.

Laetetur ecclesia tua deus martyrum tuorum dioni
sii rustici et eleutherii confisa suffragiis atque
eorum precibus gloriosis et deuota permaneat et secu
ra consistat. per

Deus qui nos conspicis ex nostra infirmitate defi

cetĕ ad amorē tuū ...

tuorū exepla per causa p.

Ut perueniat p nobis dne qs per lucas euan

gelista qui crucis mortificationē. iugiter in suo

corpore p tui nominis honore portauit. p.

Concede qs omps ds. ut sicut apostolorū tuorū simonis

et iude. gloriosa natalicia praeuenimus: sic ad tua

beneficia promerenda. maiestatē tuā pro nob ipsi

praeueniant. p. ii kl nou. sci quintini

Beati quintini martyris tui dne. nos qs: merita

praecipuantur. et tua nob indulgentia semp inp

lorent. p.

Dne ds nr multiplica sup nos gratiā tuā et quoz

praeuenimus gloriosa solemnia tribue subsequi

in sca professione laetitiā. p.

Exaudi dne famulos tuos cum multiplici scorū

tuoz tibi patrocinio supplicantes. et tempora

lis uitae eos tribue pace gaudere. et perpetuā per

cipere laetitiam. per.

Omps sempt ds. qui nos omn scoz merita sub una tri

buisti celebritate uenerari. qs ut desiderata nob

tuae propitiationis abundantiam multiplicatis intercessoribus largiaris. per

Da quaesumus domine fidelibus populis omnium sanctorum semper veneratione laetari et eorum perpetua supplicatione muniri. per

Omnipotens sempiterne deus qui nos omnium sanctorum tuorum multiplici facis celebritate gaudere. concede quaesumus ut sicut illorum commemoratione temporali gratulamur officio. ita perpetuo laetemur aspectu. per

Adesto deus populo tuo placatus ac benignus. ut eorum supplicatione qui tuae placuerunt pietati te largiente adiutam persentiat sempiternam. per

Maiestati tuae domine nos beata omnium sanctorum supplicatio conciliet. ut qui cotidie offendimus cotidiana eorum veneratione adiuvemur. per

Praesta quaesumus omnipotens deus ut continua sanctorum martyrum operatio et nobis praebeat incitamenta virtutum et multiplici nos ubique suffragia consoletur. per

Deus qui nos beata Mariae semper virginis et beatorum apostolorum martyrum confessorum atque omnium simul sanctorum continua

lætificas solemnitate. presta qs. ut quos cotidiana ueneramur officio. etiā conuersationis semper sequamur exemplo. per.

Ac nos dne ds sce mariæ sep uirginis subsidiis
attolli et gloriosa beatoꝝ aploꝝ martyrū con-
fessoꝝ atq; uirginū omniūq; simul scoꝝ prote-
tione defende. ut illū eoꝝ pariter cotidie festa celebramus eoꝝ pariter cotidiæ ab omni-
b; aduersis protegamur auxilio. per.

Adesto dne supplicationib; nris. et intercessione om scoꝝ tuoꝝ ppetuā nob misericordiā benignus inpende. per. ꝗ Salut ēpa

Da nob dne continua omniū scoꝝ uenerationē
cē ut quoꝝ gaudemus triūphis. eoꝝ protegamur
subsidiis. per ꝗ atq; om simul lus

Ds qui nos concedis scoꝝ aploꝝ martyrū confesso-
roꝝ continuis sollēnia colere sacramentis. da
nobis in aeterna laetitia de eoꝝ societate gaudere. per

Presta qs omps ds. ut qui gloriosos martyres
claudiū nicostratū simforianū castorium
atq; simpliciū fortes in sua confessione.

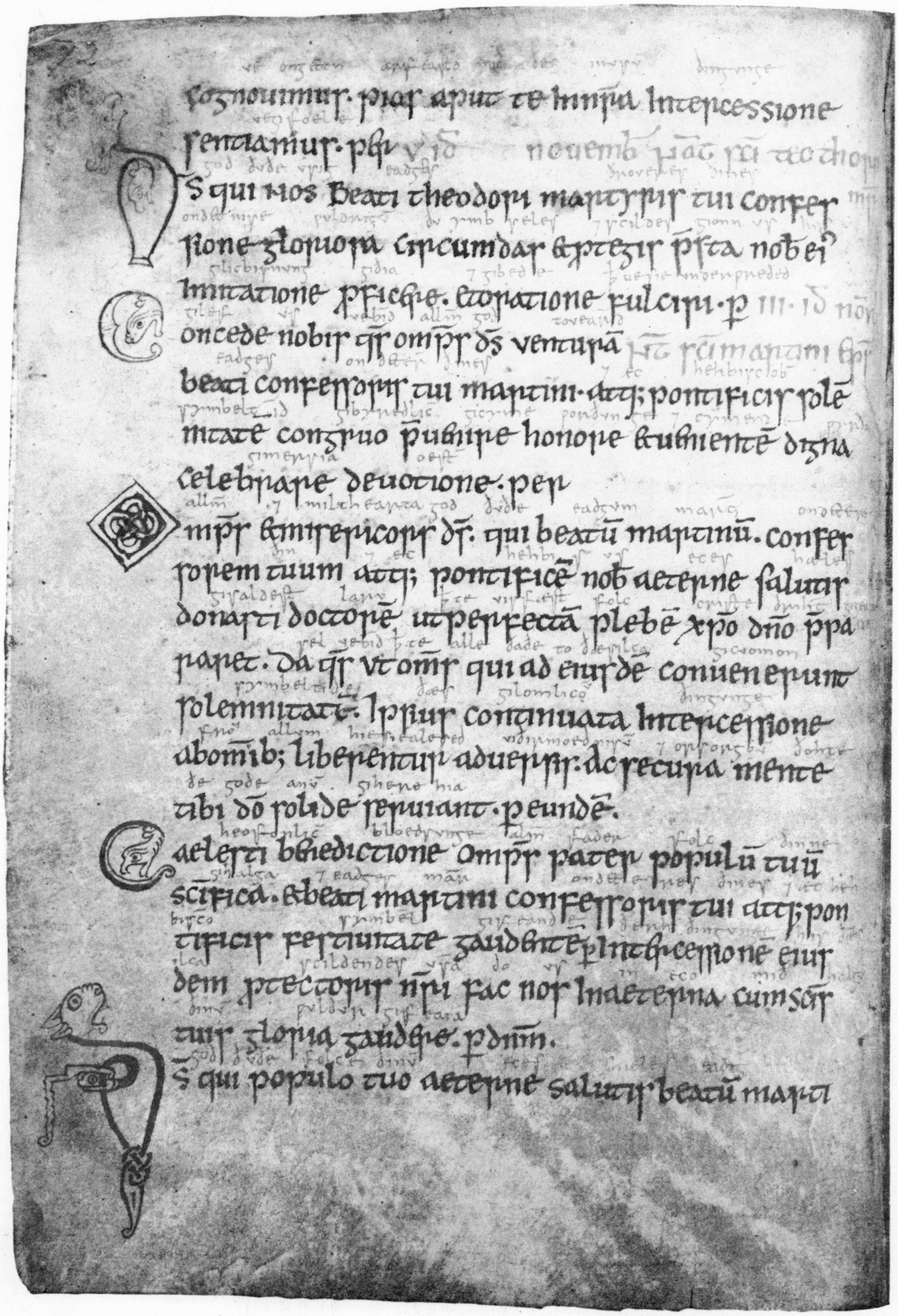

cognouimus. pias apud te iugiter intercessione
sentiamus. per. v. id. nouemb. nat. sci theodori
Ds qui nos beati theodori martyris tui confes
sione gloriosa circumdas et protegis presta nobis ei
imitatione proficere. et oratione fulciri. per. iii. id. nov.
Concede nobis quaesumus omnipotens ds ventura nat. sci martini epi
beati confessoris tui martini atque pontificis sole
mnitate congruo pietate honore et veniente digna
celebrare deuotione. per.
Omnipotens et misericors ds. qui beatum martinum. confes
sorem tuum atque pontificem nobis aeterne salutis
donasti doctorem. ut perfectam plebem xpo dno praepa
raret. da quaesumus ut omnes qui ad eius de conuenerunt
solemnitatem. ipsius continuata intercessione
ab omnibus liberentur aduersis. ac recta mente
tibi do solide seruiant. per eundem.
Caelesti benedictione omnipotens pater populum tuum
sanctifica. et beati martini confessoris tui atque pon
tificis festiuitate gaudentem per intercessione eius
dem protectoris nostri fac nos in aeterna cum sci
tuis gloria gaudere. per dnm.
Ds qui populo tuo aeterne salutis beatum marti

num ministerium concessisti. praesta quaesumus ut qui
doctorem uitae habuimus in terris. intercesso
rem semper habere mereamur in caelis. per
Exaudi domine populum tuum tota tibi mente subiectum. et beati martini pontificis supplicatione
custodi. ut corpore et corde protecti. quod pie
credidit appetat. et quod iuste sperat obtineat. per
Omnipotens sempiterne deus. Solemnitatem diei huius
propitius intuere. et ecclesiam tuam intercessione be
ati martini pontificis atque confessoris tui. con
tinua fac caelebritate gaudere. omniumque
in te credentium uota perficiat. per
Praesta quaesumus omnipotens. ut sicut diuina [illegible] laudamus
in sancti martini confessoris tui at[illegible]que ponti
ficis magnalia sic indulgentiam tuam piis
eius precibus adsequamur. per. X. kl. dec. nat. sce
Sanctae ceciliae martyris tuae cecilie mar uirg
domine supplicationibus tribue nos foueri. ut cuius
uenerabilem sollemnitatem preuenimus obsequio eius
intercessionibus commendemur. et amplius. per
Deus cui beata caecilia ita castitatis deuotione com
placuit. ut coniugem suum ualerianum affinem

que suum tibiuptatū tibi faceret consecrari iam
euangelo deferente incantatū odori fragrat florū
coronas palmā que martyrii perceperunt. qs ut ea
intercedente pro nob. beneficia tui muneris percipe mereamur. p. [VIIII kl dec sci clementis pape]
Ds qui nos annua beati clementis martyris tui atq;
pontificis sollemnitate laetificas. concede propitius ut cuius natalitia colimus uirtutē quoq; passionis imitemur. per. [VIII kl dec sci crisogoni mar]
Adesto supplicationib; nris. ut qui ex iniquitate nra
reos nos esse cognouimus beati crisogoni marty-
ris tui intercessione liberemur. p. [IIII kl dec sci saturnini]
Ds qui nos beati saturnini martyris tui concedis
natalicio [illegible] perfrui eius nob tribue meritis adiu-
[II kl dec vig sci andreae apl] uari. p
Benedictio dni super caput iusti ideo dedit illi hereditatē
et diuisit ei partē in trib; duodeci. et inuenit gratia
in conspectu omis carnis. p.
Magnificat eum in timore inimicoꝝ et uerbis suis mon
stra placuit glorificauit illū in conspectu regū
et ostendit illi gloriā suā. per.
In fide et lenitate ipsius scm fecit illū elegit eū ex
omi carne dedit illi precepta et legē uite et discipline

et excelsum fecit illum.

Statuit ei testamentum aeternum circumcinxit eum zona iustitiae et induit eum dominus coronam gloriae.

Ps. Corde creditur ad iustitiam. R. Ore autem confessio fit ad salutem dicit enim scriptura omnis qui credit in eum non confundetur.

Tuere nos misericors deus et beati andreae apostoli tui cuius natalicia sumimus semper guberna praesidiis.

Quaesumus omnipotens deus ut beatus andreas apostolus pro nobis imploret auxilium ut a nostris reatibus absoluti a cunctis etiam periculis exuamur. Per.

Beati andreae apostoli supplicatione quaesumus domine plebs tua benedictionem percipiat ut de eius memoria et feliciter glorietur et sempiternis valeat consortiis sociata laetari. Per dominum.

Adiuvet ecclesiam tuam tibi domine supplicando beatus andreas apostolus et pius interventor efficiatur qui tui nominis extitit praedicator. Per.

Da nobis quaesumus domine deus noster beati apostoli tui andreae intercessionibus sublevari ut per quos ecclesiae tuae superni muneris rudimenta donasti

38 r

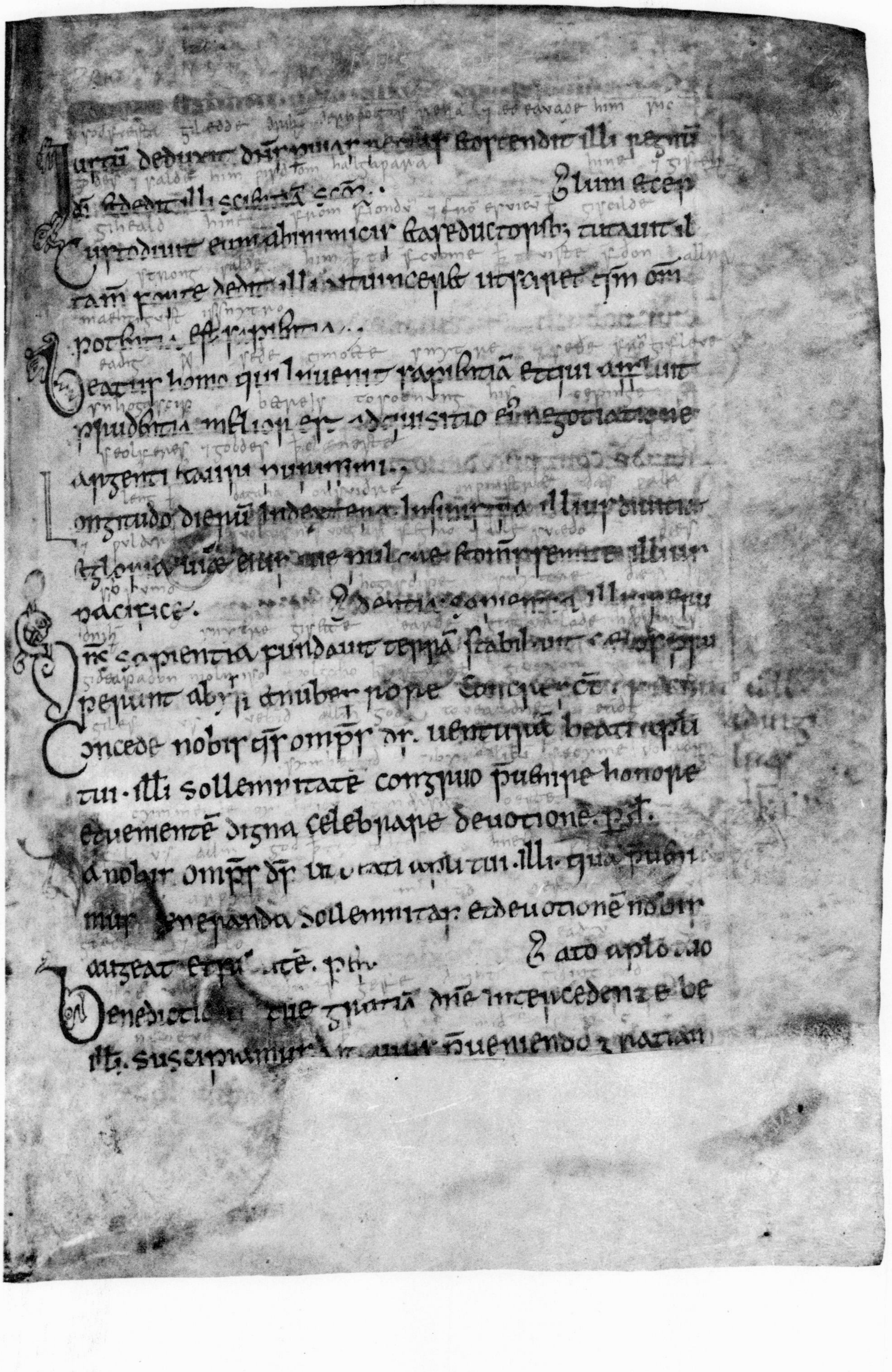

Iustum deduxit dominus per vias rectas et ostendit illi regnum
dei et dedit illi scientiam sanctorum. [illegible]

Custodiunt eum ab inimicis et a seductoribus tutavit illum et certamen forte dedit illi ut vinceret et sciret quoniam omnium
potentior est sapientia.

Beatus homo qui invenit sapientiam et qui affluit
prudentia melior est adquisitio eius negotiatione
argenti et auri purissimi.

Longitudo dierum in dextera eius et in sinistra illius divitiae
et gloria viae eius viae pulchrae et omnes semitae illius
pacificae. [illegible]

Dominus sapientia fundavit terram stabilivit caelos prudentia
eruperunt abyssi et nubes rore concrescunt.

Concede nobis quaesumus omnipotens deus ut beati apostoli
tui illi sollemnitatem congruo praevenire honore
et venientem digna celebrare devotione. Per.

Da nobis omnipotens deus ut beati apostoli tui illi quam praeveni-
mus venerandam sollemnitatem et devotionem nobis
augeat et salutem. Per. [illegible]

Benedictionem tuae gratiam domine intercedente beato
illi suscipiamus [illegible] [illegible] et gratiam

[Ip]s[e] d[eu]s dedit quosdam quidem ap[osto]los quosdam autem
p[ro]phetas alios u[er]o euuangelistas alios autem
pastores et doctores ad consummatione[m] s[an]c[t]oru[m]
in opus ministerii in aedificatione[m] corporis X[rist]i.
[F]r[atre]s. Occurramus om[ne]s in unitate fidei et agniti
onis filii d[e]i in uiru[m] perfectu[m] in mensuram
aetatis plenitudinis X[rist]i d[omi]ni n[ost]ri.
[C]oncede q[uaesumu]s om[ni]p[otens] d[eu]s. ut sic
ap[osto]lor[um] tuor[um] gloriosa natali[cia] p[rae]uenimus sic ad tua be
neficia p[ro]merenda. maiestate[m] tua[m] p[ro] nobis ipsi p[rae]ue[niant]
[S]olemnitatis apostolicae multiplicatione gaudentes. p[er]
gaudentes clementia[m] tua[m] d[e]p[re]camur om[ni]p[otens] d[eu]s. ut
tribuas iugiter nos eor[um] confessione benedici. et pat
rociniis confoueri. p[er].
[nominis]
[D]s qui nos p[er] beatos ap[osto]los tuos ad agnitione[m] tui
uenire tribuisti. da nobis eor[um] gloria[m] sempiter
na[m]. et p[ro]ficiendo celebrare. et celebrando p[ro]ficere. p[er].
[E]xaudi d[omi]ne preces n[ost]ras. et s[an]c[t]or[um] ap[osto]lor[um] tuor[um] festa
solemniter celebramus. continuis foueamur
auxiliis. p[er].
[partici]patione laetari et eor[um]
[D]a q[uaesumu]s d[omi]ne fidelib[us] populis s[an]c[t]or[um] ap[osto]lor[um] semp[er] uene
[ratione] p[er]petua suff[rag]atione muniri. p[er] d[omi]n[u]m.

40v

41 r

est iter exterminii illi sunt in pace.,
Si coram hominibus tormenta passi sunt spes illorum
inmortalitate plena est. In paucis uexati in
multis bene disponentur quoniam deus temptauit il
los et inuenit illos dignos se.
Tamquam aurum in fornace probauit illos et qua
si holocausta hostiae accepit illos. et in tempore
erit respectus illorum.
Fulgebunt iusti et tamquam scintillae in harundineto
discurrent iudicabunt nationes et dominabuntur
populis et regnabit dominus illorum in perpetuum.
Presta quaesumus omnipotens deus. ut sic beatorum
martyrum natalicia persoluimus sic auxilium mi
sericordiae tuae pro nobis semper ipsi promereantur. per
Magnifica domine beatorum martyrum tuorum quorum
sollemnia recensemus. quae praestitisti cordi
bus ambientes et suscipimus et sumimus. per.
Concede quaesumus omnipotens deus. ut sanctorum mar
tyrum tuorum quorum celebramus uictorias par
ticipemur et praemiis. per dominum.
Sanctorum martyrum tuorum nos domine precibus ad
iuuemur. ut eorum possibilitas non obtineat

eorum nobis qui ante te iusti inuenti sunt oratio
ne donetur. per dominum nostrum
Omnipotens sempiterne deus qui nos idoneos non esse perpen
dis ad maiestatem tuam sic dignum est exorandum
da sanctos martyres tuos [illegible] supplicare pec
catis quos digne possis audire.
Ad defentionem fidelium domine quaesumus dexteram tuae maies
tatis extende. ut perpetua pietatis tuae protec
tione muniantur. intercessio pro his non desit
martyrum continuata sanctorum. per. Item unius confessoris
Ecce sacerdos magnus qui
in diebus suis placuit deo et inuentus est iustus.
et in tempore iracundiae factus est reconcilia
tio. non est inuentus similis illi qui conseruaret
legem excelsi.
Benedictionem omnium gentium dedit illi et testa
mentum suum confirmauit super caput eius.
cognouit eum in benedictionibus suis conser
uauit illi misericordiam suam et inuenit gra
tiam coram oculis domini.
Magnificauit eum in conspectu regum et dedit
illi coronam gloriae. statuit illi testamentum

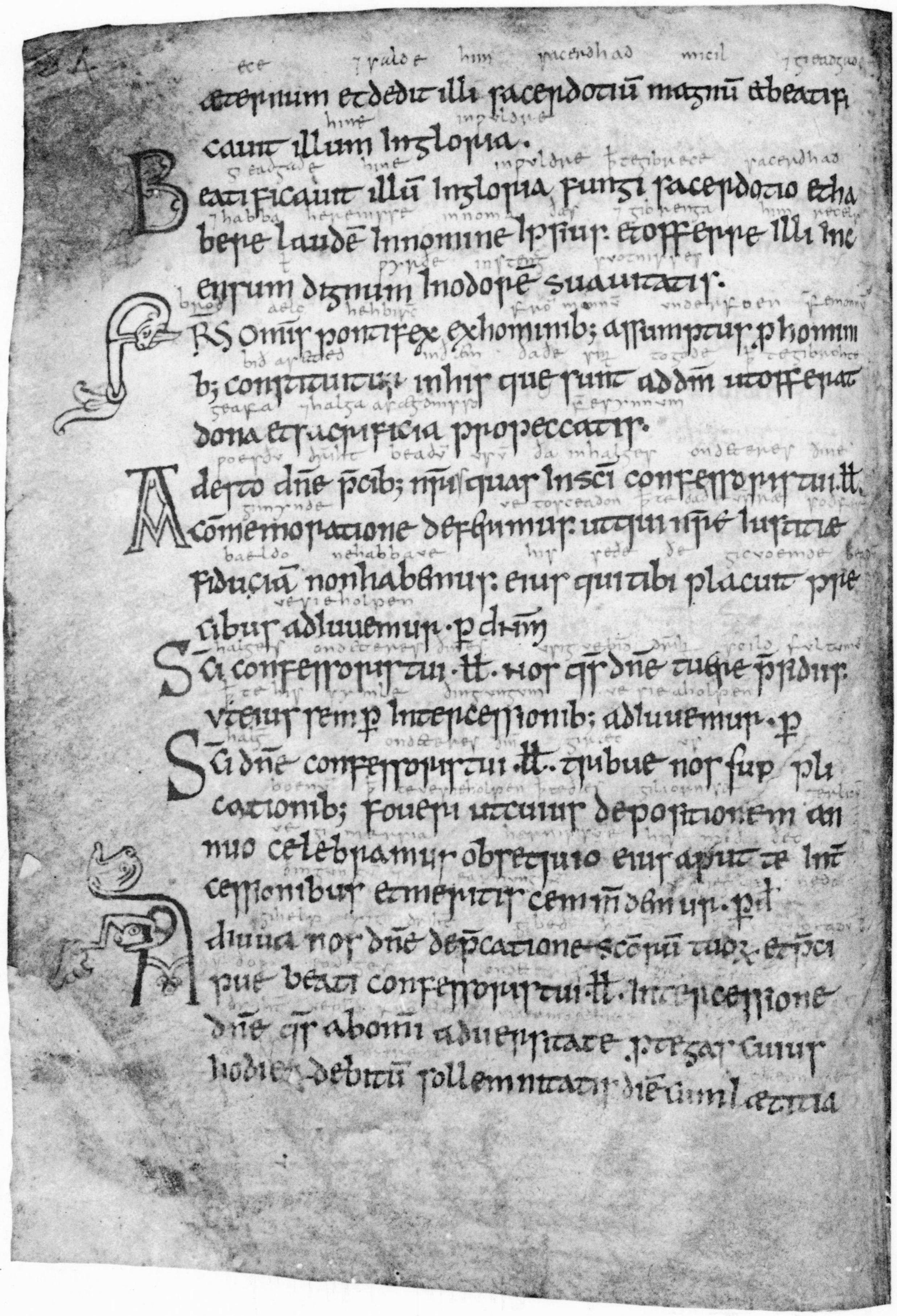

ęternum et dedit illi sacerdotiū magnū et beatifi
cauit illum in gloria.
Beatificauit illū in gloria. fungi sacerdotio et ha
bere laudē in nomine ipsius. et offerre illi in c
ensum dignum in odore suauitatis.
RS. Omnis pontifex ex hominib; assumptus. p homini
b; constituitur in his que sunt ad dm ut offerat
dona et sacrificia pro peccatis.
Adesto dne supplicib; nris qs in sci confessoris tui .ll.
commemoratione deferimus. ut qui nre iusticię
fiducia non habemus. eius qui tibi placuit pre
cibus adiuuemur. p dnm
Sci confessoris tui .ll. nos qs dne tuere presidiis.
ut eius semp intercessionib; adiuuemur. p
Sci dne confessoris tui .ll. tribue nos sup pli
cationib; foueri ut cuius depositionem an
nuo celebramus obsequio eius apud te inter
cessionibus et meritis commendemur. p d
Adiuuet nos dne deprecatione scorum tuorum et praeci
pue beati confessoris tui .ll. intercessione
dne qs ab omni aduersitate protegat cuius
hodie debitū sollemnitatis diē cum laetitia

42 v

Spiritali ueneremur. ut quorum festa gerim
us sentiamus auxilium. P.
s fidelium remunerator animarum praesta ut
beati confessoris tui .ll. cuius ueneranda cele
bramus festiuitatem. eius precibus indulgenti
am consequamur. Per.
isericordiam tuam dne nob qs interueniente
beato confessore tuo .ll. clementer inpende. et nob
peccatorib; ipsius propitiare suffragiis. P.
mps sempit ds. cui cuncta famulantur elemen
ta intercedente pro nob beato confessore tuo
.ll. exaudi propitius orationem nram et tribue nob
misericordia tua ut quecumq; precipis ut agam'
ipse adiuuante implere possim'. Per dnm

In ecclesia cuius libet. sci martyris
siue confessoris.

ropitiare qs dne nobis famulis tuis per hui
us sci tui .ll. qui in presenti requiescit ecclesia
merita gloriosa. ut eius pia intercessione ab omnibus
semper protegamur aduersis. Per.
s aeternae consolationis pater per huius sci tui .ll.
preces da populo tuo pacem et salutem ut eius

tota dilectione inhereant preceptis et que
tibi placita sunt tota perficiant uoluntate. per d.
RS. Plures facti sunt sacerdotes ideirco quod
morte prohiberentur permanere. hic autem eo
quod maneat in aeternum sempiternum habet
sacerdotium.
RS. Talis decebat ut nobis esset pontifex. sanctus inno
cens inpollutus. segregatus a peccatoribus et
excelsior caelis factus. qui non habet cotidie
necessitatem quemadmodum sacerdotes. prius
pro suis delictis hostias offerre. deinde pro popu
li. hoc enim fecit semel se offerendo dominus noster ie
sus christus.   qui penetrauit caelos iesum filium dei tene
RS. Habemus pontificem magnum qui penetrauit
amus confessionem.
RS. Non habemus pontificem qui non possit conpati
infirmitatibus nostris. temptatum per omnia pro similitu
dine absque peccato.
Sanctorum confessorum nos domine quesumus foueat preciosa con
fessio. et pia iugiter intercessio tueatur. per dominum
... domine quesumus populum tuum. continua sanctorum confes
sorum supplicatione protectum. per dominum.

[P]raesta quaesumus omnipotens deus. ut intercedentibus beatis confessoribus tuis. et a cunctis aduersitatibus liberemur
in corpore ac prauis cogitationibus mundemur in
mente. per dominum.

[P]ropitiare nobis domine. quaesumus tuorum suffragia conlata confessorum. ut quod non possumus nostris orationibus obtinere placentiam tibi precibus adsequamur. per

[D]eus qui nos sanctorum tuorum .ll. confessionibus gloriosis
circumdas et protegis da nobis et eorum imitatione
proficere et intercessione gaudere. per d.

[B]enedictionis tuae gratiam domine plebs christiana suscipiat. ut sanctorum merita gloriosa concelebrans honoris tui fructum referat pia sollemnitate pontificum. per. In natale plurimorum martirum

[I]usti in perpetuum uiuent et apud dominum est merces
eorum et cogitatio illorum apud altissimum.

[A]ccipient sancti regnum decoris et diadema speciei de manu domini quoniam dextera sua teget eos et brachio sancto suo
defendet illos. iudicium certum sument

[I]nduent sancti pro thorace iustitiam et accipient pro galea
scutum inexpugnabile aequitatem ibunt directe
promissiones et ad certum locum deducet illos dominus deus uirtutum.

... ds mercedem laborum scorum suorum et deduxit
... in uia mirabili. et fuit illis in uelamento di(ei)
et in luce stellarum in nocte.

Qui scrutatur corda scit quid desiderat sps
quia secundum dm postulat pro scis.

Rs. Scimus quoniam diligentibus dm omnia cooperantur in
bonum his qui secundum propositum uocati sunt sci.

Omnips semper ds. qui in scorum tuorum cordibus flammas
tuae dilectionis accendis. da mentibus nostris ean
dem fidei caritatisque uirtutem. ut quorum
gaudemus triumphis proficiamus exemplis.

Praesta dne qs. ut sic scorum tuorum nos nos nos nata
litia celebranda non deserunt ita iugiter
suffragiis comitentur. per.

Adesto dne populo tuo scorum tuorum patrocinio
supplicanti. ut quod propria fiducia non praesumit
eorum suffragantium meritis consequatur. p.

Magnificanter dne clementiam tuam suppliciter
exoramus. ut qui nos scorum tuorum frequentibus
facis natalitiis interesse perpetuis tribuas
gaudere consortiis. per.

Tribue nobis omnips ds. in scorum tuorum te semper com
ii.

44 v

Ds qui unigeniti tui dni nri ihu xpi. ptioso sangui
ne. humanu genus redimere. dignatus es concede
ppitius. ut qui ad adorandam uiuificam cruce
adueniunt a peccatorum suorum nexib; liberentur. p.
Ds qui unigeniti filii tui ptioso sanguine uiuifice
crucis uexillu scificare uoluisti. concede qs
eos qui eius de sce crucis gaudent honore tua
quoq; ubiq; ptectione gaudere. p eundem.
Adesto dne ds nr. ut quos sce crucis honore leta
ri fecisti. eius quoq; ppetuis defende psidiis. p.
Ds qui unicu filiu tuu p omnib; nobis in morte cru
cis sponte dedisti concede omib; nob ut per te creden
tib; ut pereande mortem & morte p tua liberemur. p.
Ds qui salute humani generis in ligno crucis constitu
isti. ut unde mors oriebatur. inde uita resurgeret.
tribue qs. ut eius dem uitalis signi tuitione ab om
bus animam aduersis. p.
Ds qui per cruce & sanguine filii tui dni di nri dedisti pa
ce hominib; & caelestiu angelorum da nob & tue pa
cis ubertate repleri. & de angelice societatis unita
te laetari. p eundem dnm.
Ds cuius filius p salute generis humani de celo descen
dit

...ciuitas et adpropinquante hora passionis suae hiero
solimam in asino uenire statuit rex appellari
et laudari uoluit. benedicere dignare hos palmarum
caeterarumque frondium ramos. ut omnes qui eos laturi
sunt. ita benedictionis tuae dono repleantur. qua
tinus et in hoc saeclo hostis antiqui temptamenta super
are et in futuro cum palma uictoriae et fructu
bonorum operum tibi ualeant apparere. per eundem.

Deus qui in hierusalem ueniens
rex appellari et a pueris adorari uoluisti benedice
re dignare has frondes diuersarum arborum et praes
ta ut sicut eas a foris in amore nominis tui ferimus
ita etiam interius cetur in aula pectoris nostri feruore
dilectionis tuae semper inardescamus. qui uiuis.

Omnipotens sempiterne deus
respice propitius super hunc famulum tuum ill. quem
ad nouam tondendi gratiam uocare dignatus es et tribue
ei remissionem omnium peccatorum atque caelestium dono
rum consortium esse perceptorum. per.

Oratio pro renuntiante saeculo et cenobio se tradentem

Praesta quaesumus omnipotens deus ut hunc famulo tuo ill. qui ad
deponenda comam capitis sui propter amorem christi

filii tui festinat. da spm scm qui habitu pe

omis in eum perpetuu custodiat a mundi impedim

to et sclari desiderio cor eius defendat. ut sicut

immutatur in uultu ita manus dextere tue

in eu uirtutis tribuat. ut ab omni caecitate hum

ana oculos aperiat. et lumen aeternitatis gr

atiae concedat. per. Dū tondis eū dicis. An

Tues dne qui restitues mihi. V Dns pars et

gloria. Item an hic accipiet benedicti an

haec est generatio. Post tonsorata ora

Presta qs omps ds. ut famulu tuu cui hodie

comam capitis sui pro diuino amore deposuimus

ut in tua dilectio pmaneat. et eu sine macu

la in sempiternu custodias. p. ora ad capillatur

Omps sempt ds. respice propitius super

hunc famulu tuu ill. que ad noua tondendi

gratia uocare dignatus es et tribue ei remis

sione omiu peccatoru atq; caelestiu dono

rum consortium esse preceptoru. per

Ds cuius spu creatura omis ora ad barbas tan

adulta congaudet. exaudi pces nras

super hunc famulum tuu iuuenali aetatis

[susc]ipe laetantem. et prosperis auspiciis adtonden-
dum. Exaudi domine ut nominibus protectionis tuae muniatur auxilio. caelestem benedictionem accipiat.
et perferentiis uitae prosperis gaudeat aeternae. per.

Omnipotens sempiterne deus insere te officiis nostris et haec
uascula arte fabricata gentilium sublimita-
tis tuae potentia ita emundare digneris ut
omni inmunditia depulsa sint tuis fidelibus tempore pacis atque tranquillitatis utenda. per.

Deus qui adventu filii tui domini nostri
omnia tuis mundasti fidelibus adesto propitius
inuocationibus nostris et haec uascula quae tuae
indulgentiae pietatis. post spatia temporum
ab origine terrae abstracta humanis usibus
reddidisti gratiae tuae largitate emunda. per

Et quos libet uasorum

Protector fidelium deus subditorum tibi pectorum
habitator. quaesumus. ut digneris tuae pietatis haec uascula ita inlustrare digneris ut descendat
super ea gratiae tuae benedictio larga et cum
salubritate utentibus ea ipse per gratiam tuam
mirificantur uasa efficere munda et licet ego

rum indignus tanti officii tuum clementissime
dne dona locupletans etiam ad meam obsec
rationem intuere pietatis tuae inclina ut per
tuo imperio hunc humani generis hostis absce
dat procul diaboli fraus absistat. procul omnis
pollutione quitiae abstersa uanescat sint
libera ab omni inpugnatione fantasmatica.
per quo operantem filium tuum dnm nrm ihm
xpm qui tecum una cu spu sco uiuit et regnat
ds in secula sclorum. super arborum
Ds qui hanc arborem pomiferam tua iussione et pro
dentia generata esse uoluisti. hunc etia eande
benedicere et sctificare digneris precamur
ut quicumque ex ea sumpserint. incolumes ee.
ualeant. per super pomorum
Benedic dne hunc fructum nouu pomoru ut
hii qui utuntur ex eo sint sctificati. p. super panis
Benedic dne creaturam ista panis noui sicut
benedixisti quinque panes in deserto. ut dno
eius dem abundans in ipsum alimentu gus
tantes que ex eo. accipiant tam corporis
quam anime sanitatem. p. ad omnia quae uolue ris

reator et conservator humani generis da
tor gratiae spiritalis largitor aeternae salu
tis tu dñe mitte spiritũ tuũ scm̃ sup hanc
creaturã aquã .ł. ut armata virtute cae les
tis defensionis qui ex ea gustaverint pfici
at illis ad aeternã salutem. p.

Benedic dñe creaturam istam ut sit reme
dium salutare generi humano p
invocationẽ nominis tui qui cumq; ex ea
sumpserint corporis sanitatẽ et animae
tutelã pcipiat. per. B. domus.

Adesto dñe supplicationib; nris et hanc domũ
serenis oculis tuae pietatis inlustra descen
dat sup habitantes in ea gratiae tuae larga
benedictio ut his manu factis cum salubri
tate manentib; ipsi tuũ semp sint habi
taculũ. per. B in eo sanitas et casti

Benedic dñe ds omps locũ istũ ut sit nob
tas virtus et victoria et scimonia et hu
militas et bonitas et mansuetudo et lenitas et ple
nitudo legis et obedientia dõ patri et filio et spi
ritui scõ haec sit benedictio sup hunc locũ et sup
omnes habitantes in eo. per ma ne at p.

I bis ne coll.

I bis ne coll :.

omnes habitantes in eo quia dñe dixisti pax huic domui benedic dñe timentes te pusillos cũ maiorib;

Ut quando iudicium de igne fit hominis

Deus qui tribus pueris mitigasti flammas ignium concede
propitius ut nos famulos tuos non exurat flamma uitiorum.

Exorcismus aque ad iudicium peragendum

Exorcizo te creatura aque in nomine dei patris omni
potentis et in nomine ihesu christi filii eius domini nostri. ut fi
as aqua exorcizata ad effugandum omnem potestatem
inimici et omne fantasma diaboli. ut si hic homo ma
num suam inde missurus innocens est. unde reputatur
pietas dei omnipotentis liberet eum. et si quod absit culpa
bilis est. et presumptiosus inde manum suam mittere
ausus fuerit. eiusdem dei omnipotentis uirtus super
eum hoc declarare dignetur. ut omnis homo timeat et
contremescat. nomen sanctum gloriae domini nostri. qui uiuit.

Domine ihesu christe qui es iudex iustus fortis et patiens et
multum misericors per quem facta sunt omnia. deus deorum dominus
dominantium qui propter nos homines et propter nostram
salutem de sinu patris descendisti. et ex maria uirgi
ne carnem assummere dignatus es. et per passionem tuam
mundum redemisti. et ad inferos descendisti et diabolum
in tenebras exteriores colligasti et omnes iustos qui

... mali peccato ibi est damnebantur magna potentia exinde liberasti. Tu domine qui mittere dignatus sum
tuum sanctum ex summa caeli arce super hanc creaturam aq-
que ab igne requiescere uidetur. qui peccatum per iudicium super hunc hominem nomine .N. comprobet ac ma-
nifestet. qui uiuis et regnas deus.

Te domine deus supplices deprecamur qui in chana galileae
ex aqua uinum fecisti. et tres pueros sidrac misac et
abdenago de camino ignis ardentis inlaesos eduxisti. et susannam de falso crimine liberasti et caeco
nato oculos aperuisti. lazarum a monumento
suscitasti et petro mergenti manum porrexisti. ne
respicias peccata nostra in hac oratione. set tu uerum et rectum iudicium coram omnibus [illegible] manifestare
digneris. ut si hic homo pro hac reprobationis causa
[illegible] [illegible] manum [illegible] hac aqua bene re-
uente [illegible] [illegible] cura non
est hoc [illegible] [illegible] ut nulla [illegible]
[illegible] inbandi [illegible] appareat [illegible]
culpa [illegible] incurrat.

Deus iudex iustus fortis et patiens qui auctor
[illegible] et [illegible] et iudicas aequitatem. iudica

...omnipotens deus confitenti tibi huic famulo tuo .N.
tua pietate peccata relaxa: ut non plus ei noc
eat reatus ad poenam quam indulgentia tuae pie
tatis ad veniam per ...
Deus qui vestimentum salutare et indumentum aeternae io
cunditatis tuis fidelibus promisisti clementiam tuam
suppliciter exoramus: ut haec indumenta humili
tatem cordis et contemptum mundi significantia
quibus famula tua .N. sancto visibiliter ÷ informan
da proposito propitius benedicas: et beatae castitatis
habitum quem te inspirante suscepit te prote
gente custodiat. per
Deus bonorum virtutum dator et omnium benedictionum
largus infusor exaudi preces nostras et hanc ves
tem quam famula tua .N. pro conservanda casti
tatis signo se adoperiendam exposcit benedice
re et sanctificare digneris. per ...
Respice domine super hanc famulam tuam quae in ma
nus tuas continentiae suae propositum colloca
ti devotione tua offerit a quo ipsa vota as
sumpsit. per   Deus super hanc famulam
Te invocamus domine sancte pater omnipotens aeterne deus.

tuam .ill. que tibi uult seruire pura me[nte] ...

mundo que corde uitam sociare digneris. Inter illa

cxliiii milia infantum qui uirgines permanserunt

et se cum mulieribus non inquinauerunt. In quorum ore dolus

inuentus non est. Ita et hanc famulam tuam .ill. facias perma

nere inmaculatam usque in finem. Per inmaculatum dominum

nostrum ihesum christum. Item oratio ab episcopo dicenda

Respice domine propitius super hanc famulam tuam .ill. ut sancte

uirginitatis propositum quod te inspirante suscepit te

gubernante custodiat. Per   Prefatio

Deus castorum corporum benignus inhabitator et incorrup

tarum amator animarum. Respice super hanc famu

lam tuam .ill. que tibi deuotionem suam offert a quo et ipsa

tandem uotum assumpsit. Sit in ea domine per donum spiritus san

prudens modestia sapiens benignitas grauis lenit

as casta libertas. Feruet in caritate et nihil ex

tra te diligat laudabiliter que uiuat et laudari

non appetat te timeat. Tibi amore seruiat tu

ei honor tu gaudium tu in merore solatium tu in am

biguitate consilium tu in iniuria defensio in tri

bulatione patientia in paupertate habundan

tia in ieiunio cibus in infirmitate sis medicina

quem diligere sup omia appetit quo e. pfer
ta custodiat. ut et hostem antiquum deuincat et
uitiorum squalores expurget quatenus cente
simi fructus dono uirginitatis decorari uirgi
num que lampadibus exornari et electarum tuarum
uirginum consortium te donante mereatur uirgi

Uota quesumus dne famulae ... admira ipsius uirgini
tate ·ll· quam uirginitatis honore dignatus es de
corare incoati operis consummatum effectum
et perfectam tibi offerat plenitudinem. Ini
tia sua pducere mereatur ad finem. per

Oblatis hostiis dne qs presentis famu sr oblata
lae tuae ·ll· perseuerentiam ppetuae uirginitatis
accommoda ut apertis ianuis summi regis ad
uentum cum laetitia mereamur intrare. i pfacio

Hanc igitur oblationem famulae tuae ·ll· tibi of
ferit ob diem natalis sui in quo eam tibi spiri
tum sacro uelamine ptegere dignatus es
qs dne ppitiatus sanctifica ut tibi dno ac
sponso suo ueniente cum lampade sua in
extinguibili placitura occurrere merea
tur dies que nsus ad compl

Respice dñe famulę tuę tibi debitam
uirtutem ut inter humanę fragilitatis incer
ta nullis aduersitatibus opprimatur quę
de tua protectione confidit. P.
Exaudi nos omnipotens et misericors ds. ut quid nostro
ministratur officio tua benedictione potius
impleatur. P. Lec. epis. beati pauli apostoli ad chor.
FRs. Nescitis quoniam corpora ura membra xpi
sunt. Tollens ergo membra xpi faciam me
bra meretricis? Absit. An nescitis quoniam qui
adheret meretrici unum corpus efficitur? Erunt enim
inquid duo in carne una. Qui autem adheret dño: unus
spiritus est. Fugite fornicationem. Omne peccatum quod
cumque fecerit homo extra corpus est; qui autem fornicatur
in corpus suum peccat. An nescitis quoniam
membra ura templum est sps sci qui in uobis est,
Quem habetis a dō et non estis uestri? Empti enim estis
pretio magno. Glorificate et portate dm in corpore
Sec. secundum mathēum Lucio.
In illo temp. loquebatur ihs cum discipulis suis
in parabolis dicens simile factum est regnum caelorum
homini regi qui fecit nuptias filio suo; et misit
seruos suos uocare inuitatos ad nuptias et nolu

... uenire. iterum misit alios seruos suos dicens
dicite inuitatis. Ecce prandium meum paraui tauri
mei et altilia occisa et omnia parata uenite. ad nup
tias. Illi autem neglexerunt. et abierunt alius in uil
lam suam alius ad negotionem suam. Reliqui uero
tenuerunt seruos eius et contumelias affectos
occiderunt. Rex autem cum audisset iratus est. et missis
exercitibus suis perdidit homicidas illos et ciui
tatem illorum succendit. Tunc ait seruis suis. Nup
tiae quidem paratae sunt. sed qui inuitati erant
non fuerunt digni. Ite ergo ad exitus uiarum. et quo
scumque inueneritis uocate ad nuptias. Et
egressi serui eius in uias. congregauerunt omnes qu
os inuenerunt malos et bonos. et impletae sunt nup
tiae discumbentium. Intrauit autem rex ut uideret
discumbentes et uidit ibi hominem non uestitum
ueste nuptiali. et ait illi. amice quomodo
huc intrasti non habens uestem nuptialem. at
ille obmutuit. Tunc dixit rex ministris. ligatis pe
dibus eius et manibus. mittite eum in tenebras exte
riores. Ibi erit fletus et stridor dentium. Multi
sunt uocati pauci uero electi.
Suscipe quaesumus domine pro sacro conubii lege munus oblatum

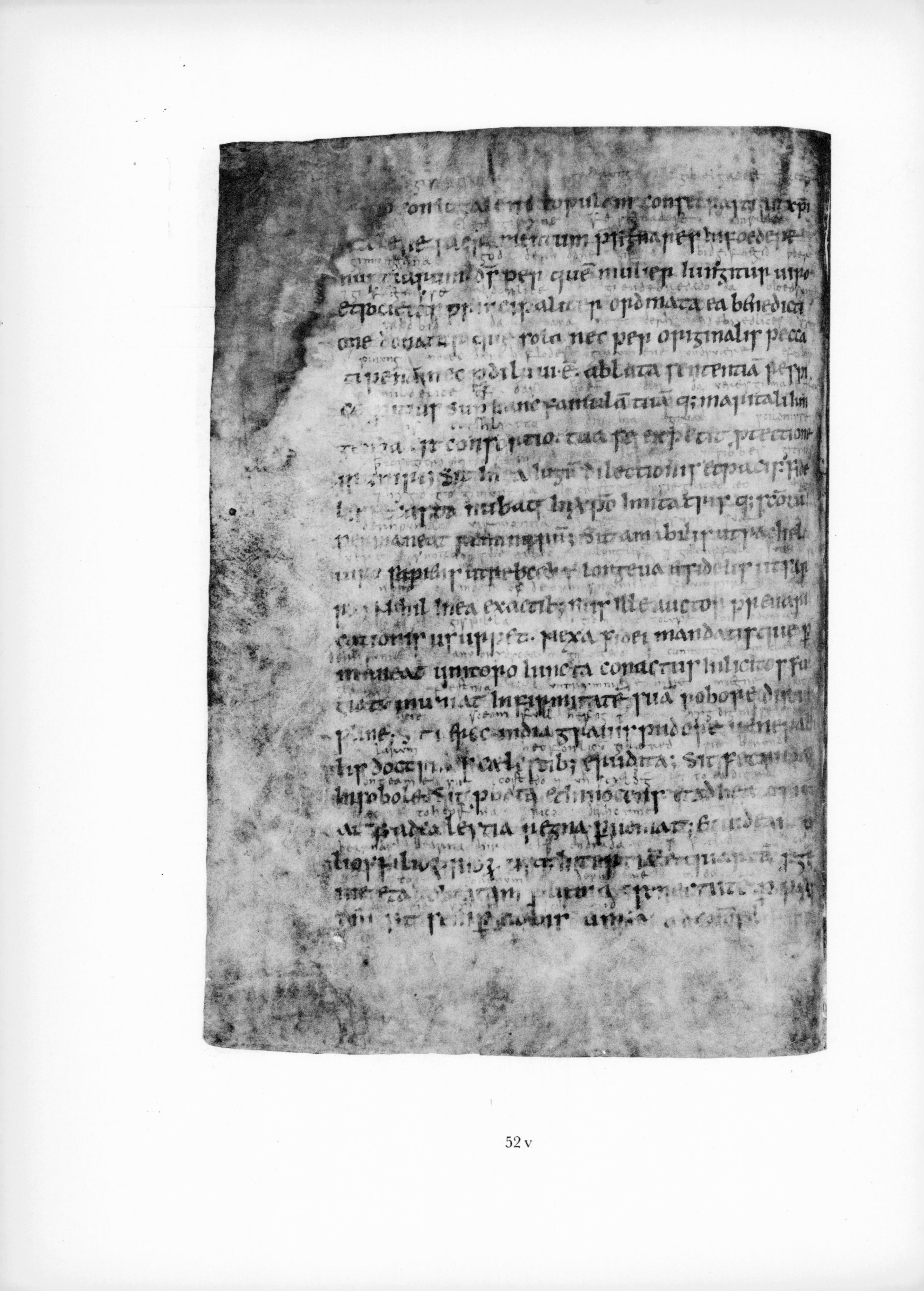

52 v

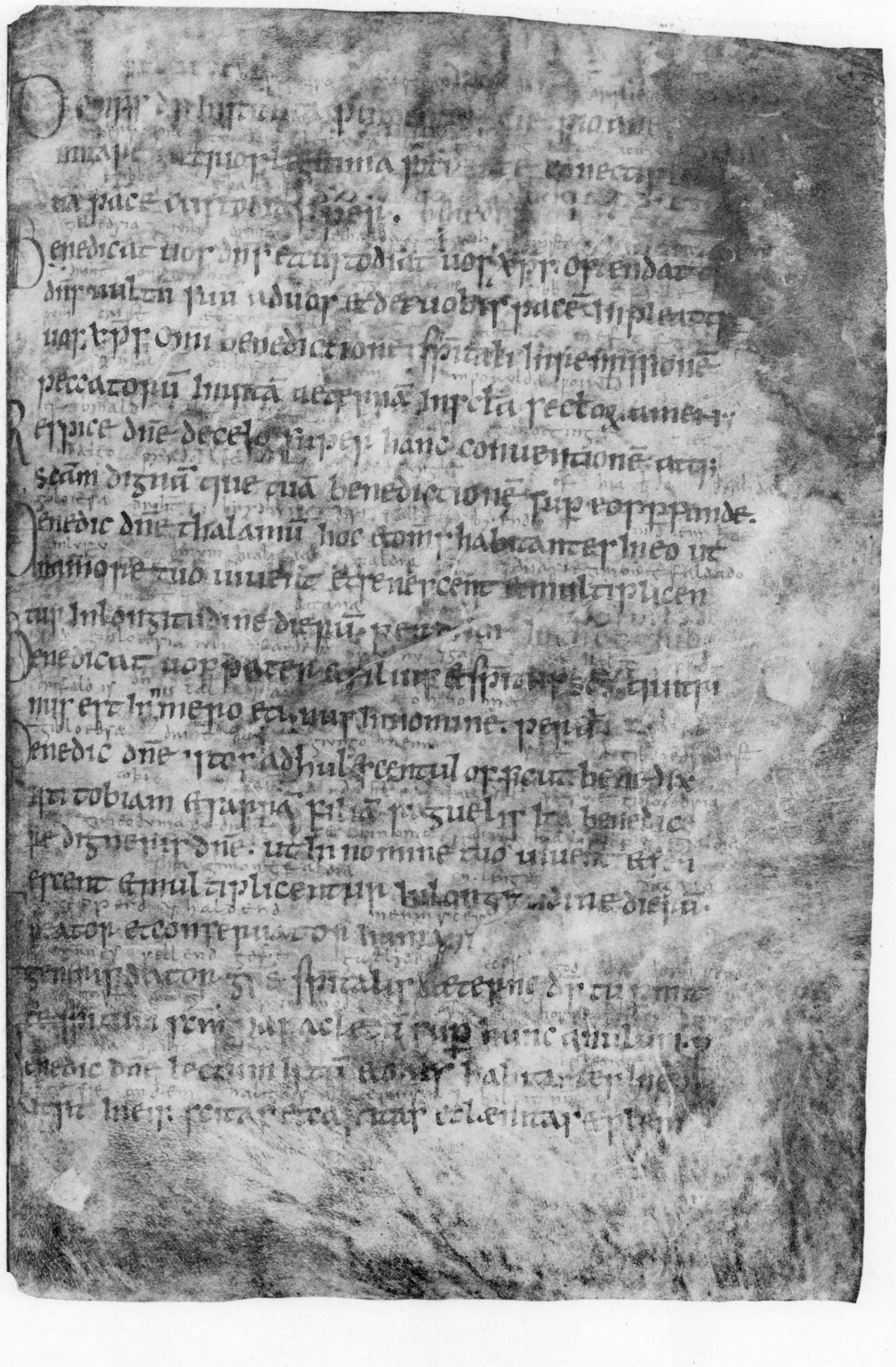

De[us] [illegible] ... [illegible]
[illegible] ... conecti[illegible]
[illegible] pace [illegible]
Benedicat uos dominus et custodiat uos. Christus ostendat
dominus uultum suum in uos et det uobis pacem. Impleat
uos Christus omni benedictione spiritali in remissione
peccatorum ... uitam aeternam in secula seculorum. amen.
Respice domine de celo super hanc conuentionem et
sicut dignum [illegible] tua benedictione super [illegible]
Benedic domine thalamum hoc et omnes habitantes in eo ut
in amore tuo uiuant et senescant et multiplicentur
in longitudine dierum. per.
Benedicat uos pater et filius et spiritus sanctus trinus
et unus in nomine. per.
Benedic domine istos adolescentulos sicut benedixisti
tobiam et sarram filiam raguelis ita benedicere
digneris domine ut in nomine tuo uiuant et senescant et multiplicentur in longitudine dierum.
[illegible]ator et conseruator humani [illegible]
[illegible] spiritalis [illegible]
[illegible] super hunc [illegible]
Benedic domine lectum hunc [illegible] habitantes in
[illegible]

Auctor salutis unicus · mundi redemptor
insignis tu xpe nobis annue crucis secunda glori[a]
sputa · colaphos · uincula · et dira passus uerbera
crucem uolens ascenderas · nostrae salutis gratia ·
hinc morte mortem diruens · uitamque uita largi
ens · mortis ministrum subdolum · deuiceras
diabulum · Nunc in parentis dextera ·
sacrata fulgens uictima · audi precamur
uirido · tuo redemptos sanguine ·
Quo te sequentes omnibus · morum pro
cessu sci · aduersus omne
scandalum · ferramus ·
laborum · Presta pater per
filium · presta per almum spm ·
cum his per euum triplici · unus
ds cognomine · amen ·

[De]us qui per ignem signa magna [illegible]
ostendens abraham puerum tuum [illegible]
caldeorum quibusdam pereuntibus eruisti et [illegible]
bum ardere in conspectu moysi et mini[me]
comburi permisisti. Deus qui ab incendio forna[cis]
caldaici plerisque succensis tres pueros [tuos]
illesos eduxisti, Deus qui incendio ignis populum sodome et gomorre involvens loht famulum tuum cum suis salute donasti; Deus qui in
adventum tuum sancti spiritus tui inlustratione ignis fideles tuos ab infidelibus [illegible] decrevisti, Ostende nobis in hoc parvitatis nostrae examine vir-
tutem eiusdem spiritus sancti et per huius ignis fervorem
discernere fideles et infideles. ut tactus eius fur-
tu criminis vel alterius cuius inquisitio agitur
conscii contremescant manus eorum aut pedes combu-
rantur aliquatenus innocentes vero ab eius
modi crimine liberi [illegible] permaneant et inlesi permaneant. Adiuro te creatura per deum patrem
et filium et spiritum sanctum et per tremendum diem iudicii
et per xii apostolos et per septuaginta discipul-
os et per xii prophetas et per xii patriarchas et per xxiiii

tione in nominis tui dñe hic com[illegible]

quod diabolo instigante ocultū nob[illegible]

innocentes iusso et inmunes ab hoc [illegible]

leros ee patiatur. Recognoscant om[illegible]

tes dm hic quia ipse est benedictus in

seculorum. amen. [illegible]

Ic eow halsige on fæder naman [illegible]

and ðurh drihten hælende crist ⁊ on

ðæs halgan gastes ⁊ for ðære cristnesse ðe

ge under fenge. ⁊ for ða halgan ðrinesse

⁊ for ða .IIII. god spelleras. matheus ⁊ marc

us ⁊ lucas et iohannes. ⁊ for ealle ða halg

an reliquias ðe gind ealne middan geard sin

don halgra martyra ⁊ for ealle ða halgan

godes ciricean ðe her on weorolde gehalgode

sien ⁊ for naman ðære halgan fæmnan sce

sca marian ðæt ge to ðis huse ne gangen ne

to ðam oðer dæle gif ge [illegible] on eow [illegible]

de eow [illegible] oððe on [illegible]

[illegible]

[illegible]

Benedic dñe ihu xpe in nomine di patris et filii

ri oculos tobie sci. & sicut aperuisti
duorum cecorum clamantium tibi in itinere
adicentium miserere nostri fili dauid & ...
et illis & aperti sunt oculi eorum perdinon.

S pater omnipotens & ihu xpe ihu fili di
uiui & sps sci porro te. ut mittere digneris
benedictionem tuam & medicinam celestem sup
hanc creaturam potionis uel unguenti. ut
prodeant omnibus hominibus uel pecoribus quibus
et sanitas fiat eis in omnibus membris illorum
corporum. ut non possit diabolus nocere eis
nec in uisu nec in risu. nec in auditu nec in am
bulando nec in gustu ciborum. nec in bibendo po
tus. sed tu dne clemens qui es saluator sa hal
nos eos facias ab omni periculo per benedictio
nem & creaturam huius unguenti uel potus
in nomine patris & filii & spi tus sci per uirtu
tem dominice passionis & resurrectionis am
ortuis ut sanctificate uerbo dei benedictione
adiuuamant aduersus omnes nequitias spiritales
et tumuras ualitudines & infirmitates
membrorum. ut qui cumque sumpserint

[illegible]tutelam mentis & corporis sumant in
[illegible] dni nri ihu xpi qui [illegible] bened
[illegible]infecta peccatorum amen.

[illegible]e pater omnips aeterne ds qui fecisti cae
lum & terram mare & omnia que in eis sunt. ro
go te & peto in nomine ihu xpi uniti filii tui
ut sanctificare digneris & benedicere epulam
istam sicut benedixisti epulationem habra
hae isaac iacob & sic benedixisti rex hydrias in
chanan galileae atque in uinum bonum conuerte
runt de aqua ita conuertere digneris mate
riam istam ceruisie in suauitatem & hilaritatem
seruis tuis his qui in fide catholicha crediderunt.

Benedictio tuo dne qs corpora sup has feras ad
ueniat. ut de uenatione bestiarum tua gratia
donante et benefitio tuo largitatis celeriter gra
tias tibi absoluere mereamur. per.

[C]oncede qs omnips ds has [illegible] passione huius [illegible]
edicti & spalis in tuo nomine significatas has
feras humano usui aptas bestias ad capien[illegible]

dari fieri iubeas ut omne quod per eam ...
ere re mereamur tibi ad laudem ...
tione perperamur. per dominum. benedictio ...

Deus omnipotens et deus abraham et deus isaac et deus iacob im
mitte in hanc creaturam tuam salis et aquae bene
dictionem tuam ad capiendas capras. et ceteris umi
odoris tui et virtute sentiant. ut sint servis
tuis munimentum tutela que defentionis et ne
liceat hostis in animas eorum et aditum credere ha
bere non possit. per.

Exorcizo te creatura salis in no
mine patris et filii et spiritus sancti qui te per helise
um in aquam mitti iussit ut sanaretur steri
litas aquae qui divina sua voce dixit. vos estis
sal terrae ad uptos ut omnes qui ex eo sumpse
rint sint sanati animis atque corporibus et
ubicumque fuerit aspersus praestet omnibus re
missionem peccatorum et sanctitatem in protectionem
salutis et ad expellendas et excludendas omnes
demonum temptationes in nomine dei patris omni
potentis et ihesu christi filii eius qui venturus est iudica
turus in spiritu sancto seculum per ignem amen.

pacis est. super animalia nostra custodiat
potestis diabolus inequitate illa habraham
atque vos per ac diuinitas dei dei ad dextram angelum
ministram propheta vos prosequentur martyres
te cedant vos pastores que prosequentur uos
todiat dominus oves et boves vitulos et equos et apar
todiant que vos hic pastores. signum crucis xpi
ihu in nomine dei summi per dominum. Oratio ad infantes
Omnipotens sempiterne qui regenerare dignatus es consignandos
et hunc famulum tuum ex aqua et spiritu sancto quique
dedisti ei remissionem omnium peccatorum tu domine inmitte
in eum septiformem spiritum tuum sanctum paraclitum de celis. da ei spiritum sapientie et intellectus. spiritum con-
silii et fortitudinis spiritum scientie et pietatis et im-
ple eum spiritu timoris dei et domini nostri ihu xpi. et con-
signa eum signo sancte crucis tuae propitiatus in vitam eternam. per dominum nostrum ihm xpm filium tuum cum
quo uiuis et regnas in unitate spiritus sancti per omnia secula
seculorum. Amen

Pax tibi. et cum spiritu tuo. ecce sic benedicetur omnis
homo. usque omnibus diebus vite tuae.

[Exorcismus] salis

[Exorciz]o te creatura salis per deum uiuum per deum
[uerum] per deum sanctum per deum qui te per heliseum prophetam
in aquam mitti iussit ut sanaretur sterelitas
aquae ut efficiaris sal exorcizatum in salutem
credentium et sis omnibus te sumentibus sanitas animae et corporis et effugiat atque discedat ab eo
loco quo aspersus fueris omnis fantasia et nequitia uel uersutia diabolicae fraudis omnisque
spiritus inmundus adiuratus per eum qui uenturus
est iudicare uiuos et mortuos et saeculum per ignem

Immensam clementiam
tuam omnipotens aeterne deus humiliter imploramus
ut hanc creaturam salis quam in usum generis
humani tribuisti benedicere et sanctificare tua
pietate digneris ut sit omnibus sumentibus salus
mentis et corporis et quicquid eo tactum uel
respersum fuerit careat omni inmunditia omni-
que inpugnatione spiritalis nequitiae per dominum

Exorcismus aque

Exorcizo te aqua in nomine dei patris omnipotentis
et in nomine iesu christi filii eius domini nostri ut fias aq-

59 r

phabitantes inea gratiae tue larga...
hīs manu factis habitaculis unum fidelium...
nentes ipsi semper habitaculum. p̄

Exaudi nos dne sce pater omps aeterne ds. ut
qua sunt adversa sic qua contraria in domo
uli tui auctoritate maiestati tuae pellentur.

In hac prima diei hora tis cne
tua nos reple misericordia. ut per tota die exul
tantes in tuis laudibus delectemur. p dnm
nr ihm xpm. Qui opa tertia diei ad crucem pro nam
pro mundi salute ductus es te supplices deprecamur
ut sua deleas peccata ut et de praeteritis malis nos
semper aput te inveniamus ubique et de futuris iugi
ter habeamus custodiam. ihu xpe qui cum

Domine ihu xpe. qui dum hora sexta pro redemptione
mundi crucis ascendisti lignum ut universus mun
dus in tenebris converteretur. illa nobis lux tua ani
ma et corpore nostro semper tribue per quam ad aeter
nam vitam pervenire mereamur ihu xpe qui

Domine ihu xpe qui hora nona in cruce pateris
confitentem latronem intra moenia paradisi transi

[...]e supplicer confitentes peccata nostra
[...] ut post obitum nostrum paradisi portas intro
[...] gaudentes concedas. ihu xpe. qui cum
[...]ias tibi agimus dne custoditi per diem gratias
tibi exsoluimus custodiendi per noctem representa nos
[...] dne matutinis horis incolomes ut nos omni tem
pore habeas laudatores. per dnm.

[D]ne ihu xpe qui nos redemisti de tuo sco pretio
so sanguine presta nob recorpore requies
cere ut tibi semp mente & corde uigilemus. p.

Exaudi nos ds salutaris nr. & apostolorum tuorum nos
tuere presidiis quorum donasti fideles esse doct
rinis. per dnm

Omps sempit ds. qui nos omnium aplorum me
rita sub una tribuisti celebritate uenera
ri. Q[uaesumus] ut celere nob tuae ppitiationis ha
bundantia multiplicatis intercessoribus
largiatur. per

Omps sempit ds. placabilis sit tibi haec oblatio
quam ego indignus pro me misero peccatore & pro de
lictis innumerabilibus meis remissione peccat[orum]

omips

arcus [...]
arcus [...]

concedas et iniquitates meas. Ne respe[illegible]
la misericordia tua pro indigno. P[illegible]
nos semper perfice has oblationes quas [illegible]
aurem clementiae tuae emitto pro me et [illegible]
is et benefactoribus meis et elemosinariis [illegible]
michi commississ seu quibus debitorum..

Et nunc sequimur in toto corde et timemus te et
querimus faciem tuam domine ne confundas nos
sed fac nobis iuxta mansuetudinem tuam et secundum
multitudinem misericordiae tuae..,

Domine deus pater et filius et spiritus
sanctus cui omnia subiecta sunt et cui omnis creatura deser-
vit et omnis potestas subiecta est et metuit et expaves-
cit et draco fugit et silet vipera et rubeta illa que dicitur
rana torpescit scorpius extinguitur regulus vincitur et spa-
lagius nihil noxium operatur et omnia venenata et adhuc
ferociora repentia et animalia noxia tenebrantur et
omnes adversae salutis humanae radices arescunt tu ex-
tingue hoc venenatum virus operationes eius morti-
feras et vires quas in se habet evacua et da in conspectu tuo
omnibus quos tu creasti oculos ut videant aures ut audiant cor et magnitudinem tuam intellegant.

Incipiunt benedictiones ad lectionem:

Ds di filius qui hodierna die de uirgine nasci
dignatus est misereatur nri. amen:

Ds uerus et homo uerus natus ex uirgine nos bndicat;

Rex regum hodie natus nos custodire dignet; amen

Regnans cum patre nat ex matre xps nos bdicat;

Saluator mundi natus ex uirgine nos saluare dignet

Redemptor mundi gentium hodie nat conseruet nos dns

Auctor uitae nat ex uirgine misereatur nobis dns;

Ds pacis et dilectionis hodie nat sit cum omnib; nobis

Ipse nos benedicat in terris qui hodie nasci dignatus
est ex uirgine; amen: + de epiphania:

Ds di filius qui hodierna die mundo apparere
dignatus est misereatur nri. amen:

+ de resurrectione: dignetur. amen

Xps di filius ab aeterna morte nos liberare

Saluator mundi pro nobis passus et a morte
resurgens nos saluare dignetur. amen:

Ds di filius qui hodie a mortuis resurgere dignatus
est misereatur nri amen + de ascensione:

Ds di filius qui hodierna di caelos ascendit
misereatur nri nunc et in secula. + de pente

Ds di filius qui hodierna die discipulis suis pro[illegible]

missis sp[iritu]m n[ost]ra inlustrare dignetur corda [illegible]

† De adventu dni.

Ds di filius quem in utero virginum colimus det nobis veniam

nostrorum delictorum. Cotidianis diebus.

Ab omni malo defendat nos dns. amen

A cunctis malis imminentibus liberet nos dns. amen

A morte secunda eripiat nos dns. am.

Divina maiestas nos tueatur. am.

Ds di filius nos benedicere dignetur. am.

Divina gratia nos benedicat. am.

De sede sca sua aspiciat nos dns. am.

Creator omnium nos benedicat. am.

Benedictionibus suis repleat nos dns. am.

Custos omnium custodiat nos xps. am.

Ipse nos benedicat qui nos creavit. am.

Protegat famulos suos omps dns. am.

Sps scs nra inlustrare dignetur corda. am.

Trinitas sca nos benedicat. am.

Sps scs aperiat nobis sensum cordis. am.

Salvet et benedicat nos omnips dns. am.

Pietas sua et gratia confirmet nos dns. am.

[illegible] sca [illegible] conservet nos dns. am.

[illegible] benedicat nobis

62 r

Intcedente pro nobis scā dī genetrice maria
ampliatam nobis omps dns · am.
Presentium sca dī genetrix maria in suo sco
partu conforta nos dns · am. omps dns · amen.
Rex regum et dns dominantium da pacem in diebus nris
Dns omps sca trinitas misereatur nri ... in
secula seculorum · amen. De apostolum
Intcedentibus pro nobis xpi apostolorum meritis
succurrat nobis omps dns. De martyrum
Intcedentibus pro nobis xpi martyrum meritis
misereatur nri omps dns · am.
Intcedentibus pro nobis xpi confessorum meritis exau
diat omps dns · amen. De omnibus scis
Omnium scorum suorum meritis eruat nos dns
a malis cunctis pro nobis xpi intcedentibus sce
salvatoris mundi misereatur nri amen.
Scis intcedentibus xpe tuorum electis succur
re nobis omps dns. benedictio lactis et mel
Benedic dne et has creaturas fontis et lactis et mel
lis et pota famulos tuos de hoc fonte perenne gi
... et reple eos de hoc melle et lacte
[illegible]
[illegible]
[illegible]
[illegible]
[illegible]

62 v

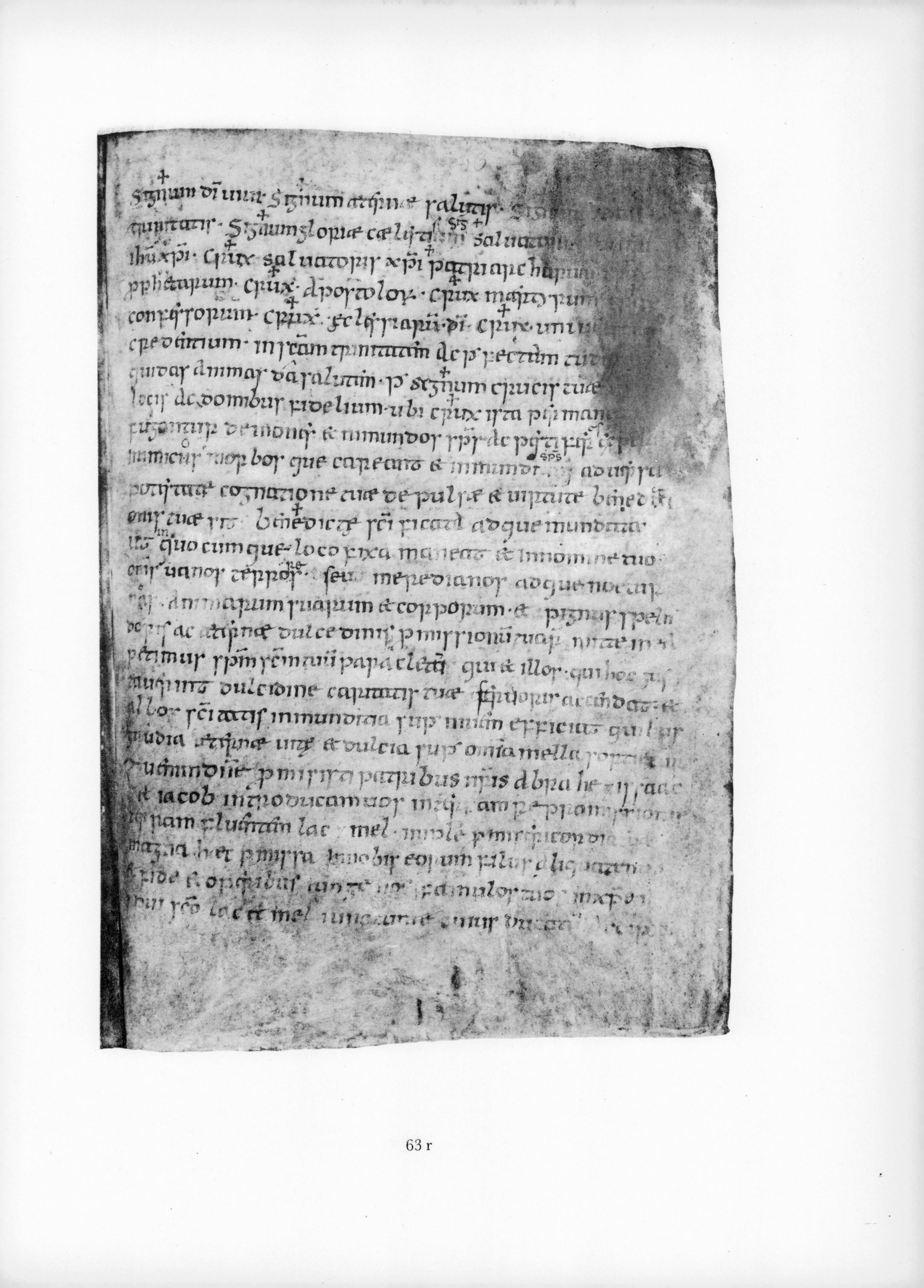

63 r

[illegible] albidinem in quam uitae passionem
[illegible] operant discipulis in monte transfiguratae
[illegible] albidinem aetherna in perruptionem suam [illegible]
[illegible] ellis commendit p quam haec omnia dne :

Benedic dne et hos fructus nouos uuae quos
tu dne rore caeli et inundatione pluuiarum
et temporum serenitate ad maturitatem per
ducere dignatus es et dedisti ea ad usus nos
tros cum gratiarum actione percipere in no
mine dni nri ihu xpi. p.

Benedic dne creaturam istam panis nouam
sicut benedixisti quinque panes in deserto
et duos pisces et .u. milia hominum saciasti
ita benedicere digneris ut sit dominis eiusdem ha
bundans in annum alimentum gustantesque quique
eo accipiant tam corporis quam animae sani
tatem per te xpe ihu qui regnas in saecula saecu
lum. p. // nucleos qui et omnibus fructum

Dne sce pater omps sci fica pomas et nuces
arbor quam herbarum qui tuo imperio us
um omnibus praebent animantibus. p.
Per quem haec omnia. Benedictio putei.

Deprecamur domine clementiam pietatis tuae [illegible]
putei huius sanctifices et ad eum cunctis [illegible] con[illegible]
salubrem esse ita ut ab eo fugare digneris omnem di[illegible]
temptationis incursum utquicumque ex eo ad hinc [illegible]
bibere uiae uel in quibus libet necessariis usibus [illegible]
hausta aquae usus fugit totius uirtutis [illegible]
mitas dulcedine perfruatur [illegible] sanctifica[illegible]
et saluatori omnium domino gratias agere mereatur. per

Praeces seruorum tuorum deus.
miserator exaudi. qui uiuis.
& regnas. per omnia saecula
saeculorum. Amen:.

Exaudi quesumus domine pre
ces seruorum tuorum.
& perduc nos ad regna caelorum.
qui uiuis & regnas deus per
omnia secula seculorum. amen:.

[illegible] salutis unicus · mundi redemptor inclitus · tu xpe nobis annuam · cunctis secundum gloriam ; Tu sputa · colaphos uincula · & dira passus uerbera · crucem uolens ascenderas · nostrae salutis gratia ; Hinc morte mortem diruens · mundumque uita largiens · mortis ministrum subdolum · deuincens diabolum ; Hunc impenetras dextera · sacrata fulgens uictima · audi precamur unido · tuo redemptos sanguine ; Quo te sequentes omnibus · morum processu seculi · aduersus omne scandalum · crucis feramus labarum ; Presta pater per filium · presta per almum spm · cum his per euum triplici · unus ds cognomine · amen :–

RESP. DE TOBI

Peto dne ut de uincula
Qui regis isrl intende
Omni tempore benedic dm
Memor esto fili qm pau.
Memor esto fili qm
fiducia magna est
Sufficiebat nobis
Heu me fili mi ut quid
Benedicite dm caeli
Tempus est ut reuertar

Tempus est ut reuertar
Benedicite dm caeli

Nos ... mittis ... dne
Omni tempore benedic
Memor esto fili qm
Tempus est ut reuertar

RESP. DE IUDITH

Adonai dne ds magnae
Qui regis isrl intende
Tribulationes ciu
Peccauimus cum patribus

Benedicite d...
Qui regis isrl
Nos alium d...
Qui regis isrl
Recordare mei d...
Exurge dne adiu...
Dominator dne
Qui regis isrl
Allide uirtutem
Adonai dne ds
Tu dne cum humili...

[illegible]

Adaperiat dns cor urm in
Exaudiat dns orationes nras
Tua est potentia tuum regnum
Qui regis isrl intende
Refulsit sol in clippeis aur
Disrumpam uincula populi
Impetum inimicorum ne timue
Memento mirabilium eius
Ornauerunt faciem templi cor
In hymnis et confessionibus
In hymnis et confessionib; be
Ornauerunt faciem templi
Congregati sunt inimici
Disperge illos in uirtute
Dixit iudas simoni fratri
Ut te ne clamemus in celum
Hic est fratrum amator
Ecce quam bonum et quam

An. unde supra.

Adaperiat dns cor urm
Da pacem dne in dieb; nris
Tua est potentia tuum reg.
Refulsit sol in clippeis
Lugebat autem iudam sup.
[illegible]
Vidi dnm se[illegible]
dentem sup solium ex
Seraphin stabat sup so
Aspice dne de sede sca
Qui regis isrl intende
Aspice dne quia facta est
Qui dicunt exinanite

Sup muros tuos ie[illegible]
Qui reminiscimini[illegible]
Muro tuo inexpugna[illegible]
Qui regis isrl intende
Sustinuimus pacem et non
peccauimus cum patrib; nris
Misit dns angelum suum
Misit ds misericordiam sua
Angustie mihi undiq;
Si enim hoc egero mors
Laudabilis populus quem
Qui regis isrl intende

An. unde supra

Vidi dnm sedentem sup
Aspice dne quia facta est
Sup muros tuos hirlm
Muro tuo inexpugnabi

Audi benigne conditor nostras
preces cum fletibus, in hoc sa
cro ieiunio, fusas quadragenario.
Scrutator alme cordium, infir
ma tu scis cordium [t uirium] ad te reuer
sis exhibe remissionis gratiam.
Multum quidem peccauimus, sed parce
confitentib; ad laudem tui nominis
confer medelam languidis; Sic
corpus extra conteri dona per
abstinentiam, ieiunet ut mens sobria
a labe prorsus criminum. Presta
beata trinitas concede simplex
unitas: ut fructuosa sint tuis
ieiuniorum munera. Amen.

ymnus infra xl ma.

Vexilla regis prodeunt. fulget crucis mysterium
quo carne carnis conditor suspensus est patibulo.
Confixa clavis viscera tendens manus vestigia.
redemptionis gratia hic immolata est hostia.
Quo vulneratus insuper mucrone diro lanceae.
ut nos lavaret crimine. manavit unda et sanguine.
t cecinit
Impleta sunt que concinit. david fideli carmine. di
cendo nationibus. regnavit a ligno deus.
Arbor decora et fulgida. ornata regis purpura
electo digno stipite. tam sancta membra tangere.
beata cuius brachiis pretium pependit seculi. statera fac
ta est corporis. predam que tulit tartari. Fundis aroma
cortice vincis saporem nectare iocunda fructu fer
tili. plaudis triumpho nobili. Salve ara salve victima
de passionis gloria. qua vita mortem pertulit. et mor
te vitam reddidit amen. :— maris rubri xpo cana
Ad cenam agni providi stolis albis candidi post transitum
mus principi. Cuius sacrum corpusculum. in ara
crucis torridum cruore eius roseo gustando vivimus deo.
Protecti pasche vespere. a devastante angelo. erepti
de durissimo pharaonis imperio. Iam pascha nostrum xps
est qui immolatus agnus est sinceritatis azima caro eius
oblata est. O vere digna hostia. per quam fracta sunt tartara
redempta plebs captivata reddita vite premia. Consurgit
xps tumulo victor redit de baratro. tyrannum trudens
vinculo et reserans paradisum. Quesumus auctor omnium in hoc pa
scali gaudio. ab omni mortis impetu tuum defendas populum.
Gloria tibi domine qui surrexisti a mortuis. cum patre et sancto spiritu in
sempiterna secula amen.

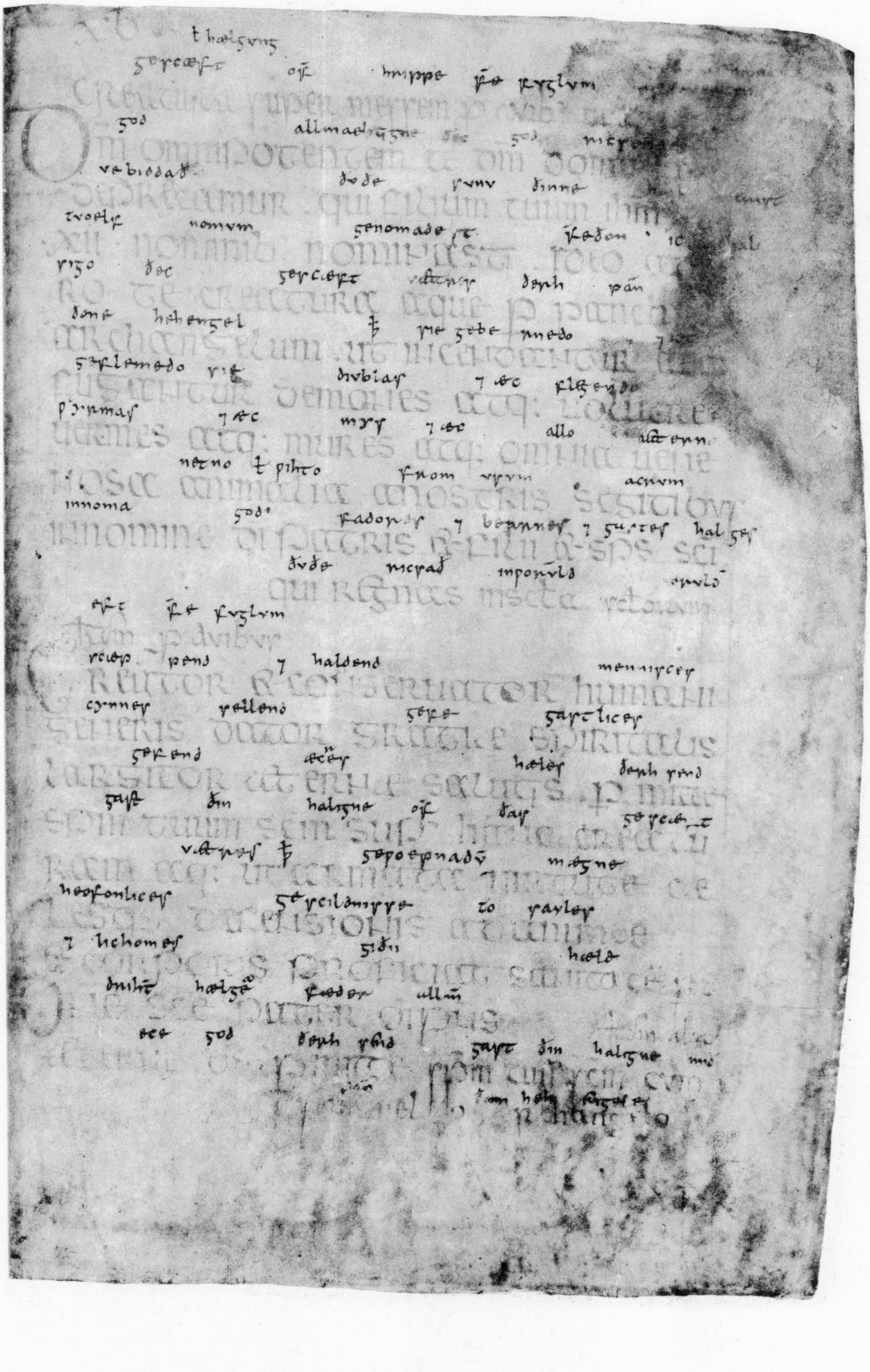

[...] perdat segites nostras uer
minibus. uolatilib. demonib. a ful
minib. ab omni temptatione dia
buli per inuocationem sci nominis
tui ihu xpe qui regnas cum patre
et cum spu sco uiuis in scla sclorum

Praecamur te dne sce pr
omnips aeterne ds. satia semen se
minatem quam uult in nomine tuo pa
nacchuhel qui est sup omnes fructus
terrae et sup semina cu quattuor
qui draginta milib. angelorum
qui hac creatura aliquid sumat
uel sup effussa tra in lesa p
maneat. ut magnificetur nomen
tuum in uniuersa tra t in oi loco
ut sciant gentes quoniam non est
alius ds praeter te. Per dnm om
nipotentem et p dominum dominan
tem et p filium suum ihm xpm
qui .xii. apostolos nominauit

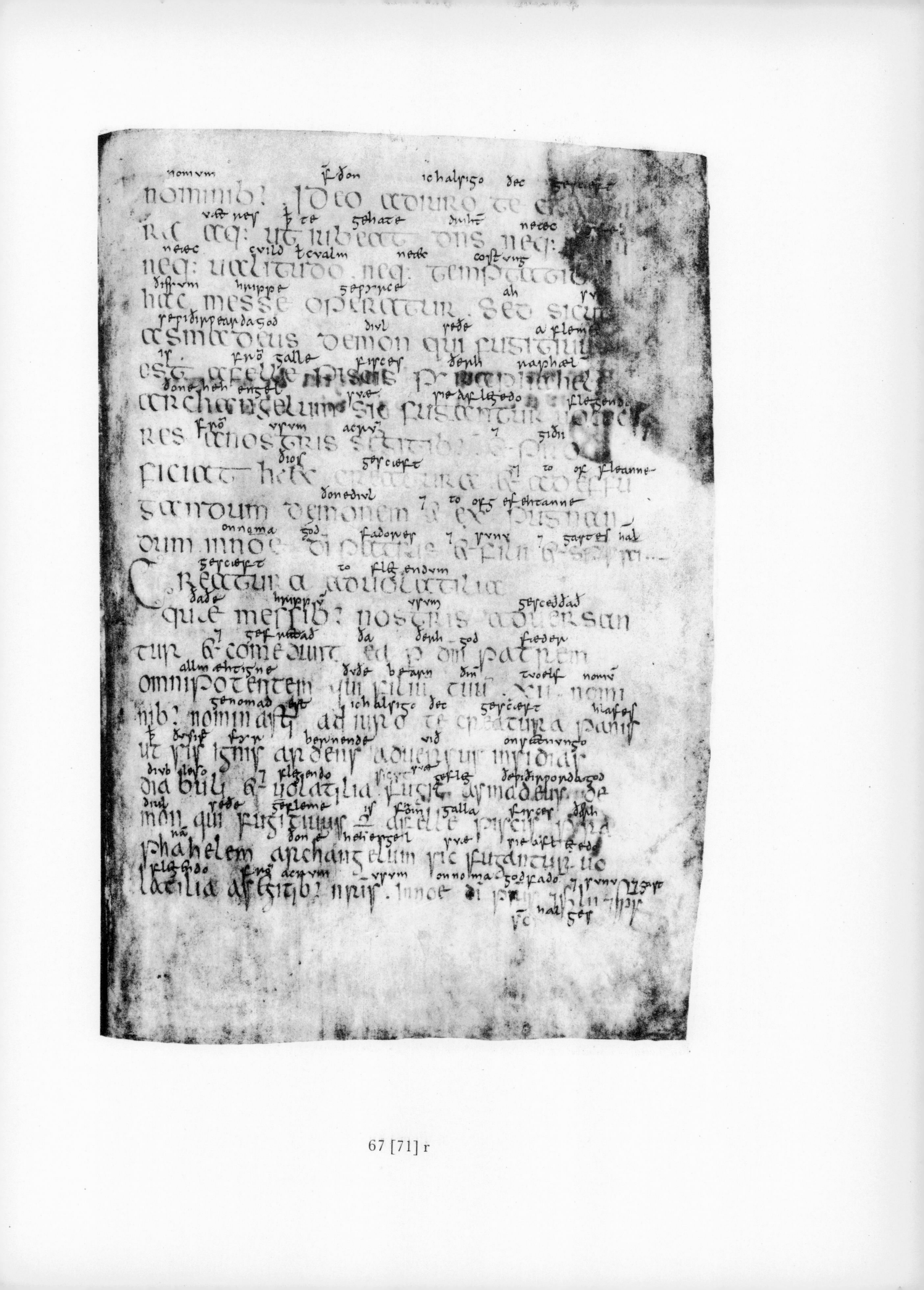

[illegible] digneris dn̄e per serenum uultum tuum [illegible] hanc creaturam aquę & per benedictionem quam benedicimus ut abiciantur uolucres caeli & aues ab ea per inuocationem nominis tui patris & filii & spiritus sci.

[illegible] mittatur sal in aqua. benedictio aquae. Or. Dn̄s uobiscum

Ds inuictę uirtutis auctor & insuperabilis imperii rex ac semper magnificus triumphator. qui aduersę dominationes uires reprimis. qui inimici rugientis saeuitiam superas. qui hostiles nequitias potens expugnas. te dn̄e trementes ac supplices deprecamur ac petimus. ut hanc creaturam salis & aquę dignanter accipias. benignus inlustres. pietatis tuę more scī fices ut ubi cumque fuerit aspersa per inuocationem scī tui nominis omnis infestatio inmundi sp̄s abiciatur. terror quoque uenenosi serpentis procul pellatur. & praesentia scī sp̄s nobis misericordiam tuam poscentibus ubique adesse dignetur. per

Oratio in domo.

Exaudi nos scē pater omnipotens aeterne ds & mittere digneris angelum tuum de celis qui custodiat foueat protegat uisitet & defendat omnes habitantes in hoc habi

[..]culo. p. bene dixio dom[..]
Adesto dne supplicationibus nris et hanc domum
sepe nis oculis tue pietatis inlustra. descendat
super habitantes in ea gratie tue larga bene dictio
ut in his manu factis habitaculis cum salubritate
manentes ipsi tuum semper sint habitaculum. p.
Exaudi nos sce pater omps aeterne ds.
Ut si qua sunt contraria in hac domo famulo
rum tuorum. ut famuli tui auctoritate maies
tati tue pellantur. p.
Benedic ds omps locum istum. ut sit nobis in eo
sanitas. scitas et castitas uirtus uictoria
et sci monia et humilitas et bonitas et mansuetudo
et lenitas. et plenitudo legis. et oboedientia do pri.
et filio et spui sco et sit semper benedictio super
hunc locum et super omnes habitantes in eo. p.
or. Vespertine laudis officia; dns uobiscum et cum spu tuo
persoluentes clementiam tuam dne humili prece deposcimus.
ut nocturni insidiatoris fraudes te protegente uincamus. p.
O[..] sempiterne ds uespere et mane et meridie omnes
maiestatem tuam suppliciter deprecamur. ut expulsis
de cordibus nris peccatorum nrorum tenebris ad ueram
lucem que xps est nos facias peruenire. p. omn[..]
or. Ds luminis aeternum et splendor siderum. claritas noctis et
illuminatio et inconprehensa tene brarum. da nobis dne
noctem hanc dominicam quietam pacificam tranquillam
et securam habere. et si qua dne hodie peccata ignorantes uel
scientes admisimus [..] clementi miseratione repelle. p.

[illegible] homo

an [illegible] am adoramus dne & s(an)c(t)am recolimus passio
[illegible] passus est pro nobis in cruce ... ds s(an)c(t)e

op Respice dne super hanc familiam tuam pro qua dns nr
[illegible] non dubitavit manibus tradi nocentium et
crucis subire tormentum p. ant. & or. ad crucem.

[illegible] ac benignus indulge p(e)cc(at)is q(uo)q(ue) supplicum tuorum
liberatos exaudi & postulata concede. omps. alia

Oratur dne noctis tenebris atque aurora iustitie
[illegible] acto die tibi supplicantes gratias agentes etiam
mane dignanter perspicias uota solventes p. alia

Concede [illegible] iustitie permanere in cordibus nostris
ad repellendas tenebras cogitationum. p. alia or.

Vespertina oratio nostra ascendat ad aures clementie
tue dne s(an)c(t)e pater omps eterne ds. & discendat gloriosa
benedictio tua super nos ut hic & in eternum te
auxiliante semper salvari mereamur. p.

[illegible] ad crucem cum oratio.

Adoramus te xpe benedicimus tibi quia per crucem tuam
redemisti mundum. V dicite in nationibus. alia or.

Adesto dne ds nr & quos s(an)c(t)e crucis letare fecisti
honore eius quoque perpetuis defende subsidiis. p.

Per signum crucis de inimicis nostris libera nos
dne ds nr; V omnis terra adoret te ds & psallat tibi

or. V [illegible] dne tua pace custodi quos s(an)c(t)e
crucis letare fecisti honore eius quoque perpetuis
defende subsidiis. p. alia an. O crux benedicta que
sola fuisti digna portare regem celorum & dominum ... ds s(an)c(t)e

or. Ds qui preclaro salutifere crucis honore eterne
redemptionis gaudia nobis dicasti tribue qs ut a
[illegible] abs omnibus semper muniamur adversis. p.

[illegible] an. Michael archangelus venit
in adiutorium populo dei. V in conspectu angelorum

·· predicamus·

or Da quesumus domine omnipotens deus beati mihaelis archangeli honore [...]
mo proficere. ut cuius in terris gloriam predicamus adiuuemur [...]
an Maria uirgo semper letare que meruisti christum portare celi
et terre conditorem. et de uentre tuo protulisti mundi saluatorem.
Diffusa est gratia in labiis tuis propterea benedixit te. oper[...]
Famulorum tuorum quesumus domine delictis ignosce. ut qui placere
de actibus nostris non ualemus. genitricis filii tui domini nostri ihesu
christi intercessione saluemur. per. an Beata mater et in
nupta uirgo gloriosa regina mundi oper[...]
or Concede nos famulos tuos quesumus domine deus perpetua mentis et
corporis sanitate gaudere. et gloriosa beate marie
semper uirginis intercessione. a presenti liberari tristicia
et futura perfrui letitia. per. antiphona de mihaelo archangelo
an Mihael gabriel raphael cherubin et seraphin qui non
cessant clamare cotidie dicentes dignus es domine accipere gloriam.
v In conspectu angelorum psallam tibi, oper[...]
or Deus qui miro ordine angelorum ministeria hominumque
dispensas. concede propitius ut quibus tibi ministrantibus
in celo semper assistitur ab his in terris nostra uita muniatur. per.
an Iohannes uocabitur nomen eius et in natiuitate eius multi
gaudebunt. v Ipse preibit ante illum in spiritu et uirtute helie.
Omnipotens sempiterne deus da cordibus nostris illam tuarum
rectitudinem semitarum quam beati iohannis baptiste in deserto uox
clamantis edocuit. per. an Beatus petrus apostolus
uidit sibi christum occurrere adorans eum et ait domine quo
uadis. uenio roma iterum crucifigi. an Tu es petrus et
super petram edificabo ecclesiam meam et porte inferi
non preualebunt aduersus eam. v In omnem terram exiuit
or Deus qui beato petro apostolo tuo conlatis clauibus
regni celestis animas ligandi atque soluendi ponti
ficatum tradidisti. suscipe propitius preces nostras
quesumus domine auxilium ut a peccatorum nostrorum nexibus libere
mur. per.

[A]ndreas xpi famulus dign͞s dō apos͞ germanꝰ
petri et in passione socius. Andreas uiro rogabat
ad populum ne impediret passionem eius;
[Maies]tatem tuam dne supliciter exoramus ut sicut eccle
siae tuae beatus andreas apos͞ tuus extitit predicator
et rector. ita apud te sit pro nobis ppetuus intercessor. p
[N]imis honorati sunt amici tui ds͞ nimis confor[tatus est principatus eorum].
[Ds͞ qui no]s per beatos apostolos tuos petrum
et paulum et andream ad cognitionem tui nominis uenire
tribuisti. da nobis eorum gloriam sempiternam et proficien
do celebrare. et celebrando proficere. p. [Corpora sanctorum]
[in] pace sepulta sunt et uiuent nomina eorum [in aeternum]
an̄ Sce paule apostoli predicator ueritatis et doctor
gentium intercede pro nobis ad dm̄ qui te elegit.
Nimis honorati sunt amici tui ds͞ nimis; [De paulo apos͞]
[Ds͞ qui] multitudinem gentium beati pauli apostoli
predicatione docuisti. da qs͞. ut cuius natalicia [t. memoriam] coli
mus huius apud te patrocinia sentiamus. p.
an̄ [Hic est] ioh̄ dilectꝰ discipl͞ qui supra pectꝰ dn̄i in cena [recubuit]
ṽ hic est ioh̄ amator castitatis et custos matris ei͞s.
or̄ Ds͞ qui per os beati iohannis euangelistae uerbi tui
nobis archana reserasti. presta qs͞. ut quod ille nostris
auribus excellenter infudit. intellegentiae conpetentis
eruditione capiamus. p. ad confessoribus;
an̄ Iustum deduxit dn̄s per uias rectas et ostendit illi regnū di.
ṽ amauit eum dn̄s et ornauit eum stola gloriae induit.
or̄ [E]xaudi dn̄e preces nostras quas in sci [tui] confessoris tui
[...]at que pontificis [quaesumus] commemoratione de[fer]im[us]
tibi [...]. ab omnib; nos absolue peccatis. p. ad martyr
or̄ [P]resta qs͞ omps͞ ds͞ ut intercedente beato [...] marti
tyre tuo a cunctis aduersitatibus liberemur
et [...] a prauis cogitationibus nos mundemur in mente. p

or Adesto dne supplicationibus nostris [illegible]
et apostolicis intercessionib; confidentes. nec m[illegible] ad
uersantium. nec ullo perturbemur incursu; per
or Ds qui per gloriosa bella certaminis ad inmortalitatem
triumphos (?) digna per eorum commemorationem laetitia gau[illegible]
ut quorum gaudemus triumphis prouocemur exemplis. per
an Iustorum animae in manu dei sunt et non tanget illos tormentum mortis. V. gloria et ho[nore]
Adesto dne supplicationib; nostris per intercessionem omnium
sanctorum tuorum. commonitis omnib; sanctis [illegible]
Concede qs omps ds ut sca nouem ordinib; angelorum
et archangelorum patriarcharum et prophetarum et
sca dei genitrix maria sci quoque tui apostoli martyres
uirgines confessores perfecti quoque tui iusti nos ubique
laetificent. ut dum eorum merita recolimus patrocinia sentiamus. per
or Ds consolationis et pacis respice propitius [illegible]
ad preces familiae tuae. et da dne uirtutum ut animae
famulorum famularumque tuarum. qui et que ab adam
usque in hodiernum diem. de hac luce migrauerunt. et
baptizati siue confessi fuerunt. et in fide catholica
perseuerauerunt. et de eorum reb; aecclesias dei ditauerunt.
et de quorum elemosinis sumus consolati. qs dne ut in si
nib; abrahe et isaac et iacob. in illa sanctorum tuorum
sede requiescant. mox que et mortuis resuscita
tur placeant in regione uiuorum. V. laetamini in dno et
or Praesta qs dne ut intercedentib; omnium
meritis quorum commemorationem puro corde capiamus. per
an Uia iustorum recta facta est et iter sanctorum praeparatum est. V. laetamini in dno
or Scorum suffragia imploremus ut a cunctis dne
liberemur offensis. per alia oratio
or Adesto dne supplicationib; nostris quas in sanctorum
tuorum commemorationem deferimus ut qui
nostrae iustitiae fiduciam non habemus eorum qui tibi.

placuisse inspicis adiuuemur. p[er] [illegible]
[illegible] leu [illegible] de p[illegible] [illegible]
[illegible] [illegible] [illegible]

Lectio

Sicut in adam omnes moriuntur ita et in christo ihesu omnes
uiuificantur. unus enim quisque in ordine suo in quo
uocatus est in eo permaneat. R. Requiem aeternam dona eis
domine et lux perpetua luceat eis. V. Audiui uocem de caelo dicentem beati mor[tui]
memoria aeterna erit iustus ab auditione mala non timebit.
preciosa est in conspectu domini mors sanctorum eius.
Redimet dominus animas seruorum suorum et non derel[inquet]
Or. Fidelium deus omnium conditor et redemptor [illegible] defunctorum
redemptor animabus famulorum famularumque
tuarum remissionem cunctorum tribue peccatorum. ut in
dulgentiam quam semper optauerunt. piis supplicatio
nibus consequantur. p[er] [illegible] nocte [illegible] et requie [illegible]
da anima mea. Requiem aeternam. Iustorum [illegible] anime
in manu dei sunt et non tanget illos; gloria et honore.
Or. Animas quaesumus quas creasti domine suscipere iubeas
in regnum tuum. et in sinu abrahe collocare facias. et
cum beato lazaro portionem accipiant; exultabunt [sancti]
Or. Deus uita uiuentium. spes morientium. Alia or. ad [illegible]
tium. salus omnium in te sperantium; praesta domine propitius
ut animae famulorum famularumque tuarum
a nexis mortalitatis tenebris absolute. in perpe
tua cum sanctis tuis luce laetentur; p[er]. Alia or. ad [illegible]
Or. Intendant quaesumus domine preces nostras intercedentibus
omnibus sanctis agminibus angelorum. ut animae
famulorum tuorum famularumque tuarum
quorum et quarum [illegible] hic sunt conscripta. gaudia
aeterna suscipiant. ut quos fecisti adoptio
nis participes. iubeas hereditatis tuae esse consortes.
[illegible]

Ds cuius misericordia non est numerus suscipe pro anima famuli tui .n. preces nostras lucem laetitiam que in regione sanctorum tuorum in pontificum societate concede. per.
Ds qui inter apostolicos sacerdotes famulum tuum .n. pontificale fecisti dignitate uigere. presta quesumus ut eorum quoque perpetuo ad gregem consortio. per.

Missa de sancta trinitate; Benedicta sit sancta trinitas atque indiuisa unitas confitemini ei quia fecit nobiscum misericordiam suam;

Omnipotens sempiterne ds qui dedisti nobis famulis tuis in confessione uere fidei aeterne trinitatis gloriam agnoscere et in potentia maiestatis adorare unitatem quesumus ut eiusdem fidei firmitate ab omnibus semper muniamur aduersis. per.

Lectio epistolae beati pauli apostoli ad corinthios.

Fratres gratia domini nostri ihesu christi et caritas dei et communicatio sancti spiritus sit cum omnibus nobis;

Sequentia sancti euangelii secundum iohannem.

In illo tempore dixit ihesus discipulis suis; Cum uenerit paraclitus quem ego mittam uobis a patre spiritum ueritatis qui a patre procedit ille testimonium perhibebit de me. Et uos testimonium perhibebitis qui ab initio mecum estis; hec locutus sum uobis ut non scandalizemini absque synagogis facient uos; Sed uenit hora ut omnis qui interficit uos arbitretur se obsequium prestare deo; Et hec facient.

Animabus quesumus domine famulorum famularumque tuarum misericordiam concede perpetuam ut eis proficiat in aeternum quod in te sperauerunt et crediderunt. per.

... nouistis patrem neque me; Sed haec locutus sum uobis: ut cum uenerit hora eorum reminis-
camini quia ego dixi uobis;

Proficiat nobis ad salutem corporis et
animae dñe ds huius sacramenti susceptio et
sempiternae scae trinitatis confessio. p.

Statuit ei dns testam... Os iusti medita...

Exaudi dñe preces nostras quas in sci confessoris tui .ill. atque pontificis solemnitate deferimus ut qui tibi digne meruit famulari ei(us)
intercedentibus meritis ab omnibus nos absolue
peccatis. p.

Ecce sacerdos magnus qui in diebus suis placuit
do et inuentus est iustus; et in tempore iracundiae factus est reconciliatio; Non est inuentus similis illi: qui conseruaret legem excelsi;
Ideo iure iurando fecit illum dns crescere in
plebem suam; Benedictionem omnium gentium
dedit illi: et testamentum suum confirmauit
super caput eius; Cognouit eum in benedictionib;
suis: confirmauit illi misericordiam suam et
inuenit gratiam coram oculis dni; Magnificauit
eum in conspectu regum: et dedit illi coronam gloriae; Statuit illi testamentum sempiternum: et dedit illi sacerdotium magnum:
et beatificauit illum in gloria; Fungi sacer-

Animae ... dne famulorum famularum quorumque ill.
oratio proficiat supplicantium ut eas et a peccatis
omnibus exuas et redemptionis facias esse participes. p.

dotio: & habere laudem innomine [illegible]

& offerre illi incensum dignum:

inodorem suauitatis:— [illegible]

Ecce sacerdos magnus [illegible]

Sequentia sci euangelii secundum matheum

In illo tempore: Dixit ihs discipulis suis; Quis putas est fidelis seruus & prudens quem constituit dns supra familiam suam ut det illis cybum in tempore; beatus [illegible] seruus ille: quem cum uenerit dns eius: inuenerit sic facientem; Amen dico uobis: quoniam super omnia bona sua constituet eum;

Sumentes dne gaudia sempiterna participatione sacramenti presta quesumus ut beati N confessoris tui cuius natalitia colimus precibus adiuuemur. p.

Letabitur iustus in dno [illegible]

Ds qui nos beati N in confessoris tui annua solemnitate letificas concede propitius ut cuius natalitia colimus etiam actiones imitemur. p. lec lib sapientiae

Beatus uir qui in sapientia sua morabitur: & qui in iustitia meditabitur & in sensu cogitabit circumspectionem di; Cybauit illum pane uitae & intellectus

Ascendant ad te dne preces nrae et animas famulorum famularumque tuarum gaudia aeterna suscipiant ut quos fecisti adoptionis participes iubeas hereditatis tuae esse consortes. p.

[illegible] sunt : [illegible] sunt : [illegible]
[illegible] in montem [illegible] ; [illegible]
[illegible] ; [illegible] ang[illegible] [illegible]
dignatus non [illegible] ; [illegible] oblationibus [illegible]
et in orationibus et in supplicationibus et [illegible]
et in omnibus [illegible] per [illegible]
in xpo ihu dno nro . [illegible]

Dix(it) ihs discipulis suis . Ponite ergo
in cordibus uestris . non praemeditari quemadmodum
respondeatis ; ego enim dabo uobis os et sapientiam
cui non poterunt resistere . et contradicere omnes ad-
uersarii uestri ; trademini autem a parentibus et
fratribus et cognatis et amicis et morte adficient
ex uobis ; et eritis odio omnibus hominibus propter
nomen meum ; et capillus de capite uestro non peribit .
In patientia uestra possidebitis animas uestras .

Exultabunt sancti in gloria laetabuntur . [illegible]

De passione martyrum celebrata solemnitate
quaesumus omnipotens deus ut sanctorum tuorum commemoratione
laetemur et tuam semper misericordiam [illegible]
[illegible] consequamur per [illegible]

Deus qui omnipotens es et qui beatam [illegible]
[illegible] uirginis [illegible]
[illegible]

73 [66] r

[illegible] mun et in templo p[lectio libri sapientiae]

[Quasi cedrus ex]altata sum in libano: et quasi
[cy]pressus in monte sion: Quasi palma exal
[ta]ta sum in cades: et quasi plantatio rosae in
[hie]richo: Quasi oliua speciosa in campis: et
[qu]asi platanus exaltata sum iuxta aquam in pla
[te]is: Sicut cinnamomum et balsamum: aromati
[za]ns odorem dedi; Quasi myrrha electa: dedi
suauitatem odoris; dilexisti iustitiam et odisti iniquitatem.

[illegible] secundum matheum.

[I]n illo tempore: dixit ihs discipulis suis parabolam
hanc: Simile est regnum celorum decem uirginibus;
que accipientes lampades suas: exierunt obuiam
sponso et sponse; quinque autem ex eis erant fatue
et quinque prudentes: Sed quinque fatue: acceptis
lampadibus non sumpserunt oleum secum; pru
dentes uero: acceperunt oleum in uasis suis cum lam
padibus; Moram autem faciente sponso: dormi
tauerunt omnes et dormierunt; Media autem noc
te; clamor factus est: ecce sponsus uenit exite
obuiam ei: Tunc surrexerunt omnes uirgines ille:
et ornauerunt lampades suas: fatue autem
sapientibus dixerunt; Date nobis de oleo uestro
quia lampades nostre extinguntur; Responderunt
prudentes dicentes; Ne forte non sufficiat

nobis & uobis: ite potius ad uendentes: & emite

Dum autem irent emere: uenit sponsus: & que parate

erant intrauerunt cum eo ad nuptias. & clausa est

ianua. Nouissime uero ueniunt & relique uirgines

dicentes: Dne dne aperi nobis; At ille respondens

ait: Amen dico uobis nescio uos; Uigilate itaque

quia nescitis diem neque horam:

Prosit plebi tue omps ds beate ill. uir

ginis uel martyris tue ueneranda sollempni

tas: ut cuius gaudet honoribus

Concede nobis qs omps ds. uenturam beati

confessoris tui ill. apostoli uel martyris sollempni

tatem congruo preuenire honore & uenientem

digna celebrare deuotione. p.

Iustus cor suum tradet ad uigilandum diluculo

ad dnm qui fecit illum: & in conspectu altissimi

deprecabitur; Aperiet os suum in oratione & pro

delictis suis deprecabitur; Si enim dns magnus

uoluerit: spu intellegentie replebit illum: & ipse

tamquam imbres mittet eloquia sapientie sue:

& in oratione sua confitebitur dno;

get consilium & disciplinam doctrine

& secreta eius

disciplinam doctrine eius: & in lege

gloriabitur

[glori]abitur; Conlaudabunt multi sapientiam eius: et usque in seculum non delebitur; Non recedet memoriam eius: et nomen eius requiretur a generatione in generationem:-

[illegible]

In illo tempore: dixit ihs discipulis suis; Vigilate ergo: quia nescitis qua hora dns vester venturus sit; illud autem scitote: quod si sciret pater familias qua hora fur venturus esset: vigilaret utique et non sineret perfodi domum suam; ideoque et vos estote parati: quia nescitis qua hora filius hominis venturus est; Quis putas est fidelis servus et prudens. quem constituit dns suus super familiam suam ut det illis cybum in tempore: beatus ille servus quem cum venerit dns eius invenerit sic facientem; Amen dico vobis quoniam super omnia bona sua constituet eum;

Benedictionis tuae dne intercedente beato confessore et martyre uel apostolo tuo ill suscipiamus ut cuius praesenti sollemnitate gloriamur celebramus ei supplicando auxilium sentiamus. p.

+ In natale unius apostoli uel martyris:-

Ds qui nos omnium sanctorum splendor mirabilis quique hunc diem beati apostoli tui ill martyrio consecrasti. da ecclesiae tuae de eius natalitio sem[per]

per gaudere ut apud misericordiam tuam [illegible]
pergamur et meritis. p. Lec. lib. sapientiae.
Beatus vir qui inventus est sine macula: et qui post
aurum non abiit nec speravit in pecuniae the-
sauris; quis est hic et laudabimus eum: fecit enim
mirabilia in vita sua, qui potuit transgredi et non
est transgressus. et facere mala et non fecit; ideo
stabilita sunt bona illius in domino: et elemosynas
illius: et enarrabit omnis ecclesia sanctorum:- Secundum Iohannem:
In illo tempore:- dixit Ihesus discipulis suis; Hoc est
preceptum meum: ut diligatis invicem sicut dilexi
vos; maiorem hanc dilectionem nemo habet: ut animam
suam ponat quis pro amicis suis; Vos amici mei estis:
si feceritis que ego precipio vobis; Iam non dicam
vos servos: quia nescit quid faciat dominus eius;
Vos autem dixi amicos: quia omnia quecumque
audivi a patre meo: nota feci vobis; Non vos
me elegistis: sed ego elegi vos; et posui vos ut
eatis: et fructum afferatis et fructus vester
maneat; ut quodcumque petieritis patrem in
nomine meo: det vobis; Ad compl.:-
Da nobis quaesumus domine deus noster beati apostoli tui Iohannis
intercessionibus (cod.) sublevari ut per quos
ecclesiae tuae suis in muneribus rudimenta donasti
per eos subsidia perpetuae salutis impendas. p.

ihs xps

Illo tempore: dixit ihs discipulis suis: parabolam
hanc; Homo quidam peregre proficiscens: uocauit
seruos suos et tradidit illis bona sua; Et uni dedit
quinque talenta: alii autem duo alii uero unum; Uni
cuique secundum propriam uirtutem: et profectus est
statim; Habiit autem qui quinque talenta acceperat:
et operatus est in eis et lucratus est alia quinque;
Similiter qui duo acceperat: lucratus est alia duo;
Qui autem unum acceperat: habiens fodit in terram
abscondit pecuniam domini sui; Post multum uero
temporis: uenit dominus seruorum illorum: et posuit
rationem cum eis; Et accedens qui quinque talenta ac
ceperat: obtulit alia quinque talenta dicens;
Domine quinque talenta tradidisti mihi: ecce alia
quinque super lucratus sum; Ait illi dominus eius;
Euge serue bone et fidelis: quia super pauca fuisti
fidelis: supra multa te constituam intra in
gaudium domini tui; Accessit autem et qui duo talen
ta acceperat et ait; Domine: duo talenta quae
tradidisti mihi: ecce alia duo lucratus sum; Ait
illi dominus eius; Euge serue bone et fidelis: quia
super pauca fuisti fidelis: supra multa te
constituam; intra in gaudium domini tui;

Dominus saluet honoret amet
aldhunum antistitem

[Lu]mini splendoris aū dne qs corda nra inlumina et ...
pro tectione omni tempore uite nre ab omni infestatione
[ini]mici inlesos nos conserua p. Alia
[In] hac prima diei hora qs dne tua nos reple misericordia
ut per tota die exultantes in tuis laudib; delectemur p. or ...
[Ti]bi subnexibus precibus xpo dno supplicamus qui hora ...
tertia spm scm apostolis tuis orantibus emisisti eiusdem
gratiam participationibus nobis poscentibus iubeas conce[dere] ...
Dne ihu xpe qui multa mirabilia fecisti et . oratio a[d]
sexta hora pro nobis in cruce ascendisti et adam de infer
no eruisti eumque in paradiso restituisti qs te ut ab omnib;
peccatis nris eripere nos iubeas et in operibus tuis scis
semper custodias ihu xpe p. oratio ad nonam :·
Nona igitur diei hora ad te dne directa supplicatione
que cultoribus tuis diuina monstrata miracula nra
quoque eorum imitatione corda purifica p. or ad completorium :
Illumina dne tenebrosa corda nra et totius noctis in
sidias inimici a nobis repelle ut te protegente ad auroram tēpu[s]
mente et corpore incolomes peruenire mereamur p. ...
Noctem hanc inlumina mentibus nris omps eterne ds et
effice nos famulos tuos dormire sine criminibus et uirtu
tibus excitari ut liberi ab omni opere tenebrarum ad diem
clarum te adiuuante peruenire mereamur p. Item alia
Dne ihu xpe qui nos redemisti de tuo sanguine precioso p̄s
ut nos hic corpore requiescere ut mente et corpore
tibi semper uigilemus p. abcdefghikl[m] ...

Dne

76 [69] v

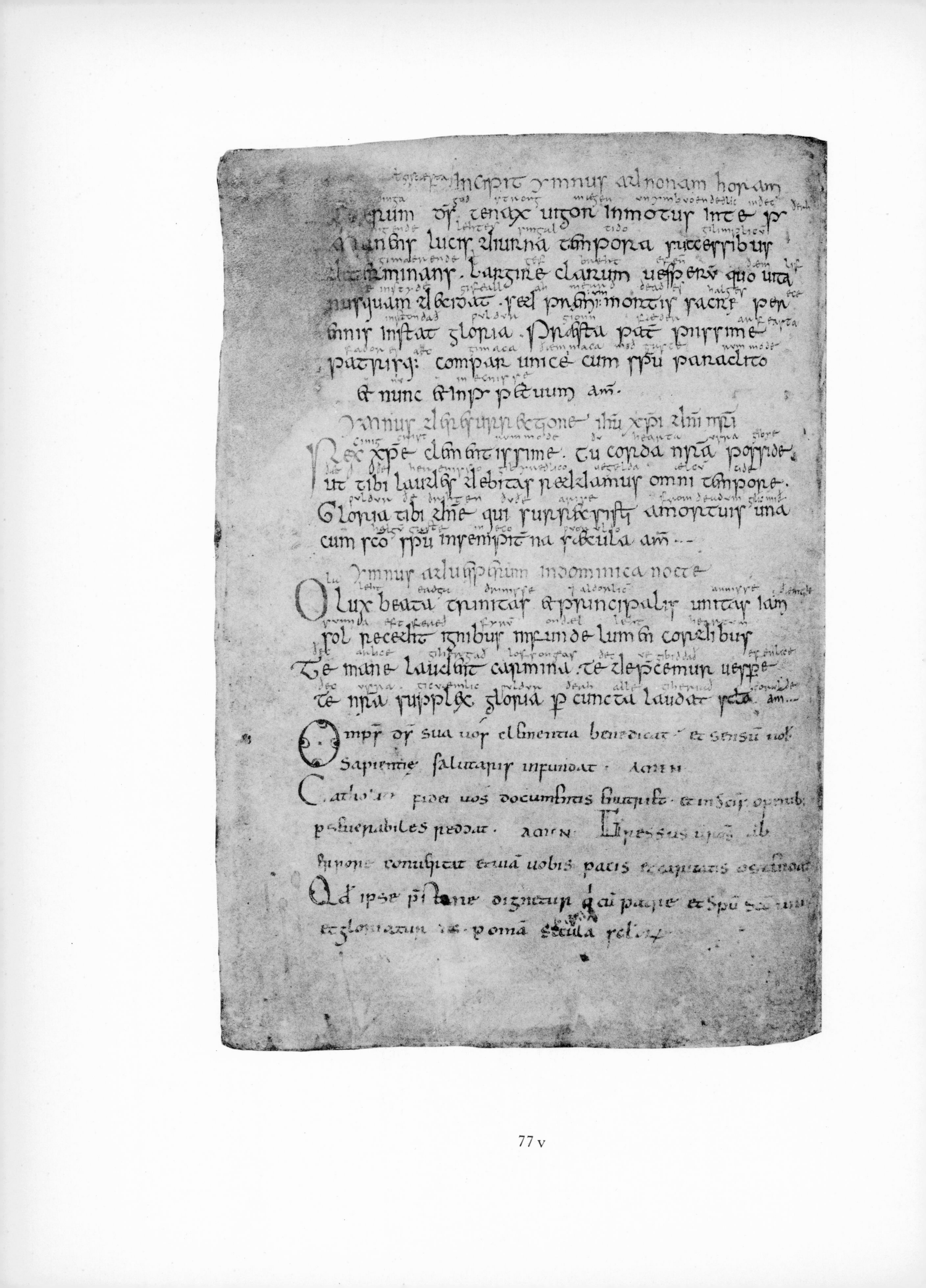

77 v

Misereatur tibi fr̄
omnip̄s ds̄. & dimittat tibi
omnia peccata tua pre
terita p̄sentia & futura
& omnia crimina atque
scelera quae gessisti a iu
uentute tua usq; in hanc
aetatis horam. & liberat
te ds̄ ab omne ope malo
& conseruat te ds̄ in omne
ope bono & perducat te
ds̄ ad uitam aeternam...
Dignare dn̄e die isto
sine peccato nos custo
Conuertere nos ds̄ salutaris
& auerte iram tuam a nobis
Dn̄e exaudi orationem meam
& clamor meus ad te perueniat
Ihs xp̄e omnium saluator
respice super nos famu
los tuos. ut miserearis
nobis qui cum patre &
sp̄u sc̄o uiuis & regnas ds̄.

Respice in seruos tuos
& in opera tua dirige fi
lios eorum. Respice sple
ndorem dn̄i di n̄ri super nos
& opera manuum nostrarum
dirige...
Gloria patri & filio
& sp̄u sc̄o.
Dirigere & sanctificare
& custodire dignare
dn̄e ds̄ rex caeli & terrae
hodie & cotidie corda
& corpora nostra in uia
tua & in operibus mandatorum
tuorum. ut hic & in aeternum
per te semper salui esse
mereamur. Saluator
mundi qui cum patre
& sp̄u sc̄o uiuis & reg
nas ds̄ per omnia s̄cla s̄clorum
Ego dixi dn̄e miserere mei
sana animam meam
quia peccaui tibi

Ab occultis meis munda
me domine et ab alienis
parce servo tuo
Converte nos deus salutaris
noster et averte iram
tuam a nobis.
Convertere domine usque quo
et deprecabilis esto super
servos tuos.
Salvos fac servos tuos
deus meus sperantes in te.
Memor esto congrega
tionis tuae quam
creasti ab initio.
Oculi domini super iustos
et aures eius in preces eorum
Confiteantur tibi domine
omnia opera tua et sancti tui
benedicant tibi.
Domine salvum fac regem
et exaudi nos in die
qua invocaverimus te.
Salvum fac populum
tuum domine et benedic
hereditati tuae.

Et rege eos et extolle
illos usque in aeternum
Memento nostri domine in
beneplacito populi tui
visita nos in salutari tuo
Fiat domine misericordia tua
super nos quemadmodum
speravimus in te
Ostende nobis domine misericordiam
tuam et salutare tuum da nobis
Pro fidelibus defunctis
Requiem aeternam dona
eis domine et lux perpetua
luceat eis.
Pro fratribus nostris absentibus
salvos fac servos tuos
deus meus sperantes in te
Mitte eis domine auxilium
de sancto et de Sion tuere eos
Nihil proficiat inimicus
in eis et filius iniquitatis
non apponat nocere eis
Dignare domine die isto
sine peccato nos custodire
Pone domine custodiam
ori meo.

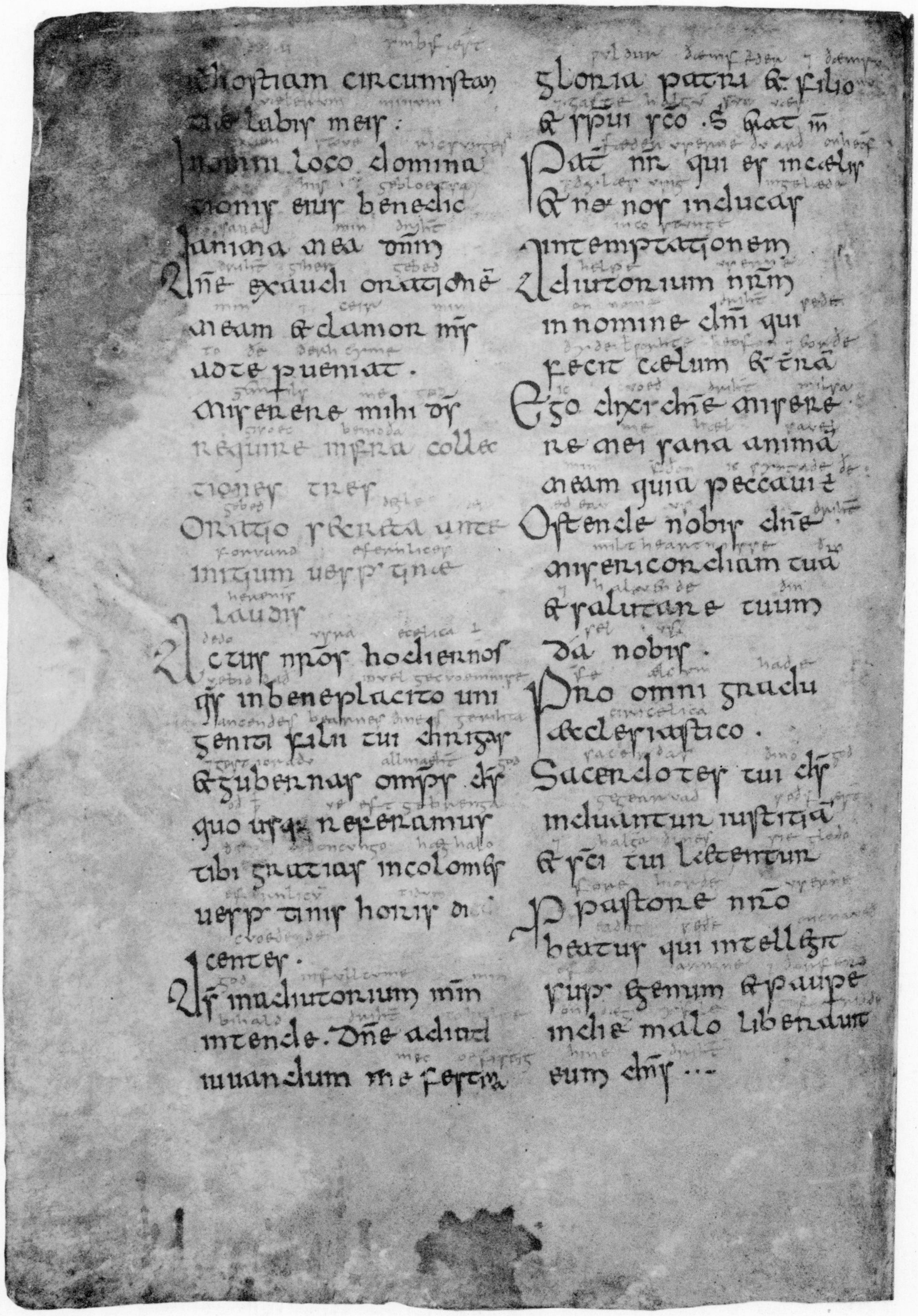

[h]ostiam circumstan
tie labiis meis :
In omni loco domina
tionis eius benedic
anima mea dominum
Domine exaudi orationem
meam et clamor meus
ad te perueniat .
Miserere mihi deus
Require infra collec
tiones tres
Oratio serotina uesp
initium uespertinae
laudis
Actus nostros hodiernos
deus in beneplacito uni
geniti filii tui dirigas
et gubernans omnes dies
quo usque referamus
tibi gratias incolomes
uespertinis horis de
centes .
Deus in adiutorium meum
intende . Domine ad adiu
uandum me festina

Gloria patri et filio
et spiritui sancto . Sicut erat in
Pater noster qui es in caelis
Et ne nos inducas
in temptationem
Adiutorium nostrum
in nomine domini qui
fecit caelum et terram
Ego dixi domine miserere
mei sana animam
meam quia peccaui tibi
Ostende nobis domine
misericordiam tuam
et salutare tuum
da nobis .
Pro omni gradu
ecclesiastico .
Sacerdotes tui domine
induantur iustitia
et sancti tui laetentur
Pro pastore nostro
Beatus qui intellegit
super egenum et paupe
in die malo liberabit
eum dominus ...

Pro rege nostro domine sal
uum fac regem et ex
audi nos in die qua
inuocauerimus te.

Pro episcopo nostro. Saluum
fac seruum tuum
deus meus sperantem in te.

Pro omni populo cris
tiano. saluum fac
populum tuum domine
et benedic hereditati
tue. et rege eos et
extolle illos usque in
eternum ...

Pro pace et sanitate
ecclesie. Fiat pax
in uirtute tua. et
habundantia in tur
ribus tuis.

Pro fratribus et sororibus
nostris. Propter fratres
meos et proximos
meos loquebar pa
cem de te. Propter domum
dei nostri quesiui bona tibi

Pro iter agentibus ...
O domine saluum me fac
o domine bene prosperare.

Pro nauigantibus in bonis
Exaudi nos deus salutaris
spes omnium finium terre
et in mari longe.

Pro omnibus aduersantibus
et calumpniantibus nobis
Domine ihesu xriste ne statu
as illis hoc in peccatum
nesciunt enim quid faciunt.

Pro discordantibus. pax
dei que exsuperat omnem
sensum et custodiat
corda et corpora illorum
in pace amen. Pro penitentibus

Pro elemosinas nobis fa
cientibus in hoc mundo
Dispersit dedit pau
peribus et iustitia eius manet
in seculum seculi. Cor.

Pro infirmis et captiuis.
Et clamauerunt ad dominum
cum tribularentur

Multae tribulationes iustorum et de omnibus his liberabit eos dominus. Dominus custodit omnia ossa eorum unum ex his non conteretur.

Pro fidelibus defunctis. In memoria aeterna erunt iusti ab auditu malo non timebunt.

Requiem aeternam dona eis domine et lux perpetua luceat eis. Animae illorum illarumque requiescant in pace. amen.

Ne tradas domine bestiis animas confitentes tibi et animas pauperum tuorum ne obliviscaris in finem.

Pro peccatis et neglegentiis nostris. Ne memineris iniquitatum nostrarum antiquarum cito nos anticipiat misericordia tua quia pauperes facti sumus nimis.

Pro nobis met ipsis. Adiuva nos deus salutaris noster propter honorem nominis tui domine libera nos et propitius esto peccatis nostris propter nomen tuum domine.

Pro benefactoribus nostris. Domine retribue pro me misericordia tua in saeculum. Inmittit dominus angelum in circuitu timentium eum et eripiet eos.

Pro fratribus nostris absentibus. Salvos fac servos tuos deus meus sperantes in te. Mitte eis domine auxilium de sancto et de sion tuere eos. Nihil proficiat inimicus in eis et filius iniquitatis non adponat nocere eis.

Pone domine custodiam ori meo et hostium circumstantiae labiis meis.

In hoc loco [illegible]

benedic anima mea domino

Domine exaudi orationem meam et clamor meus ad te perueniat.

Miserere mihi deus

ORATIO SEQUITUR

Deus qui nos uiuentes per huius diei cursum in hanc horam uespertinam peruenire fecisti conserua nos per omnium horarum spatia et per tuam magnam misericordiam fac nos semper permanere inlesos. per

Adesto nobis propitiatus omnipotens deus ut si aliquid incongruum aut ineptum rogare et petere uisi sumus, nunc propicius assumas maturus in bonum conuertas qui semper bonitatem prestas. et omnes te petentes pie adiuuas per dominum nostrum ihesum christum filium tuum qui tecum uiuit deus in unitate eiusdem spiritus sancti per infinita secula seculorum. amen.

Hymnus ad completorium

Te lucis ante terminum rerum creator poscimus ut solita clementia sis presul ad custodiam.

Procul recedant somnia et noctium fantasmata hostemque nostrum comprime ne polluantur corpora.

Presta pater piissime

82 v

Dignare dne die ista
sine peccato nos cus
todire. Oremus.
Uigilate et custodite
digneris dne ds rex
celi ac terre in ista
nocte corda et cor
pora nra. ut p te
salui esse possimus
saluator mundi q
cum patre et spu
sco uiuis et regnas
ds p omnia scla.
Pone dne custodiam
ori meo et hostiam
circumstantie labiis
In omni loco dominat
tionis illius benedic
anima mea dnm
Dne exaudi oratione
meam et clamor meus
ad te ueniat ...
Leuaui oculos meos
admontes

Post hec sequit oratio
Dne ds omnipotens
qui separasti lucem
a tenebris te sub nix
is precibus exoramus
ut p hunc sup uenturae
noctis caliginem tua nos
protegat dextera. ut in
lucis aurorum cuncti
surgamus gaudentes. p.
hii sunt vii. psalmi
poenitentiales ad .... hora
Dne ne in furore tuo .i.
Beati quorum remisse sunt
Dne ne in ira tua .ii.
Miserere mihi ds sm
Dne exaudi orationem m
et clamor meus ad te ue
De profundis clamaui
Dne exaudi orationem
meam auribus percipe
hii sunt viii. psalmi ora
tionum ad tertiam horam

Beati immaculati in uia
qui ambulant in lege domini

Omnipotens sempiterne deus
qui in meritis sancti tui
cuthberhti sacerdotis
semper et ubique mirabi
lis es clementiam tuam
ut sicut ei sempiternam
gloriam contulisti sic
ad consequendam mise
ricordiam tuam eius
nos precibus adiuua. per.

Deus qui nos sanctorum tuorum
temporali tribues
commemoratione gau
dere. presta quaesumus ut beato
cudberhto pontifice
intercedente in ea nume
rum sociemur in qua
illi sunt gratia tua
gloriosi. per.

Deus qui sanctorum tuorum
libenter suscipis uo
luntates intercedente
beato cudberhto sa
cerdote familiam
tuam quaesumus domine misera
tionis tuae dextera
semper et ubique protege. per.

Deus qui sanctorum tuorum apud
te gloriam permansuram
fidelium facis deuotio
ne clarescere. presta quaesumus
ut beatus cudberhtus
requirentibus sibi beneficia
dignanter impendat. et pro
populo tuo intercessor
existat. per dominum.

Bisuðan wudigan gæte æt aclee
on west sæxum on laurentius
mæssan dæg on wodnesdæg
ælfsige ðæm biscope in his
getelde aldred se profast
ðas feower collectæ on fif
næht aldne mona ær
undærne awrat.

[illegible] nomen dni · uii · Ecce ueniet rex · R · Aspiciens
a longe · V · Quique terrigenae · V · Qui regis isrl ·
V · Tollite portas · R · Aspiciebam · V · Ecce dominator ·
R · Missus est gabriel · V · Aue maria · R · Aue maria ·
V · Tollite portas · R · Saluatorem · V · Preocupemus ·
R · Audite uerbu · V · A solis ortu · R · Ecce uirgo con ·
V · Tollite · R · Obsecro dne · V · A solis ortu · R · Lae
tentur caeli · V · Ecce dominator · In laudibus ·
A · In illa die · A · Iocundare · A · Ecce dns ueniet · A · Oms
sitientes · A · Ecce ueniet pfeta · V · Emitte ag
nu dne · A · Spiritus scs · A · Ne timeas maria ·
A · Betlem non es minima · R · Hierusalem cito ·
V · Israhel si me audieris · R · Ecce dns ueniet et oms sci ·
V · A solis ortu · R · Ierusalem surge · V · Leua in circuitu ·
R · Ciuitas ierusalem · V · Ecce dominator · R · Ecce
ueniet dns · V · Ecce dominator · R · Sicut mater ·
V · Ds a libano · R · Ierusalem plantabis · V · Ds a libano ·
R · Egredietur dns · V · Ds a libano · R · Rex nr aduen ·
V · Ecce agnus di · In laudibus · A · Ecce in nubibus caeli ·
A · Urbs fortitudinis · A · Ecce apparebo · A · Montes et
colles · A · Ecce dns nr · A · Super solium dauid ·
A · beata es maria · III · A · Non auferetur sceptru ·
R · Ecce apparebit · V · Ecce dominator · R · Bet
lem ciuitas · V · Ds a libano · R · Qui uenturus est ·
V · Ex sion species · R · Suscipe uerbum · V · Aue maria ·
R · Egipte noli · V · Ecce dominator · R · Prope est ·
V · Qui uenturus est · R · Descendet dns · V · Ex sion ·
R · Ueni dne et noli · V · A solis ortu · R · Docebit nos ·
V · Ex sion · In laudibus · A · Ueniet dns · A · Ierusalem gau
de · A · Dabo in sion · A · Montes et oms colles · A · Iuste
et pie · A · Iohannes aut · A · Tu es qui uenturus es · A ·
Quomodo fiet istud · R · Canite tuba in sion · V ·
A solis ortu · R · Octaua decima · V · Ego sum dns ds tuus ·
R · Non auferetur · V · Pulchriores sunt · R · Me oport
[illegible] hoc est testimonium · R · Ecce iam ueni [illegible] plen[illegible]

Ap . apud . at . aut .
at . autem . acto . auc
tio . dim . actione
af . affectus . agr . au
gustus . agi . agusti .
an . ante . apli . amp
lius . brs brevius . brm
brevem . bs bene . bt
beatus . bn bonus .
bno bonorum . bf bene
ficium . bl bellum
C . cos . c causa . co
cognita . cu cuius
ci cui . cn contra
cn cum . contra .
cir . cives romanus
crim crimen : crs .
conf . fessus . crs . car
issimus . cn contra
do . deinde . d . dein
d . dum . dt . dotes
dt dant . [illegible] demum

d dixit . d dicit . dn
dicitur . de dane
dt dolus . e . est . ee
esse . edi edicti . et
etiam . en ergo . ergo
egressus . [illegible] enim .
fca facta . fo facto
fut fuerunt . fu . fugit
fau faciunt . fe facta
fas facta sunt . fx felix
fen fenisum . fc fide
commissum . fi filio [illegible]
fo fonte . f fundi .
f . fidei . fl filius
fr frater . fuit
fuerat . g gaius .
g . gaius [illegible] . gn .
gnus . gs signi . gi
gaudium . gra gratia
gl gloria . g . [illegible]
hh . heres . h . hac . h
hodie . h hunc . hedi
hereditas . h . hoc . h hec

85 v

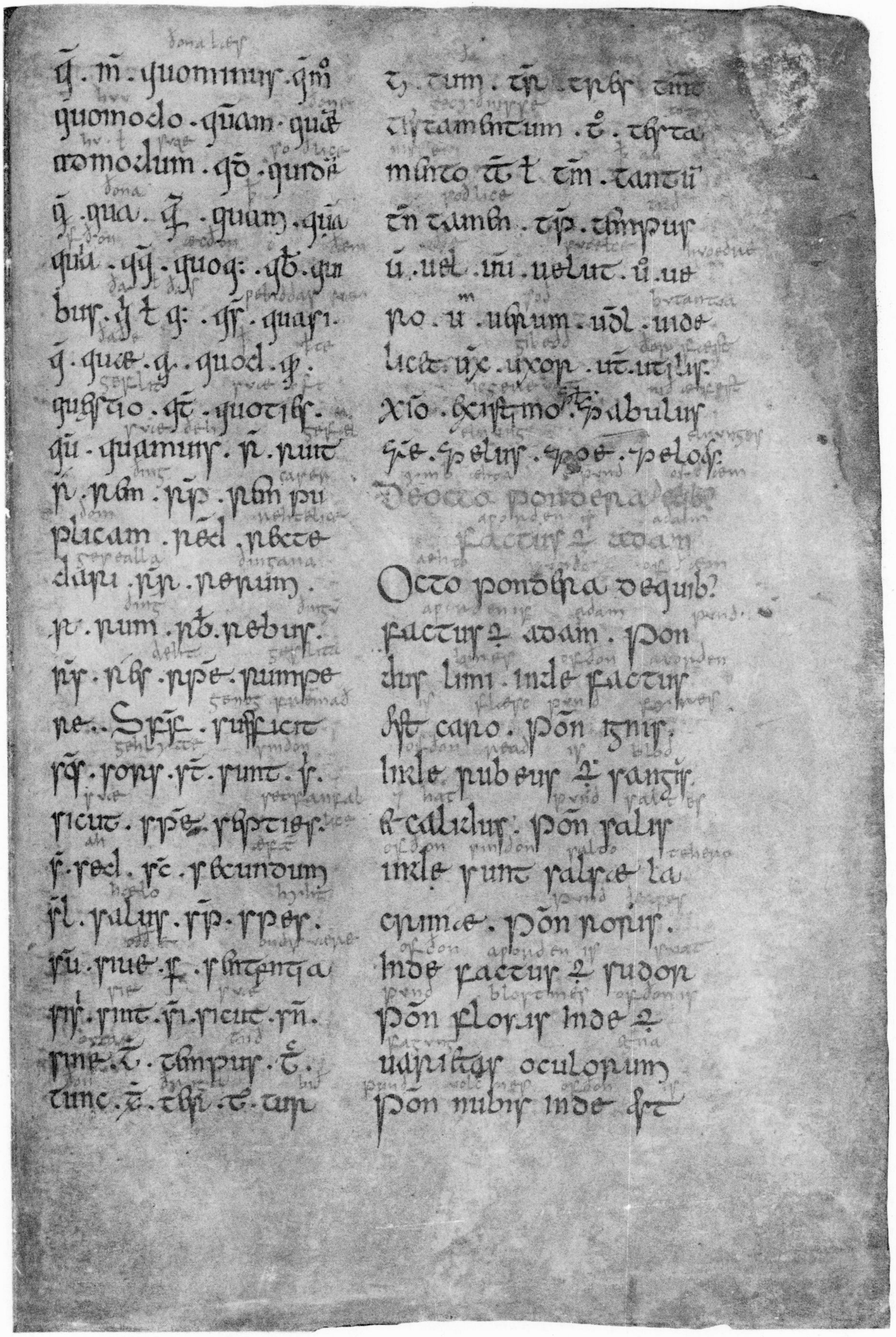

De octo ponderibus de quibus factus est adam

Octo pondera de quibus factus est adam. Pondus limi inde factus est caro. Pondus ignis inde rubeus est et sanguis et calidus. Pondus salis inde sunt salsae lacrimae. Pondus roris inde factus est sudor. Pondus floris inde est varietas oculorum. Pondus nubis inde est

in aegypto magistra-
tus prius transfertur. gre-
nos principibus inter-
pretati sumus. et quib(us)
et in exodo legimus
electos archontes
transfertur. pro quib(us)
latina simplicitas
et nos factores
transtulit ..

.I. Hostiarius
qui in uet(ere) t(estamento) testamento. ianitores sunt qui
excubabant in tab(er)-
naculo d(e)i. II.
Lector. lector a le-
gendo p(rae)cones et
clamatores sunt initium
ip(s)i fatis quib(us) dicitur
clama ne cesses
III. Exorcista [illegible]
ionis [illegible]

p(er) daemonum exeogitas
se fugans: gentilium do-
cuisse. IIII. Subdiaco-
nus quod apud grecos hypo-
diaconi uocantur. et
apud hebreos in scriptura
nathinnaei. V. Diaco-
nus qui apud hebreos le-
uitae dicti sub leui gestare
tarent arcam .. VI.
Presbyter grecum est quod
senior est aetate. grece
presbyteri uocantur. VII.
Episcopus grecum est nomen
operis non honoris. inde
dictum est. epis super et
scopus inspector.
ideo episcopi super in-
spectores nominantur. I.
VIII. Archiepiscopus
totum grecum. lati-
ne princeps super
inspectorum ..

sive summus episcopus qui
et pallio utentium.
iiii. Pr[i]ncip[es] ex l. pons popu
li ad celeste regnum
x. Chore episcopi. grece. core
latine vicarii episcopo
rum in vicis et villis con
stituti. habentes li
centiam constituere
gradum minorem sed pres
biterum neque diaconum
sine scientiam episcopi in cu
ius regione [est] ..
Papa qui et pater pa
trum. vel pater patrum
interpretatio nos[tra] [...]
Sacerdos huic nomine
fungitur et melchise
dech et aaron. primus
in lege sacerdotalem
nomen accipit et libe
ri eius. Sacerdos no
minatum qui et presbiter
nuncupatur sacerdotum
[...] presb[yteri] [...] et episcopi

sacerdotes nomin[...]
Patriarcha. pater .s. et l.
sed et hebraice abba
Archus .s. princeps .l.
Metropolitanus .s. poli
.l. urbs vel civitas
Accolithus .s. cerarius.
ad recitandum evange
Pisteuus .s. fidelis
Martyr .s. testis .l.
id est passionis et sanguinis
xpi. Epiphania .s. la[tine]
manifestatio. Ypa
pante .s. lat[ine] obviatio
id est antiqui plebis

Beatus matheus ap
ostolus & euan requi
euit intra armenia
intra amantorum
Beatus marc euange
requiescit alexand
riae in prouincia
aegypti.
Beatus lucas euan
requieuit bochtia
in prouincia meso
potamia.
Beatus iohan apost
& euange requieuit
effeso. in puinc asia
Beatus iohan babtis
ta requiescit in ciui
tate nomine sabasta
Beatus petrus apls
requiescit romae
in p uincia tuscia.

Beatus paulus apostol
requiescit romae in pro
uincia campania.
Beatus andreas apls
requiescit patras in p
uincia achaia.
Beatus iacob apls
requiescit hieros in p
uincia syria.
Beatus bartholomeus
apls requiescit licaonia
in prouincia armenia
Beat thomas ap requies
emina in india saracenor
Beat philippus ap requi
escit eriapo in prouinc
Beat symon frigia
channaneus ap requies
in bitho intra dicit
Beatus matthias / parthon
ap requies hierusal in
puincia syria
Beat stephan pri martyr
requi in prouinc syria

88 r

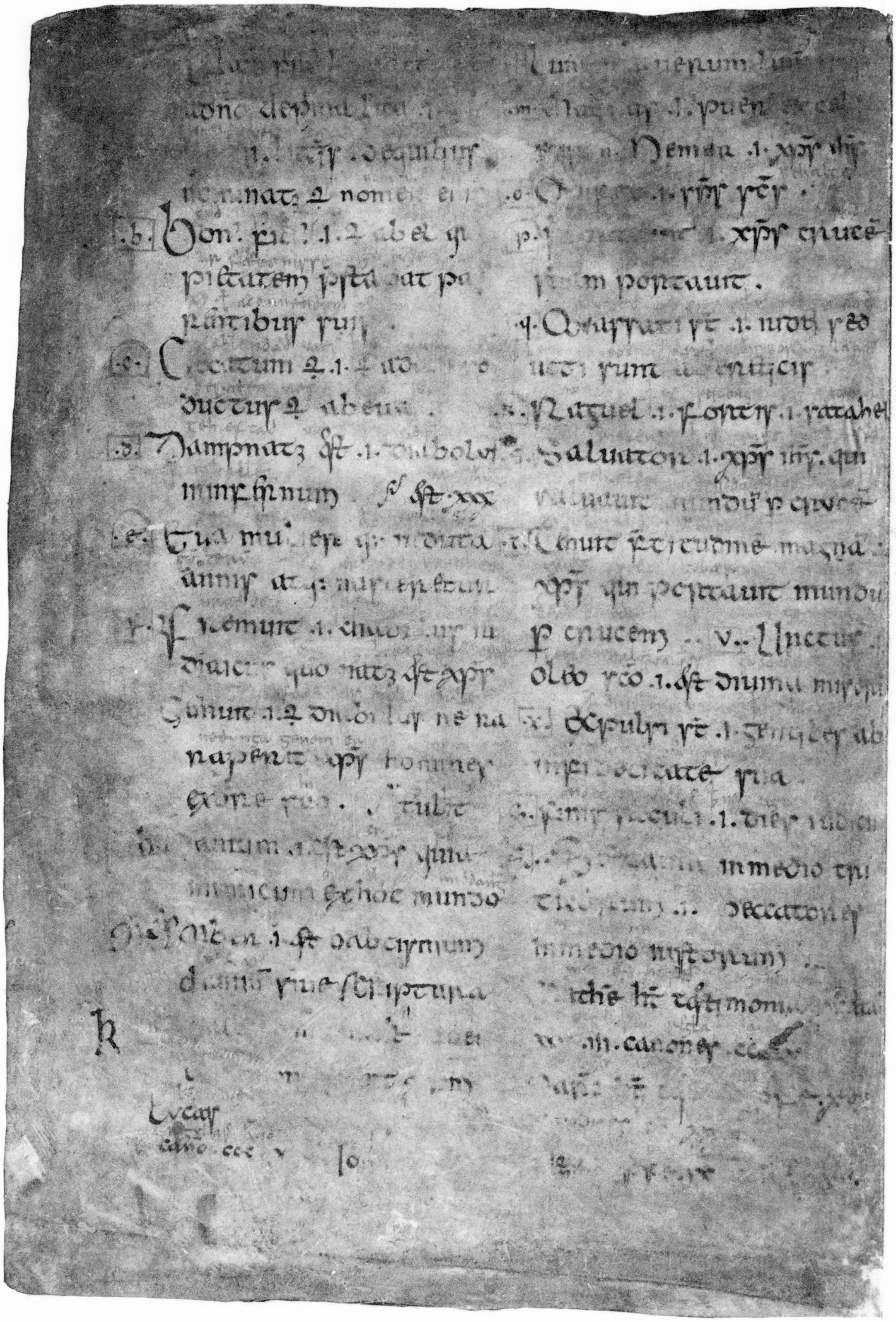

88 v

89 v